# THE AMERICAN EXPERIENCE OF BRITISH PRIZE LAW, 1776–1804

# THE AMERICAN EXPERIENCE OF BRITISH PRIZE LAW, 1776–1804

Suzanne Amy Foxley

THE BOYDELL PRESS

The book is based on a dissertation from the University of Oldenburg

First published 2025
The Boydell Press, Woodbridge

ISBN 978 1 83765 257 0

The Boydell Press is an imprint of Boydell & Brewer Ltd
PO Box 9, Woodbridge, Suffolk IP12 3DF, UK
and of Boydell & Brewer Inc.
668 Mt Hope Avenue, Rochester, NY 14620-2731, USA
website: www.boydellandbrewer.com

Our Authorised Representative for product safety in the EU is
Easy Access System Europe – Mustamäe tee 50, 10621 Tallinn, Estonia,
*gpsr.requests@easproject.com*

A CIP catalogue record for this book is available
from the British Library

*To my fabulous family and fantastic friends*

# CONTENTS

# ILLUSTRATIONS

## Figures



## Tables

# ACKNOWLEDGEMENTS

This book would not have been possible without the many kind hearts and great minds that helped me along the way. While it is impossible to list them all, I would like to express my particular gratitude to a few here.

I first started this work with the wonderful Prize Papers Project at the University of Oldenburg, supported by the German Academy of Sciences in Göttingen. The team has my greatest thanks, particularly Prof. Dr Dagmar Freist.

Equally, the staff at the National Archives in Washington and London (the latter feeling like a second home to me now) have been invaluable. They lay the foundations of historical research not merely by cataloguing and providing the documents, but through their continuous passion, motivation and exceptional knowledge on the materials that they are entrusted with and keep safe for future generations. I am especially grateful for the expertise, guidance and friendship of Dr Amanda Bevan, Head of Legal Records at the National Archives.

In addition, my sincere appreciation goes to my new team and the staff at the University of Erfurt, who have supported me throughout the publication process, as well as the competent personnel at Boydell & Brewer.

Last, but certainly not least, I would like to thank my fabulous family and fantastic friends for accompanying me along this journey. Your unwavering patience, love and belief in me laid the groundwork for this book. Thank you.

# Introduction

"The American Revolution was a legal, as well as a political revolution",[1] is how Erwin C. Surrency, founder of the American Legal History Journal, phrased it. The year 1776 spiralled into a whirlpool of blood, sea salt and independence that not only washed up on the global shores but was knitted into the maritime fabric of the law. The events ripped apart families as it stitched together new ideas and diverging concepts of loyalty. British and 'patriot'/'rebel'/American forces clashed not only on land but also at sea. While many consider the ocean a lawless space, maritime and naval warfare had a legal framework on which its players were supposed to base their actions, just as there was on land. This framework was not simply provided by the strategies and policies of politicians and military men, but it was reflected in the courts of law. Americans had no national navy upon the outbreak of hostilities, instead turning to privateering. Privateers were not national naval vessels, but private ships and their crews that had obtained licences to capture enemy vessels. To distinguish them from illegal pirates, they had to follow rules concerning how, when and whom to capture, as well as bringing the captured vessels into ports where the legality of captures was verified. These admiralty or vice-admiralty court processes enabled them to legally receive shares in the 'prizes' they had made, making privateering an act of national defence including a financial incentive for the individuals involved. Hulbert states that this "other half of the story – that is, what happened once the prize was brought to port and before a Court of Admiralty – could be just as perilous, uncertain, and complicated as the endeavour to capture an enemy vessel".[2] Although legal documents often appear as dry tomes of little interest to all but legal scholars, hiding behind the words in admiralty court books with crumbling spines lie many stories of these clashes at sea, and more generally, of the human lives affected by the violence of war.

This book will dive into how Americans experienced British prize jurisdiction from 1776 to 1804, in a time where British sea power was both great and

1 E. C. Surrency, 'The Transition from Colonialism to Independence', *The American Journal of Legal History*, 46 (2004), 55–81, at 55.

2 K. A. Hulbert, *The Untold War at Sea: America's Revolutionary Privateers* (Athens GA, 2022), p. 101.

under threat. American privateers and merchant ships captured by the British were subject to their jurisdiction and faced the consequences.[3] The capture of a vessel did not only impact those captured on board. The effect rippled on, to all the merchants whose goods the ship was transporting, to the unspoken communication trapped in captured letters, to the cargo that never reached its intended destination, and, of course, the loss of a ship. On a strategic level, the destruction of commerce (and by extension of commerce transportation) reduced the enemy's means of warfare and could be used to starve them into submission. The position of captured Americans fundamentally changed in this period, from rebels in a civil war, to an accepted international player and neutral state both suffering under and profiting from Britain's wars with France. British victory was by no means assured in the 1790s, much as British defeat had not been clear in 1776. Facing its biggest enemy on the European continent, Britain relied on its maritime forces, enacting blockades and encouraging privateering.

The law is merely a human vision of order enforced through power.[4] But, while maritime courts offered great potential to Britain as instruments of warfare, officially they were following the supranational 'law of nations', now termed 'international law'. How did this concept shape the way the British treated US citizens during the French Wars and the War of Independence? How did the American experience of British jurisdiction alter from 1776 to 1804? And what did American politicians, sailors and merchants do to enforce their interests on the international stage?

As Jasanoff phrased it, "Great histories are made up of small ones".[5] To this end, we shall be following two members of one divergent family: Robert Bayard (1739–1819) and Samuel Bayard (1767–1840), distant cousins, were uniquely placed, interacting between legal professionals, the public and leading politicians of the era in New York and London, accessing a diverse cross-section of society.[6] Their positions strongly mirror neutral trade, which

3 Throughout this work, the names of vessels have been italicised and, whenever known, the surname of the ship's captain (generally known as the master) added in brackets.

4 G. Leonard, 'A History of Violence: American Constitutional History and the Criminal System', in *The Oxford Handbook of Legal History* (Oxford, 2018), at p. 904.

5 M. Jasanoff, 'The Other Side of Revolution: Loyalists in the British Empire', *William and Mary Quarterly*, 65 (2008), 205–32, at 227.

6 See family tree in fig. 1 (Appendix). Samuel Bayard's birthdate has been disputed, but we can conclusively say, he was born on 11 February 1767, due to his wife's diary entries that recorded his age each year on his birthday; M. Bayard, *The Journal of Martha Pintard Bayard*, ed. by S. Bayard Dodd (New York, 1894), pp. 100–1.

connected "merchants, captains and naval officers, as well as politicians and lawyers, and although they did not share the same convictions, their different points of view were intertwined".[7]

The development of admiralty courts in the United States has already been the topic of many books and articles. A few key articles serve for general overview purposes.[8] In addition to these, there are a wide range of individual studies on the colonial (vice-) admiralty courts throughout the United States.[9] There has been no comprehensive study on the development of American admiralty courts in general, as their trajectories are very individual, divergent and the archival sources spread throughout the country, thus favouring the study of individual courts. Carl Ubbelohde's work *The Vice-Admiralty Courts and the American Revolution*, published in 1960, formed a watershed moment in these courts' historiography and remains a crucial read, though it cannot be viewed as a comprehensive national history of all colonial American courts.[10]

In the case of the New York Vice-Admiralty Court, known as the 'mother court'[11] of British colonial admiralty jurisdiction in North America, many studies focus extensively on the period *after* Independence, often examining the court's transition to the federal level.[12] However the continued work of the

7 S. Marzagalli and L. Müller, '"In apparent disagreement with all law of nations in the world": Negotiating Neutrality for Shipping and Trade During the French Revolutionary and Napoleonic Wars', *International Journal of Maritime History* (2016), at 115.

8 To name some particularly outstanding examples: M. P. Harrington, 'The Legacy of the Colonial Vice-Admiralty Courts: Part I', *Journal of Maritime Law and Commerce*, 26 (1995), 581–600; M. P. Harrington, 'The Legacy of the Colonial Vice-Admiralty Courts: Part II', *Journal of Maritime Law and Commerce* (1996), 323–51; H. Putnam, 'How the Federal Courts Were Given Admiralty Jurisdiction', *Cornell Law Review*, 10 (1925), 460–70; G. J. Mangone, *United States Admiralty Law* (The Hague, 1997).

9 C. M. Hough, *Reports of Cases in the Vice Admiralty of the Province of New York and in the Court of Admiralty of the State of New York, 1715–1788: With an Introduction and Appendix* (New Haven CT, 1925); D. S. Towle, *Records of the Vice-Admiralty Court of Rhode Island, 1716–1752: With an Introduction by Charles M. Andrews, American Legal Records* (Washington DC, 1936), III; K. L. Wroth, 'The Massachusetts Vice Admiralty Court and the Federal Admiralty Jurisdiction', *American Journal of Legal History*, 6 (1962), 250–68.

10 C. Ubbelohde, *The Vice-Admiralty Courts and the American Revolution* (Chapel Hill NC, 1960).

11 John D. Winter and Richard Maidman, 'Retelling the History of the United States District Court for the Southern District of New York', *NY Litigator*, 17 (2012), 1.

12 Federal Bar Association of New York, New Jersey and Connecticut, *History of the United States District Court for the Southern District of New York* (New York, 1962); C. M. Hough, *1789–1919, The United States District Court for the Southern*

(British, loyalist) Vice-Admiralty Court of New York under Robert Bayard's tenure (1776–83) has not been analysed by scholars until now. Robert Bayard's tenure remains an unwritten chapter of American admiralty jurisdiction, a research gap that this book will start to fill.[13] The very existence of this court is not mentioned in the US National Archives and Records Administration or in many national admiralty histories. This is down to providence, with many excellent works on American privateers focusing exclusively on sources found in America, thus excluding documentation such as Robert Bayard's records, which are preserved in the National Archives, London.[14] This national focus on archival material has meant a large chunk of the American privateer experience has thus far been neglected in scholarship, a bias that this book will begin to rectify.

A similar trend can be noticed in examining early works on Anglo-American relations in the 1790s. John Bassett Moore compiled two legal history digests on the Jay Treaty (officially termed the Treaty of Amity and Commerce, 1794) and recognised the importance of Samuel Bayard's role in this process. In his governmentally sponsored works published in the 1890s, the first US professor for International Law and Diplomacy worked with the American archival records, but, in congruence with contemporary academic practice, no references were given and large passages quoted without indication. His work also mirrors a traditional legal history approach, chronicling the legal precedents set out by cases with much attention being paid to the legal opinions of the commission's members, while the boxes of merchants' correspondence were neglected. These aspects, addressed in this book, are important for our understanding of the treaty's impact on Americans. They reveal the personal stories of those involved as well as the communication cycles that prevailed

*District of New York: Its Growth, and the Men Who Have Done Its Work* (New York, 1934); New York County Lawyers' Association Committee on the Federal Courts, *The United States District Court for the Southern District of New York: A Retrospective (2000–2010)* (New York, 2012); J. D. Winter and R. Maidman, 'Retelling the History of the United States District Court for the Southern District of New York', *NY Litigator* (2012).

13 The HCA 49/92 series was partially used by Martin in his 2014 dissertation, however New York was not the centre of the study; E. J. Martin, 'Prize Game in the Borderlands: Privateering in New England and the Maritime Provinces, 1775–1815' (dissertation, University of Maine, 2014); see also Richard D. Pougher, '"Averse … to Remaining Idle Spectators": The Emergence of Loyalist Privateering During the American Revolution, 1775–1778 Volume I. Introduction to Chapter 8' (dissertation, University of Maine, 2002), http://digitalcommons.library.umaine.edu/etd/207 (accessed 18 August 2024). Pougher mainly focused on the Loyalist Claims Commission records and those of the Treasury Board in the British archives; however, his work examines New York from the viewpoint of loyalist privateers, though it does not focus on legal practice.

14 As an example, see Hulbert, *Untold War*.

across the Atlantic, highlighting the entangled nature of privateering as well as offering glimpses into the onshore impact that American maritime policies had. From the nineteenth century onwards, the Jay Treaty was celebrated as a milestone in international arbitration, as the first introduction of a systematic negotiation of legal cases between two countries. Today, its place in the development of international law is clearly cemented. [15] While Anglo-American relations overall have been studied extensively for the period, the Jay Treaty has mainly been studied regarding the development of the public sphere and American political debate culture.[16] But maritime affairs were hugely important to the early republic and reflect US governmental objectives, to the point that they contributed to the outbreak of the War of 1812, and they made up large sections of Jay's negotiations with Britain.

Privateering and 'prize' were a major component of maritime policy and hard for the American maritime community to avoid, whether as active privateers in wartime or as subjects of foreign maritime predation during peace. The tensions around prize reflected in the Anglo-American relationship are echoed in US foreign relations with other countries, as the field of international law and the sphere of the open ocean was a contested space between all European nations, especially during the French Wars. Regardless of how capriciously national borders or nationality itself could be defined, it is important to maintain a national framework when examining prize jurisdiction, as this was the reality faced by claimants in court: their ascribed nationality determined their losses and gains. Privateering, often studied for its economic and military impact, founded on the principles of international law (known as the law of nations), was entirely based on a system of nationalities. While many historians criticise national histories, this was the legal framework with which claimants were confronted, and by examining it, we actually reveal the contested nature of this very concept.[17] Admiralty courts had a highly complex vision of what

15 S. F. Bemis, *Jay's Treaty: A Study in Commerce and Diplomacy, The Making of Modern Law: Foreign, Comparative, and International Law, 1600–1926* (Gale, 2013); B. Perkins, *The First Rapprochement* (Oakland CA, 1967); J. M. Trautsch, *The Genesis of America: US Foreign Policy and the Formation of National Identity, 1793–1815* (New York, 2018); C. G. Roelofsen, 'International Arbitration and Courts', in B. Fassbender, A. Peters and S. Peter (eds), *The Oxford Handbook of the History of International Law*, 1st edn (Oxford, 2012), pp. 145–69, at p. 160.

16 J. A. Combs, *Jay Treaty: Political Battleground of the Founding Fathers* ([S.l.], 2022); T. Estes, *The Jay Treaty Debate, Public Opinion, and the Evolution of Early American Political Culture, Political Development of the American Nation* (Amherst MA, 2006); N. C. Green, '*The focus of the wills of converging millions': Public Opposition to the Jay Treaty and the Origins of the People's Presidency* (Philadelphia PA, 2017).

17 Especially microhistorical approaches should be noted in this regard, often explicitly used to subvert "the primacy of the nation state". C. G. de Vito, 'History

determined nationality, ranging from birthplace and residency to the location of one's business, the residencies of the crew and many other factors.[18]

Scholars of prize thus need to follow the same trajectory as those in the field of international law in general, which is gradually moving away from traditional, clear-cut depictions, to acknowledging how the law was open to negotiation and interpretation.[19] Much like neutrality, it needs to be re-envisioned, not as a policy of waiting and restraint, of dealing with indisputable laws, but as an active political, diplomatic and legal battle field. As Leos Müller phrased it: "Neutral maritime states fought for their rights to trade and navigate freely during wartime, with anyone and anywhere. They also employed legal arguments for ensuring the freedom of the sea, and they took steps to enforce their trade rights."[20]

This book strengthens his statement, showing how the United States attempted to reshape international law in its favour and followed up its national interests through the British admiralty court system in the 1790s. At present, much attention and funding has been applied to make admiralty records produced in the London courts (the High Court of Admiralty and its appellate court) more accessible, with the so-called 'prize-papers' drawing a diverse range of scholarly attention.[21] Yet most works on British prize juris-

Without Scale: The Micro-Spatial Perspective', *Past and Present* (2019), 348–72, at 371.

18 This becomes blatantly clear when dealing with prize jurisdiction and can already been seen from the set of questions that were issued to captured crews (the so-called 'Standing Interrogatories').

19 B. R. Clark and A. J. Bellia, *The Law of Nations and the United States Constitution* (Oxford, 2017); B. Fassbender, A. Peters and S. Peter (eds), *The Oxford Handbook of the History of International Law*, 1st edn (Oxford, 2012); M. W. Janis, *America and the Law of Nations, 1776–1939* (Oxford, 2010); M. W. Janis, 'North America: American Exceptionalism in International Law', in Fassbender, Peters and Peter (eds), *The Oxford Handbook of the History of International Law*, pp. 525–52; P. Onuf and N. Onuf, *Federal Union, Modern World: The Law of Nations in an Age of Revolutions 1776–1814* (Madison WI, 1993); G. W. Paulsen, 'An Historical Overview of Development of Uniformity in International Maritime Law', *Tulane Law Review: Devoted to the Civil Law, Comparative Law and Admiralty Law* (1983), 1065–91.

20 L. Müller, *Neutrality in World History, Themes in World History* (New York and London, 2019), p. 3.

21 The court's records also encompass general correspondence, which was confiscated as evidence during captures. This material, consisting partially of letters unopened since their original capture, are of interest to a wide range of researchers, as can be seen in this small selection of publications using the collection: S. Aslanian, 'Trade Diaspora versus Colonial State: Armenian Merchants, the English East India Company, and the High Court of Admiralty in London, 1748–1752', *Diaspora: A Journal of Transnational Studies*, 13 (2004), 37–100; J. Cronshagen, '"A Loyal Heart to God and

diction are outdated or focus on the history of admiralty jurisdiction more generally.[22] There is a dire need for scholars outside legal history to understand how the court worked, so that they can competently conduct research on its records. This book will give an overview of the workings of the London prize system in the 1790s, considering the microcosm of British prize law professionals at 'Doctors' Commons', the maritime law court centre, and uncovers an almost sociable history in this regard. Aligning with the critical and liberal legal history movement, these human and social factors, along with political pressures they faced, cannot be neglected when regarding 'the law'.[23]

To this end, a methodology was chosen to connect individual, sociable and political histories of the American experience of British prize jurisdiction. The book specifically alternates between very different sized units of analysis, known as a scalar approach, and exaggeratedly described as transitioning "from the micro to the global and back again".[24] To give a complex depiction of the American experience it is necessary to shift from national to international relations, from individuals to communities, from lobby groups and governments to the legal professionals they interacted with, and understand how different interests and realities collided in the court rooms. The challenge, as always faced by historians, is to try to bridge the gap between the value

the Governor": Missions and Colonial Policy in the Surinamese Saramaccan Mission (c. 1750–1813)', *Journal of Moravian History,* 19/1 (2019); J. van Lottum, J. Lucassen and L. H. van Voss, 'Sailors, National and International Labour Markets and National Identity,1600–1850', in R. W. Unger (ed.), *Shipping and Economic Growth, 1350–1850* (Leiden, 2011), pp. 309–52; A. Raapke, '"Dieses verfluchte Land"', transcript Verlag (2019); E.-M. Wagner and M. A. H. Ahmed, 'From Tuscany to Egypt: Eighteenth Century Arabic Letters in the Prize Paper Collections', *Journal of Semitic Studies, 62/2* (2017); For more about the collection and its history, see, Amanda Bevan and Randolph Cock, 'High Court of Admiralty Prize Papers, 1652–1815: Challenges in Improving Access to Older Records', *Archives* (2018), 34–58.

22 For example, L. W. Cowrie, 'Doctors' Commons: "A cosey, dosey, old-fashioned little family party", wrote Dickens in 1849', *History Today*, 20 (1970), 419–26; G. D. Squibb, *Doctors' Commons: A History of the College of Advocates and Doctors of Law* (Oxford, 1977). A notable exception is A. Brinkman, *Balancing Strategy: Sea Power, Neutrality, and Prize Law in the Seven Years' War, Cambridge Military Histories Series*, 1st edn (Cambridge, 2024).

23 Following in line with two attitudes to legal history as described by Jonathan Rose, 'Studying the Past: The Nature and Development of Legal History as an Academic Discipline', *The Journal of Legal History*, 31 (2010), 101–28, at 120–1.

24 J. de Vries, 'Playing with Scales: The Global and the Micro, the Macro and the Nano', *Past and Present,* 242/14 (2019), 23–36, at 23.

of the "uniqueness"[25] of individual experiences and their "exemplariness".[26] Using the standardised sets of data provided by legal records and Wertheimer's common sense quantification method, individual cases can be analysed within a larger bedrock of the national experience.

The narrative thread binding all these layers together is the Bayard family, who provide us with unique insights into the American experience of prize from 1776 to 1804 and beyond, due to their unique involvement in prize jurisdiction. Special attention is paid to Robert and Samuel Bayard.

The Bayard family is not an unknown entity in scholarly research.[27] Stephen Hess devoted a chapter to them in *America's Political Dynasties*, but Robert and Samuel Bayard both feature as minor characters only in what genealogists see as the larger family success story. [28] Very little research has been done on Robert and Samuel in particular, with other family members stealing the spotlight.[29]

[25] J. Leopore, 'Historians Who Love Too Much: Reflections on Microhistory and Biography', *Journal of American History*, 88 (2001), 129–44, at 133.

[26] Ibid., 141–2.

[27] J. G. B. Bulloch, *A History and Genealogy of the Families of Bayard, Houstoun of Georgia: And the descent of the Bolton family from Assheton, Byron and Hulton of Hulton Park, by Joseph Gaston Baillie Bulloch* (Washington DC, 1919); L. J. Fosdick, *French Blood in America* (Boston MA, 1911).

[28] It is the Asheton branch of the Bayard family that became particularly well known for their connection to American governmental service. There was a Senator Bayard of Delaware for more than fifty-three consecutive years, spanning four generations, and including the election of both a father and son to the Senate on the same day, "the only time in American history". S. Hess, *America's Political Dynasties: From Adams to Clinton* (Washington DC, 2016), p. 281; Fosdick, *French Blood in America*, p. 308.

[29] Founders Online and NARA, *LeRoy, Bayard & McEvers to Thomas Jefferson, 19 March 1816*, https://founders.archives.gov/documents/Jefferson/03-09-02-0400-0001 (accessed 17 August 2023); S. Nagel, *Patriotism and Profit: Washington, Hamilton, Schuyler and the Rivalry for America's Capital City* (New York, 2021); in Lorenzo's work, *Biographical Sketches of Loyalists of the American Revolution*, Robert Bayard is not even mentioned. While research from the twenty-first century rarely mentions him, his family's standing as part of the old New York elite and his status as a member of the British gentry makes it possible to superficially trace him through nineteenth and early twentieth-century genealogical works, as well as some works on the history of New York. L. Sabine, *Biographical Sketches of Loyalists of the American Revolution, with an Historical Essay: In Two Volumes*, 2 vols (Boston MA, 1864), vol. 1; L. Sturm-Lind, *Actors of Globalization: New York Merchants in The Global Trade, 1784–1812* (Leiden and Boston mA, 2018), vol. 10; J. Burke and J. B. Burke, *Dictionary of the Landed Gentry of Great Britain and Ireland: Vol. II, M to Z* (London, 1847), vol. 2; R. J. Caliendo, *New York City Mayors: Part I: The Mayors of New York City before 1898* (Bloomington IN, 2010); G. J. Tucker, *New York Marriages previous to 1784:*

Robert Bayard was a loyalist, who accepted the post of the British New York vice-admiralty Judge in 1776, fully integrating into the imperial policies of London.[30] His position placed him squarely in the middle of courtroom events, while connecting him to the mercantile realities of a nation in disarray, fighting its own citizens. By the end of his tenure in 1783, Robert sailed for Britain, the country that he had represented all his life, never to return.

Samuel Bayard also traversed the courtrooms, dealing specifically in cases of prize. However, his presence was felt in London, not in New York, and his clients were fresh American citizens trying to navigate the British system of admiralty law. He lived on the fringes of a newly devised system of international arbitration, conceived as a commission of the Jay Treaty. As the first "Agent appointed by the Government of the United States of America, to prosecute Claims and Appeals in Prize Causes, on Behalf of Citizens of the

---

*A reprint of the original edition of 1860 with additions and corrections* (Clearfield, 1999); N. W. Wallace, *A regimental chronicle and list of officers of the 60th, or the King's Royal Rifle Corps: Formerly the 62nd, or the Royal American Regiment of Foot* [Mikrofiche-Ausg.] (London, 1879). Samuel Bayard and his wife, on the other hand, have been researched a little. As a Princetonian, several works give rough outlines of Samuel's biography, but none examine him in depth. He is the focal point of an article by David Sterling, examining his unusual political stance. Samuel and his family were also showcased in James Wilson's works, as prominent local figures. An article focusing on their family estate, published in 1931, gives many useful insights into their family life. These follow the lines of some, equally superficial, nineteenth-century works. Samuel's wife, Martha Pintard Bayard, has also been featured in the context of women's literature and the history of the family; W. F. Craven and R. L. Woodward, *Princetonians, 1784–1790: A Biographical Dictionary (Princeton NJ, 1991)*; J. G. Wilson, *Colonel John Bayard (1738–1807) and the Bayard family of America: The anniversary address before the New York genealogical and biographical society, February 27, 1885* (New York, 1885); J. G. Wilson, 'Judge Bayard of New Jersey and his London diary of 1795–96: Read before the New Jersey Hist. Soc. May 21, 1885', *Proceedings of the New Jersey Historical Society* , 8 (1885), 203–16; H. H. Stockton, '"Cleremont" – Historic Mansion', *Daughters of the American Revolution* (1931), 546–50; F. S. Drake, *Dictionary of American Biography: including Men of the Time, containing nearly ten thousand natives of Persons of both Sexes, of Native and Foreign Birth, who have been Remarkable, or Prominently Connected with the Arts, Sciences, Literature, Politics, or History of the American Continent* (Boston MA, 1879); M. Culley, *A Day at a Time: The Diary Literature of American Women from 1764 to the Present* (New York, 1985); E. H. Pleck, *Celebrating the family: Ethnicity, Consumer Culture, and Family Rituals* (Cambridge MA, 2000).

30 New York Historical Society Museum and Library, 'Robert Bayard (1739–1819) commissions and letters, 1757–1830', New York Historical Society MSS Collection, https://bobcat.library.nyu.edu/permalink/f/22u4kq/nyu_aleph004034186 (accessed 11 March 2025).

said United States",[31] he acted in the regular admiralty courts and the appeals court, fighting for American rights in Britain on the legal frontline. These battles not only led him to meet with the aggrieved, the captured US maritime community in London, but also to the movers and shakers of this reality, such as American and British politicians and lobby groups. Moreover, he needed to interact with the elite microcosm of British admiralty professionals at Doctors' Commons, whom the US government needed to ascertain the rules of combat that they hitherto did not understand.

It is surprising that up until now Robert and Samuel Bayard have received so little scholarly attention, particularly regarding the wealth of archival sources connected to them and their importance in prize jurisdiction. This is down to historiography in a dual sense; Robert was neglected as American historiography discounted his tenure from their history and British historiography had no interest in him. Samuel was sidelined as he was not one of the 'great men' of history, not one of the official commissioners and his position not even recognised by Congress.

When following their trails, we can find a plethora of archival sources for both their lives and works in prize jurisdiction. Although the focus of this book is on the American experience of British prize jurisdiction, archival sources on both sides of the Atlantic were consulted in order to prevent a biased analysis and to understand the motivations on both sides.

The main source body consists of legal records, records whose standardisation has sometimes masked their "violent"[32] contexts, despite actually materialising these systems of power that were enacted by imposing "the law".[33]

The basis of the research on Robert Bayard is formed of High Court of Admiralty records 49/92–96 in the National Archives, London (hereafter TNA).

According to Charles M. Andrews' *Guide to the Materials for American History, to 1783, in the Public Record Office of Great Britain*, Robert Bayard delivered an assignation book to the deputy register of the High Court of Admiralty on 29 November 1784.[34] Assignation books are lists of court orders,

31 TNA, HCA 45/20/8: *Salome (Wassen)* 91r.

32 J. Leane and N. Harkin, 'When Records Speak we Listen: Conversations with the Archive', in K. Biber, T. Luker and P. Vaughan (eds), *Law's Documents: Authority, Materiality, Aesthetics* (London and New York, 2022), pp. 51–70, at p. 54.

33 K. Biber, T. Luker and P. Vaughan, 'Law's documents: Authority, Materiality, Aesthetics' in Biber, Luker and Vaughan (eds), *Law's Documents: Authority, Materiality, Aesthetics*, pp. 3–25, at pp. 6–7.

34 No. 1823, C. M. Andrews, *Guide to the Materials for American History, to 1783, in the Public Record Office of Great Britain* (Washington DC, 1914), vol. 2, p. 330. Andrews believed this book to be mistakenly referring to a packet of nine books, now

structured chronologically by court day, and are not exclusive to the New York Vice-Admiralty Court; however, "the practice of writing up acts from Assignation Books was apparently general in civilian tribunals",[35] making it a typical feature of admiralty law. In simple terms, these New York assignation books (HCA 49/92) can be considered very similar to minutes of the court, as becomes particularly apparent when examining the two volumes of Registers from the New York Vice-Admiralty Court HCA 49/93 and HCA 49/94, in which the form of entries is practically identical. Moreover, the wrapper of HCA 49/92/2 reveals that the label/description of 'assignation books' may not be correct, as the book is titled *Minutes of the Court of Vice Admiralty for the Province of New York.*[36]

HCA 49/92/1–9 span almost continuously (following the pattern of court dates), from 31 December 1777 to 10 July 1783 and are absolutely crucial to this work. HCA 49/93 and HCA 49/94 date from 16 September 1777 to 9 October 1778 and form a set of bound volumes, with significant spinal damage, their covers both bearing the same design, intended to represent a unit.[37] On the former, *Register of Vice Admiralty of New York, September 17, 1777,*[38] has been written with ink. This volume starts by reiterating Bayard's commission, alongside that of the Register, David Mathews, dating from the same day, 6 December 1776. The entries in HCA 49/93 and /94 are practically identical to those in the assignation books, though varying in time and scope. In this manner almost all of Bayard's tenure has been recorded for posterity.

In addition, two volumes HCA 49/92/10–11 include a list of fees and cases. Further records from the Vice-Admiralty Court of New York in TNA's

catalogued as the assignation books HCA 49/92/1–9 at TNA. Andrews's interpretation of the receipt of a book being mistaken for a packet of books seems unconvincing. Two further volumes of 'A list of Causes and Fees and by whom paid' are included at TNA as HCA 49/92/10 and 49/92/11. Andrews's volume mentions three; ibid; The latter of these two volumes contains a loose, contemporary label, reading "Box No 4: 8 Assignation Books Unbound. Sent from New York. No 9 received the 19th November 1784"; TNA, HCA 49/92/11. If we assume that this label belonged to the assignation books as opposed to the lists of fees, where it is presently inserted, we can infer that Bayard delivered the ninth book on 19 November, after the other eight had already been received. In this case, the source that Andrews refers to would have been correct in mentioning one, singular book, as opposed to a packet of books. Either way, one can deduce that all nine assignation books had been received by November 1784. These nine books have been numbered on their respective front pages.

35 G. I. O. Duncan, *The High Court of Delegates* (Cambridge, 1971), p. 225.

36 TNA, HCA 49/92/2.

37 TNA, HCA 49/93: *Register for the Vice-Admiralty Court of the province of New York*; TNA, HCA 49/94: *Register for the Vice-Admiralty Court of the province of New York.*

38 TNA, HCA 49/93.

collection also include HCA 49/95 and /96. They are compiled registers of letters of agency; that is, of powers of attorney for prize agents acting before the New York Court. A quick look into these books reveals that conditions for prize agents could vary widely and that the legal phrasing of terms and conditions was equally diverse. They are "well filled",[39] not only with the names of authorised attorneys, but also with vast lists of seamen and officers attached to these powers of attorney, thus giving insights into the culture of the Royal Navy and its participants. It was not enough for the officers on board the naval vessel to authorise the power of attorney, individual signatures (copied out for the registers) were required from all the subordinates on their vessels. Many of the attorneys were notable merchants from New York. HCA 49/96 has been catalogued in greater depth, to include the names of vessels and prize agents, which is a useful reference work for researchers examining both maritime law and the history of New York.[40] The cataloguing of the HCA 49 series (Vice-Admiralty Court Proceedings) was supported by the William Nelson Cromwell Foundation, who have already recognised its potential for American legal history.[41]

The manuscript papers of more than 1,300 cases from the New York Vice-Admiralty Court can be found within the HCA 32 series.[42] As the appeals court was also located in London, these proceedings shed additional light on the vice-admiralty court during this time, so HCA 45 (printed appeals) and HCA 42 (manuscript appeals) likewise have references to the colonial court.[43]

[39] No. 1824; Andrews, *Guide to the Materials for American History*, vol. 2, p. 330.

[40] TNA, *Volume 2 of 'Letters of Agency', compiled by the registry of the British New York Vice-Admiralty Court*, Catalogue Description of HCA 49/96, https://discovery.nationalarchives.gov.uk/details/r/C3301416 (accessed 6 June 2023).

[41] TNA, *Vice-Admiralty Courts: Proceedings*, Catalogue description HCA 49, https://discovery.nationalarchives.gov.uk/details/r/C8647 (accessed 11 September 2023); William Nelson Cromwell Foundation, *William Nelson Cromwell Foundation*, https://cromwellfoundation.org/ (accessed 11 September 2023).

[42] For example, TNA, HCA 32/350/9: *Hawke* (Yell). Projects identifying American captures from the American Revolutionary War and the Fourth Anglo-Dutch War (1780–4) and their corresponding papers in this series are also being supported by the William Nelson Cromwell foundation, see TNA, *High Court of Admiralty: Prize Court: Prize Papers*, Catalogue Description HCA 32, https://discovery.nationalarchives.gov.uk/details/r/C8630 (accessed 23 March 2023).

[43] For example, TNA, HCA 42/331/1224: *Sally (Choate)*; TNA, HCA 45/19/9: *Sally (Choate)*. Many manuscript appeals from the HCA and other vice-admiralty courts alongside New York can be found in HCA 42/110–165, as yet uncatalogued. Some of the HCA 45 series has also been catalogued with support from the William Nelson Cromwell Foundation and made accessible on the Prize Papers Portal; TNA, *High Court of Appeals for Prizes: Case Books (Printed Appeal Papers)*, Catalogue Description

In addition to these records, Robert Bayard can be found in the Loyalist Claims Commission as well as in sundry colonial correspondence papers throughout the American Revolution.[44] His will and entry in the death duties have also been preserved.[45] The commissions that Robert Bayard was furnished with for his military and legal career are part of the New York Historical Society's collection.[46] All these records were used for this study to gain a rounded impression of his life and work.

Both Samuel Bayard and his wife Martha left diaries behind.[47] Martha's original diary has been lost, but extracts from it were published by her son, Lewis, and have thus survived.[48] These extracts outline her experiences in London, where she lived with Samuel for the duration of his mission from 1794 to 1798. Although the original document no longer survives, her son's editorship seems to have been unusual in its inclusion of several traumatic events, such as Martha recording her feelings upon the deaths of two of her children in London and her strong feelings of isolation and loneliness. Nevertheless, her diary must be regarded with the critical eye of an edited document as opposed to an original, archived journal. Samuel Bayard, a prolific writer, also left a diary for posterity. Here, it seems to have been one of several, however the others are lost.[49] This diary is focused exclusively on his work, with very few references to private events in his and his family's life. It was never published

HCA 45, http://discovery.nationalarchives.gov.uk/details/r/C8643 (accessed 26 May 2021); Prize Papers Portal: Appeals, https://portal.prizepapers.de/search/-/%28ISWORK%3Atrue+ISANCHOR%3Atrue%29+-IDDOC_PARENT%3A*/1/SORT_ALL_NAME/MD_DOCUMENT_DOCUMENT_TYPE%3ACase+book+of+prize+appeals%3B%3B/ (accessed 19 July 2023).

44 TNA, AO 12/20: *American Loyalist, Claims Series I, Evidence, New York*; TNA, AO 13/63: *American Loyalist Claims, Series II, Temporary Support, New York, A–B*; TNA, AO 13/113 A: *American Loyalists Claims, Series II, Temporary Assistance, New York, A–D*; For some examples of colonial correspondence, see TNA, PRO 30/55/41: *Thomas Murray to Robert Bayard, 29 March 1782*; TNA, PRO 30/55/44: *Robert Bayard to Maurice Morgan, 3 July 1782*; TNA, T 1/557: *Robert Bayard to John Robinson, 9 December 1780.*

45 TNA, IR 26/772, 1003: *Death Duties of Robert Bayard*; TNA, PROB 11/1621/289: *Will of Robert Bayard.*

46 New York Historical Society Museum and Library, *Robert Bayard (1739–1819) commissions and letters, 1757–1830.*

47 Some family furniture and crockery (mainly soup plates) also survive from the Bayards in the New York Historical Society's collection; New York Historical Society, *Works by Martha Pintard Bayard and Lewis Pintard*, https://emuseum.nyhistory.org/people/1849/martha-pintard-bayard/objects (accessed 19 July 2023).

48 Bayard, *Journal of Martha Bayard.*

49 The front cover of the diary has been marked "No I.", suggesting other diaries were either written or conceived of at the time of its marking.

and is part of the American Philosophical Society's collection.[50] Bayard's diary is riddled with changing abbreviations and personal judgements, which has made it both very challenging and rewarding. In addition, Bayard's private and business correspondence can be found in various American archives.[51]

The HCA 45 series, mentioned in brief above, was thoroughly analysed for the duration of the commission's work (1794–1804) and integrated with the hand-written appeals papers from HCA 42 to gain insights into Bayard's contribution and the success of the American venture in general. This series consists of various printed appeals papers, laying out each case on behalf of the respondents or claimants.[52] The papers were originally printed for the Lords of Appeal and later also used by commissioners of the Jay Treaty. They have been catalogued in great depth and are in large part available for digital access through the Prize Papers Portal.[53] Their manuscript equivalents can be found in HCA 42, though not all manuscript appeals also went on to be printed. In addition, the HCA records, comprising of original court and ships' papers, have also been preserved in many original cases files. These records are found in HCA series 30 and 32.[54] This collection of HCA records, created or preserved through the prize law system, consists of both papers produced by the court process and documents taken from an estimated 35,000 captured ships, and is kept in about 4,000 boxes at TNA. It has also been termed the 'Prize Papers'.[55]

50 S. Bayard, *London Diary of Judge Samuel Bayard: contained in 'Samuel Bayard Papers', American Philosophical Society* (1795).

51 A few letters have been printed; for example, correspondence between Bayard and Boudinot in Sterling's article; others can be found distributed in different collections across the United States; for example, Founders Online and NARA, *To Alexander Hamilton from Samuel Bayard, 23 April 1794*, https://founders.archives.gov/documents/Hamilton/01-16-02-0246 (accessed 7 October 2020); S. Bayard, *Letter to John Jay, 16 May 1796*, https://dlc.library.columbia.edu/jay/ldpd:78762 (accessed 11 March 2025); E. Boudinot, *Letter to Sammuel Bayard, 2 April 1796*, www.gilderlehrman.org/collection/glc03627 (accessed 11 March 2025). More correspondence can be found in the Collection of the American Philosophical Society.

52 TNA, Catalogue Description HCA 45.

53 Prize Papers Portal 2023.

54 TNA, *High Court of Admiralty and Supreme Court of Judicature: Admiralty Miscellanea*, Catalogue Description HCA 30, https://discovery.nationalarchives.gov.uk/details/r/C8628 (accessed 19 July 2023); TNA, Catalogue Description HCA 32; TNA, *High Court of Appeals for Prizes: Papers*: Catalogue Description HCA 42, https://discovery.nationalarchives.gov.uk/details/r/C8640 (accessed 26 May 2021); TNA, Catalogue Description HCA 45.

55 Prize Papers Project, *What is the Prize Papers collection?* www.prizepapers.de/what-is-the-price-papers-collection (accessed 13 July 2020).

To show how different visions of international law collided under Article VII of the Jay Treaty, the commission's records on both sides of the Atlantic have been examined for this study.[56] To limit the scope of this undertaking, Samuel Bayard's time in London (1794–8) was used as the reference framework for analysing these papers. At the National Archives and Records Administration, Washington (hereafter NARA), seven series are connected to the commission. One of these comprises Samuel Bayard's despatches to the Secretary of State, informing him of the status of his mission and current political development.[57] Alongside these are two bound volumes of commissioners' (legal) opinions,[58] two bound volumes of lists of claims compiled by Samuel Bayard in 1797,[59] and four volumes of commissioners' correspondence.[60] In addition, three series consist of boxes with loose paperwork: the series *General Records* consists of two boxes of further commission papers and Bayard's memorials.[61] The series *Records Relating to Claims* is almost exclusively connected to later cases.[62] Finally, the series *Records Relating to British Spoliations* was particularly valuable for this study. It encompasses six boxes sorted roughly alphabetically by the name of the vessel. These papers are in disarray, with some papers concerning vessels of the same name unintentionally placed together and sometimes individual papers belonging to the same vessel strewn throughout a box entirely. Another four boxes in the series have not been sorted at all and contain a wild mix of French captures, merchant correspondence, pamphlets and much more.[63] To puzzle scholars further, all the boxes are labelled differently from their online catalogue entries, with the *General Records* box 1 labelled *Records of Boundary and Claims Commissions and Arbitrations RG 76/International Claims/Great Britain Treaty of 1794 (Article VII) Unbound Records, Ca. 1790–1820*.[64] These NARA records were supplemented with

56 It appears that Moore did not access the British archive materials for his work.

57 NARA, *Letters Received from Samuel Bayard, ca. 1796 – NAID: 1170268.*

58 NARA, *Opinions Filed by the Commissioners, 1797 – NAID: 1170266.*

59 NARA, *List of Claims, 1797, dated 12 May 1797 – NAID: 1170192.*

60 NARA, *Vol. 1 – Papers Relative to the Commissioners, 1796–1804 – NAID: 1170191.*

61 NARA, *Box 1, General Records, ca. 1790–ca. 1820 – NAID: 1170269: Unbound Records.*

62 NARA, *Box 1, Records Relating to Claims, ca. 1796–1804 – NAID: 1438808: Miscellaneous Records Relating to Claims.*

63 NARA, *Records Relating to British Spoliations, ca. 1796–ca. 1824 – NAID 1170270*, Catalogue Description, https://catalog.archives.gov/id/1170270 (accessed 23 March 2023).

64 NARA, *Box 1, General Records – NAID: 1170269.*

published documents and memories found in the biographies and personal collections of the US commissioners.[65]

At TNA, the commission is archived as FO 304.[66] This collection is significantly larger than that at NARA.[67] As it consists of thirty-one record groups, not every subgroup will be detailed here.[68] Many of the catalogue entries and documents themselves overlap; for example, the British also maintained and copied commissioners' correspondence.[69] However, the minute books[70] and assessors' reports[71] are entirely lacking in the US archive, though some minute extracts from the commission can be found in the *General Records* series.[72] A much larger selection (eighteen boxes) of alphabetically sorted ships' cases can be found at TNA.[73] These have been maintained in a more orderly fashion, probably since they were originally set aside as they are, still in their original court structure. A specific collection of merchant correspondence is lacking in FO 304, though partially merchant correspondence is integrated into the alphabetic ship records.

Some of the British records beautifully encapsulate the development of the commissioners' work; for example, with FO 304/1/1 recording official awards in cumbersome and exceedingly large hand-written documents, whereas FO 304/25 and /26 contain compiled awards in streamlined printed forms, where only minimal entries needed to be entered by hand.[74] Such materials showcase how, over time, the processes involved in the commission's work were made more efficient as they became regular practice. A special highlight at TNA

65 W. Pinkney and H. Wheaton, *Some account of the life, writings, and speeches of William Pinkney* (New York, 1826); J. Trumbull, *Autobiography, Reminiscences, and Letters of John Trumbull from 1756 to 1841* (1841).

66 TNA, *Archives of American Claims Commission (1794)*, Catalogue Description FO 304, https://discovery.nationalarchives.gov.uk/details/r/C7618 (accessed 23 March 2023).

67 The distribution of papers was detailed by the commission on 23 February 1804. Copies of some books and journals were to be made for the US government, but the originals were to be kept in London, Minute Extracts of the commission, 23 February 1804, NARA, *Box 1, General Records – NAID: 1170269*.

68 To be precise there are thirty-four record groups, but FO 304/32–35 concern the other commissions of the Jay Treaty.

69 TNA, FO 304/31.

70 TNA, FO 304 19–24.

71 TNA, FO 304/28–30.

72 For example, Minute Extracts of the Commission, 20 July 1799; NARA, *Box 1, General Records – NAID: 1170269*.

73 TNA, FO 304/1–18.

74 TNA, FO 304/1/1: *Polly (Smith), Atlantic (Marshall), Industry (Grozer)*; TNA, FO 304/25: *Office Copies of Awards, volume I*; TNA, FO 304/26: *Office Copies of Awards, volume II*.

is FO 304/27, a large register with data entered for each recorded case. This register was exhaustively analysed to gain quantitative impressions of the commission's work. Undoubtedly, even more data can be gathered from the private collections of the British commissioners.[75]

All these sources naturally come with their own challenges. The legal records generally depict the visions of the empowered party. Certainly, some of the claimants would have disagreed with the way they were labelled and processed; however, they give us insight into the system and its conduct. While claimants may not have agreed with the nationality or political affiliations they were ascribed, the financial outcomes denoted in the records can generally be accepted, as they were often based on proofs, invoices and appraisals. As the saying goes: follow the money.

Regardless, merchants may have overstated their losses in a bid for compensation. Their anger may have clouded their complaints, leading to exaggerations. They may have found solutions outside court, bribed appraisers or engaged in illegal or illicit activities. A proclamation of innocence may have masked an intentional smuggling operation. Equally, corrupt vice-admiralty courts may have been engaging in similar practices. The HCA 45 series is invaluable as it provides us with the narratives both parties presented before court. Yet while we can use these sources to understand the arguments that were made and to follow the decrees that were issued, we will never know what really happened at sea and although the legal argumentation and national policies enacted by Britain have been reconstructed, there is a notable absence of the British mercantile voice in this study. Yet the methodology has clearly turned the sums and case files of these legal documents into the voices of affected American individuals, which lie at the heart of this study: understanding how British prize jurisdiction affected Americans.

The first chapter will provide an overview of British (or English) prize jurisdiction in colonial America and is ideally suited for those new to this subject matter. How did prize work? What baggage did it come with? And why did historiography lose sight of Britain's last American vice-admiralty judge, Robert Bayard?

These questions are followed by a close examination of this missing link, analysing Robert Bayard's tenure during the Revolution in Chapter 2 and comparing the New York Vice-Admiralty Court with its imperial counterpart. How did prize work in loyalist New York and what did this mean for rebels/patriots/those caught in the crossfire?

Chapter 3 transitions from war and rebellion to independence and peace. Which objectives did American politicians strive for in this new republic?

75 For example, TNA, HCA 30/464–467 and HCA 30/475.

What role did prize and international law play for them? And how did relations outside the Anglophone realm impact on these goals?

Tracing Samuel Bayard's efforts in the lower courts, we examine how the first American agent for aiding in disputed prize claims began his operations in London (Chapter 4) and delve deeper into the conflicts his work and the American objectives brought claimants into (Chapter 5).

We then follow American objectives up the judicial ladder, into the appellate court, into an entirely different judicial body (Chapter 6). How many Americans chose this path and why? Which strategies could they use in their defence? The global connections and entanglements caused by the web of British prize courts, particularly in the Caribbean, played a crucial role in this regard.

While the Lords of Appeal offered the highest form of British legal redress, the Jay Treaty had created another chance for Americans to gain compensation under Article VII, providing a binational arbitration commission. In Chapter 7, the impact of this commission is examined, questioning the celebrated nineteenth century vision of Jay's success. How did American politicians try to instrumentalise the law of nations to their advantage and what consequences did this bring for American claimants? Moreover, the Chapter 8 delves into the American mercantile and maritime experience of the commission's work: the communication cycles required in this first large-scale transatlantic governmental effort show the pitfalls and chances the commission offered, highlighting the voice of affected American citizens. What did it feel like to be trapped in British admiralty jurisdiction? Was it all a question of economics, of losses and gains, or was there more to American merchants' claims?

In Chapter 9, we look beyond the commission, shining a light from the developments in prize jurisdiction post-1804 up until the present day, before drawing our final conclusions. When American politicians, intelligence firms and naval historians refer to prize law as a method to combat the Chinese and the Russians in the twenty-first century, we must realise that prize law is not a thing of the past, but a story still waiting to be written. And the pen is never far away.

# 1

# Looking Back: Prize Jurisdiction in New York and Colonial America

Many studies have been published on the development of maritime courts. Maritime courts[1] (including admiralty jurisdiction) and their existence as part of an international network of common legal ground have been traced back in time through the ages. Some researchers trace this common European legal practice through the codifications of the Consulato de Mare, the Black Book of the Admiralty, Rhodian sea law, to the Tabular Amalphitana, the Rôles d'Oléron, Jerusalem or the Baltic and Hanseatic states.[2]

Other experts emphasise that merchant and consular courts had been prevalent previously.[3] Merchant courts reflect how commercial communities found measures to ensure their interests in maritime trade.[4] Such measures were gradually taken over by the state.[5] Consular courts show a different approach to issues of the marine, not focusing on commercial business as a common denominator, but instead highlighting the international character of maritime trade interactions. Consular courts reduced the possibility of individuals later claiming to have been wronged as foreigners and gave leeway to different legal practices as enacted in different countries, regions or cities.[6] Both merchant and consular courts would be replaced by admiralty courts

1 Grant and Gilmore define admiralty and maritime law as "virtually synonymous", a definition to which this work will adhere. However, while this work will consider maritime law to include admiralty law, it will not use the term 'admiralty law' to include all other forms of maritime law. G. Gilmore and C. L. Black, *The Law of Admiralty*, 2nd edn (Mineola NY, 1975), p. 1.

2 For a thorough overview of historical sources, see *J. H. W. Verzijl, W. P. Heere and J. P. Offerhaus, The Law of Maritime Prize, Nova et vetera iuris gentium. Ser. A, Modern international law* (Leiden, 1992), vol. 16, Chapter 1, Section 1.

3 F. Deák and P. C. Jessup, 'Early Prize Court Procedure: Part One', *University of Pennsylvania Law Review*, 82/7–8 (1934), 677–94, at 679.

4 Paulsen, 'An Historical Overview of Development of Uniformity in International Maritime Law', 1067.

5 Ibid., 1073.

6 F. M. Kert, *Prize and Prejudice: Privateering and Naval Prize in Atlantic Canada in the War of 1812* (St John's, Newfoundland, 1997), vol. 11, pp. 41–2; Paulsen,

in the long term, with the consular prevailing significantly longer. Consular courts continued to be used regularly as alternatives to prize courts well into the eighteenth century, mainly due to the practicalities of international jurisdiction.[7] Whatever their origins, the demand for maritime courts was a direct result of international trade and its expansion. Admiralty jurisdiction was to solve this demand by addressing maritime law in a more standardised, regulated and clear fashion.[8]

According to the Black Book of the Admiralty, the High Court of Admiralty was established during the reign of Edward I (1272–1307), with Durston tracing its first case back to 1357.[9] Legal historian Holdsworth described the court's jurisdiction as "wide and vague",[10] comprising criminal, civil and prize law, as well as the regulation of droits, salvage and wrecks. Criminal, instance and prize law would become distinct branches – 'sides'[11] in judicial jargon – of the admiralty court with separate rules and processes to follow.[12] Its jurisdictional limitations were the tide and a 'doctrine of salt', meaning they had no jurisdiction over inland waterways.[13]

With the expansion of trade and seafaring beyond European waters, especially under Elizabethan rule, maritime law and warfare gained a new importance.[14] Diplomatic tensions could easily arise from maritime disputes,

---

'An Historical Overview of Development of Uniformity in International Maritime Law', 1067.

7 For an example of consuls' roles in general procedure, see HCA 32/216/10. For a case involving consulates and ambassadors, see HCA 32/250/5.

8 R. Hill, *The Prizes of War: The Naval Prize System in the Napoleonic Wars, 1793–1815* (Stroud, 1998), p. 7.

9 G. Durston, *The Admiralty Sessions, 1536–1834: Maritime Crime and the Silver Oar* (Newcastle-upon-Tyne, 2017), p. 6; Other scholars date its first nominal existence to 1360 and first traceable session to 26 July 1361, for example, G. H. M. Thompson, *Admiralty Registrars: Some Historical Notes* ([London], 1958), p. 7.

10 W. S. Holdsworth, A. L. Goodhart, H. G. Hanbury and S. B. Chrimes, *A History of English Law*, volume 1, 4th edn (London, 2009, 1938), p. 548.

11 H. C. Black, *Black's Law Dictionary: Definitions of the Terms and Phrases of American and English Jurisprudence, Ancient and Modern*, 4, rev. edn (St Paul MN, 1968), p. 1551.

12 The National Archives, London, Guide to the High Court of Admiralty Records, www.nationalarchives.gov.uk/help-with-your-research/research-guides/high-court-admiralty-records/#4-pre-1535 (accessed 11 March 2025).

13 T. M. Etting, *The Admiralty Jurisdiction in America* (Philadelphia PA, 1879), p. 12; Though a significant dispute between civil and common law professionals would erupt, prize was never a disputed area of jurisdiction. Harrington, 'Legacy, Part II', 588, fn 28.

14 D. Scott, 'The Spanish Armada and England's Conflict with Spain, 1585–1604', in J. Davey (ed.), *Tudors and Stuart Seafarers: The Emergence of a Maritime Nation, 1485–1707*, 1st edn, 1 vol. (London, 2018), pp. 55–79.

whose international jurisdictional issues could have far-reaching implications.[15] The creation of the letter of marque and reprisal exemplifies this. Letters of marque and reprisal were originally created to right individual grievances that could not be sorted through diplomatic measures or consular courts.[16] In this manner, an English captain who had, for example, been captured and robbed at sea by a Frenchman, applied to the English government. If they in turn could not receive or incentivise the French government to give compensation, the applicant could be issued a letter of marque and reprisal instead. With this letter, authorised by the monarch, the English captain had permission to capture a French ship at sea and thus 'correct' the miscarriage of justice that had befallen him on an individual level. This practice was originally rooted in common law and was not considered a breach of peace as it was on a private, individual level.[17] Over time, the measure evolved from a redressing of individual wrongs to a collective measure, dropping the 'reprisal' aspect to become the simple 'letter of marque'.[18] This meant that it no longer addressed the wronging of a private individual by another, but of one state against another, turning the letters into "instruments of warfare".[19] From this point of view, an entire nation had allegedly been 'wronged', and therefore there was no limit to the amount of captures that could be undertaken to 'redress' this international imbalance, thus allowing governments or monarchs to issue as many letters of marque as they wished against their alleged aggressor.[20] The development of the letter of marque created privateering as an established principle of European maritime warfare.[21] Accordingly, the office of the Admiral, which was responsible for issuing such letters and governing the actions of the privateers who owned them, was strengthened.[22]

English/British admiralty jurisdiction, as well as privateering, was exported to the nation's colonies in the shape of inferior vice-admiralty courts. After the introduction of (English) admiralty jurisdiction in the British Isles, a global

15 Holdsworth, Goodhart, Hanbury and Chrimes, *A History of English Law*, vol. 1, p. 533.

16 D. J. Starkey, 'Voluntaries and Sea Robbers: A Review of the Academic Literature on Privateering, Corsairing, Buccaneering and Piracy', *The Mariner's Mirror*, 97 (2011), 127–47, at 129.

17 T. M. Cooperstein, 'Letters of Marque and Reprisal: The Constitutional Law and Practice of Privateering', *Journal of Maritime Law and Commerce, 40/2* (2009), at 223.

18 Starkey, 'Voluntaries and Sea Robbers', 130.

19 D. A. Petrie, *The Prize Game: Lawful Looting on the High Seas in the Days of Fighting Sail* (New York, 1999), p. 3.

20 Hill, *The Prizes of War*, pp. 6–7.

21 Starkey, 'Voluntaries and Sea Robbers', 132–3.

22 D. J. Starkey, *British Privateering Enterprise in the Eighteenth Century* (Exeter, 1990), vol. 4, p. 23.

web of vice-admiralty courts was set up. Previously, maritime business in North America had been taken on by non-specialised courts out of necessity. Often these courts would style themselves as 'Courts of Admiralty'; for example, in Maryland and Virginia, where the courts even undertook prize jurisdiction, but they were not officially sanctioned at this point.[23] As the imperial legal system established itself and became more complex, admiralty jurisdiction was officially allocated to courts in the system, local courts being replaced by new, state-sanctioned vice-admiralty courts from the end of the seventeenth century; for example, in Maryland (1694), New York (1697), South Carolina (1697), Pennsylvania (1698), Virginia (1698), Massachusetts, (1699), New Hampshire (1704/1715), Rhode Island (1716), North Carolina (1729) and Georgia (after 1745).[24] The 1696 Act for Preventing Frauds, and Regulating Abuses in the Plantation Trade determined that all vice-admiralty court judges were to be appointed from London.

In theory, all the vice-admiralty courts based their decisions on the same judicial principles. The vice-admiralty courts were not independent, colonial courts, they were supposed to be extensions of the High Court of Admiralty, part of the same organism, following the same legal precedents.[25] In 1711, this principle, confirming the High Court of Admiralty's legal superiority and cementing its status as the court whose decisions were to be the model for all other admiralty courts, was enshrined in British law.[26] But in practice, this was difficult to achieve, as the judgments from the High Court of Admiralty and the appeals court were not published for colonial judges to refer to. Throughout their establishment appealing decrees from vice-admiralty courts was costly and time-consuming. At first, the appeals jurisdiction for vice-admiralty causes lay with the reigning monarch, but was later it was transferred to the Privy Council and subsequently to the Lords of Appeal.[27] In all cases, distance created costs.

Moreover, some of the vice-admiralty courts were staffed by qualified personnel that had experience at Doctors' Commons and could fall back on their doctorates of Civil Law, but most of these courts were run by the

[23] H. J. Bourguignon, *The First Federal Court: The Federal Appellate Prize Court of the American Revolution, 1775–1787, Memoirs of the American Philosophical Society* (Philadelphia PA, 1977), vol. 122, p. 21.

[24] Mangone, *United States Admiralty Law*, p. 26.

[25] J. P. van Niekerk, 'The Story of the Silver Oar Mace of the Vice-Admiralty Court of the Cape of Good Hope', *Fundamina*,18 (2012), 135–73, at 151.

[26] M. J. Carton, 'The Caribbean Vice Admiralty Courts 1763–1815: Indispensable Agents of an Imperial System' (dissertation, 1968), p. 38.

[27] Kert, *Prize and Prejudice*, vol. 11, p. 44; Cooperstein, 'Letters of Marque and Reprisal', 225; cf., C. J. Colombos, *A Treatise on the Law of Prize*, 2nd edn (London, 1940), p. 16.

governors of the colonies in question.[28] They were often accused of abusing the system, of being in league with either privateers or illegal traders, who were often viewed as their counterpart.[29] The imperial regulation of such courts was not very strong and, over time, with the strengthening of its Empire, British admiralty jurisdiction also attempted to gain more control over its jurisdictional players abroad.[30]

Due to a regular stream of wars and incurred war costs throughout the first half of the eighteenth century, the British government started looking for new, additional forms of revenue.[31] Various duties enacted by parliament to collect taxes in the North American colonies seemed a suitable stream of income. It was argued that wars, both in and outside Europe, were conducted to protect said colonies, thus, increased taxation was seen as justifiable.[32] Local interest of course was not in favour. Colonial taxation could be viewed as simply "for the benefit of the Imperial coffers"[33] or to line the "pockets of various Crown officers"[34] as well as Britain-based merchants. Thus, various methods of evading customs officials ensued. The easiest of which were cooperation, bribery or intimidation of the Crown officials, including vice-admiralty court judges.[35] But these could not withstand long-term pressure from London. The commissions of vice-admiralty judges, for example, were frequently issued "at the pleasure" of the Crown, as opposed to being based on "good conduct".[36] Their judgeship was therefore dependent on delivering the desired results. In addition, their tenures were not salaried positions, their incomes relied on fees and percentages of condemnations, as was the usual practice in Britain.[37] Hence, the enforcement of the government regulations was regularly seen as evidence for personal greed.[38] Whether acting in collusion with the locals or

28 Kert focuses the Vice-Admiralty Court at Halifax; Kert, *Prize and Prejudice*, vol. 11, pp. 56–7.

29 Ubbelohde, *The Vice-Admiralty Courts and the American Revolution*, p. 26.

30 For more on this phenomenon in general, see L. A. Benton and L. Ford, *Rage for Order: The British Empire and the Origins of International Law, 1800–1850* (Cambridge MA, London, 2016).

31 Mangone, *United States Admiralty Law*, p. 27.

32 C. B. Yirush, 'The Imperial Crisis', in J. Kamensky and E. G. Gray (eds), *The Oxford Handbook of the American Revolution* (Oxford, 2012), pp. 85–102, at p. 86.

33 C. A. Ying, 'Colonial and Federal Admiralty Jurisdiction', *Federal Law Review*, 12 (1981), 236–70, at 242.

34 Wroth, 'Massachusetts Vice Admiralty Court', 262.

35 Ubbelohde, *The Vice-Admiralty Courts and the American Revolution*, pp. 24–6.

36 W. F. Pratt, 'Judicial Disability and the Good Behavior Clause', *Yale Law Journal*, 85 (1976), 706–20, at 708.

37 Mangone, *United States Admiralty Law*, pp. 29–30.

38 One utterance of this can be found in the *Boston Gazette*, 5 October 1772, stating: "Rejoice O America, in the Blessings of His [George III] Auspicious Reign –

not, the inability of customs officials of the Crown to prosecute revenue cases before common law courts became increasingly apparent. Wherever trials were conducted by jury, there was a risk that local (financial) interests would trump the intention of the (imperially) issued acts. Simply put, the situation put Crown officials, especially in the realm of customs, in a very difficult position.

A clause of the Navigation Act of 1696 therefore gave vice-admiralty courts "equal jurisdiction with common-law courts in trade and revenue cases".[39]. In the same year, the Act for Preventing Frauds, and Regulating Abuses in the Plantation Trade determined that all vice-admiralty court judges were to be appointed from London.[40]

Taking trade-violation or customs cases to vice-admiralty courts was an attempt to remedy the inability to prosecute in common law courts, as according to civil law admiralty courts were presided over by a single judge and did not feature any jury.[41] Chances for condemnations were therefore significantly improved. As Friedman put it, "from the English standpoint, the lack of a jury was icing on the cake".[42] In England/Great Britain, the High Court of Admiralty was also headed by a single judge with the title of "Supremae Curiae Admiralitatis Angliae locum tenens Judex, sive Praesidens".[43] He was in the position to pronounce sentences, both interlocutory and final, after hearing a case in court without the assistance of a jury. By employing merely one judge, the court hoped to achieve a higher consistency and credibility in its rulings.[44] However, in Britain, trade law violations would not have fallen to the

in which your Property is so wisely Justly & Mercifully taken care of by Courts of Admiralty", quoted in Ubbelohde, *The Vice-Admiralty Courts and the American Revolution*, p. 189.

39 Ibid., p. 15.

40 Bourguignon, *The First Federal Court*, vol. 122, p. 25.

41 R. S. August, 'Trial by Jury in a Court of Admiralty: A Constitutional Right Buried Under Historical Ignorance', *Journal of Maritime Law and Commerce*, 13 (1982), 149–76, at 163.

42 L. M. Friedman, *A History of American Law*, 3rd edn (New York, 2005), p. 21.

43 J. Chamberlayne, *Magnæ Britanniæ Notitia: Or, The present state of Great-Britain: With diverse remarks upon the ancient state thereof. By John Chamberlayne, Esq; The thirty-seventh edition of the south part, called England; and the sixteenth of the north part, called Scotland. To which is added, a compleat list of their Royal Highnesses the Prince and Princess of Wale's household; as also those of their Royal Highnesses the Duke of Cumberland, the Princess Amelia, and the Princess Caroline. In two parts. With His Majesty's royal privillege*, Eighteenth Century Collections Online (London, 1748), p. 232.

44 Hill, *The Prizes of War*, p. 162. A secondary result of the single judge policy was that the entire workload fell to one person, as well as resulting in confusing rulings should a judge change his legal point of view or be unsuited or unqualified for the job. In the cases of admiralty and especially prize jurisdiction, this workload could

High Court of Admiralty but to the Court of Exchequer, where hearings were conducted before a jury.[45] These colonial rulings therefore clearly demonstrate how wider jurisdiction was permitted in the vice-admiralty courts across the Atlantic, than was tolerated at home with the High Court of Admiralty.[46] They were, simply put, being used to solve a problem caused by lack of authority. These differences also founded colonial inhabitants' belief, that they were illegally being deprived of a jury and their natural rights were thus being infringed.[47] It is this role that has provided vice-admiralty courts with the label "controversial".[48]

Some legal historians have felt the need to point out that the work conducted in the vice-admiralty courts was "integral"[49] to the functioning of the maritime community and was "more often beneficial than it was oppressive".[50] Indeed, before 1776, it is generally the grievances against the vice-admiralty courts that are highlighted by historians, perfectly epitomised in Carl Ubbelohde's work. In it, the criticism of the system is at the forefront, in order to show how these attitudes to vice-admiralty courts contributed to the American Revolution.[51] Harrington in contrast sees many historians as having taken on the rhetoric of revolutionaries without question, painting the vice-admiralty court as a "universally-hated institution",[52] and overshadowing its maritime functions. Certainly, that prize jurisdiction lay with admiralty courts was "virtually unchallenged",[53] and not an issue of political contention.

Either way, its function as a place for prosecuting violations of acts of trade, among other things, was highly contested. This procedure was further

---

vary from more than 2,000 cases per year in wartime (for example, in 1806), to an "occasional morning's" work in times of peace; H. C. Coote, *The New Practice of the High Court of Admiralty of England: With the Rules of 1859, and a collection of forms, and bills of costs, &c., &c*, p. 5, http://galenet.galegroup.com/servlet/MOML?af=RN&ae=F106188149&srchtp=a&ste=14 (accessed 11 March 2025).

45 TNA, *Court of Exchequer: Research Guide*, www.nationalarchives.gov.uk/help-with-your-research/research-guides/court-exchequer/ (accessed 1 February 2023).

46 Bourguignon, *The First Federal Court*, vol. 122, p. 24.

47 Mangone, *United States Admiralty Law*, p. 26.

48 Harrington, 'Legacy, Part I', 581.

49 Harrington, 'Legacy, Part II', 337.

50 Towle, *Records of the Vice-Admiralty Court of Rhode Island*, III, p. 2.

51 Ubbelohde, *The Vice-Admiralty Courts and the American Revolution.*

52 Harrington, 'Legacy, Part II', 338.

53 Wroth, 'Massachusetts Vice Admiralty Court', 264.

enshrined in the Revenue Act of 1764 and the Stamp Act of 1765.[54] And this, despite the Stamp Act having "nothing to do with the sea".[55]

New York's Vice-Admiralty Court had been founded in 1697, exactly fifty years after the Bayard family emigrated to America due to their Huguenot faith.[56] It has been described as the "mother court"[57] of the American colonies and was well known for having "the heaviest concentration of maritime lawyers outside of London".[58] During the Revolution, New York was the place where "the problem of revolutionary political choice [was] at its most complex".[59] The Crown had many supporters here, a relationship that is exemplified by the city's acquirement of a silver admiralty oar, a symbol of the vice-admiralty court's power inspired by the original oar still preserved in London today. The New York silver admiralty oar was crafted in *c.* 1725 by local silversmith Charles Le Roux. It had its locality and a fouled anchor engraved on its hilt and blade, but also displayed the Royal Coat of Arms.[60] By the 1760s, the New York court would be located on Wall Street.[61] Robert Bayard's grandfather had served on the New York Vice-Admiralty Court and his great-grandfather had worked in the administration that set up a vice-admiralty court even before the official sanctioning of such an undertaking had been granted.[62] His father became the mayor of New York from 1744 to 1747 and married the daughter of the Royal Governor of Nova Scotia, Alida Vetch.[63] In general, the family

54 In the Stamp Act, admiralty jurisdiction is guaranteed next to "any court of record", in the Sugar Act, the vice-admiralty courts specifically were "authorized and required to proceed, hear and determine" such cases; An Act for Granting Certain Duties in the British Colonies and Plantations in America: The Sugar Act (1764); An Act for Granting and applying Certain Stamp Duties, and Other Duties, in the British Colonies and Plantations in America: Stamp Act (1765).

55 Friedman, *A History of American Law*, p. 21.

56 An overview of the Bayard genealogy can be found in figure 1. Mangone, *United States Admiralty Law*, p. 26; Fosdick, *French Blood in America*, p. 308.

57 John D. Winter and Richard Maidman, 'Retelling the History of the United States District Court for the Southern District of New York', *NY Litigator*, 17 (2012), 1.

58 Van Niekerk, 'Story of the Silver Oar', 154.

59 N. E. H. Hull, P. C. Hoffer and S. L. Allen, 'Choosing Sides: A Quantitative Study of the Personality Determinants of Loyalist and Revolutionary Political Affiliation in New York', *The Journal of American History*, 65 (1978), 344–66, at 344.

60 Southern District Court of New York, *Proceedings: Gift of Silver Oar* (1941).

61 M. J. Lamb, *Wall Street in History* (New York, 2005), p. 29.

62 Burke and Burke, *Dictionary Landed Gentry*, vol. 2, p. 1361; Caliendo, *New York Mayors*, pp. 6–7, 10; Niekerk dates the first court slightly later, considering Colonial Governor Edmund Andros as the responsible founder in 1678; van Niekerk, 'Story of the Silver Oar', 153.

63 Alida Vetch's parents were Robert Livingston and Alida Schuyler Van Rensselaer, families of large wealth and high standing in the New York area.

was very well connected and established in the New York area by the time of Bayard's birth in 1729.[64] Being the ninth of ten children and not the eldest son, Robert Bayard decided to enter government service too.[65] He was "ever from his Youth [...] a Crown Officer",[66] soon serving in the British army. On 26 December 1757, he was promoted to the rank of Lieutenant.[67] Two years later he was a Captain in the 60th Royal American Regiment of Foot.[68] By 1766, the year that the Stamp Act was repealed, his position in the officer corps of that regiment was firmly cemented and he was promoted to the rank of Major.[69] Now he had only six direct superior officers within his unit, commanding a force of more than 2,000 men.[70] This regiment, previously numbered the 62nd Royal American Regiment of Foot, had been renumbered in 1756 after a restructuring of the (royal) American armed forces led to the dissolution of two other regiments.[71] It saw active duty in the French and Indian wars in forested territories of Canada, and would again fight in Pontiac's Rebellion in 1763, combating various Native American tribes in the Great Lakes Region.[72]

In 1766, Bayard had not only been promoted, but had also married Rebecca Apthrop, the daughter of Charles Apthrop, allegedly the richest man in Boston.[73] Bayard's new brother-in-law was James McEvers, the stamp and

64 William described his family line as "among the first Settlers of that Province [of New York], under the British Government in point of Rank, as well as fortune". Testimony of Willliam Bayard, TNA, AO 12/20, 130r. As Bulloch would phrase it, "In New York the [Bayard] family descended from or was allied to the foremost families, among whom were the Stuyvesants, Van Cortlandts, Livingstons, Van Rensselaers, Schuylers, Cuylers, Van Brughs and others"; Bulloch, *A History and Genealogy of the Families of Bayard, Houstoun of Georgia*, p. 2.

65 J. Cornell, *Genealogy of the Cornell family: Being an Account of the Descendants of Thomas Cornell* (New York, 1902), p. 381.

66 TNA, AO 13/113 A, 104r.

67 New York Historical Society Museum and Library, *Robert Bayard (1739–1819) commissions and letters, 1757–1830*.

68 Wallace, *Regimental Chronicle*, p. 84.

69 New York Historical Society Museum and Library, *Robert Bayard (1739–1819) commissions and letters, 1757–1830*; Despite his varied and continuing career as a Crown official, the title of Major would stick to him during and beyond his lifetime. While his grandfather, Samuel Bayard, would generally remain 'Judge Bayard' in genealogical research, Robert remained known as the 'Major Bayard'; W. S. Pelletreau, *Historic Homes and Institutions and Genealogical and Family History of New York: Volume I*, 4 vols (New York and Chicago IL, 1907), vol. 1, p. 109.

70 Wallace, *Regimental Chronicle*, pp. 86–7.

71 Ibid., pp. 1–2.

72 Ibid., pp. 9–12.

73 HouseHistree, *Charles Apthorp (1698–1758)*, https://househistree.com/people/charles-apthorp (accessed 20 May 2023). He supposedly left a fortune of £150,000 after his passing; Pelletreau, *Historic Homes*, vol. 1, p. 109.

tax collector in New York during the Stamp Act crisis.[74] Crown officials there would describe the situation as verging on anarchy, with various mobs, often spearheaded by the radical Liberty Boys, taking part in public resentment over and the demand for the repeal of the Stamp Act.[75] A pseudonymously penned article in the New York *Mercury* had warned stamp distributors "to look for Nothing but the Hatred and Detestation of all the Good and Virtuous".[76] News reached the town of riots in Boston over the Stamp Act in August 1765.[77] Bostonians had forced their stamp agent, Andrew Oliver, to resign, while a second mob had burnt their vice-admiralty court records and ransacked the house of the Massachusetts Chief Justice.[78] An effigy of Oliver had been paraded through town, before the mob destroyed his home.[79] An effigy of Governor Colden had been ceremoniously hung from a gallows, before being burnt, along with his carriage, and furniture of one of the town's Majors.[80] McEvers resigned in the summer of 1765.[81] In November 1765 about 200 Liberty Boys, having discovered the Maryland stamp collector's whereabouts, forced him to renounce his commission. One month later, the Liberty Boys forced James McEvers to publicly confirm his resignation once more.[82] Appointed stamp distributors had "come to symbolize the tyranny of legislation".[83] Thus, they had joined the ranks of civil and military leaders in the wrath over British (imperial) policies. Robert Bayard thus gained a close, familial impression of the public pressure faced by officials.

Nevertheless, in 1769, he sold his commission to Captain John Wharton.[84] Subsequently, he received a commission to act as Collector of His Majesty's Customs at the Port of Philadelphia from 7 February 1772 onwards.[85] He must have understood the antipathy and risk that his new position would bring him. But Bayard had other factors to consider; he may have been preoccupied with

74 HouseHistree, *James McEvers (1763–1818)*, https://househistree.com/people/james-mcevers (accessed 23 May 2023).

75 J. S. Tiedemann, *Reluctant Revolutionaries: New York City and the Road to Independence, 1763–1776* (Ithaca NY, 2008), p. 78.

76 *Mercury*, 26 August 1765, quoted in B. A. Jones, *Resisting Independence: Popular Loyalism in the Revolutionary British Atlantic* (Ithaca NY, 2021), p. 53.

77 Tiedemann, *Reluctant Revolutionaries*, p. 66.

78 Ibid., pp. 71–2.

79 Jones, *Resisting Independence*, p. 53.

80 B. L. Carp, *The Great New York Fire of 1776: A Lost Story of the American Revolution* (New Haven CT, 2023), p. 15.

81 Jones, *Resisting Independence*, p. 53.

82 Tiedemann, *Reluctant Revolutionaries*, p. 84.

83 Jones, *Resisting Independence*, p. 52.

84 'War Office announcement 12 April', *London Gazette*, 18 April 1769.

85 TNA, AO 12/20, 117r; New York Historical Society Museum and Library, *Robert Bayard (1739–1819) commissions and letters, 1757–1830*.

the burial of his first wife and his second marriage, this time to her sister, Elizabeth.[86] As tension around taxation and other 'rights' of colonial Britons residing in America rose, Bayard was "often threatened and his house [...] watched and Surrounded by Arm'd Men".[87] In May 1773 the Tea Act was issued, ringing in another era of tension and conflict between the British motherland and her colonial North American subjects. While some feared these would mirror events from the Stamp Act crisis, others believed the new Governor, Tryon, would easily deal with the unrest.[88] However, the latter far underestimated the public reaction. A committee of fifty (swiftly expanded to fifty-one) was set up to coordinate a joint response with the other colonies and decided on a joint response; for example, with economic sanctions, such as non-importation agreements. It drafted a letter condemning British reactions to the Boston Tea Party, such as the Boston Port Act, and agreed to join a Continental Congress to determine further steps.[89]

Robert's older brother, William, earnt his living as the head of the mercantile house William Bayard & Co., alongside his income from the Bayard estates.[90] He had served as a member of the Assembly in the Stamp Act Crisis.[91] A few years later, he was elected as a member of the New York Committee of Fifty, which was filled with a considerable number of moderates attempting to curb the radical drive for a general non-importation agreement. Yet when New York decided to join other provinces in the sanctioning of British imports and the refusal of exporting, in part, even to the West Indies, William Bayard continued to harbour Whig sentiments. He was closely associated with John Jay and other committee members and continued to host delegates of the Continental Congress up until 1775.[92] But something changed. In December 1775, the Prohibitory Act was issued by the British parliament. Declaring war in all but name on the American colonies, it gave permission to treat the vessels and cargo of rebellious Americans like "open enemies, and [they] shall be so adjudged, deemed, and taken, in all Courts of Admiralty", more specifically, "taken as prize" for the profit of the British capturing parties, unless those captured could prove they were conducting a legal, licensed trade.[93]

86 Tucker, *New York Marriages*, p. 247.

87 TNA, AO 13/113 A, 104r.

88 Tiedemann, *Reluctant Revolutionaries*, p. 179.

89 Ibid., pp. 187–90.

90 Sabine, *Biographical Sketches*, vol. 1, p. 217.

91 Pelletreau, *Historic Homes*, vol. 1, p. 109; E. S. Morgan and Helen M. Morgan, *The Stamp Act Crisis: Prologue to Revolution* (Chapel Hill NC and London, 1995), p. 304.

92 Sabine, *Biographical Sketches*, vol. 1, p. 217.

93 *An Act to Prohibit all Trade and Intercourse with the Colonies* (1775).

By June 1776, William Bayard was identified as a probable domestic enemy by the Provincial Congress and was summoned to appear before them.[94] If he could not prove his innocence – that is, his allegiance and support of the independence movement – he could be removed from his home, arrested and his property confiscated. Similarly, Robert Bayard was also identified as an enemy in the New York area. The specific reason for Robert (or indeed William) Bayard's summons is unclear. It could have been based on:

> reason of their holding Offices from the King of Great Britain, from their having neglected or refused to associate with their fellow citizens, for the defence of their common Rights, from their having never manifested, by their conduct a zeal for and attachment to the American cause, or from their having maintained an equivocal neutrality, have been considered by their countrymen in a suspicious light.[95]

A vague definition, giving little hope to an honest trial for those who dared appear before Congress. But as it was, neither of the Bayard brothers would try their luck. William Bayard fled first to an estate further afield, then to Britain from whence he never returned. Robert Bayard fled on the night of 20 June 1776, the day before his summons to Congress.[96] He rowed to the British vessel *Dutchess (of) Gordon*, which was lying at Sandy Hook.[97] William Tryon, the governor of New York, had already fled the city and taken refuge aboard what has been termed his "floating headquarters"[98] on 14 October 1775.[99] Both the Bayards decided to leave their families behind. Robert Bayard reported that his wife and ten children were threatened to be turned out of their house and become destitute by rebel forces.[100] In the end, they were permitted to stay, while plans were enacted to turn their home into a hospital.[101] This places Robert Bayard into the category of what New York historian Flick termed "chief loyalists",[102] whose homes were often early examples of appropriation and confiscation, repeatedly with the stated aim of being converted into hospitals. William Bayard, on the other hand, described his wife's utter state of shock almost as an attempt on her life, when she was

94 H. B. Dawson, *Westchester County, New York, During the American Revolution* (New York, 1886), p. 167.

95 Ibid., p. 169.

96 TNA, AO 12/20, 117r.

97 TNA, AO 13/113 A, 104r.

98 Carp, *Great New York Fire*, p. 42.

99 Ibid., p. 21.

100 TNA, AO 13/113 A, 104r.

101 TNA, AO 12/20, 117v.

102 A. Flick, *Loyalism in New York During the American Revolution, Studies in History, Economics and Public Law* (New York, 1901), XVI/1, p. 137.

awoken by armed men in the middle of the night, taking possession of their family home.[103]

On 4 July 1776, the Declaration of Independence was issued.[104] Robert Bayard remained on the *Dutchess (of) Gordon* until New York was recaptured by British troops on 15 September, though his exact role in this time is unclear.[105] Having lost his income, he "must have been reduced with his numerous Family to Extreme want"[106] had he not been furnished with a commission to become Vice-Admiralty Judge of New York by Governor Tryon, who Bayard not only described as a compassionate humanitarian, but also as a personal friend. The latter would appear to be confirmed by the name of his youngest son, Tryon Bayard, born in 1782.[107] He received his official commission as judge of the vice-admiralty court 6 December 1776, after the Governor of North Carolina, Josiah Martin, had applied to the British government for the official instalment of a vice-admiralty court in the New York area.[108] Maybe Bayard was already acting as a temporary judge at this point, as cases of prize are documented as coming before a New York Vice-Admiralty Court before this date.[109]

In the historiography of the Vice-Admiralty Court of New York, Robert Bayard is often overlooked. The tenures of previous judges have been the subject of historical study, particularly those three of the Morris family, who preceded him.[110] In the New York region, individual Vice-Admiralty case files from 1685 to 1774 can be found at NARA in Washington, as well as chronologically arranged minutes from the court spanning the time 1701 to 1774, though the latter item does not even have a description in the catalogue.[111] In addition, a minute book spanning 1753 to 1770 can be found in the New York

[103] Robert's wife was advised to remove some of their furniture at her own discretion to prevent its removal as part of the hospital conversion plans. However, this seems to have been a scheme, as the removed furniture could never be recovered once sent underway to a 'safe location' elsewhere; TNA, AO 12/20, 60v.

[104] *Declaration of Independence* (1776).

[105] Ibid., 117v.

[106] TNA, AO 13/113 A, 104r.

[107] New York Genealogical and Biographical Society, *The New York Genealogical and Biographical Record: Devoted to the Interests of American Genealogy and Biography* (New York, 1890), XXI, pp. 26–7.

[108] New York Historical Society Museum and Library, *Robert Bayard (1739–1819) commissions and letters, 1757–1830*; Governor Martin to Secretary of State, 7 August 1776; TNA, CO 5/330/022, pp. 276–83.

[109] For example, TNA, HCA 32/401/20: *Mercury* (Banker).

[110] For example, M. Watson, 'Judge Lewis Morris, the New York Vice-Admiralty Court, and Colonial Privateering: 1739–1762', *New York History*, 78 (1997), 117–46.

[111] NARA, Catalogue Entry: *Records created by the Organizational Unit New York (State) Court of Vice Admiralty: 4 Series*, https://catalog.archives.gov/search?q=record.creators.naId:10490821 (accessed 26 May 2023).

Public Library under the Archives and Manuscripts division, fully digitised. These records, however, mainly focus on the Seven Years' War (1756–63) during Judge Lewis Morris Jr's tenure.[112]

Richard Morris had previously served as a surrogate Vice-Admiralty Judge for his father, Lewis Morris Jr, in New Jersey, and took over the judgeship in New York in 1762.[113] Although the time of his resignation is unclear, Richard Morris gave up his position as Vice-Admiralty Judge due to his leaning towards independence and against loyalty to the Crown.[114]

In October and November 1775, Continental Congress permitted the fitting out of armed vessels.[115] Yet the biggest warships sailing under the American flag during the Revolution would actually be French (allied) ships.[116] The Continental Navy on the whole consisted of few vessels. However, privateering was a useful and known solution to supplementing a national navy.[117] 'American' waters had already been viewed as a training ground for colonial sailors by the British government, a source of skilled labour ready for impressment into the British Navy should wartime create the need.[118] About one-third of British merchant vessels were being built in the American colonies in 1775 due to more competitive pricing.[119] Thus, personnel and vessels were, in theory, available. At least one delegate to the Continental Congress had gained wealth through privateering investments, Robert Morris (no relation to Richard Morris), as did George Washington. Two delegates, Nathaniel Gorham and John Langdon, also invested in privateers. Letters of marque and reprisal were considered "both a natural component of the national war power and a concurrent aspect of the authority to raise a navy or enforce

112 New York Public Library, *Minute Book of the New York Court of Vice Admiralty*: MssCol 2230, https://archives.nypl.org/mss/2230 (accessed 31 January 2023).

113 Watson, 'Judge Lewis Morris', 146.

114 He was still actively serving in his position in June 1774. Historians have placed his resignation sometime between this date and 1776; for example, A. B. Street, *The Council of Revision of the State of New York: Its History, a History of the Courts with which its Members were connected, Biographical Sketches of its Members and its Vetoes* (Albany NY, 1859), p. 77; T. G. Bergen, *Genealogies of the State of New York: A Record of the Achievements of her People in the Making of a Commonwealth and the Founding of a Nation, Long Island Edition* (New York, 1915), p. 220.

115 Bourguignon, *The First Federal Court*, vol. 122, p. 43.

116 J. R. Dull, *American Naval History, 1607–1865: Overcoming the Colonial Legacy* (Lincoln NE, 2012), pp. 24–5.

117 J. C. Bradford, 'The First United States Navy', in J. P. Greene and J. R. Pole (eds), *A Companion to the American Revolution*, 1st edn (Malden MA: Blackwell Publishers, 2000), pp. 326–32, at p. 327.

118 Harrington, 'Legacy, Part I', 592.

119 Dull, *American Naval History*, p. 7.

international law".[120] Aside from Congress, individual states also issued privateering commissions. In total, more than 2,000 privateers were authorised in this manner, capturing more than "2,200 British merchant ships (not including those recaptured by the British)",[121] therefore increasing British insurance rates, causing convoy protections to be installed and adding to 'war-weariness'. In November 1775 Congress declared itself the sole authority for issuing privateering commissions. It also recommended the states establish courts to deal with captured prizes, suggesting trials by jury, with the jurisdiction lying with the state court where the prize had been captured.[122]

The New York Provincial Congress recommended establishing its own, new, American admiralty court to deal mainly with cases of prize on 31 July 1776. Richard Morris was offered the judgeship of this new court, called the Court of the Admiralty of New York.[123] However, he declined, attempting to shield his property and his family from the danger the position would bring. Upon resigning his tenure as British vice-admiralty Judge, Governor Tryon had asked him to reconsider, only to be rebuked.[124] In retaliation, Governor Tryon had confiscated Morris's property, Mount Fordham in Westchester County, approved it for use for the British army and finally, ordered its destruction upon their removal.[125] Lewis Graham would take on the new judgeship for the American cause in Morris's stead.[126] The void left by the disbanded vice-admiralty courts was thus quickly filled by individual states creating their own systems of adjudication, some of these even being established before Congress's declaration. Ubbelohde describes the death of the vice-admiralty courts as the birth of the "first American admiralty courts".[127] Nine states, including New York, created courts of admiralty and a further four created them under the name of 'Courts Maritime'.[128] Procedure and adjudication varied immensely in these different institutions.[129] Some states continued in what had previously been vice-admiralty courts, simply changing the name

[120] Cooperstein, 'Letters of Marque and Reprisal', 230.

[121] Dull, *American Naval History*, p. 28.

[122] Bourguignon, *The First Federal Court*, vol. 122, p. 48.

[123] Street, *Council of Revision*, p. 77.

[124] Historical Society of the New York Courts, *Richard Morris*, https://history.nycourts.gov/figure/richard-morris/ (accessed 26 May 2023).

[125] R. Bolton, *The History of the Several Towns, Manors, and Patents of the County of Westchester: From its First Settlement to the Present Time, Volume II* (New York, 1881), vol. 2, p. 524.

[126] Historical Society of the New York Courts, *The New York Court of Admiralty, 1775–1789*, https://history.nycourts.gov/case/court-admiralty/ (accessed 26 May 2023).

[127] Ubbelohde, *The Vice-Admiralty Courts and the American Revolution*, p. 194.

[128] August, 'Trial by Jury in a Court of Admiralty', 168.

[129] E. C. Benedict, *The Law of Admiralty: Its Jurisdiction and Practice with Forms and Directions*, 6th rev. edn (New York, 1940), vol. 4, p. 438.

and personnel, others determined common law courts to hear admiralty cases in special sittings.[130] However, though "not universally used, juries were definitely the rule and not the exception in prize litigation".[131] The legal basis for adjudication also varied widely with states referring to maritime law, the law of nations, the rule of the Continental Congress, state laws, the rolls of Oléron, Rhodian sea law and previous rules of the English admiralty in a variety of combinations.[132]

When examining the further development of the North American vice-admiralty court system it is also important to keep in mind that:

> The tradition of prize practice in America, within which American lawyers were trained, was already different from English practice before the American Revolution. When the Americans came to establish their own prize courts during the Revolution, it was very natural for them to continue the type of procedures (probably thinking them to be standard English procedures) with which they had become familiar in their own vice-admiralty court.[133]

However, due to the state of war in New York, the new Court of the Admiralty of New York never conducted any business until the British had evacuated the area after the peace of 1783. From 1784 to 1788, the only time during which the court functioned, no records remain.[134] In 1789 the court was replaced by the new District Court of New York.[135] This was not only another change of title, but reflected a nationwide change, moving admiralty courts from a state to a federal level.

Under the Articles of Confederation of 1777, Article IX gave the Continental Congress, among other things, the power to establish rules for the adjudication of legal prize alongside appellate jurisdiction, but did not confer the power of creating admiralty courts throughout the states.[136] Thus, clashes about admiralty jurisdiction and how admiralty business should be conducted, continued between the states and Congress.[137] The parallel existence of very different forms of admiralty litigation in the different American states led

[130] Bourguignon, *The First Federal Court*, vol. 122, p. 58.

[131] Ibid., p. 192.

[132] Benedict, *Law of Admiralty*, vol. 4, pp. 439–41.

[133] Bourguignon, *The First Federal Court*, vol. 122, p. 171.

[134] NARA, *New York (State), Court of Vice Admiralty: Organizational entity*, https://catalog.archives.gov/id/10678313 (accessed 11 March 2025).

[135] J. D. Winter and R. H. Maidman, *The Federal Court in New York: 225 Years and Counting (2014)*, p. 2.

[136] Putnam, 'Admiralty Jurisdiction', 464.

[137] Janis, 'North American Exceptionalism', 530.

to many complications and anomalies for domestic claimants.[138] But it also caused friction with citizens of other nations, which could ultimately have been a cause for war. Consequently, the states' behaviour has been described as a "threat to the survival of the nation".[139] It was "a disaster, as juries in a number of the new state courts frequently ignored traditional admiralty rules and awarded prizes on the basis of local sentiment [... placing] Congress in a difficult position".[140] The conduct of state admiralty jurisdiction did not showcase a respect of international law precedent.[141] Aside from local biases, admiralty law was highly complex, and its procedure required persons with legal or specifically admiralty law training, making it unsuitable for jury trials.[142] Along with the international legal rights that the United States was lobbying for overseas, came international legal duties at home.[143]

While Congress had been awarded the power over international affairs, many historians have thus described a natural consensus to moving admiralty power to the federal level.[144] Friedman describes admiralty law as "not a game; it was, among other things, a branch of foreign policy".[145] The need for a "stronger national government"[146] thus became apparent. In what became the federalist faction of the early Antebellum American Republic John Jay, James Madison and Alexander Hamilton vouched for this strategy.

In *The Federalist Paper* No. 3, Jay wrote that:

> [u]nder the national government, treaties and articles of treaties, as well as the law of nations, will always be expounded in one sense and executed in the same manner – whereas adjudications on the same points and questions in thirteen states, or in three or four confederacies, will not always accord or be consistent.[147]

138 Benedict, *Law of Admiralty*, vol. 4, p. 441.

139 M. A. Giunta, *The Emerging Nation: A Documentary History of the Foreign Relations of the United States under the Articles of Confederation 1780–1789* (Washington DC, 1996), vol. 3, p. 2.

140 Harrington, 'Legacy, Part II', 344.

141 Clark and Bellia, *The Law of Nations and the Constitution*, p. 49.

142 Ubbelohde, *The Vice-Admiralty Courts and the American Revolution*, p. 199.

143 Janis, 'North American Exceptionalism', 530.

144 W. R. Casto, 'The Origins of Federal Admiralty Jurisdiction in an Age of Privateers, Smugglers, and Pirates', *The American Journal of Legal History*, 37 (1993), 117–57, at 132; for example, Harrington, 'Legacy, Part II', 345; Putnam, 'Admiralty Jurisdiction', 469; T. J. Schoenbaum, *Admiralty and Maritime Law, Hornbook Series*, 6th edn (St Paul MN, 2019), p. 1.

145 Friedman, *A History of American Law*, p. 190.

146 Harrington, 'Legacy, Part II', 344.

147 Quoted in Janis, 'North American Exceptionalism', 532.

Madison simply stated that "As our intercourse with foreign nations will be affected by decisions of this kind, they ought to be uniform"[148] and Hamilton agreed.[149]

Finally, at the Constitutional Convention of 1787 it was decided to give federal jurisdiction to all maritime and admiralty cases.[150] Calls for a federal admiralty court system were expressed; for example, in the Virginia Plan, New Jersey plan and Hamilton's plan. Edmund Randolph served on the five-person Committee of Detail which had been set up by the Constitutional Convention. Here he helped draw up "the Constitution's admiralty clause, and had previously aided in drafting regulations for prize adjudication in the Continental Congress".[151] In a draft report on the current state of admiralty jurisdiction conducted for the House of Representatives, Randolph wrote nineteen lines on prize and criminal prosecutions and added a mere six on private litigation and revenue offences. Thus, Randolph feared that if left unchecked, the result could be an ensuing war for the confederation of states, regardless of whether other states agreed with this undertaking.[152]

Especially with regard to prize, the allocation of jurisdiction at the federal level seems to have been considered a given.[153] However, there was a fear that such a jurisdiction would take over the right to individual state admiralty jurisdiction as a whole.[154] Privateering itself was also not necessarily popular. William Paterson, the creator of the New Jersey plan, wrote that "privateering ought to receive no encouragement; it is a sort of licensed depredation; and it is to be wished, that it could be utterly abolished. Activated by a predatory spirit, how often do privateers perpetrate outrages, that shock the moral sense, and disgrace the human character".[155]

In this manner, some have seen Congress as bowing down to international law, uprooting what they consider to be a uniform system of state admiralty trials by jury.[156] However, it must be noted that there was no such uniformity in the state courts, despite the overall prevalence of jury trials. Colonial admiralty practice in North America had already diverged from international law, and certainly from British admiralty practice, at this time.[157] It was a chequered cloth

148 Quoted in Casto, 'Origins of Federal Admiralty Jurisdiction', 139.

149 Quoted in ibid., p. 136.

150 Clark and Bellia, *The Law of Nations and the Constitution*, p. 122.

151 Casto, 'Origins of Federal Admiralty Jurisdiction', 129.

152 Ibid., pp. 130–1.

153 Mangone, *United States Admiralty Law*, p. 204.

154 Casto, 'Origins of Federal Admiralty Jurisdiction', 137.

155 Quoted in ibid., p. 124.

156 August, 'Trial by Jury in a Court of Admiralty', 176.

157 Bourguignon, *The First Federal Court*, vol. 122, p. 171.

of many different shades of procedures and jurisprudence. Congress brought it back in line with what was described as the uniformity of international law.[158]

The final result was Section 2 under Article III of the US Constitution, describing the federal judiciary and its authorities: "The judicial Power shall extend to all Cases, in Law and Equity, arising under this Constitution, the Laws of the United States, and Treaties made, or which shall be made, under their Authority; [...] to all Cases of admiralty and maritime Jurisdiction."[159]

Such a grant of jurisdiction over an entire subject matter is singular within the Constitution.[160] It should also be noted that the tenure of federal judges was decreed to be salaried and based on good conduct.[161]

When George Washington signed the Judiciary Act of 1789, thirteen federal district courts, under the tenure of one district judge each, were established to take on said admiralty jurisdiction as inferior courts to the Supreme Court. The District Court of New York would be headed by James Duane, who had previously served in the colonial vice-admiralty period.[162] Interestingly, part of the Committee of Detail's work had also been focused on the revenue potential of admiralty courts, which they linked to national defence.[163] This meant drawing a similar pattern of jurisdiction as had led to the unpopularity of the vice-admiralty courts in their colonial past. "Once free from British control, American legislators seemed to have forgotten most of the rhetoric about the evils of trying trade cases in admiralty."[164] While the amount of litigation coming before the New York court was initially small, it rapidly increased.[165] In 1814 it was split into two districts, southern and northern, that still exist today.[166]

When looking back at the transition from the vice-admiralty courts to the first state admiralty courts, a tradition in American historiography prevails

158 Schoenbraum phrases it as such "Metaphysical discussions do not contribute to the solution of the problem" of the discussion of the right to a trial by jury in admiralty and simply concludes that "since the early years of the republic, the general rule applies that there is no right to trial by jury". Schoenbaum, *Admiralty and Maritime Law*, p. 86.

159 Library of Congress and United States Congress, *Constitution Annotated: Article III*, https://constitution.congress.gov/constitution/article-3/ (accessed 2 February 2023).

160 Schoenbaum, *Admiralty and Maritime Law*, p. 1.

161 Library of Congress and United States Congress, *Constitution Art. III.*

162 Hough, *1789–1919 Southern District Court New York*, p. 7.

163 Casto, 'Origins of Federal Admiralty Jurisdiction', 134.

164 Harrington, 'Legacy, Part II', 349.

165 Federal Bar Association of New York, New Jersey and Connecticut, *History of the District Court of New York*, pp. 1–3.

166 New York County Lawyers' Association Committee on the Federal Courts, *Court for the Southern District of New York*, pp. 1–2.

of depicting Lewis Graham as Richard Morris's successor.[167] However, the (British) Vice-Admiralty Court of New York did not cease to exist merely because Judge Richard Morris resigned. In reality, Robert Bayard was the true successor of Richard Morris, and he continued his work until Britain officially recognised American independence in 1783.[168] Viewing Robert Bayard in this light can also be regarded as a reflection of the traditional historiography of American admiralty jurisdiction, in which some historians have drawn a fictitious line between English and colonial precedents, regarding one as endemic and more valued than the other.[169]

What most of the above-mentioned historiography fails to reflect, is that they are portraying an image of 'American jurisdiction' that includes the colonial period but excludes British jurisdiction from 1776 onwards. This version of history brings the colonial court adjudicating British law in America to an end with the Revolution, even though it continued throughout the war until 'America' had established itself. In this manner, Robert Bayard's tenure has been almost entirely omitted from history. Even Charles Merrill Hough, regarded as one of the most eminent scholars on the New York admiralty court, who was *aware* of Robert Bayard's records, stated that Richard Morris was the last judge of that court. He wrote "the last known official act of the Vice Admiralty Judge was [...] on March 29, 1775",[170] only to list the existence of the records of Bayard's tenure without explanation in a footnote attached to said statement. Much like in the case of the fire that burnt down one-fifth of New York days after the British took possession of the city, it was not in the interest of the British to highlight that the fire was most likely started by American rebels/patriots wishing to deny Britain the strategic benefit of the city.[171] Britain after 1783 had no need to correct American versions of the history of the Revolutionary war, especially not in regard to admiralty history. Much like the narrative on the British treatment of American prisoners of war was glossed over, Britons left the vision of a continued American admiralty history dating back to colonial days untouched. And so, Richard Morris is, to this day, listed as the last Judge of the New York Vice-Admiralty Court on the website of the National Archives and Records Administration, Washington DC.[172]

[167] E. A. Werner, *Civil List and Constitutional History of the Colony and State of New York* (New York, 1886), p. 276.

[168] New York Historical Society Museum and Library, *Robert Bayard (1739–1819) commissions and letters, 1757–1830*.

[169] For example, Casto, 'Origins of Federal Admiralty Jurisdiction', 154.

[170] Hough, *Reports New York, 1715–1788*, p. 12.

[171] Carp, *Great New York Fire*, p. 247.

[172] NARA, *New York (State)*.

However, the British Vice-Admiralty Court of New York continued to function during the war, with Robert Bayard at its head. He received his commission with great seal to act as Vice-Admiralty Judge of New York on 6 December 1776 from Governor Tryon and continued in this position until the conclusion of peace in 1783.[173] Superficially, it may appear that he received his commission solely through personal connections and being in the right place at the right time: his military background is certainly unusual for the New York court, his lack of civil law training was not. Still, his family had long been embedded in public service, some had even aided in New York admiralty jurisdiction or been judges themselves, much like the three generations of Morris judges that preceded Robert.[174] In this regard, Bayard's appointment doesn't seem particularly irregular. In fact, what makes his tenure unusual is his predominant lack of surrogate throughout his tenure.[175] Once the peace of 1783 was concluded, he personally delivered the records of the court into the hands of the deputy register of the High Court of Admiralty in 1784.[176]

173 New York Historical Society Museum and Library, *Robert Bayard (1739–1819) commissions and letters, 1757–1830*.

174 Burke and Burke, *Dictionary Landed Gentry*, vol. 2, p. 1361; Caliendo, *New York Mayors*, 6–7, 10; Niekerk dates the first court slightly later, considering Colonial Governor Edmund Andros as the responsible founder in 1678; van Niekerk, 'Story of the Silver Oar', 153.

175 From this point until the dissolution of the court, Sampson Salter Blowers became more and more present as 'Deputy Judge' in Bayard's stead; TNA, HCA 49/92/9 559r.

176 No. 1823, Andrews, *Guide to the Materials for American History*, vol. 2, p. 330.

# 2

# "The Loyal American": Colonial Prize Jurisdiction in the Vice-Admiralty Court of New York, 1776–1783

While Bayard was ostensibly to act as a neutral wartime judge, he had much to gain by aiding the British, and was, in his official capacity, woven into the web of British governmental operations. Indeed, a provenance note regarding a portrait of Robert Bayard's second wife documents that he was not only known as Major Bayard but would later also be known as "the Loyal American"[1] by family descendants. Correspondence can be found in which British military commanders enquired about the status of cases, with Bayard acting as a hub of knowledge, regardless of whether the cases fell into his official jurisdiction.[2]

Other correspondence, however, shows a far closer link to the British government, with Major Thomas Murray, the aide-de-camp of William Tryon's successor to the governorship of New York, James Robertson, writing to Bayard, that, "I am directed [...] to request that you will give the necessary Orders that the Vessel [...] mentioned may not be condemned till the matter is enquired into".[3] Though it is hard to discern from the lack of context, it appears from this letter that Bayard as the vice-admiralty judge, was receiving orders from officials who definitively expected condemnations before any due process had taken place.

To understand Bayard's role in military operations, it is important to examine his court and the realities faced by claimants facing him.

One of the main challenges in examining vice-admiralty court proceedings is that American colonial practice had diverged from British procedure, growing

1 When the portrait of Mrs Bayard was given to the Museum of the City of New York, the family nickname for her second husband, Robert Bayard, was noted as the "Loyal American" during the accession process. This provenance note can be seen as one of the images connected with the portrait's entry in the Frick Digital Collections' database. The Frick Digital Collections, 4107100224500: Mrs James McEvers (Elizabeth Apthrop) (Later Mrs Bayard). https://digitalcollections.frick.org/digico/#/details/ContainerID/b10879055/Photoarchive (accessed 1 August 2024).

2 TNA, PRO 30/55/44: Deposition of John Barlow, 12 July 1782 p. 92; TNA, PRO 30/55/42: Robert Bayard to Major Murray, 6 June 1782 p. 67.

3 TNA, PRO 30/55/41, p. 66.

apart due to colonial conditions.[4] Michael Craton describes the procedures concerning prize in Caribbean vice-admiralty courts as subject "to an almost infinite degree"[5] of variation, despite the British legal framework supposedly ensuring uniformity.[6] This chapter will examine whether such a divergence can also be found in the loyalist Vice-Admiralty Court of New York.

Specific attention has been paid to one year of Bayard's tenure, ranging from 31 December 1777 to 31 December 1778. The start date was chosen as this is the first entry recorded in HCA 49/92/1, the first assignation book of the New York Vice-Admiralty Court (HCA 49/92) in Bayard's tenure.[7]

Four volumes of the HCA 49/92 papers were used, including the first third of HCA 49/92/4, to examine twelve months of Bayard's tenure.[8] The 'December period' referred to in this chapter thus consists of the data from 31 December 1777 and 1778 until December 31 of that year. The HCA 49/94 Register overlaps with the entries in some of the 'Assignation books'. However, in all but one case, the Register was *missing* entries from the HCA 49/92 papers; that is, the HCA 49/92 papers contained all but one of the Register's entries alongside a significant number of additional court actions. Therefore, it was chosen to examine a year's worth of entries from the assignation book series as opposed to the Registers, following Wertheimer's commonsense quantification approach.[9] Although the results drawn are sketchy, giving very little information and barely any content for the cases mentioned, they do provide us with insights into the machinations and workings of the court, by chronicling the actions taken in it.[10]

4 Bourguignon, *The First Federal Court*, vol. 122, p. 171.

5 M. J. Craton, 'The Caribbean Vice Admiralty Courts, 1763–1815: Indispensable Agents of an Imperial System' (dissertation, 1968), p. 68.

6 Ibid., pp. 47–9.

7 The books were bound in a variety of materials, including a coarse material like burlap. The wrapper of the sixth book, now ripped into several pieces, consists of a blank, printed privateering commission from Robert Bayard's tenure, the only document of this kind to be found in archives. TNA, HCA 49/92/6.

8 TNA, HCA 49/92/1 3r; TNA, HCA 49/92/4 158r.

9 The missing case was dated 26 August 1778 Robert Sheddon/Black Prince. Although the Black Prince is listed in the Assignation Books, this specific step is not; TNA, HCA 49/94, 200v.

10 For example, it is hard to trace cases of recapture. While several cases are marked as "in lieu of salvage" (TNA, HCA 49/92/2, 46r), potentially referring to cases of recaptured vessels, some of these are also referring to actual salvage cases. By using the original HCA 32 records, we can attempt to cross-reference the vessels, however the cross-referencing is difficult as the HCA 49/92s generally don't record the masters of the ships, only the claimants in their case, not always making a positive identification possible. In addition, the HCA 32s are still being catalogued. *Le Fortune* (Masse), for example is clearly marked as a probably recapture in HCA 49, but

For the studied time frame, the HCA 49/92 volumes recorded 1,607 individual entries.[11] From the comparison with the Register, one can deduce that the number of total actions may have been slightly higher in total, yet the difference in values can be considered insignificant to the overall analysis of the data. The court sat very regularly, 100 times in the studied time frame, meaning court dates amounted to just over a quarter (27%) of the year and was never absent for more than six days. Most frequently, Robert Bayard conducted public business on a Wednesday (forty-two weeks out of the year), though the court also regularly sat on Fridays (thirty-four) and Mondays (eighteen). No business was ever conducted on a Sunday, respecting religious practice, though the court also sat on three Saturdays.[12] The range of court actions conducted per sitting varied from four to forty-seven.[13] The busiest time of the year was May, in which 187 court actions were recorded. The least busy was August. However, this may simply be down to the amount of court sittings per month. In August, there was an all-time low of seven sittings, in May, a calendar high of ten, which is reflected in the data. Two other months also only had seven court sittings, one of which displays the second-lowest number of court actions (March; ninety-four). Yet April, the third in this dataset, produced 140 court actions, significantly more than even months with nine court dates (for example, October; 122; nine sittings), showing that it was not that simple.[14] Though the completion of court actions was reliant on court dates, productivity (defined here as number of court actions per sitting) varied, depending on the cases and circumstances at hand.

To determine the average duration of a case in the Vice-Admiralty Court of New York, only *complete* cases were taken into account. These encompassed the whole process from the first proclamation to the decree and totalled 220 cases. Theoretically, the libel was the first action instituted in court after the captured vessel was brought into the port of New York by the captors. In it, the captor stated that he wished the captured vessel to be condemned, on what grounds (for example, enemy property) and added some cursory notes on the circumstances of capture (for example, date, place of capture).[15] A libel could

termed a French "contested cause" in the HCA 32 catalogue as it was captured prior to the declaration of war. TNA, HCA 49/92/2, 50r; TNA, HCA 32/333/7: *Le Fortune* (Masse). https://discovery.nationalarchives.gov.uk/details/r/C13505832 (accessed 12 March 2025). In the time frame, thirty-one vessels were indicated as either salvage cases or recaptures.

11 See table 1.

12 Ironically, two of the Saturdays were the least productive days of the year examined. See fig. 3 (Appendix).

13 See fig. 3.

14 See fig. 4.

15 For example, TNA, HCA 32/350/9, p. 1.

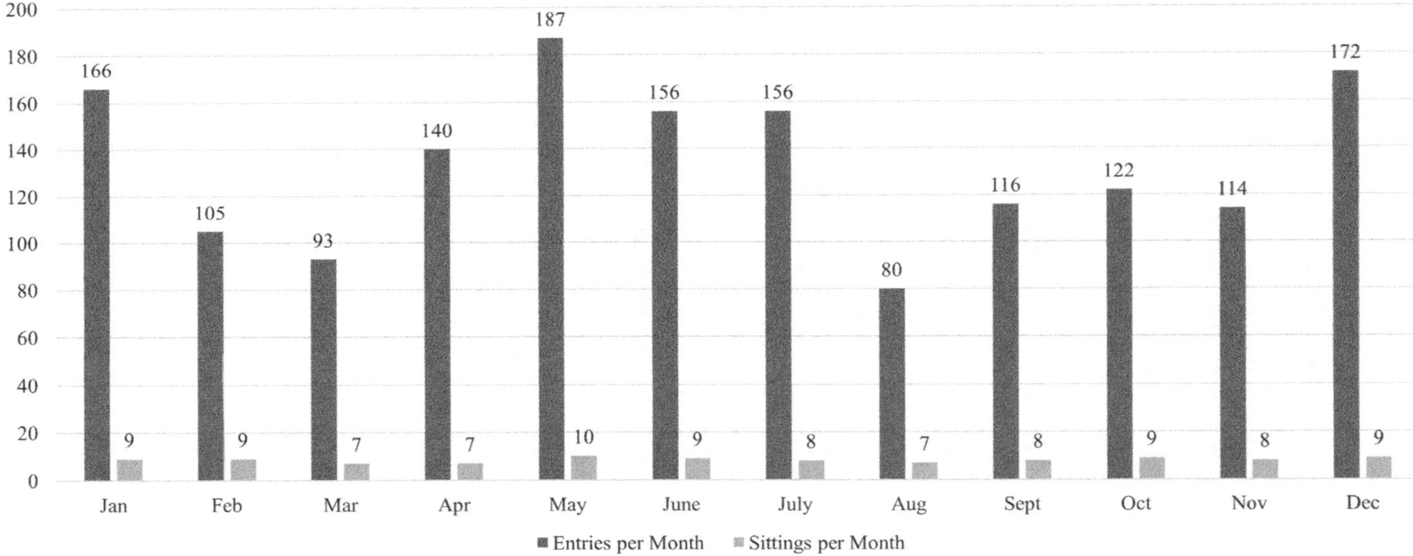


Fig. 4: Productivity of the New York Vice-Admiralty Court measured per month in Court Actions and Sittings, from 31 December 1777 to 31 December 1778 according to the Minute Books HCA 49/92/1–4.

be conducted by a representative attorney or prize agent.[16] It was also often accompanied by the first instance of a public proclamation and a monition, sometimes even preceded by them.[17] Both these procedural steps essentially stated that, if there were any reason for a specific vessel not to be condemned or restored, those in the know should come forward and declare them. In the case of *La Assumption* the proclamation was noted down as: "if anyone can shew any Cause why Sentence of Restitution of the said Brigantine should not pass to Charles Morris & John Church that they should come forth."[18] In the case of the *Hawke* (Yell), an original monition has been preserved stating:

> whereas […] our Advocate General for […] Thomas Symonds […] of our Ship of War the Soleby […] hath exhibited a certain Libel […] against a certain Schooner called the Hawke, her Apparel, Furniture and Cargo praying that the same may be by Decree and Sentence of our said Court condemned as lawful Prize, therefore we command you [the Marshal] that without Delay you cause publick Monition & Notice to be given to Moses Yall late Master of the said Schooner and all and every other Person and Persons having or knowing any Thing to say why the said Schooner Hawke her Apparel, Furniture & Cargo ought not to be condemned according to […] the said Libel that they be and appear before our said Court […] on or before the thirty first Day of August […] and […] make their Allegations in that Behalf.[19]

Monitions were served in 315 cases, of which the Marshal was explicitly noted as responsible in 96% of all cases, single-handedly accounting for just under 19% of all entries by serving and returning monitions.[20] The duration given to the monition was variable, but was limited to twenty days according to the Prohibitory Act, whereupon an automatic condemnation was to be executed by the judge.[21] Sometimes, these verbal proclamations were accompanied by written publications (51%), but usually, the publication was issued after the decree had been issued (81.5%).[22] It appears that publications were not requisite in advance. The Judge could also block a motion to proclaim

16 Alexander Hamilton was noted in the minute books twenty-one times during the studied time frame; for example, TNA, HCA 49/92/1, 25r; TNA, HCA 49/92/2, 88v; TNA, HCA 49/92/3 106v; TNA, HCA 49/92/4, 148r.

17 See table 2.

18 TNA, HCA 49/92/1, 9r.

19 TNA, HCA 32/350/9, p. 27.

20 See table 2.

21 This rule had been especially issued "for the more speedy proceeding to condemnation or other determination", *An Act to Prohibit all Trade and Intercourse with the Colonies* (1775), Article V.

22 See table 2.

or publish.[23] If nobody came forward upon a proclamation, a default was entered in the minute books.[24] Generally, three proclamations and defaults were made. The monition was usually returned on the same day as the third proclamation was issued (in 96.5% of cases).[25] Upon the entering of the third default, a hearing *instanter* (immediately) could be motioned for, enabling a condemnation to be decreed on the same day as the last proclamation. A regular hearing could proceed at any later date after the third proclamation. For example, one can look at the case of the *Eliza* (Vicary). Her first proclamation and default were entered on 1 May 1782. The second on 3 May, the third on 22 May, the same day that she was condemned in a hearing *instanter*.[26] If we examine a different, earlier case, such as the *Hawke* (Yell), captured on 28 July 1778, with no involvement of another Bayard family member, her proclamations were entered into the minute book on 7, 14 and 31 August 1778.[27]

Why was the libel not taken as the starting point in this examination? Of 272 cases of filed libels, 247 libels were filed on the same day as the first proclamation was issued. Of the remaining twenty-five cases, six were filed *after* a proclamation had already been made, meaning they did not actually initiate the process at court. The rest was listed without the number of proclamations registered in the court minutes. Thus, the first proclamation appears to be the most sensible starting point for an investigation of average case duration. There were 244 cases of first proclamations in the studied time frame, however only 220 of these were carried through to the final decree.[28] On average, each of these completed cases lasted 29.6 days. The shortest case required five days from start to completion (for example, *Betsy*/Becher), the longest 191 days (*St Jago*/Cleary). However, when examining the data, it becomes apparent that only twenty-eight cases took thirty days or longer. If one instead examines the arithmetic mode, a duration of twenty-one days from first proclamation to decree was the most common.[29]

These values reflect the number of days from the first proclamation until the decree (condemnation/restitution) was issued by the Judge. Only complete cases were evaluated. Cases that were dropped or resolved by consent outside

23 For example, TNA, HCA 49/92/3, 113v.

24 Aside from the clear correlation between the steps in the minute books, their unity can be demonstrated in these two examples, where the default is entered as the 'first' of three and the phrase 'Procl. and Default' is employed as a usual term: TNA, HCA 49/92/1, 29v, 33r.

25 See table 2.

26 TNA, HCA 49/92/8 509v, 513r, 518r, 520r.

27 TNA, HCA 49/92/2, 98v; TNA, HCA 49/92/3, 102r, 106v.

28 See table 2.

29 See fig. 5.

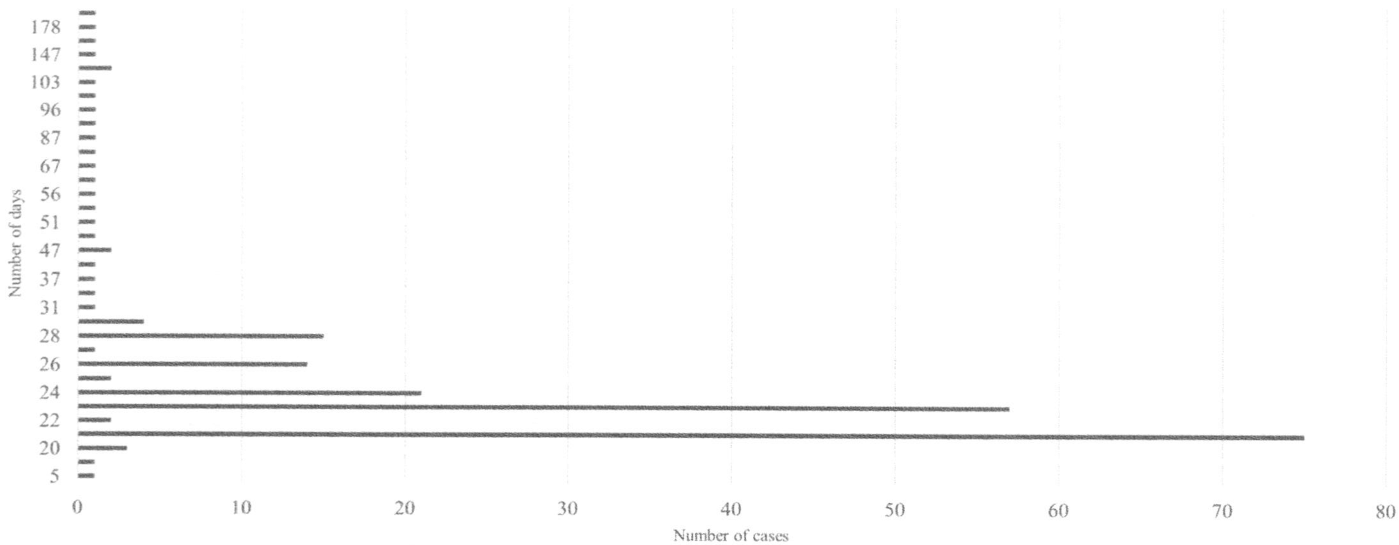


Fig. 5: Duration of a court case in the Vice-Admiralty Court of New York in days, from 31 December 1777 to 31 December 1778 according to the Minute Books HCA 49/92/1–4.

of court were not included, even if the court took on the formalities of the distribution of moneys.

This process seems very swift and efficient. The court also took great pains to maintain this efficiency. In one case concerning the *Lady Margeritta* legal counsel asked for time to examine witnesses in Spain.[30] After six days of consideration, the Judge turned down the request, stating that permission would have "occasion[ed] a great and unnecessary Delay".[31] Legal counsel also used the matter of delay in their favour, portraying time taken by the other party as a selfish strategy to prolong cases they were going to lose and demanding quick judgments to prevent such behaviour.[32]

If nobody came forward in the proclamations, the vessel was generally condemned, its guilt precluded. In the contested case of the ship *Rifleman*, the cargo was condemned as there had been "no person [...] to claim or defend the same".[33]

When the libel, proclamations and monition had been completed, a hearing could take place. Every hearing, regular and *instanter*, followed a clear set of standardised procedures.

Some 443 hearings were recorded in the total time frame. Not all these hearings led to an immediate decision. Sometimes the court would need a second date to hear further council and/or evidence on the case. Occasionally, the Judge desired more time to consider the case at hand. About 75% of all hearings, however, concluded definitively on the first court date. Of these cases, Robert Bayard ordered nineteen restorations of the vessel and/or cargo, whereas he ordered a partial or complete condemnation in 313 counts. In other words, approximately 94% of decrees resulted in condemnations.[34] Partial restorations were rare and generally down to individual pieces of cargo being exempted from the condemnation.[35] It appears the odds were thus stacked vastly against those brought into court.

The procedure during a hearing generally started by reading out sets of papers in a particular order. First, the affidavit as to papers, in which the captor generally swore to not have tampered with the papers found on board. It was usually sworn before the Register of the Court, and the papers found on board the captured vessel handed over to the vice-admiralty court at this

30 TNA, HCA 49/92/1, 43v.

31 Ibid., 44v.

32 For example, ibid., 26r.

33 TNA, HCA 49/92/4, 154v.

34 See table 3.

35 TNA, HCA 49/92/1, 25v; TNA, HCA 49/92/4, 154v.

point.[36] One hundred per cent of affidavits as to papers were read out on the date of the hearing.[37]

Second, the preparatory examinations. These were answers, more specifically sworn depositions, to a set of questions asked to members of the seized crew, sometimes also of the prize crew. These were to follow the standard (or standing) interrogatories, a series of questions determined by British officials and distributed throughout the empire.[38] In the case of the *Mehitabel* (Jackson),[39] it was noted that these preparatory examinations showed that "the sloop was armed, manned with 10 men, officers included, and that she was commissioned by the Continental Congress".[40] This schooner was one of nine rebel privateers explicitly described as such in the court minutes, which had received a commission either from one of the states or the Continental Congress. The time to process such privateers until their condemnation does not vary significantly from those of other cases.[41]

Third, the papers found on board. These could give clear indications as to the nationality of the vessel or its 'guilt' of rebel trade. From the minutes, it is nearly impossible to glean the reasons for which vessels were condemned as legal prize. This is much more easily deduced from the actual papers, which were preserved in the HCA 32 series. However, sometimes, snippets of information can be gleaned from the minute books. Several times, alleged French ownership was specifically recorded (for example, sloop *Congress*).[42] At other times, the civil war character of the American Revolutionary War was highlighted. In the case with the snow *L'Amitié* (Pascal),[43] the vessel had been illegally captured by a British ship lacking a privateering commission. Despite this, the evidence provided through *L'Amitié*'s papers was such that the Judge condemned the vessel, although he condemned it to the use of His Majesty, as opposed to the captors.[44] In most cases, the vessels brought before the court were related to the 'rebel' cause. An edited passage in the

36 For example, TNA, HCA 45/7/4: Appeal of Thomas Symonds against the *Hawke* (Yell) 52r.

37 See table 2.

38 The standing interrogatories were supposed to be concluded within five days according to the Prohibitory Act. An act to prohibit all trade and intercourse with the colonies, Article V. Prize Papers Portal, Document Types: Standing Interrogatories, https://portal.prizepapers.de/documenttype/ (accessed 9 June 2023).

39 The name of the master was omitted in the HCA 49/92, but could be found in the manuscript papers: TNA, HCA 32/401/11: *Mehitabel* (Jackson).

40 TNA, HCA 49/92/2, 95r.

41 See table 4.

42 TNA, HCA 49/92/2, 82r.

43 The name of the master was omitted in the HCA 49/92, but could be found in the manuscript papers: TNA, HCA 32/267/10: *L'Amitié* (Pascal).

44 TNA, HCA 49/92/3, 136v.

case of the sloop *Exchange* reveals the conflict made court officials adapt their terminology: "it appearing from the said prepatory examinations that the said Sloop and her Cargo was the Property of some [crossed out] British Subject or Subjects, [replaced with] Person or Persones remaining and continuing under his Majesty's Protection"[45] The question of subjecthood – or dare one say nationhood – raised by the United States independence movement, permeated everyday court procedure.

Should none of the papers above be present, a statement that no papers were found on board was read. This was the case in only sixteen hearings; in other words, about 4% of all hearings. None of these hearings was prolonged by the fact that no papers were presented at court. On the contrary, all of them were condemned. In most cases the affidavit as to papers was simply replaced with an "Affidavit that no Persons or Papers were found on Board".[46]

Of course, there was also the option that a person would appear after the monition, proclamations and/or publications had been made. If the reclaimant missed the announcements on the capture of their vessel, they could still belatedly appear before the court. It appears to have not been unusual for owners of vessels to hear of their condemnation after the business had already been conducted in the admiralty court, not surprising when regarding the swift process. To reclaim such condemned vessels, the original owners or their legal representatives had to take the captors to court. Thus, the minutes of the Vice-Admiralty Court of New York are speckled with *in personam* (against a person) cases linked to prize, despite prize law itself being *in rem* (against an item, specifically in prize, against the vessel). Due to the *in rem*/*in personam* distinction, at first glance an analysis of the minute books should allow all *in personam* cases to be excluded from prize jurisdiction. In this form 115 actions were originally considered unrelated to this case study.[47] However, upon uncovering this practice, none of these actions could be excluded from the realm of prize. Taking captors to court in order to reclaim previously condemned prizes must be considered a relevant and integral part of New York's Vice-Admiralty Court procedure. This is one of the main weaknesses of working with the HCA 49/92 papers. It is difficult to distinguish between cases of prize and instance jurisdiction. In the minutes, cases are merely identifiable through the names of the parties, their representatives and/or the vessels/defending parties and their representatives. Cases *in rem*/*in personam* can also be distinguished through the 'v'/'ad' label in the first column. Nevertheless, one can clearly state that a majority of the cases featured in the HCA 49/92 minutes were prize cases. Some of these were also clearly labelled as 'prize'[48]

45 TNA, HCA 49/92/2, 73r.

46 Ibid., 73r.

47 See table 1.

48 TNA, HCA 49/92/1, 31v.

in, for example, the decrees. Only one case on the instance side of admiralty jurisdiction, concerning sailors' wages, could be clearly identified.[49] As the *in rem/in personam* distinction is unreliable for this American vice-admiralty court, it is hard to know without thorough study of each case, how many instance cases have masked themselves as 'prize'. In theory, the prize causes should have been instigated with a monition, not a libel, but this intermingling of instance and prize procedure is characteristic of American colonial admiralty jurisdiction, making this another unreliable form of differentiation.[50]

Due to the haphazard nature of conservation, an in-depth study of all cases is impossible, as papers have not been preserved in every case; however, sometimes this cross-referencing can be used very effectively, such as in the case of the *Hawke* (Yell), which we shall examine in greater detail here. Alongside the entries in the minute books, the original vice-admiralty court papers, some of the ship's papers and its appeals papers have all been preserved at TNA, showcasing the potential that lies in the combinational value of these sources.[51]

The *Hawke* was captured near Cape Henlopen, Delaware, by HMS *Solebay* on 28 July 1778.[52] HMS *Solebay* was commanded by captain Thomas Symonds.[53] He had already libelled the *Hawke* and entered two defaults on her account when Samuel Fairlamb, the owner of the schooner and her cargo, appears to have heard of the capture. On 14 August 1778, the day of the second proclamation and default, Fairlamb's legal counsel requested time to file a claim.[54] One week later, the claim was entered: Samuel Fairlamb instigated an *in personam* case against the Advocate General representing Thomas Symonds.[55] Nevertheless, a third proclamation and default ensued, causing two parallel suits *in rem* and *in personam* to be pursued by the court about the same vessel.[56] Both parties agreed by consent to a publication prior to the decree, yet ultimately the case would go on to be appealed.[57] But what was actually the case prosecuted against the *Hawke*?

The *Hawke* was an American schooner of 70 tons burthen, manned by six to seven men under the direction of Moses Yell (sometimes Yale).[58] She was

49 TNA, HCA 49/92/3, 139v.

50 Bourguignon, *The First Federal Court*, vol. 122, p. 141.

51 TNA, HCA 32/350/9; TNA, HCA 45/7/4.

52 Libel: TNA, HCA 32/350/9, p. 1.

53 C. Harrison, *Thomas Symonds (c.1720–1792)*, https://threedecks.org/index.php?display_type=show_crewman&id=13868 (accessed 8 June 2023).

54 TNA, HCA 49/92/2, 98v; TNA, HCA 49/92/3, 102r.

55 TNA, HCA 49/92/3, 103r.

56 Ibid., 106v.

57 Ibid., 131v, 132r.

58 TNA, HCA 45/7/4, 52r.

loaded with flour and tobacco.[59] At the time of her capture, she was travelling from Annapolis to St Eustatius. At least, this was the route she was cleared for when leaving (American-controlled) Maryland.[60] It was also the route entered by the master, Yell, in his logbook.[61] However, allegedly, this route had been chosen to mask her true destination: Philadelphia. The tobacco had been bought, literally, as a cover, to hide the flour, which, according to the owner, Samuel Fairlamb, had been promised as provisions to the British Army and was to be smuggled to the troops from rebel territory.[62] Her name, *Hawke*, could already have been pointing to this political, loyalist stance, potentially referencing Edward Hawke, First Lord of the Admiralty from 1766 to 1771.[63] However, Royal Navy Captain Thomas Symonds wasn't convinced. HMS *Solebay* carried the *Hawke* (Yell) into New York and the Advocate General libelled her on Symond's behalf in the vice-admiralty court, staking out his personal as well as his crew's claim to the prize.

In a majority of cases, the captor(s) would be represented by the Advocate General.[64] In the High Court of Admiralty, the King's Advocate was the second highest official of the court after the Judge, who would generally become his successor upon resignation or death.[65] He represented the government's interest in the High Court of Admiralty and the ecclesiastical courts, as well as drafting opinions on international law for the Foreign Office.[66] In London, captors could not choose their own means of representation in court and were instead represented through the Crown.[67] This practice was strongly criticised by some (for example, Admiral Alexander Cochrane) due to the high workload consequently suffered by the King's Advocate. The fear was that this workload would be reflected in a poor representation, while claimants were able to choose their own representative.[68] In the Vice-Admiralty Court of New York, it was the Advocate General who undertook the defence and

59 Libel: TNA, HCA 32/350/9, p. 1.

60 TNA, HCA 45/7/4, 52v.

61 Logbook TNA, HCA 32/350/9, pp. 35–6.

62 See Claim of Samuel Fairlamb TNA, HCA 45/7/4, 52v; and Logbook, TNA, HCA 32/350/9, p. 37.

63 For more information, see M. Burrows, *The Life of Edward Lord Hawke: Admiral of the Fleet, Vice-Admiral of Great Britain and First Lord of the Admiralty from 1766 to 1771* (London, 1896); M. Grossman, *World Military Leaders: A Biographical Dictionary*, 1st edn (New York, 2007), pp. 147–8.

64 See table 1.

65 See table 5.

66 N. S. Marsh, 'Lord Stowell: A New Assessment', *International and Comparative Law Quarterly*, 37, 668–74, at 668.

67 Starkey, *British Privateering Enterprise in the Eighteenth Century*, vol. 4, pp. 26–7.

68 Hill, *The Prizes of War*, pp. 164–5.

prosecution on behalf of the Crown. He represented the complainants in 59.3% of all examined cases, and the defending party in an additional 5.4%. This meant that he was involved in roughly two-thirds of all court actions in the Vice-Admiralty Court of New York.[69] It also demonstrates, how captors had more freedom in this colonial system than in the London one.

Both parties, Symonds of the HMS *Solebay* and Fairlamb of the *Hawke* had to stipulate that that they were financially capable of prosecuting their case in court through the provision of £200 New York currency. In the High Court of Admiralty in London, private persons offered themselves as sureties, attesting to the claimants' ability to pay up and essentially determining his financial value and pledging their own riches should the party at court be unable to cover the costs. In the New-York Vice-Admiralty Court these sureties were referred to as stipulants. The sum of £200 New York currency was the amount required for regular prize cases here. Stipulations composed only about 4% of all entries in the court minutes. Of these stipulations, most can be found in *in personam* cases (approximately 63%). The *in rem* cases that required stipulations to be made during the court case (that is, before the decree was issued) were all but one for £200 New York currency.[70] Regarding *in personam* cases, values of £100 and £60 New York currency were also stipulated, but these made up only about 7% of running court cases. Stipulations could also be made after a decree had been issued. Such stipulations were enforced by the court when there was a chance the decree would be overturned on appeal. They ranged from £1,000 to 4,000 New York currency, covering the value of the vessel and/or cargo.[71]

Often, the persons appearing before the Register to stipulate in their case would be the claimants themselves. However, with Thomas Symonds back at sea, his stipulation was provided by Henry White, the later general prize agent for the Navy.[72] Samuel Fairlamb in turn was represented by William Backhouse.[73] Financial viability was therefore exclusively vouched for by New York merchants. This may have been down to the practicality of New Yorkers being able to appear before the Register of the Court, David Mathews, for their stipulation with less difficulty than brethren with longer distances to travel. But it also seems to have been due to the jurisdiction of the court. In the studied time frame, the court only registered the stipulation of residents outside of New York in a single case: that of the *Hawke* (Yell). Alongside New York merchants Samuel Fairlamb and William Backhouse, three men from other

69 See table 1.

70 The sum of £200 New York currency made up 75% of all stipulations in the New York Vice-Admiralty Court.

71 See table 6.

72 TNA, HCA 49/92/3, 108v.

73 Ibid., 103r.

American provinces stipulated to the joint sum of £4,000 New York currency. The minutes of the court specifically added that these three non-residents were "submitting themselves to the Jurisdiction of this Court".[74] This may be a reference to the fact that it was difficult for British authorities to force stipulants to pay up if they resided outside the court's jurisdiction, especially considering the court's position not far from active military operations.

In total, every tenth stipulation at court went towards an appeal. Six appeals were lodged during the time frame examined.[75] Appeals had always been a contentious issue in the American colonies. As the vice-admiralty courts became spaces of conflict, especially through their role in the enforcement of British imperial trade acts, the option of appealing decrees became more important. Having to lodge appeals in London before the Lords Commissioners of Appeals in Prize Causes was a costly and expensive affair, as has already been clearly demonstrated in this work, and also showed little regard to legal expertise in the colonies.[76]

London had attempted a series of reforms to change the appeals process, instituting appellate courts in America, introducing staff with civil law decrees from London and reducing their financial gain from condemnations, breaking with the traditional dependency of judges being paid out of condemned proceeds from their own courts. But these reforms came too little too late, so that the *Hawke* (Yell) needed to be appealed in London.[77] Appeals were inherently risky and costly, but judges could amplify these risks. In the case of the *Lively*, Robert Bayard decreed that the appellants were to "pay treble Costs as shall be awarded in Case the Sentence given in this Cause shall be affirmed".[78] Nothing alike has been found for the *Hawke*. Sometimes the court minutes also recorded how the Vice-Admiralty Court in New York reiterated the final decrees issued by the Lords of Appeal; for example, in the case of the *Polly*, where the court was able to proudly state that their own decree had been upheld in the metropolis.[79] Despite this, Symonds took on the risk

74 Ibid., 141r.

75 See table 6.

76 Harrington, 'Legacy, Part II', 325.

77 A single appellate American vice-admiralty court had been established at Halifax under Dr William Spry, LLC. Spry's court was not accepted by the general population. In 1768, Halifax was to become one of four American vice-admiralty courts with appellate jurisdiction with Boston, Charleston and Philadelphia, but this reform proved equally unsuccessful. Ubbelohde, *The Vice-Admiralty Courts and the American Revolution*, pp. 56, 62, 69–70; Kert, *Prize and Prejudice*, vol. 11, p. 58; Mangone, *United States Admiralty Law*, p. 27; Harrington, 'Legacy, Part II', 325.

78 TNA, HCA 49/92/2, 88v.

79 TNA, HCA 49/92/7 429v.

and lodged an appeal regarding his capture of the *Hawke*.[80] Two days later, Henry White stipulated £200 British sterling on his behalf.[81] Reviewing the evidence, Robert Bayard had decreed the restitution of the *Hawke* (Yell) and its cargo on 4 November 1778. But, generously, he did consider the seizure of the vessel legitimate. The event was unusual, to say the least, and he declared it a case of probable cause, meaning Samuel Fairlamb was to pay Symonds' costs for the court case.[82] The ship's papers, though limited in number, were lodged with the Register when John Symonds, Thomas Symond's First Lieutenant on board HMS *Solebay* came in and swore his affidavit as to papers.[83] Sadly, for Symonds, the papers were not marked, listed or numbered, so that Fairlamb's counsel could simply discredit them, stating they had never seen these documents before. The ship's papers, alongside the original court papers from the Vice-Admiralty Court of New York can be found in HCA 32/350/9 at TNA. The respondent's case (Fairlamb) clearly rested on one piece of evidence: the special licence, attached to the vessel's clearance documentation (referred to in the court records as Exhibit A and B, respectively).[84] It read as follows:

> Samuel Fairlamb has the Permission of the Commander in Chief to import into Philadelphia from Baltimore a Vessel & Cargo of flour for the Use of his Majesty's Army & Navy Provided he shall put the said vessel under the Protection of the first King's Ship nearest to the Port sail'd from. Head Quarters Feb[ruar]y 2 1778 – By Order of the Commander in Chief, Robert McKenzie Secretary.[85]

This scrap of paper, allegedly hidden on board by Fairlamb so as to go unnoticed if searched by rebel forces, was the only piece of evidence that could truly save the *Hawke* (Yell) from loyalism or treason.[86] Samuel Fairlamb described himself as "is now and always hath been a good, true, loyal and faithful Subject of his Majesty, the King of Great Britain",[87] whose support of the Crown had been "well known".[88] The master of the *Hawke*, Moses Yell, was "a well known Friend to His Majesty's Government".[89] Given the special

80 Appeal TNA, HCA 32/350/9, p. 30.

81 TNA, HCA 49/92/3, 132r.

82 Ibid., 131v.

83 TNA, HCA 45/7/4, 52r; TNA, HCA 32/350/9, p. 28.

84 TNA, HCA 45/7/4, 51r–v (captor's case), 59v (owner's case); currently SP 33 TNA, HCA 32/350/9.

85 TNA, HCA 32/350/9, p. 33.

86 TNA, HCA 45/7/4, 58r.

87 Answer of Samuel Fairlamb, TNA, HCA 32/350/9, p. 37.

88 TNA, HCA 45/7/4, 58r.

89 Ibid., 59r.

dispensation issued by General Howe, it seems astonishing that Symonds would even attempt to question the decree made by Bayard. However, upon closer inspection, some loopholes in Fairlamb's story emerge.

Conveniently for the captor, the reliability of Fairlamb's primary piece of evidence was questionable, as "Sir William Howe and his Secretary were not at New York – The Proof of an Exhibit admits of Latitude".[90] Several crew members of the *Hawke* believed that they had signed up for a voyage to St Eustatius and deposed as much upon questioning.[91] Incidentally, these were also two of the three people questioned on the standing interrogatories. The logbook entries supported this. The crew consisted mainly of Americans.[92] The customs officer of the "rebel Custom house"[93] at Annapolis, John Davidson, had cleared them. Yell had stipulated to the amount of £1,000 that their vessel would neither land in British territory, nor sell (part of) their cargo to "the Enemies of *America*".[94] If Fairlamb was such a notorious loyalist, how had he been allowed to buy provisions, load them onto a vessel and then leave when Congress had just issued an embargo?

Fairlamb argued that he had snatched up the opportunity of leaving his life behind in rebel-controlled territory. He had sold all his belongings, had travelled from his hometown in Chester, Pennsylvania, to a "very retired Place in the Country",[95] where nobody knew him. He had allegedly been loading the cargo, 330 barrels of flour, when news of Congress's embargo on provisions broke. But the secluded nature of the backwater town had meant the inhabitants had not known his political outlook on current events.[96]

In reality, while Samuel Fairlamb depicted himself as a clear-cut loyal British citizen, he *had* been an active member in Chester County enforcing the economic sanctions against the British ordered by the Continental Congress in 1774/1775.[97] He had also acted as a contractor to Congress in 1776, receiving an advance for $600 in February.[98] This early political activity echoes back to William Bayard's position on the edge of both political movements. Nevertheless, Fairlamb's support of loyalism won over in the end. He lost

90 Ibid., 60r.

91 Depositions of William Hale and Peter Peterson, TNA, HCA 32/350/9, 9, 19.

92 Ibid., p. 35.

93 TNA, HCA 45/7/4, 52r.

94 TNA, HCA 32/350/9, p. 33.

95 TNA, HCA 45/7/4, 58r–v.

96 Ibid., 58r.

97 W. H. Egle, *Pennsylvania in the War of the Revolution: Associated Battalions and Militia 1775–1783* (Harrisburg PA, 1892), vol. 2, p. 132.

98 L. E. Horgan, Forged in War: *The Continental Congress and the Origin of Military Supply and Acquisition Policy* (Westport CT, 2002), vol. 219, p. 16.

his estate and, historiographically, has even ended up listed in *Pennsylvania's Traitors and Criminals During the Revolutionary War*.[99]

As to the logbook of the *Hawke*, master Yell had been in on the plot.[100] The logbook was therefore an intentionally falsified document.[101] Three other men, Lewis Lewis, John Fairlamb (Samuel's brother) and James Hill had also been party to the plot.[102] They had hidden ammunition and arms on board, so as to forcibly control the vessel, should the 'American' mariners, who had signed up believing the Caribbean to be their destination, attempt to alter the vessel's course once its true route became apparent.[103] In this manner, a ship with no guns all of a sudden seemed like a floating powder keg. The main piece of evidence relied on by the captor and appellant, Symonds, was the clearance document from Annapolis, Exhibit B and essentially part of the same document relied on by the claimants. Yell had obtained the clearance paper from Annapolis without the customs official thoroughly examining the vessel.[104] The cargo the two innocent American seamen spoke of in their depositions on the standing interrogatories was flour and tobacco.[105] The clearance was just for tobacco, sixty hogsheads containing 51,000 pounds of the crop.[106] In reality, there was only 1,600 pounds of tobacco loaded, amounting to about 3% of the stated amount on the clearance paper. Fairlamb explained that he had bought the product to hide the flour barrels.[107] Yet, this circumstance was one angle that proctors Wynne and Wedderburn, representing the captor, Symonds, focused on in their case.[108] The special licence spoke only of provisions, not of an illegal trade in tobacco![109] In addition, there was an introductory note especially written by merchant Richard Curson to the Governor of St Eustatius.[110] Why would introductions be necessary if New York had been the true destination? To this, the respondent's counsel merely stated that the affidavit as to papers had not listed any of the papers

99 D. Corbly, *Pennsylvania's Traitors and Criminals During the Revolutionary War* (Raleigh NC, 2013), p. 357.

100 TNA, HCA 45/7/4, 59r.

101 Incidentally, the logbook is a very interesting source. It was not only used by Yell on multiple voyages, previously on the vessel *Black Joke*, but is also sprinkled with religious affirmations, thanking God for deliverance on, quite literally, stormy seas.

102 TNA, HCA 45/7/4, 58v.

103 Ibid., 59r.

104 Ibid., 58v.

105 TNA, HCA 32/350/9, 9, 19.

106 TNA, HCA 45/7/4, 52v.

107 Ibid., 58v.

108 Ibid., 53v.

109 Ibid., 58v.

110 Ibid., 55r.

found on board. The *Hawke*'s master, Yell, deposed that he had never seen the introduction letter to the Governor, suggesting that it was doctored, incriminating evidence inserted after the event of capture.[111] While the ship's papers in HCA 32/350/9 are indeed few and far between, the court papers are not. In typical New York admiralty court fashion, the court papers were turned over horizontally when being written upon. Once bound together in the top corner to keep multi-paged documents together, this creates the unusual material feature of having to rotate each paper 180 degrees when now examining the reverse side.[112] While the original libel, answer and rejoinder can thus be found at TNA, the large part of the court papers consist of something entirely different: depositions. In another step different from London procedure, Robert Bayard repeatedly permitted additional depositions to be taken. Both parties were able to file additional questions to be asked of witnesses to strengthen their claim. Commissions for examining witnesses in other countries were occasionally entered in the minute books.[113] But the court repeatedly noted giving extra time for additional interrogatories to be conducted.[114] The three normal, standing interrogatories were conducted by the Register of the court on 7 August 1778.[115] Bayard, it seems, permitted both sides leave for additional witnesses to be questioned, though this is not explicitly recorded in the minute books for the *Hawke* (Yell). Ten different people gave depositions for the case, some twice, being questioned individually by both parties.[116] These depositions were not, strictly speaking, permissible evidence; although Bayard had permitted them, they were "irregular"[117] to say the least. The court papers at TNA even include a set of directions issued to the Register by Samuel Fairlamb, stressing how additional, individual interrogatories were to be conducted on his behalf.[118]

In summary, the case was, in more ways than one, the opposite of the daily appeals grind. Eight members of the Lords were present on 18 March 1780, as they issued their final decree on the case: they upheld Bayard's decision. Moreover, they even noted their reasons for following this line of thought, referring firstly to the fact that Samuel Fairlamb as sole owner of the vessel and cargo had clearly been proven to be a "Subject of Our Sovereign Lord

111 Ibid., 62v.

112 See, for example, any deposition in TNA, HCA 32/350/9.

113 Some examples of foreign commissions being discussed include TNA, HCA 49/92/2, 61v, 93r.

114 Some examples of irregular interrogatories being permitted by the judge, TNA, HCA 49/92/1, 28r; TNA, HCA 49/92/2, 53r, 66v.

115 TNA, HCA 45/7/4, 59r.

116 HCA 32/350/9

117 TNA, HCA 45/7/4, 60r.

118 TNA, HCA 32/350/9, p. 34.

the King".[119] Secondly, "the Trade the said Schooner was employed in, was highly laudable and meritorious, and it was professedly to furnish his Majesty's Army, Navy, and the Inhabitants [...] with Provision at a Time they were in great Want of them".[120] They did not follow up the reasoning employed by Fairlamb's counsel that the conducting of irregular interrogatories should already be seen as an intent to manipulate the evidence in the captor's favour. They did not condemn the captor in costs either.[121]

The case of the *Hawke* (Yell) thus remains one of the most unusual cases in the examined time frame. While it is commendable that a higher body could be appealed to, Symonds's chances of a reversal of decree seemed slim from the beginning. The evidence was not in his favour and Fairlamb's tale would seem a very odd one to invent if entirely fictional. Of course, if only General Howe had deigned to confirm the licence, the court case may have been avoided. At the same time, it is astonishing to note that no costs were ever issued against Thomas Symonds, not even when he appealed the case, having reviewed the evidence and spoken to the crew members on board.

Thomas Symonds had sought out a career in the British Navy once he understood his elder brother would inherit the family estate. After being warned by his mother not to sponge off him in later life, he:

> left the house immediately, with his clothes tied in a bundle over his shoulder, and keeping his intentions to himself, trudged off to Harwich [Essex, Britain], where he was invited to try his luck at sea, by the captain of a vessel of war, who had been staying with his father. He was not heard of again until he had become a Master and Commander in the Navy, when he paid a short visit to his brother.[122]

Symonds continued his naval career undeterred, while the case of the *Hawke* (Yell) was passing through the courts. At the Battle of Yorktown in 1781, the last major battle in North America during the Revolutionary War, Symonds signed the Articles of Capitulation on 18 October 1781 as the most senior Naval officer present.[123] He became a prisoner of war, continuing his

119 TNA, HCA 45/7/4, 60v.

120 Ibid., 60v.

121 Ibid., 60v.

122 Quote in W. Symonds and J. A. Sharp, *Memoirs of the Life and Services of Rear-Admiral Sir William Symonds: Surveyor of the Navy from 1832 to 1847* (London, 1858), pp. 2–4; I was made aware of this quote through a Wikipedia article: Thomas Symonds (Royal Navy officer, died 1792), https://en.wikipedia.org/wiki/Thomas_Symonds_(Royal_Navy_officer,_died_1792) (accessed 12 March 2025).

123 R. A. Selig, 'Washington, Rochambeau, and the Yorktown Campaign of 1781', in E. G. Lengel (ed.), *A Companion to George Washington* (Hoboken NJ, 2012), pp. 266–87, at p. 285; Articles of Capitulation; 18 October 1781: Avalon Project –

service as the Commander of HMS *Diadem* more than a year later.[124] He gained nothing from his case against the Salem-built schooner, but he lost nothing either.

Samuel Fairlamb on the other hand, followed his long-term emigration plans. In the summer of 1783, he was appointed as an agent to represent "refugees […] in many cases persons not strictly speaking in the category of loyalists",[125] often religious Quakers like himself, who wished to migrate from the United States to New Brunswick and Nova Scotia. In this capacity, he continued working with British officials and seeking a new home within the confines of the Empire, although he did not move to Britain like other loyalists; for example, the Bayards.[126] His fortune and that of his family would have been altered massively, had his vessel and cargo, carrying all his belongings and the money from the sale of his old life in Chester, been condemned as prize.

The true losers of the capture of the *Hawke* (Yell) appear to have been Peter Peterson and William Hale, the two mariners that had thought the schooner was travelling to the Caribbean. They found themselves led into a trap by their employers, suddenly and unintentionally supporting the enemy in a civil war. The winners were most definitely the inhabitants of New York, as well as some soldiers in the British Army and Navy stationed there. They did not have to deal with any of the legal complexities of the case, instead, they swiftly gained access to the flour and tobacco on board: by consent, the Marshal had been permitted to sell the cargo and vessel on 4 November 1778.[127] On 1 December 1778 he brought the proceeds, totalling £1761 7s 1d New York currency, into court and paid them into Samuel Fairlamb's hands.[128]

The role of the Marshal in the New York admiralty court is not to be underestimated. He regularly sold goods and vessels, as well as taking them into custody, conducting general or specific searches of vessels and, occasionally, drawing up inventories of the cargo on board.[129]

---

Documents in Law, History and Diplomacy, Yale Law School/Lillian Goldman Law Library, https://avalon.law.yale.edu/18th_century/art_of_cap_1781.asp (accessed 8 June 2023).

124 Harrison, *Thomas Symonds*.

125 A. J. Mekeel, 'The Quaker-Loyalist Migration to New Brunswick and Nova Scotia in 1783', *Bulletin of Friends' Historical Association*, 32 (1943), 65–75, at 65.

126 TNA, PRO 30/55/77/72: 8672.

127 TNA, HCA 49/92/3, 131v.

128 Ibid., 141r, 142r.

129 For further examples, see TNA, HCA 49/92/1, 13v; TNA, HCA 49/92/3, 103v, 105v, 121v or table 5. Moreover, if the Marshal found that vessels or their cargoes had been tampered with, it was also his task to "make Inquiry for the Goods taken out, and the Persons by whom the same was done, and that he make report of the same"; (HCA 49/92/3, 107v).

Sometimes, he also needed to summon "witnesses"[130] or bring summoned people to court to bear oath.[131] A large part of his work was also connected to the underlying finances, much like those of the Register of the court. It is therefore not surprising that when the Treasury wrote to inform Robert Bayard of the appointment of John Jackson as British Naval prize agent, they also addressed the Marshal and the Register.[132] For every sale, the Marshal had to bring an account of sales into court. If he did not bring it in "with all convenient speed",[133] the Judge promptly reminded him to do so.[134] Alongside this account, he would generally bring the proceeds of the sale, which he would pass on to the respective parties. In some cases, the proceeds were directly handed to the court parties, or their agents/legal counsel.[135] Often, the proceeds were paid directly "into the hands of the judge".[136] This was the case, for example, when a vessel was condemned to the use of His Majesty (the Judge would forward the amount to the government at a later date).[137] It was also the case when parties involved were not present. In the examined time frame alone, at least £48,196 15s 10d (New York currency) were lodged in the hands of Robert Bayard by the Marshal.[138] These were some of the "large sums lying for a long Time in his hands"[139] that were mentioned in Bayard's claim before the Loyalist commission. Sometimes the Register also fulfilled this function, although it is very rarely noted in the minute books.[140] In London, the High Court of Admiralty's Register, also referred to as the Registrar, was responsible for keeping money awaiting collection.[141] In 1813 the maximum sum the Register could take charge of was set at £10,000 (Sterling).[142]

While the sums involved were large on both sides of the Atlantic, there are two notable differences that must be mentioned regarding the Vice-Admiralty Court of New York. The first concerns the distribution of costs. It has already been shown that Bayard generally condemned those before his court. However,

130 TNA, HCA 49/92/3, 103v.

131 Ibid., 102v.

132 Henry White also worked closely with John Jackson, and it appears was active in this role until September 1780. TNA, T 1/557: *Commissioners for the Office of Lord High Admiral of Britain and Ireland to the Judge, Register and Marshal at New York*, undated.

133 TNA, HCA 49/92/1, 22v.

134 For example, ibid., 7r.

135 For example, ibid., 34v; TNA, HCA 49/92/2, 94r.

136 See table 7.

137 For example, TNA, HCA 49/92/3, 104r.

138 See table 7.

139 TNA, AO 12/20, 114r.

140 For example, TNA, HCA 49/92/1, 33r.

141 Thompson, Admiralty registrars, p. 23.

142 Ibid., pp. 16–17.

it was very rare for him to decree costs and damages to either party. Of the 332 decrees issued from 1777 to 1778, only eight mention the distribution of costs, three in favour of the captors, five in favour of the owners/reclaimants. Generally, the reclaimants were condemned in costs when the Judge identified a probable cause of seizure.[143] This was also a way to encourage privateering, as it did not penalise the captors despite the seized vessel not being condemned as legal prize. One of Bayard's predecessors had consequently issued judgments along this line to increase the appeal of the New York Vice-Admiralty Court and to promote the privateering trade in the city.[144]

The distribution of cases of costs, though skewed towards the captors, seems to have been more or less balanced regardless of decree: three cases of costs were declared in condemnation decrees, five in restoration cases.[145] Whereas the Appeals Court in London almost exclusively dealt in 'costs and damages', the New York Vice-Admiralty Court focused mainly on 'costs'.

The reason why damages were infrequent, can be attributed to the more open 'microcosm' of the New York Admiralty Court. Although the regular court staff consisted of Robert Bayard, the Judge, David Matthews, the Register, John Tabor Kempe, the Advocate General and two regular proctors, Mr Jones and Mr Kissam, the court was not a microcosm at all. Whereas Doctors' Commons was an elitist club of select members, representation in the vice-admiralty court was an open playing field, where claimants could represent themselves. More than 130 people represented themselves in court throughout the time frame, forming 36% of all actions taken in the court during this year of study.[146] The rest was undertaken by people acting as agents on behalf of others.[147]

In London, the admiralty courts were highly structured social spaces. Procurators[148] – also known simply as 'proctors' – and advocates had become distinct groups of legal professionals in the seventeenth century.[149] Advocates were civilian trained lawyers (that is, the actual civil law Doctors of Doctors' Commons) and thus also referred to as civilians. They had to study civil

143 See table 8.

144 Watson, 'Judge Lewis Morris', 128, 144.

145 See table 8.

146 See table 1.

147 One of these private agents was Alexander Hamilton, TNA, HCA 49/92/1, 25r; TNA, HCA 49/92/2, 89v; TNA, HCA 49/92/3, 106v; TNA, HCA 49/92/4, 156r. Another was William Bayard Sr, Robert's older brother, as we can tell from his power of attorney listed in TNA, HCA 49/96: Volume 2 of 'Letters of Agency', compiled by the registry of the British New York Vice-Admiralty Court marked no. 47, 53, 70, 84, fol. 70r–71r, 80v–81v, 111r–112r, 128v–129r.

148 Chamberlayne, *Magnæ Britanniæ*, p. 232.

149 H. J. Bourguignon, *Sir William Scott, Lord Stowell, Judge of the High Court of Admiralty, 1798–1828* (Cambridge, 1987), p. 9.

law at either Cambridge or Oxford and were required to absolve a 'year of silence', during which they were not allowed to practise before the court, after receiving their degree. This meant that they often came from wealthy family backgrounds and were capable of supporting themselves throughout this time.[150] They were a select, even elitist, few, recognisable by their "scarlet robes, academic hoods and round black velvet doctors' bonnets",[151] although in admiralty procedures they were generally dressed all in black.[152]

Proctors, on the other hand, were not allowed to practise in court themselves.[153] Equivalent to modern day solicitors, they prepared cases for trial.[154] They wore black robes and hoods with white lamb furs to distinguish them from advocates, as furs were worn by those without university degrees.[155] In Doctors' Commons, the professional distinction was further reflected in the fact that proctors sat almost at ground level while the Judge and advocates were seated on a raised platform in the courtroom.[156] Despite their subordinate position, they also made up a legal elite, with only nineteen practising proctors sharing a monopoly of maritime legal activity in 1833.[157]

But in the American vice-admiralty courts proctors often argued cases before the court.[158] In the Vice-Admiralty Court of New York, instances could be found where proctors Jones and Kissam both argued before the court on behalf of their clients.[159] In some of the American vice-admiralty courts, the terms such as libellant, complainant, appellant, proponent and plaintiff were all used interchangeably without differentiation, while legal counsels were described as attorneys or advocates, instead of proctors.[160] In the case of the Massachusetts admiralty court, no formal distinction between *in rem* and *in personam* cases were drawn, though both were employed.[161] Generally, American colonies lacked civilian lawyers, making the admiralty processes, even in court, reliant on common law lawyers.[162]

While these distinctions may seem trivial, it seems that in New York, the flat hierarchies and liberal court structure enabled claimants to swiftly and directly

150 Ibid., p. 13.

151 F. L. Wiswall, *The Development of Admiralty Jurisdiction and Practice Since 1800*, 2nd edn (Cambridge, 1970/2011), p. 82.

152 Ibid., p. 77.

153 Bourguignon, *Sir William Scott* (1987), pp. 6–7.

154 Hill, *The Prizes of War*, p. 164.

155 Chamberlayne, *Magnæ Britanniæ*, p. 232.

156 Wiswall, *Development of Admiralty Jurisdiction*, p. 82.

157 Ibid., p. 80.

158 Bourguignon, *The First Federal Court*, vol. 122, p. 156.

159 For example, TNA, HCA 49/92/1, 26r; TNA, HCA 49/92/2, 92v.

160 Wroth, 'Massachusetts Vice Admiralty Court', 267–8.

161 Ibid., p. 266.

162 Harrington, 'Legacy, Part II', 325.

contact the Marshal of the Court and thus cause less damages to cargoes and vessels. If either party stated in court that the cargo was at risk of spoiling or being damaged, the court could order the Marshal to sell the affected goods and bring the proceeds into court. This procedure, so straightforward, enabled parties at court to regularly sell parts of their cargo. On average, a case of partial sale was ordered every third court sitting.[163] In the case of the *Polly*, the cargo had taken some water damage due to "several hard Gales of Wind at Sea"[164] *en route* to New York and there was a risk of the rest of the cargo being spoilt. Bad weather was listed as the reason for sale in 9% of the cases.[165] In 34% of all cases, it was the leakiness of the vessel that was listed as the issue. Sometimes it was also the bad quality of casks and containers, or the manner of their stowing that meant substantial parts of the cargo would be lost if not sold quickly.[166] This reason was given in 12.5% of the studied cases. Some cargoes, such as fruit, were perishable by nature and could not be stored for weeks prior to condemnation. This was cited as a reason for sale in 19% of cases.[167] In the case of the *Polly*, an infestation of pests was also listed as a reason to sell the cargo.[168] Generally, the reason for the sale of parts of the cargo by the Marshal could be found on a scale between limiting existing damage and preventing potential damage. In the case of the *Success*, it was pleaded that the cargo was "already damaged and is likely to become more damaged".[169] Often, the potential loss that was emphasised, such as in the case of the *Three Friends*, where the complainant highlighted that a "great Part of it [the cargo] will be lost if it is not taken out",[170] or in the case of the *Exchange,*[171] where it was emphasised that "some of the sugar on Board is already damaged and the Rest of the Same in Danger of being Damaged"[172] without decisive action. The worst scenario was voiced in regard to the *Betsy*'s cargo which was "in great Danger of being totally spoiled".[173]

If the risk of damage to the cargo was noted far enough in advance, it did not even have to be sold. Its removal from the vessel could be ordered by the court instead; for example, in the case of *Le Hardie*, where it was "ordered

163 See table 9.
164 TNA, HCA 49/92/4, 154r.
165 See table 9.
166 For example, in the case of another Polly; TNA, HCA 49/92/4, 155r.
167 See table 9.
168 TNA, HCA 49/92/3, 105r.
169 Ibid., 140r.
170 Ibid., 136r.
171 For more information on this case, see the manuscript papers: TNA, HCA 32/327/3A: *Exchange* (unknown).
172 TNA, HCA 49/92/2, 62r.
173 TNA, HCA 49/92/1, 38r.

that the said cargo be unloaded and that it be stored under Joint Custody of the Agent for the said Prize, and the Collector of this Port"[174] to prevent spoliation. In some cases, even the vessel itself was sold by the Marshal for fear of not being able to maintain it in custody without damage.[175]

Such processes were not only efficient in their conduct; they also saved everyone money: in the case of partially spoilt cargo, the owners could still obtain some value for their property, while the rest of the cargo was ideally preserved through swift action. Perishable cargo was simply exchanged for preservable currency. Thus, no further charges against the captors could be produced for negligence or loss of product, hindering increased court fees and rises in case complexity. Even the inhabitants of New York profited, as they were able to purchase such goods from captured vessels while their military and economic situation seemed dire.

From the study of the period 1777–8, one can conclude that admiralty jurisdiction in New York was very different from the British admiralty process, despite, in theory, being a mere extension of the High Court of Admiralty's power. The cosmos of the New York court was far more liberal than its British, traditionalist superior. This was not only reflected by the people in the court and in its loose terminology, but also by the liberties applied to procedure; for example, through individualised interrogatories and *in personam* prize cases. At the same time, the court seems to have been remarkably efficient, dealing swiftly with those cases before it. Robert Bayard, as Judge, was a clear representative of British imperial power, and his rate of condemnation clearly supported imperial, loyalist policy. However, without a clear analysis of the merits of such cases, one cannot say whether this was the result of a bias or whether he was following the precedents set by 'international law' (as envisioned by the British).

When daring to peer into subsequent volumes of the HCA 49/92 series, it seems that in the long-term another procedural trend ensued. While in the studied time frame most libels were for vessels and their cargo (with the exception of privateers), later volumes record two separate libels, one against the vessel and one against its cargo. This may have made decrees faster in particular cases, while reducing the opportunity for partial restoration or condemnation decrees. It also means that at first glance far more decrees were issued in later years than in 1778. The value of stipulations also increased in later volumes, reaching over £5,000 New York currency.[176] The number of court actions and decrees undoubtedly also rose and fell, parallel to wartime developments, with the series offering great potential for military historians. It would also be highly interesting to compare Bayard's tenure in detail to

174 Ibid., 22v.

175 TNA, HCA 49/92/3, 116r.

176 TNA, HCA 49/92/6, 360r.

that of his predecessors, to understand the continuities and discrepancies in the development of colonial admiralty law and procedure in the region. His reluctance to issue costs against privateers has already been noted as in line with his predecessors. At the same time, how Bayard's tenure was removed from historiography should give us warning. Maybe comparisons between Caribbean vice-admiralty courts would be more fruitful, examining whether there was one general culture of vice-admiralty court jurisdiction, separate from London, or whether each court had a unique tradition. Either way, it is important that Bayard, his records and his tenure are reinserted into the historiography of the New York Vice-Admiralty Court. Nationalist historiographies portraying an American admiralty jurisdiction in that location from 1697 until the present day, yet excluding the loyalist court during the War of Independence, have persisted in ignoring not only the experience of their own ships and seamen in a continued colonial jurisdiction, but also the complex realities facing admiralty law throughout the conflict. Robert Bayard's tenure, especially in light of the rich source material still available to researchers today, must be actively used in the sense of positive, transnational and global history, rather than being relegated to the footnotes of an uncomfortable truth in a nationalist agenda.

About 60–80,000 loyalists left the United States during the War of Independence. For many of them, their first stop was London, about 7,000 choosing to remain in England.[177] These émigrés included Robert Bayard, and his brother, William, along with much of their families. They left their native country alongside many others, including John Tabor Kempe, the Advocate General from the Vice-Admiralty Court of New York. Most of the New York loyalists migrated to Britain, Nova Scotia or Canada.[178]

177 J. Flavell, *When London was Capital of America* (New Haven CT, 2010), p. 242.

178 Flick, *Loyalism in New York*, XVI/1, p. 171.

# 3

# Independent and Neutral: US Objectives in British Prize Jurisdiction in the 1790s

Some of the captured sailors from vessels condemned in the Vice-Admiralty Court of New York would have been sent to detention facilities under British control. These men, often from low social backgrounds with no military training, were considered to be regular rebels as opposed to soldiers by the British armed forces, meaning they were not recognised as prisoners of war and thus were not subject to the standards of treatment required for prisoners of war by international agreements.[1] Up to 18,000 Americans died in British captivity during the conflict.[2] When the American Commissary General of Prisoners, Elias Boudinot, signed the preliminary articles of peace in 1783, the British treatment of American prisoners of war was glossed over.[3] It was not conducive to the establishment of peaceful relations and the treaty declared that "all past Misunderstandings and Differences that have unhappily interrupted the good Correspondence and Friendship"[4] between the now independent United States and Britain were to be put aside.

John Jay had been one of the negotiators of the 1783 peace treaty and had, in this capacity, travelled to London. In mid-December 1783, Jay noted that he had met his cousin, William Bayard (Sr), on the street there. Cousin 'Billy' was a loyalist, John Jay a patriot civil servant. Loyalists were often looked down upon as "fools and traitors",[5] their conduct during the war considered worse than that of the British. The different political outlooks and choices that

1 E. G. Burrows, *Forgotten Patriots: The Untold Story of American Prisoners During the Revolutionary War* (New York, 2008), pp. 26, 80.

2 J. W. Chambers, F. Anderson and G. K. Piehler, *The Oxford Guide to American Military History* (New York, 1999), p. 560.

3 *A Century of Lawmaking for a New Nation: U.S. Congressional Documents and Debates: 1774–1875, Journals of the Continental Congress; American Memory* (Washington DC, 2003), vol. 24, p. 243.

4 National Archives, *Treaty of Paris (1783)*: Milestone Documents Series, www.archives.gov/milestone-documents/treaty-of-paris#transcript (accessed 19 July 2024), foreword.

5 Flick, *Loyalism in New York*, XVI/1, p. 162.

the two cousins had made were, at this point, insurmountable. They passed each other on the street as if they were strangers.[6]

Although Great Britain had acknowledged US independence in the Treaty of Paris, many grievances remained in the late eighteenth century, as can be seen in the Jay Treaty.[7] Not only were British troops still stationed on American soil and the boundaries of that soil still being debated, but the maritime realm also required a shift in thinking. With the emergence of the United States, the primary mode of identifying seamen as English (or British) through their language, behaviour and types of vessel, became unreliable.[8] While American merchants were fighting for their valuable cargoes, ships and crews, US seamen's fortunes in the face of British impressment depended entirely on the recognition of their nationality as non-British subjects. The imprisonment and impressment of US sailors would remain one of the most contested issues in the Anglo-American relationship. Much like Samuel Bayard, who was sent out to be US agent for disputed prize jurisdiction, another US agent was sent to London to undertake work assisting impressed Americans sailors in the 1790s too.[9]

Especially in the early period, the United States struggled to be seen as an equal player on the world stage. The US government possessed barely any naval forces and was generally a militarily weak state. After the War of Independence, the new government was still a loose confederation of states without strong taxation powers. As a result, there was a lack of funding to maintain or indeed create a national naval service. While a standing army was often considered a liability and danger to the new republic, the navy was considered an asset worth building. This division between land-based and naval forces can be clearly traced in early American political thought. Both Jefferson and Madison felt a navy posed no inward threat, with the former stating "a naval force can never endanger our liberties, nor occasion bloodshed; a land force would do both".[10] To some American politicians, the navy was an

6 G. Pellew, *John Jay* (Boston MA and New York, 1890), p. 227.

7 *Treaty of amity, commerce, and navigation, between His Britannick Majesty and the United States of America: Signed at London, the 19th of November, 1794* (London, 1795).

8 N. Perl-Rosenthal, *Citizen Sailors: Becoming American in the Age of Revolution* (Cambridge MA and London, 2015), p. 81.

9 David Lenox was appointed to protect American seamen in London and his work mirrored that of the American agent for claims and appeals in prize causes in many regards. He also introduced a system of sorting the vast amount of paperwork, regularly wrote to persons in America to attain evidence to forward to British institutions and even suggested publishing the forms in which these proofs would be accepted. Ibid., pp. 211–16.

10 Quoted in M. J. Crawford and C. F. Hughes, *The Reestablishment of the Navy, 1787–1801: Historical Overview and Select Bibliography*, www.history.navy.mil/

integral part of a "respectable Nation"[11] from the very beginning, but the Act to provide a naval armament was only passed by Congress in 1794. For many others, naval forces were not a priority. Once the Treaty of Paris seemed to guarantee peace and Britain had acknowledged US sovereignty, reestablishing trade with Britain seemed more important: maybe investments were needed more for state-building rather than for the creation of armaments.

Strong mercantile relations, including a large part of financial credit and insurance, continued between London and America, despite independence.[12] Economically, US reliance on British trading networks remained high. About 75% of US commerce relied on trade involving British import and export goods, effectively propping up the new nation's credit and economy.[13] The importance of the American market had also increased in Britain, with American trade (including the West Indies) accounting for 57% of exports and 31% of imports by 1797–8.[14] Moreover, all the belligerent parties during the French wars were also reliant on neutral carriers, which provided badly needed goods, reduced transaction costs, weakened blockades and who prevented "the wholesale collapse of Atlantic commerce during the era".[15] Wartime led to increases in mariners' wages and shipping insurance, as well as additional costs for armaments, convoy travels, and so forth. However, these expenses did not rise as much for neutrals as they did for the belligerent parties. In addition, shipping capacities destroyed in battle or through the loss of captured vessels could be taken over by neutral carriers, which meant that neutral shipping became "extremely profitable"[16] in times of war. Even Samuel Bayard admitted as much in his private correspondence, writing: "Were all the property I have claimed to be condemned by Great Britain, I apprehend it is nothing when compared with the money our merchants have

---

research/library/bibliographies/reestablishment-navy-1787-1801.html (accessed 12 March 2025).

11 Quoted, ibid.

12 Flavell, *When London was Capital of America*, p. 246.

13 S. F. Bemis, 'The United States and the Abortive Armed Neutrality of 1794', *The American Historical Review*, 24 (1918), 26–47, at 34.

14 M. Robson, *A History of the Royal Navy: The Napoleonic Wars* (London, 2014), p. 75.

15 J. Land, 'Trade and the New Republic: American Trade During the Napoleonic Wars, 1783–1839', Chapter provided as an e-resource by the University of Helsinki in J. Eloranta, E. Golson, P. Hedberg and M. C. Moreira (eds), *Small and Medium Powers in Global History: Trade, Conflicts and Neutrality from the 18th to the 20th Centuries* (London and New York, 2019), at p. 5.

16 L. Müller, 'Nordic Neutrals and Anglo-French Wars: 1689–1815', The Northern Mediterranean, XIVth International Economic History Congress (Helsinki, 2006), p. 4.

made in consequence of our neutrality."[17] America was one of the great neutral winners during the French Wars until the War of 1812 and the need to protect its international trade is undeniable when one looks at its impact: between 1790 and 1807 alone, the value of exports, imports and re-exports in US trade increased sixfold, from $20 million to $120 million. The tonnage of US ships, from 1789 to 1807, rose from *c.* 100,000,000 to 1,100,000,000 tons.[18] Generally, the period can be described as "one of the highest rates of growth ever recorded"[19] in the American economy, with an undeniable "U.S. dependency on Britain as a trading partner".[20]

Britain, on the other hand, was fighting adversaries across the globe in a series of costly wars, in which victory was far from certain. The impressment of American sailors did not simply display a British disregard for US sovereignty, it reflected the British need for maritime manpower. In 1793 the Royal Navy had required 36,000 personnel. By 1805 the number had risen to 115,000 men.[21] At its height, the British armed forces encompassed 400,000 men (126,000 in the Navy), three times the magnitude of those employed in the American Revolutionary War.[22] "The [...] struggle was immense in its scale and intensity. Never before had European states resorted to a mobilization of civilian and military resources as total as during this period."[23] The French Wars have been considered a "total war of the will".[24] For more than twenty years, France remained at war with Britain.[25] Britain had been flourishing throughout the 1780s and '90s, with the population increasing by 1.5 million from 1781 to 1791 and the economy growing at about 6% per year from 1781 to 1802 with the onset of industrialisation.[26] Now, it faced a European rival (later rivals) on a huge scale and did not only require manpower, but also a whole chain of logistical efforts to organise enough supplies and weapons to utilise those men. The British national debt more than tripled from the outbreak

17 Bayard to Boudinot, 12 December 1795, in D. L. Sterling, 'A Federalist Opposes the Jay Treaty: The Letters of Samuel Bayard', *William and Mary Quarterly*, 18 (1961), 408–24, at 423.

18 Müller, *Neutrality in World History*, p. 77.

19 Land, 'Trade and the New Republic', 10.

20 S. Moats, *Navigating Neutrality: Early American Governance in the Turbulent Atlantic* (Charlottesville NC and London, 2021), p. 133.

21 J. C. Bradford, *America, Sea Power, and the World* (New York, 2016), p. 27.

22 R. Knight, *Britain against Napoleon: The Organization of Victory 1793–1815* (London, 2014), p. 154.

23 A. Mikaberije, *The Napoleonic Wars: A Global History* (New York, 2020), p. 11.

24 M. Broers, 'The Concept of "Total War" in the Revolutionary-Napoleonic Period', *War in History*, 15 (2008), 247–68, at 248.

25 Mikaberije, *The Napoleonic Wars*, p. 13.

26 Knight, *Britain against Napoleon*, p. 3.

of the French Wars, rising to £659.5 million by 1815.[27] During the American Revolutionary War (1775–83), Britain had borrowed about £91.9 million. The French Wars would result in a borrowing sum of £423.5 million, with the first phase (1793–1801) alone accounting for £184.9 million.[28]

The United States had very few naval forces to speak of. It has thus been classified as a 'weak state' alongside other neutral nations such as Sweden or Denmark, but this is misleading considering their economic impact and also due to neutral ports acting as privateering harbours.[29] At this point in time, Britain did not need to risk further stresses on its already stretched wartime resources.

Almost a decade since his estranged encounter with William Bayard in the 1780s, John Jay travelled to Britain again, this time to negotiate another treaty, resolving the outstanding issues from the Treaty of Paris. Time had healed some wounds, and a smattering of correspondence between Jay and his cousin proves that this was at least true for the two of them.[30] Hearing of Jay's arrival in Britain, William Bayard Sr sent him a letter, asking him to visit. He wished Jay the best in his endeavour to establish a lasting "Peace and friendship"[31] between both countries.

The treaty Jay negotiated would be termed the Treaty of Amity and Commerce, but is more well-known as the Jay Treaty. Although Britain and the United States had officially concluded peace in 1783, several issues remained contentious and had not been implemented by either government. The aim of the treaty was to ensure future peaceful relations between the two countries in the light of these stresses.[32] Some of the most prominent among these were that British troops had not been recalled from forts along the Northwest Territory and were thus still stationed on US soil.[33] On the other side, American citizens had not paid British creditors' debts they had taken

27 Mikaberije, *The Napoleonic Wars*, p. 13.

28 J. F. Wright, 'British Government Borrowing in Wartime, 1750–1815', *Economic History Review*, 52 (1999), 355–61, at 356, 361.

29 Land, 'Trade and the new republic', 5; A. L. Wold, *Privateering and Diplomacy, 1793–1807: Great Britain, Denmark-Norway and the Question of Neutral Ports* (Cham, 2020), p. 231.

30 For example, Founders Online and NARA, *From John Jay to William Bayard, 24 August 1794*, https://founders.archives.gov/?q=Recipient%3A%22Bayard%2C%20William%22&s=1111311111&r=1 (accessed 18 August 2023).

31 W. Bayard, *Letter to John Jay, 16 August 1794*, https://dlc.library.columbia.edu/jay/ldpd:54720 (accessed 18 August 2023).

32 P. C. Hoffer, W. Hoffer and N. E. H. Hull, *The Supreme Court: An Essential History, 2nd edn* (Lawrence KS, 2018), p. 36.

33 J. P. Kaminski, 'Honor and Interest: John Jay's Diplomacy During the Confederation', *New York History*, 83 (2002), 293–327, at 325.

up prior to the Revolution.[34] In addition, the issues of British impressment of American sailors and their prizetaking of allegedly neutral American vessels all plagued the relationship between the two nations.[35] With the Jay Treaty these main issues were addressed, although the issue of impressment remained unresolved.[36] Three mixed commissions, consisting of American and British participants, were set up to deal with the most contentious topics, an idea that is considered crucial to the development of international arbitration. The tradition of referring to the Jay Treaty in this light originated in the second half of the nineteenth century.[37] It expanded with some authors going so far as to refer to Grotius as the father of international law and John Jay as "the legitimate parent of international justice".[38] In contrast, other researchers remark that the system of mixed commissions was riddled with pitfalls and "inherent defects".[39] The Article IV Commission was to make a survey of the Mississippi River and thus determine the boundaries/borders outlined in the Treaty of Paris 1783, but hotly contested afterwards.[40] The second mixed commission was introduced in Philadelphia under Article VI to deal with the claims of British creditors regarding pre-Revolutionary debts owed by American citizens.[41] Under Article VII, a commission in London was to be set up to deal with disputed prize cases from either jurisdiction.

It was also stated that the commission under Article VII was to base its decisions upon the law of nations. The law of nations offered a great framework to these neutral states and players like the United States, placing them all as equal parties in a supranational construct that adhered to an idea of 'the law' placed beyond the reach of national desires. It would be the framework within which the US government tried to act in all cases of British prize adjudication, despite the independence of the British admiralty courts repeatedly being questioned.

34 Ibid., p. 317.

35 Jay to Lord Grenville, 30 July 1794; H. P. Johnston, *The Correspondence and public papers of John Jay: Vol. 4 (1794–1826)* (New York, 1893), pp. 45–6.

36 G. H. Clarfield, 'Postscript to the Jay treaty: Timothy Pickering and Anglo-American relations, 1795–1797', *William and Mary Quarterly*, 23 (1966), 108–20, at 117–8.

37 R. B. Lillich, 'The Jay Treaty Commissions', *St John's Law Review*, 32 (1963), 260–83, at 261; G. Schwarzenberger, 'Present-Day Relevance of the Jay Treaty Arbitrations', *Notre Dame Law Review*, 53 (1978), 715–33, at 716–17.

38 J. E. Read, *The Rule of Law on the International Plane: The W. M. Martin Lectures* (Toronto, 1961), vol. 1960, p. 11. Quoted in Schwarzberger, 'Present-Day Relevance of the Jay Treaty Arbitrations', 715.

39 Lillich, 'The Jay Treaty Commissions', 261.

40 *Treaty of Amity, Commerce, and Navigation, between His Britannick Majesty and the United States of America*, Article 4.

41 Ibid., Article 6.

The law of nations was held in high esteem by the political leaders of the early American republic.[42] A large part of the US mercantile community also refused to regard their court cases as personal pleas depending on British political and judicial goodwill. Instead, they saw their treatment as an international right they felt entitled to as members of a sovereign nation. When writing to the Secretary of State about the capture and condemnation of the *Rossetta*, one complainant launched into his message as follows: "Sir, I take the liberty of informing you of a late violation of the law of nations."[43] Similarly, Joshua Barney phrased it this way: "how far such [British] proceedings are agreeable to Justice or the law of Nations I must leave to"[44] the US government to decide. Others described their treatment simply as "enormous violations of the Maritime Law".[45] The Jay commissioners would even consider it "an indisputable right"[46] of the nation.[47]

The Jay Treaty was full of articles relating to maritime affairs, several of which explicitly dealt with piracy, privateering and the Courts of Admiralty in attempt to curb the conflict encapsuled in these contentious issues.[48] That disputed prize cases were not just mentioned alongside these, but considered important enough to receive their own commission is a clear reflection of American policies and international objectives. On the one hand, the economic importance of international trade for US citizens shaped US governmental interest in the results of prize jurisdiction and in its execution. On the other hand, international law was an angle to enter the arena of sovereignty and to

[42] Janis, *America and the Law of Nations, 1776–1939*, p. 24.

[43] [Illegible] to Pickering, 14 August 1798; NARA, *Box 5, Ships O-R; British Spoliations, ca. 1796–ca. 1824 – NAID: 1170270.*

[44] Barney to Jefferson, 17 February 1794; NARA, *Box 10, Unsorted Papers; British Spoliations, ca. 1796–ca. 1824 – NAID: 1170270.*

[45] Petition of the Subscribers of the Committee of the Sufferers by British Spoliations in the State of Massachusetts, to the President of the United States, 15 December 1801; NARA, *Box 9, Unsorted Papers; British Spoliations, ca. 1796–ca. 1824 – NAID: 1170270.*

[46] J. B. Moore, *History and digest of the international arbitrations to which the United States has been a party: Vol III, The Miscellaneous Documents of the House of Representatives, 1893–94* (Washington DC, 1898), vol. 212, p. 3197.

[47] Historian Andrew Lambert described the US government policy of attempting to gain neutral rights from a war-waging Britain at a time when neutrals were also profiting the enemy as "remarkably naïve". However, the effort and money the US government invested in the venture clearly show this was not their impression. A. D. Lambert, *The Challenge: America, Britain and the War of 1812* (London, 2012), p. 13.

[48] Piracy: Article 20, Privateering: Article 21, 22, 24, Courts of Admiralty: Article 19; *Treaty of Amity, Commerce, and Navigation, between His Britannick Majesty and the United States of America.*

prove one's independence on the international stage. In the case of the *Sisters*, American merchants highlighted:

> our Government, [...] will now determine whether our Commerce is to be regulated by the common standard of the law of nations, or by the conveniences or caprice of a foreign people [and] whether the Citizens of America are to be secure in the prosecution of a fair & lawfull commerce.[49]

The treatment of US citizens in the British prize courts was seen as a reflection of the British treatment of US sovereignty and the maritime rights the US claimed under international law. In this manner, the US agent for prize and the Jay commission on contested prizes, were additional cogs in a wider US foreign policy. [50]

However, as becomes clear in Rufus King's correspondence, the commission's work under Article VII was more reliant on the relationship and development of wider Anglo-American politics, than on the theoretical principles of the law of nations. King wrote that the commissions of Articles VI and VII were "considered as reciprocal checks upon each other in the hands of the respective Governments".[51] It went without saying that British financial interests would be the focus of Article VI (debts owed to British citizens), whereas the compensation of disputed captures was clearly geared towards American interests. When cooperation ceased under Article VI, the commission of Article VII was put on hold. It would take a political negotiation by King to conclude the failed work of the commission under Article VI to set in motion the machinery in London under Article VII.[52]

[49] Ludlow to Randolph, 28 May 1795; NARA, *Box 8, Unsorted Papers; British Spoliations, ca. 1796–ca. 1824 – NAID: 1170270*.

[50] This becomes blatantly apparent when examining, for example, Bayard's integration into foreign policy. As a member of the State Department, Bayard regularly sent dispatches and maintained contact with personnel there. He was also in contact with the other American consuls; for example, forwarding them papers. Some of these consuls, like Joshua Johnson, who had been posted in London since August of 1790, had not only been providing the State Department with political intelligence, but had also represented American claimants in admiralty court cases prior to Bayard's appointment. Bayard to Sec. State, 11 July 1795: NARA, *Letters Received from Samuel Bayard – NAID: 1170268*, p. 42; N. M. Keegan, *US Consular Representation in Britain since 1790* (London, 2018), p. 1.

[51] C. King and R. King, *The Life and Correspondence of Rufus King: Comprising his letters, private and official, his public documents and his speeches, Vol. IV 1801–1806* (New York, 1897), p. 50.

[52] Lillich, 'The Jay Treaty Commissions', 277.

While negotiating in April 1794, John Jay was secretly approached by Laurent von Engeström, the Swedish minister to London, with an offer for the United States to join the Swedish-Danish neutrality compact instead.[53] Jay had been told to examine the probability of such an alliance, as well as a more general support of the League of Armed Neutrality, should negotiations with Britain fail. That the League was pledged to "abundantly"[54] protect neutral rights and attempt to strengthen the economic free trade policies that neutrals desired, was considered a viable alternative, but only if the great threat posed by Britain could not be solved by Jay on a diplomatic level first. The fear was that a closer alliance with the other neutrals would antagonise as opposed to ease the tension between the two countries. Indeed, Lord Grenville received intelligence of the Scandinavian offer. Consequently, considerably more favourable drafts of what would become the Jay Treaty were scrapped on the British side of the negotiating table.[55] In response to Swedish minister Engeström's offer, Alexander Hamilton declared: "that it was the settled policy of this government [...] to avoid entangling itself with European connections, which would only tend to involve this country where it might have no possible interests."[56] In his 1786 Farewell address, Washington echoed the sentiment: "Why, by interweaving our destiny with that of any part of Europe, entangle our peace and prosperity in the toils of European ambition, rivalship, interest, humor, or caprice?"[57]

In contrast, Samuel Bayard felt this was the time to strike. He worried that British seizures of American vessels were "a prelude to general Hostilities between Great Britain and America".[58] He even considered the delays in the admiralty court system to be calculated steps undertaken by the British government to draw out court decisions until the beginning of another war with the United States.[59] The joint connection between all these assumptions was Samuel Bayard's conclusion that the British admiralty court system was a political institution, governed flexibly by policy, as opposed to the rigid and impartial law of nations that it aspired to enact.[60] Unusually, he was a Francophile and an Anglophobe. Despite working for Jay, Samuel Bayard

[53] Bemis, 'Abortive Armed Neutrality', 37.

[54] Randolph to Jay, 6 May 1794, in ibid., pp. 42–3.

[55] Ibid., p. 44.

[56] Ibid., p. 44.

[57] Washington, *Farewell Address, 1796*, in C. C. Hodge and C. J. Nolan (eds), *U.S. Presidents and Foreign Policy: From 1789 to the Present* (Santa Barbara CA, 2007), p. 388.

[58] Undated Memorial, *c.* February 1796, NARA, *Letters Received from Samuel Bayard – NAID: 1170268*, p. 87.

[59] 15 May 1796, ibid., p. 104.

[60] 3 February 1796, ibid., p. 83.

considered his work and the treaty flawed and unrealistic. In letters to America, he pointed out that while he believed justice was unobtainable in the British courts:

> we [the US government] *can* obtain *prompt* and *full* justice. The [British] nation is not now in a state to refuse it. [...] You will not hence infer that I am [an] advocate for war; far from it. I would avoid it if *possible*. But if we cannot without it prevent the establishment of the principle, that [...] so large a portion of our shipping [...] must be recovered only through the medium of their complex, expensive, dilatory and *political* courts of admiralty, it is our *interest*, our *duty* in *self defense* to seek redress by force of arms.[61]

This sentiment seems to have only been a fleeting one, but it did permeate Samuel Bayard's work. In a conversation about the importance of Sir William Scott in the undertaking of solving disputed Anglo-American prize cases to maintain peace through justice in the admiralty courts, the latter assured Bayard there was a strong wish to keep an alliance between the two countries. Samuel Bayard had responded that a lack of British judicial cooperation, indeed judicial "provocation",[62] could cause the opposite effect.

Samuel Bayard also urged America to ally with other neutrals, such as Russia or Prussia against Britain. While many neutral nations suffered from British seizures at sea, there was a certain power in the shared victimisation of neutrals and an entanglement that was impossible to avoid (see Chapter 5 on compensation regulations). The authors of a letter about the US vessel *Charlotte* voiced their outrage and questioned why their vessel or cargo should even fall under suspicion, declaring "we being a Neutral Nation and had a right to go to a Neutral port"![63] As another American merchant phrased it in his letter to the Secretary of State, there may be many insecurities, but: "this I am certain of: that my Property is illegally stopped. & you must be convinced that the Commerce, Independence & Neutrality of these State, are insulted by this Act."[64]

Neutrals faced a range of shared challenges in the face of British admiralty jurisdiction. The British vehemently insisted on what they considered their legal right to detain, search and adjudge neutral vessels, and also clearly expressed suspicion towards neutral vessels and merchants. A 1758 pamphlet

61 Samuel Bayard to Elias Boudinot, July 1795; quoted in Sterling, 'A Federalist Opposes the Jay Treaty', 415–16.

62 5 July 1795; Bayard, Diary of Samuel Bayard, p. 18.

63 Brothers Coster & Co. to Pickering, 19 July 1799; NARA, *Box 1, Ships A–C; British Spoliations, ca. 1796–ca. 1824 – NAID: 1170270.*

64 John Proctor to Secretary of State, 21 September 1795, NARA, *Box 3, Ships G–K; British Spoliations, ca. 1796–ca. 1824 – NAID: 1170270.*

titled *The Case of the Dutch Ships, Considered*, summed up: "an impartial Conduct is the very Idea of Neutrality. It is incumbent upon Neutrals to remove a Presumption that is against them, by a Justification of themselves, and by submitting to a proper Enquiry, without Fraud, or Resistance."[65] Jenkinson's *A Discourse on the Conduct of the Government of Great-Britain in Respect to Neutral Nations during the Present War*, first printed in 1758 and republished in 1794, contains another colourful depiction of the British attitude towards neutrality at this time:

> What can Neutral Nations desire more, than to remain amid the Ravages of War in the same happy Circumstances, which the Tranquillity of Peace would have afforded them? But can any Right from hence arise, that you should take Occasion from the War itself to constitute a new Species of Traffic, which in Peace you never enjoyed, and which the Necessity of One Party is obliged to grant you, to the Detriment, perhaps Destruction, of the Other? If this Right was admitted, it would become the Interest of all Commercial States to promote Dissention among their Neighbours; the Quarrels of others would be a Harvest to Themselves; and from the Contentions of others They would gather Wealth and Power.[66]

A British consul in Norway wrote to Lord Grenville in 1794, that: "A maritime war wherein Great Britain is concerned is ever the Harvest of the Northern States; […], is a glad Tidings to these so called neutral Spectators as the loss of a Revenue Cutter is pleasing to a Smuggler […] extraordinary gain is in view."[67]

Not just were neutrals jointly subjected to this British depiction of neutrals as greedy individuals, profiting from war, they also were confronted with similar obstacles in the legal system.

The elitist community of maritime legal professionals in Britain, known as Doctors' Commons, guarded knowledge on prize adjudication jealously: they were likened to a religious faction only functioning through the spoken word or secret scripts.[68] There were no publications of the decisions made by the Judge

65 TNA, HCA 45/3/3: *The Case of the Dutch Ships, Considered* (London, 1758), p. 3.

66 TNA, HCA 45/3/1: *A Discourse on the Conduct of the Government of Great-Britain in Respect to Neutral Nations during the Present War* (London, 1758), p. 28.

67 Quoted in Wold, *Privateering and Diplomacy*, p. 230.

68 *Decisions in the High Court of Admiralty: During the time of Sir George Hay, and of Sir James Marriott, late Judges of that Court, vol. 1. 1776 to 1779* (London, 1801), vol. 1, p. i.

or the Lords of Appeal, not even to other inferior British courts abroad.[69] This unshared knowledge meant that it was not possible for claimants or (potential) appellants to understand decrees, as the legal principles they were founded on were often not explained or set down, only vaguely grasped.[70] Some precedents could be followed through research in the maritime community or the press, such as the Swedish ship *Maria* (Paulsen), reports of which could be followed in American, Danish, Swedish and British newspapers.[71] But these reports were not legal reports, and might not reflect important criteria in diverging decisions.[72] This led to a large amount of risk, frustration and insecurity in taking cases to court.

Samuel Bayard especially pointed out that his focus in attending hearings lay on American cases only. Still, he did attend other nations' cases when they promised to be relevant to American procedure. One example is the Bremen ship *Orion* (Christoffers), which Bayard attended on 28 November 1795.[73] Here, the Lords of Appeal decreed that the transportation of potash was to be considered as contraband from that point forward, as the method for extracting saltpetre from it (for the use in gunpowder) had, according to the Lords, not been "generally known thro Europe" [74] up until that date.[75]. Thus, while the *Orion* was not considered to be carrying contraband goods, potash would be considered as such on all ships afterwards. Samuel Bayard jotted this down in his dairy and communicated the change in policy to the Secretary of State two days later. Similarly, he also forwarded notes and printed appeals cases to Washington regarding various Danish cases.[76] A memorandum was also

69 J. D. Gordan, 'Publishing Robinson's Reports of Cases Argued and Determined in The High Court of Admiralty', *Law and History Review* (2014), 1–49, at 16.

70 Colombos, *A Treatise on the Law of Prize*, p. 28.

71 Müller, *Neutrality in World History*, p. 74.

72 According to Hill, the periodical *Naval Chronicle* offered many insights into court rulings (p. 263), but would often highlight their impact on maritime communities and individuals working in the sector, as opposed to legal distinctions (p. 18); Hill, *The Prizes of War*. As a result, prize cases "were avidly followed by the press and public", Petrie, *The Prize Game*, p. 1.

73 Bayard falsely denoted it as a Hamburg vessel, 28 November 1795; Bayard, *Diary of Samuel Bayard*, p. 41; TNA, HCA 45/18/15: *Orion* (Christoffers).

74 Bayard to Pinckney, 30 November 1795: NARA, *Letters Received from Samuel Bayard – NAID: 1170268*, p. 66.

75 This decision by the Lords is astonishing as the use of potash in making saltpetre was traditional in Europe throughout the eighteenth century. The extraction method was identified by Bayard as the key reason for considering potash an item of contraband. R. P. Multhauf, 'The French Crash Program for Saltpeter Production: 1776–94', *Technology and Culture*,12 (1971), 162–81, at 177–8.

76 Bayard to Pinckney, 29 December 1795: NARA, *Letters Received from Samuel Bayard – NAID: 1170268*, p. 68.

drafted concerning Danish and American vessels in regard to freight and expenses.[77] Before Samuel Bayard's work had even begun, Jay had already applied for instructions from the British government on the administration of prize law.[78]

These instances show a persistent American desire for gaining (access to) knowledge on prize law. It was this consistent drive that was finally put into action by Rufus King, the US Minister to Great Britain who succeeded Thomas Pinckney in 1796. He contacted Sir William Scott, now Judge of the High Court of Admiralty, and, once he had received permission from British politicians, it was agreed to collect and publish his judgments.[79]

The resulting reports, *Reports of Cases Argued and Determined in The High Court of Admiralty* – generally referred to as *Robinson's Reports*, were penned by Sir Christopher Robinson in 1799.[80] The book, also available as pamphlets, described various cases from the High Court of Admiralty and noted down important precedents as well as the reasoning for the decrees.[81] In this manner, it gave insights into the workings and principles that governed the court. Its success caused the continual publication of further cases, and even case summaries of prior judges, such as the decrees of George Hay or James Marriott, to be printed.[82]

The original *Robinson's Reports* were published almost simultaneously in Britain and the United States. To achieve this, King passed the English edition of Scott's judgments to the Secretary of State, who passed it on to a US district Judge, who in turn organised the printing process on American soil.[83] Fifty copies were printed on US government expenses to cover some of the costs, but the report series also sold very well on the open market, mainly to the "American legal intelligentsia"[84] as well as to mariners and middlemen in the prize system.[85] The publication was, however, also successful outside

77 Memo respecting Danish and American vessels, 19 July 1793: NARA, *Box 10, British Spoliations – NAID: 1170270.*

78 John Jay to Edmund Randolph Johnston, *Correspondence and Public Papers of John Jay*, p. 86.

79 King and King, *The Life and Correspondence of Rufus King*, p. 150.

80 C. Robinson, *Reports of cases argued and determined in the High Court of Admiralty; commencing with the judgments of the Right Hon. Sir William Scott, Michaelmas term 1798. By Chr. Robinson* (London, 1799).

81 Gordan, 'Publishing Robinson's *Reports of Cases Argued and Determined in The High Court of Admiralty*', 8.

82 *Decisions in the High Court of Admiralty*, vol. 1.

83 Gordan, 'Publishing Robinson's *Reports of Cases Argued and Determined in The High Court of Admiralty*', 6.

84 Ibid., p. 31.

85 Ibid., p. 15.

the United States.[86] The success of Scott's published decrees has to be linked to the high demand for such a publication, not just from the point of view of legalists, but also from businesspeople, sailors and politicians.[87] The need for the knowledge contained in the reports had already been expressed openly by Marriott in his *Collectanea Juridica*, where he wrote:

> while the Common Lawyers are continually drawing the attention of the public, by printing what passes in their Courts, the Civilians have persisted in preserving an uniform silence. No Reports of adjudged Cases, no Arguments of Counsel [...]; the learned and unlearned are equally uninformed of what is there transacted.[88]

In a letter to James Madison, dated 21 July 1802, King outlined his reasoning for financing the publication of the reports with US government funds as follows:

> Dear Sir,
>
> [...] It has not, as you may well know, been the practice of this country to publish Reports of the decisions of its prize Tribunals; and while a pretty general opinion has prevailed that England administers the Law of Nations in matters of prize with great rigour, Englishmen have uniformly asserted that these Tribunals have manifested greater moderation in that respect than those of any other Nation. *So long as the decisions of the English prize Courts remain unpublished, this Disagreement would continue to exist, and so long likewise foreign States would remain without precise notion of the maxims of Public Law by which these Tribunals profess to regulate their Decisions.* [emphasis added][89]

86 H. C. Coote, *Sketches of the Lives and Characters op [sic] Eminent English Civilians, with an historical introduction relative to the College of Advocates, and an enumeration of the whole series of academic graduates admitted into that society, from the beginning of the reign of Henry VIII. to the close of the year 1803; by one of the members of the College [i.e. C. Coote]* (London, 1804), p. 137.

87 The reports form the main building block for Scott's lasting reputation as an excellent legalist. However, it must be mentioned that while the publication of his judgments cemented Scott's success, they most certainly profited from Robinson's excellent reporting skills. H. J. Bourguignon, *Sir William Scott, Lord Stowell* (Cambridge, 2009), p. 249.

88 J. Marriott, *Collectanea Juridica: Consisting of Tracts relative to the Law and Constitutions of England* (London, 1792), vol. 1, p. 82.

89 King and King, *The Life and Correspondence of Rufus King*, p. 150.

Taking the opposite view, some saw the publication of the reports as a propaganda move by Britain to strengthen the perception that its own decrees represented international, not municipal, law.[90] Complaints calling British vice-admiralty courts' integrity into question were numerous and included the American government, which actively employed this strategy as part of the Jay Treaty's prize commission.[91] Regarding this backdrop, the publication of British prize law precedents and legal foundations may have been particularly opportune. However, the publications also weakened the court in a two-fold manner, enabling opponents to call out decisions they were unable to grasp, questioning the judgments made there, and, at the same time, permitting government interference, which was able to put more pressure on court decision without set precedents and principles being available for public examination.[92]

To a large extent, Scott's decrees built upon the work of prior British/English judges (for example, of Lord Mansfield), whose decrees were also cited in American cases.[93] They relied on the oral tradition in Doctors' Commons, as well as the access to private notebooks and individual notes, and Scott's ability to recall cases from memory.[94] Most of this material was inaccessible to outsiders. Scott's decisions thus "created a reservoir of judicial precedents for the court and made its work accessible to a wider audience".[95] Scott's biographer goes so far as to conclude: "One contribution he [Scott] made to admiralty law was to gather these loose stones of all shapes and sizes and to start reshaping and fitting them together to build a coherent body of law."[96] Moreover, Scott intended to cultivate his international reputation through these publications, opening his decrees up not only to American and British citizens, but also to other neutral and belligerent parties.[97]

On at least one occasion, Samuel Bayard combined forces with the consuls of neutral Denmark (George Wolff), Sweden (Elias Grill) and Prussia

[90] *Decisions in the High Court of Admiralty*, vol. 1, pp. 2–4.

[91] See Chapter 6.

[92] Bourguignon, *Sir William Scott* (2009), p. 155; E. S. Roscoe, *A History of the English Prize Court* (London, 1924), p. 50.

[93] J. Oldham, *English Common Law in the Age of Mansfield* (Chapel Hill NC, 2004), p. 178; Bourguignon, *Sir William Scott* (1987), p. 130.

[94] Prior advocates' notebooks were also available in the Society of Advocates' library, as were some printed editions of previous cases. Petrie, *The Prize Game*, p. 130; Squibb, *Doctors' Commons*, pp. 94–6; Bourguignon, *Sir William Scott* (1987), p. 130; TNA, PRO 30/26/9: Doctors' Commons Library Accounts; Bourguignon, *Sir William Scott* (2009), p. 246.

[95] Kert, *Prize and Prejudice*, vol. 11, p. 53.

[96] Bourguignon, *Sir William Scott* (2009), p. 249.

[97] Gordan, 'Publishing Robinson's *Reports of Cases Argued and Determined in The High Court of Admiralty*', 14.

(Sebastian Fridag), uniting their shared interests as parties involved in British prize adjudication. A joint letter on their behalf was forwarded to the proctors Bush, Crickett and Townley, and Slade, enquiring how many cases were pending in the court. The strategy was a simple one: How many cases did the admiralty court system currently have pending? How many had it been able to process to date? Hoping to attain simple sums for both these questions, the consuls and Bayard would be able to give an estimate of the expected delays and duration required per case, in order to reinforce their claims about costly delays and strengthen their demands for faster process.

On 1 February 1797, Samuel Bayard and the consuls received an answer:

> contested matters remaining unadjudged in the Court of Admiralty amount in number to four hundred and upwards [...] the total of contested Causes determined by the Judge since the war commencing in Feb[ruar]y 1793 to the sixteenth Jan[uar]y 1797 [....] about four hundred and twenty [...] the number of Restitutions and other Decrees by consent before a surrogate exceeds 1600.[98]

While neutral nations were metaphorically all in the same boat, they were also rivals for the limited time allotted to the British admiralty court system. The admiralty court was already constantly and chronically dealing with delays and overwork, making every case compete for its own slot. Several times, Samuel Bayard noted in his diary that American cases were waiting for other cases to be determined first; for example, on 9 July 1796, when his irritation became palpable through the lines of "a Danish case took up all the morning. The Sally not brought on".[99]

It was therefore key to maintain a distance between the United States and other neutral nations. In a letter to Rufus King, Samuel Bayard decidedly referred to the joint neutral venture as one by "the consuls for the different neutral powers & myself",[100] allying American interest with other neutrals, yet still keeping a clear distinction between the two. This was the key to maintaining American neutrality, which had already been established as a desired foreign policy, attempting to prevent any entanglement not just in the war, but also in neutral alliances. The publication of *Robinson's Reports* was not an effort organised for the benefit of neutral states, but an undertaking aimed at US independence from British legal counsel.

98 Crickett and Townley, Slade, Bush to Wolff, Grill, Fridag and Bayard, 1 February 1797: NARA, *Box 10, British Spoliations – NAID: 1170270.*

99 9 July 1796; Bayard, *Diary of Samuel Bayard*, p. 79.

100 Bayard to King, 3 February 1797: NARA, *Box 10, British Spoliations – NAID: 1170270.*

The strong interest the US government took in prize jurisdiction was also reflected in the caseload at the London Appeals Court: American cases made up a majority of all appeals cases between 1793 and 1804.[101] This does not necessarily mean that the United States was also the nation that was captured most often, but it does show that Americans were following up on (British) prize jurisdiction and considered the risks of appeals procedure tolerable, pushing their agenda on a judicial level.

Historian David J. Starkey refers to those going on to appeal as "aggressive parties".[102] Indeed, Samuel Bayard considered it his personal and political mission to redress what he judged to be illegal decisions regularly made in the British prize courts. His work offered an alternative for those unable to afford redress, with government funds being used to fight cases of American citizens abroad. For claimants, it not only reduced the financial burden of appealing against what was considered an unjust sentence, it should also have reduced the amount of work, organisation and fear involved in the process (see Chapter 6). Yet this only applied to claimants captured by British vessels.

While the Jay Treaty secured peace with Britain, it had created distance towards what had been a staunch US ally: France. During the Revolutionary War, Louis XVI had promised to uphold the "liberty, sovereignty and independence"[103] of the United States, as well as funding the Revolutionary war effort and providing military assistance.[104] In the French Treaty of Amity and Commerce of 1778, Article XVII guaranteed French and American vessels exclusive rights to enter each other's ports with prizes, and principles of free trade were enshrined under Article XXIII.[105] However, after the peace of 1783, mercantile relations veered back to known patterns, strengthening British, rather than French economic relations.[106] Some US citizens may have "feared British power, but were open to cultural and commercial ties between the

[101] See table 10.

[102] Starkey, *British Privateering Enterprise in the Eighteenth Century*, vol. 4, p. 26.

[103] National Archives, *Treaty of Alliance with France (1778)*: Milestone Documents Series, www.archives.gov/milestone-documents/treaty-of-alliance-with-france (accessed 19 July 2024), Article II.

[104] It is estimated France provided 10.5 million livres' worth of subsidies to Congressional forces, as well as loaning 35 million livres to the United States. N. Desmarais, *America's First Ally: France in the Revolutionary War* (Newburyport, 2019), p. 318; G. A. King, 'The French Spoliation Claims', *The American Journal of International Law*, 6 (1912), 359–80, at 360.

[105] Articles referring to the redacted version, Treaty of Amity and Commerce Between the United States and France; February 6, 1778: *Avalon Project – Documents in Law, History and Diplomacy*, Yale Law School/Lillian Goldman Law Library, https://avalon.law.yale.edu/18th_century/fr1788-1.asp#1 (accessed 19 July 2024).

[106] Desmarais, *America's First Ally*, p. 319.

two countries".[107] At the same time, British protection of its colonial trade forced Americans to travel father in patterns of "economic adjustment",[108] to the Mediterranean and the Far East, coming into conflict with Barbary privateers off the North-African coast.[109] Nevertheless, the exclusive privateering cooperation with France was confirmed by the United States again in the Consular Convention of 1788.[110] While on the Western side of the Atlantic the US Constitution was being drafted, ratified and its first president sworn into office, back in France famine was raging, debts were mounting and the Estates-General collapsed. France became a republic, war erupted with the first in a series of continental victories for the French Revolutionary army and the execution of Louis XVI ushered in a new era of terror. These turbulent events are encapsulated beautifully in a conversation Samuel Bayard had with the aide-de-camp of French Revolutionary General Dumouriez in 1794 (after his defection), in which he probed the Frenchman's "immense information on the subject of the characters & events of the late Revolution in France",[111] including Beurnonville, Breteuil, Brissot, Danton, Dumouriez and the Marquis de Favras, as well details on the execution of the royal family, French military operations and the foreign policies of Britain, Prussia and Spain.[112]

However, when France declared war on Britain in February 1793, the United States issued a proclamation of neutrality, rather than assisting its old ally in the conflict.[113] In the face of a lack of American military power, diplomacy was to safeguard the new nation: John Jay was dispatched to London, James Monroe to Paris.

The United States and France quickly clashed over privateering and neutrality in the so-called Citizen Genêt affair of 1793–4. This éclat centred around the French minister to the United States, Edmond-Charles Genêt, who called himself 'citizen' to reinforce his pro-revolutionary politics and ideals. He had started outfitting 'French' privateers in American ports, consisting of US vessels and American mariners, armed with French letters of marque. He

[107] D. Kilbride, *Being American in Europe, 1750–1860* (Baltimore MD, 2013), p. 48.

[108] Chambers, Anderson and Piehler, *The Oxford Guide to American Military History*, p. 613.

[109] I agree with Boot that these captures should be classified as privateering rather than piracy. M. Boot, *The Savage Wars of Peace: Small Wars and the Rise of American Power* (New York, 2014), p. 8.

[110] G. H. Williams, *The French Assault on American Shipping, 1793–1813: A History and Comprehensive Record of Merchant Marine Losses* (Jefferson NC, 2009), pp. 8–9.

[111] 31 May 1794; Bayard, *Diary of Samuel Bayard*, p. 9.

[112] 31 May 1794; ibid., pp. 9–10.

[113] Chambers, Anderson and Piehler, *The Oxford Guide to American Military History*, p. 280.

did this against the wishes of the US government, which in consequence found itself directly implicated in the war, as opposed to maintaining the neutrality it desired.[114] Additionally, his actions violated the Jay Treaty, which had come to fruition in 1794 and in violation of the US–French treaties, now granted exclusive privateering cooperation to Britain.[115]

From October 1796, France changed its maritime policy to open hostilities, permitting thousands of French privateers to seize American vessels, often setting off from French ports in the West Indies.[116] It was the beginning of the undeclared Quasi-War between the two republics.[117] According to American economist Larry Sechrest, from October 1796 to June 1797 French privateers captured about 6% of the entire US merchant fleet.[118] Alongside Britain, France was regularly invoked as one of the main violators of neutral rights in the American public sphere.[119] Repeatedly, the United States levied accusations against France that captures were illegal, the judicial grounds unfounded and the process unfair. The Swedish consul at the French prize court in Marseilles agreed that "Americans, […] Danes, Swedes, Russians, Genoises etc. etc. are almost all condemned".[120] The US State Department began preparing files such as "the claim of Joha Tiefet, Joshua Harlan and others, citizens of the United States, residents at Philadelphia, against the French Republic, for the capture of the Schooner Two Sisters and her cargo by the Privateer called de Razoir

114 Estes, *The Jay Treaty Debate, Public Opinion, and the Evolution of Early American Political Culture*, p. 37.

115 Dull, *American Naval History*, pp. 40–1; *Treaty of Amity, Commerce, and Navigation, between His Britannick Majesty and the United States of America*, Article XXVII.

116 Jenkins has shown how French privateering increased in Guadeloupe at this time, showing a rise of privateering vessels from fewer than fifty issued privateering licences from July 1795 to June 1796, to more than 200 licences in the next twelve months. H. J. K. Jenkins, 'The Heyday of French Privateering from Guadeloupe, 1796–98', *The Mariner's Mirror*, 64 (1978), 245–50, at 246.

117 To make matters more complex, some American citizens were serving on French privateers during the Quasi-War and aided in the capture of US vessels, leading to what Marzagalli has termed "a nuanced approach to national allegiance". S. Marzagalli, '"However illegal, extraordinary or almost incredible such conduct might be": Americans and Neutrality Issues in the Mediterranean during the French War', *International Journal of Maritime History* (2016), at 124.

118 L. J. Sechrest, 'Privately Funded and Built U.S. Warships in the Quasi-War of 1797–1801', *The Independent Review*, 12 (2007), 101–13, at 103.

119 Perl-Rosenthal, *Citizen Sailors*, p. 265.

120 Quoted in *Naval Documents related to the Quasi-War*, I, 79, in: Marzagalli, 'However illegal', 123.

National".[121] In 1797, when the Jay commission on disputed prizes had already taken up its work in London, the US government drew up a list of maritime grievances that needed to be addressed by France. They grouped them into classifications of cases (including disputed prize cases), as had already been done for the Jay Treaty commission in London.[122]

Unlike Jay, Monroe, who had been sent on the diplomatic mission to France, was a Republican, a Francophile and supporter of the Revolution, who began "making unauthorized [...] speeches about an American alliance"[123] upon arrival. His secretary, Fulwar Skipworth would be responsible for the settlement of some of the disputed prize claims in 1797, but many dragged on as the so-called 'French Spoliation Claims' until the last cases were settled in 1914.[124]

The French-American vessels organised by Genêt would be discussed by the Jay Commission in London, as some had successfully captured British vessels. Four out of the five cases mentioned in this context were clearly labelled as 'French privateer' in the records and resulted in the US government paying Britain $30,045.72 of compensation by 1799.[125]

Aside from France, the US government was also embroiled in disputed prize cases with Chile, Peru and Spain.[126] Arbitration committees and commissioners, following the example set by Samuel Bayard's work and the commission under Article VII of the Jay Treaty in London, were also set up elsewhere. Additionally, throughout the first half of the nineteenth century, a variety of binational treaties granted summary restorations to prevent long-winded claims procedures in cases of prize.[127]

121 Statement of the claim of Joha Tiefet, Joshua Harlan and others, citizens of the United States, residents at Philadelphia, against the French Republic, undated; NARA, *Box 7, Unsorted Papers; British Spoliations, ca. 1796–ca. 1824 – NAID: 1170270.*

122 J. H. Scattergood and B. Henry, *The French Spoliation Claims: With special reference to insurance companies* (Washington DC, 1910), p. 165. For more on this subject, see Chapter 4.

123 R. G. Kennedy, *Mr. Jefferson's Lost Cause: Land, Farmers, Slavery, and the Louisiana Purchase* (Oxford, 2003), p. 182.

124 Williams, *French Assault on US Shipping*, pp. 3–4. Although by this point the claims were levied domestically against the US government. King, 'The French Spoliation Claims', 371; G. W. McGinty, 'Reviewed Work: The Parisian American: Fulwar Skipwith of Virginia by Henry Bartholomew Cox', *Louisiana History: The Journal of the Louisiana Historical Association*, 6 (1965), 410–2, at 411.

125 See cases numbered 19B, 38B, 41B, 50B and 88B, in TNA, FO 304/27: *Register of Awards*.

126 Barttet to Pickering, 2 December 1796; NARA, *Box 8, British Spoliations – NAID: 1170270*; NARA, *Box 1, Records Relating to Claims – NAID: 1438808.*

127 Williams, *French Assault on US Shipping*, p. 3; in the Treaty of Ghent that closed the War of 1812 with Britain, deadlines for the restoration of prize cases were

Further study needs to be conducted on these international dimensions of prize-taking and disputed claims, not just to compare the treatment American claimants received in different countries and courts, but also to compare that treatment to other (neutral) nations and the foreign policies these nations enacted.

Leos Müller, one of the leading academics researching (active) neutrality, states the following: "In practice, the Jay Treaty meant British acknowledgement of US neutrality- and treating that neutrality in a special, benevolent way. Compared to how the British behaved against the Scandinavian neutrals, the Americans were treated much more amicably."[128]

The data provided by the appeals at first glance seems to refute Müller's claim: American cases made up over half of the total printed cases in the appeals court. If we add the manuscript appeals that were never printed, the total amount of American appeals still accounts for over 38% of all appeals between 1794 and 1805. Danish and Swedish vessels combined only totalled about 30% of printed appeals and 26% of never printed manuscript appeals, totalling just under 21% of all appeals cases.[129] Yet the appeals do not necessarily reflect the total number of captured prizes, as it was a special US policy to follow up a large percentage of its cases in the superior court through government aid and at considerable expense.

On the other hand, one of Samuel Bayard's dispatches seems to back up Müller's hypothesis. In it, Bayard described the Lords of appeal, whose:

> judicial determinations are said often to be influenced [...] by the relations which this Country bears to those Neutral States or Kingdoms whose Subjects or Citizens appear before them to demand Justice, Since however the English Government and Nation begin fully to appreciate the importance of maintaining a friendly intercourse with the United States I hope the work of conciliation which Mr Jay has so ably & so happily begun may progress and terminate finally to the satisfaction of both countries. To this desirable end nothing can [be] more directly contributed than facilitating the recovery of property illegally taken from our citizens in the course of the present war. And I am happy in being able to sure you that all the decisions that have

---

determined depending on geographical location "to prevent all causes of complaint" (Article II), alongside a whole host of articles setting up further international arbitration committees (Article IV–VIII). Treaties with France and Spain followed similar lines. National Archives, *Treaty of Ghent (1814)*: Milestone Documents Series, www.archives.gov/milestone-documents/treaty-of-ghent (accessed 19 July 2024).

128 Müller, *Neutrality in World History*, p. 68.

129 Danish and Swedish cases for 1794 to 1804 totalled 342 cases, compared to the American data chronicled in table 10. For the never printed manuscript appeals and totals, see tables 11 and 12.

> lately taken place on American claims or appeals point immediately to this object.[130]

It thus becomes apparent, that at least to a quasi-member on the periphery of Doctors' Commons, nationality was key to the success or failure of prize cases in the British appeals court and prize jurisdiction could be adapted to fit practical, national, political needs.

In summary, the United States itself did not find it easy to navigate prize law. The objective was to remain independent and neutral while pushing the international rights of American citizens within the framework of international law, simultaneously not antagonising Britain into a war that the United States had little chance of winning. Although rare cases of US cooperation with other neutrals could be traced, the shared resources of the Doctors' Commons' microcosm caused a rivalry between claimants, and the US desire for neutrality limited these interactions. The British government was trying to maintain neutral nations as carriers of needed supplies throughout the French Wars, but also wanted to prevent them from doing the same for the enemy. This made prize jurisdiction in the 1790s a relevant, high-stakes and contested diplomatic issue on all sides. Though the extent of the 'special relationship' between the United States and Great Britain in the realm of prize remains hard to judge at this time, the influence US policy had on the future development of prize jurisdiction by initiating the publication of the court's decrees cannot be overstated.

130 Bayard to Sec. State, 14 March 1795: NARA, *Letters Received from Samuel Bayard – NAID: 1170268*, p. 17.

# 4

# "In a Lion's Mouth": The American Agent for Claims in the High Court of Admiralty

For many Londoners, the American Revolution had been a conflict far away, to be observed, not actively participated in.[1] But for James Marriott (1730–1803) it was a matter of personal and professional importance. Sir James Marriott was the Judge of the High Court of Admiralty in London from 1778 until his resignation in 1798.[2] The son of a London attorney, he was admitted to the College of Advocates in November 1757 and fulfilled the position of King's Advocate for four years from 1764 to 1768.[3] He resided over the court throughout the course of four different wars, often struggling with the amount of work created by them.[4]

Marriott was or certainly styled himself a zealous patriot and ardent anti-Americanist, both in the field of politics and in international law; for example, describing Britain as a "Nation [...] too dazzling not to be seen by some of the Maritime Powers with Malevolence".[5] According to him, the civilian united the characteristics of "the scholar, the gentleman and friend of their country".[6] This patriotic flair can also be found in his judgments, such as in one case before the High Court of Admiralty, where he went so far as to say:

> That this [British] nation (now fighting for its domestic preservation, as well as empire) had its cruelest enemies within its own bowels [America]; that he [Marriott] would be bound by the act in regard to

1 Flavell, *When London was Capital of America*, pp. 241–2.

2 Lewis Namier and John Brooke (eds), *The History of Parliament: The House of Commons 1754–1790, III Members K–Y*, 2nd edn (London, 1984), p. 110.

3 Cambridge Alumni Database, *Marriott, James*, http://venn.lib.cam.ac.uk/cgi-bin/search-2018.pl?sur=&suro=w&fir=&firo=c&cit=&cito=c&c=all&z=all&tex=MRT746J&sye=&eye=&col=all&maxcount=50 (accessed 13 July 2020); *R. Thorne, Marriott, Sir James (1730–1803)*, www.historyofparliamentonline.org/volume/1790-1820/member/marriott-sir-james-1730-1803#footnote1_81440wp.+ (accessed 13 July 2020).

4 Thorne, *Marriott, Sir James*.

5 J. Marriott, *A Letter to the Dutch Merchants in England* (London, 1759), p. 2.

6 Marriott, *Collectanea Juridica*, vol. 1, p. 86.

> costs. The American prohibitory act regulated, like other prize acts, the modes of proceeding, but did not take away the general powers of the Court; that the act required bail for double costs from the claimants [Americans]; but there were other costs beside those upon bail. He would not condemn the claimants upon their bail, but he would condem them in treble cost generally, *ex officio*, and as much as the proctors could swear to; that it was his duty to do as much justice as he could to the whole kingdom in this instance, in putting a check to every sort of support and encouragement from home of a system involving the ruin of all good men's lives and properties; a system treasonable and traitorous. That here was a clear fact proved from the evidence of the guilty party, of aiding, abetting, and having intercourse with the self-established and declared enemies of the King and nation; and he only wished his Court had a longer arm to reach such a sort of treason that if Mr. Macurdy, Mr. Johnson, and Mr. Ridley [claimants], were dissatisfied with the decree, they might appeal if they dared.[7]

At the time, he was labelled a "very eminent civilian"[8] by his contemporaries, and his work would exert a lasting influence on the development of Admiralty jurisdiction in the United States.[9] However, by the nineteenth century, even Associate Justice of the Supreme Court of the United States Joseph Story is credited to have said that "[Marriott's] decisions were such as no other person would ever follow".[10]

Sir James Marriott has not retained a reputation as a qualified or talented judge to the present day. Instead, his career can be traced back to "numerous and voluminous, fawning, self-important letters"[11] to important politicians of his day. These political connections, not his talent or qualifications as a judge, formed the backbone of Marriott's career. At the end of his tenure, his erratic behaviour was seen as such a liability by his own government that he was offered £2,000 to accept early retirement, in a post usual vacated only through death or serious illness.[12]

In the 1790s, Samuel Bayard was responsible for representing American interests before this man, who had so prominently decreed against what he considered illegal, dangerous rebels in the War of Independence. Samuel Bayard was the son of Colonel John Bubenheim Bayard, a passionate supporter

7 *Decisions in the High Court of Admiralty*, vol. 1, pp. 144–5.

8 J. Nichols, *Literary Anecdotes of the Eighteenth Century* (London, 1812), p. 617.

9 Wiswall, *Development of Admiralty Jurisdiction*, p. 12.

10 W. Senior, 'Judges of the High Court of Admiralty', *The Mariner's Mirror*, 13 (1927), 333–47, at 347.

11 Namier and Brooke (eds), *The History of Parliament*, p. 109.

12 Thorne, *Marriott, Sir James*.

of American independence, who was also active in the judicial sphere.[13] His contribution to the Revolutionary War has been described as follows: "He was neither an original thinker, nor an outstanding legislator, nor a great soldier. But he was a brilliant host […] his home became a rallying place for Revolutionary leaders […] John Adams […] Hancock, Sam Adams, Gerry, Lafayette, the Livingstons, Stockton, Hopkinson, Witherspoon, and James Wilson"[14] all met at his home, where his son, Samuel Bayard, grew up fully embedded into the founding fathers' generation. Born in 1767, Samuel left grammar school in 1781 and graduated from Princeton college with his cousin, James Asheton Bayard, in 1784. He received various prizes as a freshman and junior, performing the valedictorian speech at their graduation ceremony.[15] Bayard then studied with William Bradford Jr (Attorney General for the United States 1794–5) in Pennsylvania and was admitted to the bar there in 1787.[16] This was the usual form of legal education in America at the time.[17] He married Martha Pintard in 1790, whose cousin was married to Bradford, before becoming a clerk at the Supreme Court a year later, where he acted as Chief Justice Jay's private secretary.[18] While it was expected that Samuel Bayard would accompany him on his diplomatic mission for the treaty negotiations, John Trumbull was selected, as his prior experience and connections in Britain made him more suitable.[19]

Instead, Samuel Bayard received the new position of government agent in disputed prize cases. In this capacity, he came before the British prize court at Doctors' Commons. He considered Marriott unreliable, stating "there is no saying what will be the opinion of the Judge of the Admiralty for two days on the same subject".[20] In the Martinique cases, which will be examined in depth in Chapter 5, Bayard sadly concluded: "From the vast accumulation of business before this Court, its continual increase & the age & infirmities of

13 For an overview of the Bayard genealogy, see fig. 1. Wilson, *Colonel John Bayard*, pp. 10, 17.

14 Hess, *America's Political Dynasties*, p. 285.

15 Craven and Woodward, *Princetonians, 1784–1790*, pp. 9–10.

16 Ibid., p. 10; Sterling, 'A Federalist Opposes the Jay Treaty', 408.

17 J. Henrietta, 'Magistrates, Common Law Lawyers, Legislators: The Three Legal Systems of British America', in M. Grossberg and C. L. Tomlins (eds), *The Cambridge History of Law in America* (Cambridge and New York, 2008), vol. 1, pp. 555–92, at pp. 571–2; A. Forsyth, *Common Law and Natural Law in America: From the Puritans to the Legal Realists* (Cambridge and New York, 2019), p. 21.

18 Wilson, *Colonel John Bayard*, p. 15; B. Dye, G. Genel-Gonzalez, L. L. Lawry, C. Hannan and J. L. Herman (eds), *Georgia Biographical Dictionary, 2008–2009* e (Hamburg MI, 2008), p. 103; Fosdick, *French Blood in America*, p. 309.

19 Craven and Woodward, *Princetonians, 1784–1790*, p. 11.

20 3 February 1796, NARA, *Letters Received from Samuel Bayard – NAID: 1170268*, p. 84.

the Judge, I fear there is little chance of our obtaining compensation thro[ugh] the medium of this Court."[21]

Samuel Bayard's mission was to last somewhere between eighteen and twenty-four months.[22] His yearly salary was set at $1,600, on top of which he received a daily allowance of $6 for expenses abroad as well as the coverage of his travel expenses to and within England.[23] He landed on British soil at Falmouth on 5 December 1794 aboard the *Adriana*. His wife and eldest son, Lewis Pintard Bayard, accompanied him.[24] Lewis was enrolled in a boarding school throughout their time in England.[25]

Samuel Bayard did not only aid in the work of the commission, but was also entrusted with regular prize cases, and appellate work. His work therefore helped pave one of the first cornerstones of American international law.

Before setting off on the *Adriana*, Edmund Randolph, the Secretary of State, had instructed Bayard to apply to Jay for instructions "immediately on his arrival"[26] in Britain. Bayard had also been given various letters from persons in America to pass on to addressees in Britain, a quite usual practice for the time.[27] Among these was a letter from George Washington to John Jay, so a face-to-face meeting would probably have been required urgently once they had reached their lodgings.[28] After their arrival in London on Sunday, 12 December 1794, Jay had cases delivered to him within a matter of days.[29] On 13 December, in a letter to Quincy Adams, Jay referred to the fact that Bayard had arrived, but did not specifically record a meeting between the two of them. Bayard's dispatches, directed to the Secretary of State, start on 15 December, with Bayard informing Randolph that Jay himself did not actually

21 28 February 1797, ibid., p. 170.

22 Bayard to Rufus King, 10 August 1797, ibid., p. 203.

23 Ibid., p. 97.

24 5 December 1794, Bayard, *Journal of Martha Bayard*, p. 22.

25 B. T. Onderdonk, *Memorial of the Rev. Lewis P. Bayard: Containing a memoir of his life, extracts from his journals and correspondence, notices of his tour through Europe and the Holy Land, selections from his sermons, and the discourse preached on the occasion of his decease* (New York, 1841), p. 22.

26 Edmund Randolph to John Jay, 29 October 1794; W. Lowrie and M. St Claire Clarke (eds), *Class I – Foreign Relations: Documents, legislative, and executive, of the Congress of the United States, From the first Session of the First to the Second Session of the Twenty-Second Congress, Inclusive: Commencing March 3 1789 and Ending March 3, 1833, American State Papers* (Washington, 1833), vol. 1, p. 500.

27 Bayard, *Journal of Martha Bayard*, p. 27.

28 George Washington to John Jay, 1 November 1794; Johnston, *Correspondence and Public Papers of John Jay*, p. 122.

29 J. Jay, Letter to Edmund Randolph, 7 January 1795, https://dlc.library.columbia.edu/jay/ldpd:29908 (accessed 12 January 2021).

know what Bayard's work would practically entail.[30] However, Bayard was sure he would grasp the concept of British admiralty jurisdiction swiftly and had a positive outlook, saying: "From all I have seen or heard thus far I am happy to say that there seems to be a sincere deposition in the constituted authorities here to do us full & impartial justice."[31] From the dispatch dated 15 December, one can deduce that the first meeting between Bayard and Jay had already taken place, though it is not specifically recorded anywhere. Martha Bayard's diary first notes her husband and Jay having dinner together on 30 December 1794.[32]

In January 1795 Bayard received detailed instructions from John Jay on how he was to go about his mission: Bayard was to keep meticulous records, entering every case into a register, noting down the papers involved in the case, the costs precured, the judicial steps taken and the persons and vessels involved.[33] A similar register, in its completed form, was twice provided by Bayard at the end of his tenure in 1797 to the Department of State, but only for the claims under Article VII of the commission.[34] Another register fitting this description, can be found in FO 304/27, as part of the British archive on the commission's work. However, unlike the American lists of claims that solely record the commission's work, it also features the American appeals and, in a limited capacity, regular prize cases.[35] But it is doubtful whether this register was written by Bayard at all, as it was completed in one hand and includes cases until April 1798, almost a year after he had resigned from his position. It seems the original register prepared by Bayard has thus been lost.

It is not surprising that Jay, who, although repeatedly referred to as a politician in this work due to his responsibility for negotiating the treaty with Great Britain, did not simply instruct Bayard to swiftly process each case laid before him. Aside from the fact that this would have barely been possible due to the volume of cases for which Bayard was responsible, Jay was not merely a politician, but had presided over a successful law practice throughout much of his adult life and would only resign his position as Chief Justice of the United States Supreme Court in June 1795.[36] He thought like a judge. Bayard was to work his way through all the cases he had been presented with,

[30] 15 December 1794, NARA, *Letters Received from Samuel Bayard – NAID: 1170268*, p. 1.

[31] 15 December 1794, ibid., p. 2.

[32] Bayard, *Journal of Martha Bayard*, p. 41.

[33] J. Jay, *Letter to Samuel Bayard, 5 January 1795*, https://dlc.library.columbia.edu/jay/ldpd:29908 (accessed 13 March 2025).

[34] NARA, *List of Claims, 12 May 1797 – NAID: 1170192*; NARA, *List of Claims, 1797–1797, dated 18 May 1797 – NAID: 1170192.*

[35] TNA, FO 304/27.

[36] Hoffer, Hoffer and Hull, *The Supreme Court*, pp. 36–7.

classifying them according to "discriminating and governing principles and merit"[37] into groups of similar cases. One or two exemplary cases of each group were then to be counselled with professional, British admiralty lawyers, generally Doctors Scott or Nicholl, discussing their chances of success and taking a summary statement in writing to send to the Secretary of State. Should a case have good chances of succeeding, it was to be moved quickly through the courts. This classic work shows how Jay was thinking in terms of precedent, hoping to win a few cases prominently in the courts and thus enable a quick processing of all other similar cases in the group or at least increasing their chance of victory by being able to refer to the exemplary case's prior success in court. This method was also intended to save the US government a significant amount of costs, by speeding up the process of adjudication and methodically laying the steps to be taken for every case with the same characteristics. If cases had little chance of success, Bayard was to leave the decision on whether to prosecute up to the Secretary of State. Key elements, repeatedly stressed by Jay were Bayard's need to be thorough, exact and well organised, as well as adhering to the permanent mantra of "[b]y all means avoid delay".[38] Should further proofs be required from America, claimants were to be contacted immediately. Bayard was also to interact with private agents, should they have already been employed by American merchants.

Bayard followed this strategy, even enhancing its vision of stream-lined cost efficiency by detailing how evidence was to be taken and which evidence would be permissible in the Admiralty Court and Court of Appeals in a letter to the Secretary of State. The idea was for knowledge on admiralty court procedures, which at this time remained the privileged knowledge of an elite club, to trickle down to the merchants, enabling them to follow correct procedure, add missing documents or proofs to their cases and understand how to back up their claims or allegations on a procedural level.[39] To Bayard, every American claimant was trapped in the British prize court system. He phrased it as such: "what can one do. When the hand is in a Lion's mouth one must get it out with as little injury as possible."[40] Through the proposed strategy Bayard and the US government were attempting to learn the anatomy of the wildcat's mouth, to help American citizens navigate the pitfalls and fangs of British prize jurisdiction.

About three months after Bayard's initial instructions from Jay, he sent a preliminary list of classifications, listing five groups of cases, much like would be done two years later in the French spoliation cases:

37 Jay, *Letter to Samuel Bayard, 5 January 1795*.

38 Ibid.

39 S. Bayard, *Letter to John Jay, 27 January 1795*, https://dlc.library.columbia.edu/jay/ldpd:29850 (accessed 12 January 2021).

40 17 February 1796; Bayard, *Diary of Samuel Bayard*, p. 55.

1. Where our vessels have been taken & condemned under the orders of the 6 of Nov. 1793
2. Under colour of those of the 8th Jany 1794
3. Under pretence of being French property – or as belonging to American citizens resident within the Territories of France
4. Under pretence of trading with blockaded places
5. Where both vessel & cargo – or only one of them has been restored, but without costs or damages.[41]

Specifically the fifth group, that of costs and damages, were later taken up with some success. To “save the delay and expense attending the prosecution before the judiciary tribunals” both governments agreed to let Sir William Scott as King’s Advocate General and Doctor Nicholl as counsel of the United States agree to sums to be paid out as “referees”.[42] This class of cases was therefore settled out of court by mutual agreement. The sums awarded were paid out on 28 July 1798. By this date, sums had been awarded in fifty-seven cases. The costs spent on reaching this agreement amounted to £1,034 7s 4d, but the sums awarded by far outweighed these costs, reaching £34,389 13s 11d. By avoiding the court system, an average case cost slightly over £18.[43] This was less than the advance given to proctors for their collaboration in a single court case. The list of classifications would later be expanded to encompass fifteen.[44]

Jay’s theoretical framework and instructions were followed meticulously by Bayard, as he documented thoroughly in his correspondence. Important parts of this interaction were preserved through Jay’s letter books and notes. However, more concrete steps were seldom spoken of between Bayard and Jay. While the practical steps undertaken by Bayard can only be guessed at from his correspondence with Jay, they are well documented in his work diary. It is a great shame that Bayard either stopped writing his diary after 12 December 1796, or, more likely, his other diaries have been lost as the diary is marked “No. I”,[45] but no others have at present been found. Yet, while his diary gives insights into the everyday working of this judicial process, they in no way, shape or form mention the grand strategy envisioned by Jay. It

41 S. Bayard, *Letter to John Jay, 31 March 1795*, https://dlc.library.columbia.edu/jay/ldpd:78754 (accessed 12 January 2021).

42 Timothy Pickering to John Adams, 16 February 1798; W. Lowrie and M. St Claire Clarke (eds), *Class I – Foreign Relations: Documents, legislative, and executive, Congress of the United States, From the first Session of the First to the Third Session of the Thirteenth Congress, Inclusive: Commencing March 3 1789 and Ending March 3, 1813, American State Papers* (Washington DC, 1832), vol. 2, p. 119.

43 See table 13.

44 See Index, NARA, *List of Claims, 18 May 1797 – NAID: 1170192.*

45 Bayard, *Diary of Samuel Bayard*, p. 3.

is therefore very fortunate that both these sources have survived in order to reconstruct Bayard's mission during his time in London.

Bayard's regular workload, as described in his diary, encompassed practically all steps in prize jurisdiction once local commissioners had questioned crew members. One of the first issues facing Bayard was how to get in touch with American merchants and captains or ship owners upon their capture. He attempted to "see the captains as early as I can & give them every assistance and information in my power".[46] To achieve this, Bayard visited the Royal Exchange on a regular basis, several times a week if not daily. This place is referred to as "Change"[47] in his diary, as well as in those of other contemporaries.[48] It had been "erected so that merchants no longer need conduct their business in shops, taverns and even under the open skies".[49] It was a location not only known for trading and offering legal services, but also specifically catering to maritime needs through institutions such as Lloyd's or the Merchant seamen's offices.[50] In addition, monitions detailing recent captures were posted there, making it an ideal meeting place for maritime professionals. Bayard noted "went to 'change in expectation of meeting some of the sent in captains".[51] Thus, many captains of captured vessels, including those with American nationality, congregated at the Royal Exchange.

Located close to the Exchange were various coffee houses. The coffee houses of London were highly specialised with each one being frequented by specific intellectual or mercantile circles. Regarding American trade, there were several geographically specialised houses, with at least one New England Coffee House, Georgia Coffee House, Virginia Coffee House, Maryland Coffee House, New York Coffee House and Philadelphia Coffee House being available in London's city centre.[52] Bayard attended them with the stated purpose of making the acquaintance of captured American captains and discussing their cases.[53] Although of course captains did attend his office in Doctors' Commons too.[54] Moreover, by February 1795, he and his family

46 12 June 1795, NARA, *Letters Received from Samuel Bayard – NAID: 1170268*, p. 35.

47 30 May 1795, Bayard, *Diary of Samuel Bayard*, p. 9.

48 Flavell, *When London was Capital of America*, p. 125.

49 Ibid., p. 122.

50 W. Thornbury, *Old and New London: A narrative of its history, its people, and its places, A new edition, carefully revised and corrected* (London, Paris and New York, 1881), p. 503.

51 16 June 1795, Bayard, *Diary of Samuel Bayard*, p. 14.

52 Houses from Bayard's diary have been added to Flavell's list; Flavell, *When London was Capital of America*, p. 125.

53 20 June 1795, Bayard, *Diary of Samuel Bayard*, p. 15.

54 24 July 1795, ibid., p. 22.

had moved into lodgings in 50 Hatton Street, as this was "easy to access to my American Brethren".[55] Hatton Street lay at the centre of what is now Hatton Garden. Located close to legal institutions such as the Inns of Court, it was less crowded than the centre and provided easy access to other parts of the city, such as Westminster, the Royal Exchange or Doctors' Commons. It therefore quickly established itself as a popular area for legal professionals.[56] Nevertheless, Bayard conducted large parts of his work outside these two premises. His coffee house of preference was the New York Coffee House, although he occasionally attended the Philadelphia Coffee House as well.[57] Here, he could not only meet other American citizens, whom he might later represent in court or give legal counsel to as their state representative, but also discuss and gain news from other Americans in London. For example, Bayard's diary specifically mentions hearing news of American vessels at his coffee house.[58] Coffee houses also functioned as places to post and receive sundry letters and newspapers, as Bayard often jots down in his diary. The coming and going of vessels is repeatedly mentioned in his notes.[59] On the one hand, Bayard would impatiently wait for a vessel to arrive.[60] He even went so far as to take note of weather patterns to judge his chances of the vessel's speedy or slow travel; for example, "the wind at S.W. hope for letters from America tomorrow".[61] After a ship's arrival, he would regularly visit the coffee houses and await post, sometimes remarking in irritation that nothing had yet arrived.[62] On the other hand, the departures of vessels forced his hand in when to write, acting as a deadline by which post for the United States had to be on board or be delayed waiting for the next vessel to depart.[63] When vessels set off with a delay, this also offered a convenient chance to add further

55 2 February 1795, NARA, *Letters Received from Samuel Bayard – NAID: 1170268*, p. 8; Some of the Bayards' original furnishings from this residence can be found in the collection of the New York Historical Society; New York Historical Society Museum and Library, *Works by Martha Pintard Bayard: Overview*, https://emuseum.nyhistory.org/people/1849/martha-pintard-bayard/objects (accessed 27 July 2024).

56 P. Hunting, 'The Survey of Hatton Garden in 1694 by Abraham Arlidge', in A. Saunders (ed.), *London Topographical Record* (London, 1985), pp. 83–110, at pp. 103–4.

57 6 August 1796, Bayard, *Diary of Samuel Bayard*, p. 83.

58 29 June 1795, ibid., p. 17.

59 9 November 1795, ibid., p. 38.

60 18 February 1796, ibid., pp. 56–7.

61 1 May 1796, ibid., p. 71.

62 18 April 1796, ibid., p. 67.

63 11 July 1796, ibid., p. 79; 16 July 1795, NARA, *Letters Received from Samuel Bayard – NAID: 1170268*, p. 43.

letters.[64] Interestingly, Bayard's diary also shows that certain vessels were repeatedly used for sending post. For example, the captain of the *Adriana* (Clapp), on which the Bayard had arrived in England, dined with the Bayards several times.[65] He is also recounted as having delivered and/or taken post to London/the United States five times by the end of 1796.[66]

As part of Bayard's position, he also advised American citizens on their cases. A good example is entered in his diary on 11 June 1795, describing how Bayard attended a New York merchant whose vessel had been captured and explained to him how to regain his cargo and vessel as well as receiving compensation.[67] When Bayard could not make his clients' personal acquaintances, he would send papers out to them, sometimes sending more than 140 letters in fourteen days.[68]

Along with this correspondence, he was also responsible for large parts of the judicial paper trail in the High Court of Admiralty. He filed and dealt with claims, swore to affidavits, prepared cases, attended and counselled with proctors, handed evidence on to this extended team, registered the transfer of such papers from one team member to another, wrote to claimants and attended cases at Doctors' Commons. Naturally, he also needed to spend some time on the organisation of his paperwork.

Among the papers he received from the New York Coffee House or through persons arriving from American vessels, were many case files, on one occasion even a box containing eighty-one cases.[69] One must note, however, that a considerable part of these were not regular cases, but more complicated appeals, generally from the vice-admiralty courts.[70]

Occasionally, Bayard would also attend the market to oversee the sales of American vessels and cargoes.[71] On one such occasion he foresaw issues with the further process after the sale had been significantly more successful than a financial estimate had thought.[72] Concerning the amount of costs incurred by the courts and the vessels/cargoes discussed in them, trips to the admiralty registrar and various merchants were unavoidable in Bayard's position.[73]

64 9 February 1796, Bayard, *Diary of Samuel Bayard*, p. 53.

65 For example, 15 May 1795, ibid., p. 6.

66 8 May, 1 August, 9 November, 9 December 1795 and 5 March 1796, ibid., pp. 5, 22, 38, 44, 60.

67 11 June 1795, ibid., p. 13.

68 10 October 1796, ibid., p. 91.

69 10 July 1795, ibid., p. 19.

70 26 February 1796, ibid., p. 58.

71 26 June 1795, ibid., p. 16.

72 See TNA HCA 32/803/55.

73 7 July 1795, Bayard, Diary of Samuel Bayard, p. 19.

As the first American agent prosecuting claims and appeals in prize causes, Bayard had to face various challenges; for example, whether he was authorised to take on the work envisioned for him, or whether he could be held financially accountable for the costs involved in the process. There were numerous issues dealing with financing from the US government, which especially concerned Bayard's role, with some of his alleged decisions still being disputed between British and American parties in 1805, several years after his return to the United States.[74] The fact that his appointment was in a grey zone, instead of being wholly official, probably did not aid this.

Bayard never received an official commission for his position but was rather considered an "informal appointment"[75] indirectly recognised by Congress. Instead of being directly appointed by Congress, he had received his directions from the President of the United States. Bayard addressed his dissatisfaction with this state of affairs several times to the Secretary of State and was encouraged to make things "proper"[76] by Jay.[77] However, nothing came of it and the position remained the same until Bayard's departure. Allotting government funds to this mission, that was still in a grey zone between presidential power and an act of Congress, therefore caused significant political irritation, with one member of the House remarking: "Should it be said [...] that the PRESIDENT OF THE UNITED STATES has the power, whenever a vessel should be seized with contraband goods, to apply the public money in bringing the cause to trial?"[78]

Congress did not pass an appropriation bill taking on the costs of Bayard's mission until 3 March 1797, when it capped the expenditure at £50,000, a mark that was quickly overstepped.[79] An act to regulate the appointment of agents under Article VI was only passed on 30 June 1797.[80]

74 Founders Online and NARA, *To James Madison from Robert Slade, 24 September 1805*, https://founders.archives.gov/documents/Madison/02-10-02-0343 (accessed 13 March 2025).

75 Sterling, 'A Federalist Opposes the Jay Treaty', 408.

76 Jay, Letter to Samuel Bayard, 5 January 1795.

77 Sterling, 'A Federalist Opposes the Jay Treaty', 409.

78 *The debates and Proceedings in the Congress of the United States with an Appendix containing Important State Papers and Public Documents, and all the Laws of Public Nature with a Copious Index: Fourth Congress-Second Session; Comprising the Period from December 5, 1796, to March 3, 1797, inclusive*, Compiled from Authentic Materials, Annals of the Congress of the United States (Washington DC, 1849), p. 2297.

79 Library of Congress, Law Library, *Fourth Congress, Sess II, Ch. 23: 3 March, 1797*, www.loc.gov/law/help/statutes-at-large/4th-congress/session-2/c4s2ch23.pdf (accessed 17 January 2021).

80 Library of Congress, Law Library, *Fifth Congress, Sess. I, Ch. 6: June 30, 1797*, www.loc.gov/law/help/statutes-at-large/5th-congress/session-1/c5s1ch6.pdf (accessed 13 March 2025).

A similar issue was that the High Court of Admiralty at first refused to recognise Bayard's authority to represent any American citizen. In April 1795, Bayard was informed by British proctors that he would require a power of attorney for each claimant/appellant or their executors/administrators/agents he represented in court.[81] One month later, Bayard described his powers of attorney as "certainly addressable".[82] His hope was that by providing the British government, more specifically, the British admiralty court system with proof that the claims were forwarded to him by the State Department in an official capacity, he could abate this requirement. However, this never materialised.[83] Pickering shared Bayard's impression, arguing that as American claimants had already agreed in writing to let the US government take on their case, an additional paper specifying that Bayard, the delegate of the US government, could represent them, would not be necessary. Sir William Scott and Lord Grenville, however, disagreed.[84] In the long run, the issue settled and was no longer questioned further by the courts. As Bayard phrased it in 1796: "The Question as to my authority I hope therefore has gone to sleep."[85] Ten days later his authority to represent American claimants in court was questioned again by the Judge of the High Court of Admiralty.[86] A notarised power of attorney listing Bayard would have to be provided in every single case brought to court.

The main issue with Bayard's informal position, tolerated as opposed to endorsed by Congress, was that he became personally liable in every case he undertook.[87] This created one of the largest challenges posed to Bayard's mission in London: the question of the financial viability of his undertaking in general. As has been mentioned previously, Bayard's work entrusted him with vast amounts of financial loss or gain, depending on the outcome of a case. Either way, spending money to build a case was always a necessary first step. Bayard himself pointed out that in every instituted case, the proctors would expect an advance of £30, which they themselves would need to distribute between their advocates, register and further staff.[88] Generally,

81 17 April 1795, NARA, *Letters Received from Samuel Bayard – NAID: 1170268*, p. 23.

82 19 June 1795; Bayard, *Diary of Samuel Bayard*, pp. 14–5.

83 2 November 1795, NARA, *Letters Received from Samuel Bayard – NAID: 1170268*, p. 61.

84 J. B. Moore, *History and digest of the international arbitrations to which the United States has been a party: Vol IV, The Miscellaneous Documents of the House of Representatives, 1893–94* (Washington DC, 1898), vol. 212, pp. 59–60.

85 4 March 1796; Bayard, *Diary of Samuel Bayard*, pp. 59–60.

86 14 March 1796, NARA, *Letters Received from Samuel Bayard – NAID: 1170268*, p. 100.

87 2 November 1795, ibid., p. 64.

88 Bayard, *Letter to John Jay, 27 January 1795*.

proctors did not require any money in advance, but this changed when the American government became their client, as the case load was so high that individual proctors did not have the cash reserves to take on the work without advanced payments.[89]

When considering the fact that Jay instructed Bayard to give a minor proctor fifty cases or that Bayard on a single day could receive upwards of eighty-one cases, these numbers quickly add up.[90] The costs Bayard was required to cover were consequently vast.

Normally, private persons were able to act as stipulants or sureties financially vouching for the party at court. It would have been difficult, if not downright impossible, for Bayard to follow this procedure. For every case he took on, he would have had to find private sureties to pledge themselves to him financially and that person would only be able to do so for as many cases as they themselves could vouch for with their personal fortune. To add fuel to the fire, Bayard's position was not officially recognised, and it was questionable whether he even had the authority to pledge government money for his mission, as that power lay with Congress, not the President.[91]

Nevertheless, Jay and Lord Grenville had already discussed this issue during the treaty negotiations and had come up with a solution. A tailor-made alternative was agreed upon by the British and American politicians, switching Bayard's financial resolutions from the private to the cooperative.[92] In association with Pinckney,[93] Jay arranged that the company of Bird, Savage & Bird would attest to the financial promises of the US government, or concretely to the cases Bayard vouched for on behalf of the American nation.[94] This family company mainly gained its wealth from trade with South Carolinian and New York merchants, as well as marketing US government bonds.[95] Persuading the partners to take on this risk may at first seem a difficult task, especially as Congress had not yet passed any act to guarantee that the costs incurred by Bayard's mission would be reimbursed. Thus, the risk taken on by the banking

[89] 16 May 1795, NARA, *Letters Received from Samuel Bayard – NAID: 1170268*, p. 31.

[90] 10 July 1795, Bayard, *Diary of Samuel Bayard*, p. 19; J. Jay, *Draft of Letter to Samuel Bayard, 27 January 1795*, https://dlc.library.columbia.edu/jay/ldpd:78792 (accessed 12 January 2021).

[91] 20 December 1794, NARA, *Letters Received from Samuel Bayard – NAID: 1170268*, p. 2.

[92] Jay, *Letter to Edmund Randolph, 7 January 1795*.

[93] Ibid.

[94] J. Trumbull and J. Jay, *Draft of Samuel Bayard's indemnity, 5 January 1795*, https://dlc.library.columbia.edu/jay/ldpd:78802 (accessed 12 January 2021).

[95] Bird, Savage & Bird, *Letter to James Madison, 10 February 1803*, https://founders.archives.gov/documents/Madison/02-04-02-0385 (accessed 12 January 2021).

house was not insignificant, considering that both Pinckney and Jay could not vouch for the reimbursement of government expenditures that had not yet received governmental approval.[96] But, in fact, the company itself had offered to act as a surety. It had felt "an anxious desire to serve both countries, by assisting in paving the way for your obtaining full justice to your citizens".[97] An arrangement was swiftly drafted.[98] Once Bayard had received formal authority to pledge financial assurances on behalf of the US government, the agreement was formalised and Bayard regularly met with members of the Bird family.[99] In addition, to get Bayard going while this financial arrangement was being organised, both Pinckney and Jay put £500 each into a small fund for him to access at the beginning of his mission.[100] The investment was well worth the while for the American government and its people. By September 1796, Bayard had already taken on more than 300 cases. In every case, proctors were advanced £20 – that is, £10 less than had originally been stipulated to Bayard a year earlier – and the total costs estimated at about £250 per case. The costs for these cases alone can be estimated at about £70,000. However, successful cases were to pay for themselves. If a case was successful in court, the costs incurred from pursuing it would be deducted from the sum awarded. This meant that only unsuccessful claims or appeals cost the government money, while – at least in theory – successful claims did not.[101]

In the face of the 'experiment' of American democracy, Bird, Savage & Bird's trust seems to have been astonishing. A correspondence from the Secretary of State, James Madison, in 1801, referred to Bayard's successor, Samuel Williams, as having taken advances from Bird, Savage & Bird in the space of six months – without notifying the Department of State – amounting to "upwards of 88,000 dollars".[102] Bird, Savage & Bird went bankrupt in 1803.[103]

96 Jay, *Letter to Edmund Randolph, 7 January 1795.*

97 H. M. Bird to John Jay, 25 December 1794; *The debates and Proceedings in the Congress of the United States with an Appendix containing Important State Papers and Public Documents, and all the Laws of Public Nature with a Copious Index*, pp. 2484–5.

98 2 February 1795, NARA, *Letters Received from Samuel Bayard – NAID: 1170268*, pp. 4–5.

99 Copy, undated, *c.* April 1795, ibid., pp. 13–14.

100 Jay, *Letter to Edmund Randolph, 7 January 1795.*

101 *The debates and Proceedings in the Congress of the United States with an Appendix containing Important State Papers and Public Documents, and all the Laws of Public Nature with a Copious Index*, p. 2293.

102 James Madison to Samuel Williams, 29 June 1801, quoted in Keegan, *US Consular Representation in Britain Since 1790*, p. 186.

103 Cf fnl; Bird, *Letter to James Madison, 10 February 1803.*

Doctors' Commons was a microcosmic community, consisting of a small number of legal professionals. The fact that everyone knew everyone there made diplomacy and tact more important and difficult than ever. When Bayard arrived in London and took up his post, which proctors would be entrusted with the valuable and vast amount of American casework became a topic of conversation. Before January 1795 had passed, Jay had already been asked to recommend proctors Jenner and Bush to Bayard.[104] He had received a complaint from proctors Crickett & Townley that rival proctor, Mr Slade, had allegedly been promised a large cut of the cases.[105] Bayard had assured Jay that he had not promised or handed over any cases to anyone.[106] However, he would recommend Mr Slade.[107] Bayard in turn had been refused a recommendation of a specific proctor by Sir William Scott, but had been recommended Crickett & Townley by Pinckney and Johnson. In the end, the recommendations of other American civil servants won out, with Jay instructing Bayard to employ Crickett & Townley as the proctors to be turned to. Furthermore, in a move which clearly demonstrates Jay's tact, he suggested passing some, but not many, cases to Mr Slade, as Slade had probably gained the impression he would be receiving some work through his interactions with Bayard and was not to be disappointed.[108] By May 1795, more than £600 had been paid out to Crickett & Townley, £500 to Slade, and Jenner & Bush were still waiting to receive American cases as soon as possible.[109]

Such interactions showcase two of the three social circles with which Bayard mainly interacted. First, the maritime community must be named, as has already been demonstrated through Bayard's communications with his clients both personally and through the written word. Second, he regularly met many members of Doctors' Commons. Third, he regularly interacted with politicians both British and American. The interconnection of the latter two groups must be stressed in this regard.

As previously mentioned, Doctors' Commons was a community. Its microcosmic quality resulted in a constant interconnection of the legal, the social and the political sphere. Bayard regularly met up with the United States'

[104] J. M. Adair, *Letter to John Jay, 19 December 1794*, https://dlc.library.columbia.edu/jay/ldpd:35688 (accessed 12 January 2021).

[105] Crickett and Townley, *Letter to John Jay, 20 January 1795*, https://dlc.library.columbia.edu/jay/ldpd:48732 (accessed 12 January 2021).

[106] S. Bayard, *Note to John Jay, 20 January 1795*, https://dlc.library.columbia.edu/jay/ldpd:78784 (accessed 12 January 2021).

[107] S. Bayard, *Letter to John Jay, 27 January 1795*, https://dlc.library.columbia.edu/jay/ldpd:29850 (accessed 12 January 2021).

[108] Jay, *Draft of Letter to Samuel Bayard, 27 January 1795*.

[109] 16 May 1795, NARA, *Letters Received from Samuel Bayard – NAID: 1170268*, p. 29.

legal counsel. This was provided by Sir William Scott, referred to in Bayard's shorthand of his diary as "S.W.S."[110] or more frequently as "Sir W.S.".[111] It was also provided by Sir John Nicholl.

William Scott was born on 17 October 1745[112] as the eldest son of William and Jane Scott.[113] Scott grew up in a family of significant means, his parents being members "of power and prestige in the community".[114] Among his many siblings, his brother, John Scott, would go on to have a successful career in law and Tory politics, becoming Lord Eldon and taking on positions such as Attorney General from 1793 and Lord Chancellor of Great Britain from 1801 to 1806 and 1807 to 1827.[115] William and John Scott retained a close bond throughout their lives, navigating both political and judicial spheres together.[116] In 1794, for example, they collaborated to prevent a reform of the vice-admiralty court system. William Scott had enrolled as an advocate at Doctors' Commons after receiving his Doctorate of civil law (D.C.L.), and moved to Doctors' Commons with his wife, Anna, in 1781.[117] He chose to specialise in ecclesiastical and admiralty law due to their exclusivity and consequent financial security as well as, specifically in cases of prize, profitability.[118] However, he kept up a teaching post as Camden Reader until 1785 to provide an additional source of income.[119] In 1788, he took on the position of King's Advocate, which he filled until Marriott's resignation. Sir William Scott's tenure as Judge is probably the period of the High Court of Admiralty that has received the most scholarly attention, and his reputation has gone so far as to be considered a legacy. Roscoe describes Scott's attainment of the judgeship as "a noteworthy moment in the history of the Prize Court"[120] from every angle. He is not alone in that Scott, in contrast to Marriott, is depicted by many (legal) historians as "the greatest of the civilians".[121] Holdsworth

110 15 June 1795; Bayard, Diary of Samuel Bayard, p. 14.

111 4 August 1796; ibid., p. 83.

112 Although due to the change in dating (old style/new style) William Scott would go on to celebrate his Birthday on the 28 October each year from 1752 onwards.

113 H. Twiss, *The public and private life of Lord Chancellor Eldon, with selections from his correspondence: Vol. III*, 2nd edn, 3 vols (London, 1844), pp. 513–14.

114 Bourguignon, *Sir William Scott* (2009), p. 31.

115 R. Thorne, *Scott, Sir John (1751–1838)*, www.historyofparliamentonline.org/volume/1790-1820/member/scott-sir-john-1751-1838 (accessed 26 August 2020); R. A. Melikan, *John Scott, Lord Eldon, 1751–1838: The Duty of Loyalty* (Cambridge, 1999), p. 142; Mangone, *United States Admiralty Law*, p. 38.

116 Ibid, p. 21.

117 Bourguignon, *Sir William Scott* (2009), p. 37.

118 Marsh, 'Lord Stowell', 669.

119 Bourguignon, *Sir William Scott* (2009), p. 37.

120 Roscoe, *A History of the English Prize Court*, p. 53.

121 Bourguignon, *Sir William Scott* (2009), p. ix.

phrases it this way: "It was Lord Stowell,[122] who by his decisions [...], settled the principles of Prize jurisdiction of the admiralty."[123] Colombos adds that Scott "laid down, not only for his country, but also for a great part of the civilized world, the rules and principles of prize law".[124] He was described as "a great civil lawyer, whose judgments laid the basis of modern admiralty law and the international law of war"[125] in the *Oxford Dictionary of National Biography*, while Thorne simply sums up his judicial career as "brilliant and lucrative".[126] This appreciation for Scott is not only a phenomenon of historical retrospect, but was also shared by many of his contemporaries. In 1837, shortly after his death, a sixty-one-page biography was published on his life and work.[127] Two years later he was depicted in *Historical Sketches of Statesmen* in the following manner:

> Few names are more intimately connected either with classical or judicial recollections than the one which has just been mentioned. There has seldom if ever appeared in the profession of the Law any one so peculiarly endowed with all the learning and capacity which can accomplish, as well as all the graces which can embellish, the judicial character, as this eminent person.[128]

It is worth noting how, while Marriott's obituaries were kind to him and history was not, Scott's legacy continues to flourish in present times.[129] While his wealth, as well as the financial, political and social means of his family will have contributed to the creation of his legacy, the extent and longevity of his reputation can be attributed to the publication of his judgments. These case reports, first prepared by Christopher Robinson, and later followed by

[122] He was raised to the peerage in 1821; Thorne, *Scott, Sir John*.

[123] Holdsworth, Goodhart, Hanbury and Chrimes, *A History of English Law*, vol. I, pp. 561–2.

[124] Colombos, *A Treatise on the Law of Prize*, p. 28.

[125] Cited from R. Thorne, *Scott, Sir William (1745–1836)*, www.historyofparliamentonline.org/volume/1790-1820/member/scott-sir-william-1745-1836#footnoteref3_uxjdk4y (accessed 26 August 2020).

[126] Ibid.

[127] *The annual biography and obituary for the year 1837: Part I – Memoirs of celebrated persons, who have Died Within the Years 1835–1836, Vol. XXI* (London, 1837).

[128] H. Brougham, *Historical sketches of statesmen who flourished in the time of George III: Volume II, Works of Henry Brougham* (London Glasgow, 1856), vols 4 and 3, p. 67.

[129] A. Shoenberger, 'Loyola Law School, State Secrets, the American Revolution, the War of 1812: The Maritime Connections of the Middle Temple', *Journal of Maritime Law and Commerce* (2012), 293–300, at 297–8.

Thomas Edwards, John Dodson, John Haggard and William Robinson/George Minot, took on a life of their own.[130]

John Nicholl was born in South Wales on 16 March 1759. Like Scott, he went to Oxford, where he obtained his D.C.L. in April 1785 and was admitted as an Advocate into Doctors' Commons six months later.[131] He would take over from Scott first as King's Advocate in 1798, became Dean of the Arches in 1809, and also took on the judgeship of the High Court of Admiralty after Scott's retirement in 1833.[132] Moreover, he played an active part in the development of prize relations between Britain and America in the 1790s, as he was chosen to be a (British) commissioner.[133] Unlike Scott, Nicholl received very little scholarly attention. Although the judgments of his significantly shorter tenure (until his death in 1838) were also published in the *Reports* series, he has not left a lasting legacy, treasured by the admiralty law community.

The cost of obtaining counsel from both these reputable men was significant to the US government, especially as only one counsel could be heard in court without extra charge. Nevertheless, the United States continued obtaining the opinions of both men, which Bayard collected into a book.[134] This book can now be found at NARA.[135]

But aside from these 'grand men' of Doctors' Commons, Bayard also regularly met with the clerks, advocates and proctors of the microcosm.[136] Next to frequent business meetings, consultations and similar events, regular social interactions with other members of this prize court were usual, including

130 T. Edwards, *Reports of cases argued and determined in the High Court of Admiralty: Commencing with the judgments of the right hon. Sir William Scott, Easter term, 1808* (London, 1812); J. Dodson, *Reports of cases argued and determined in the high court of admiralty: Commencing with the judgments of the right hon. Sir William Scott, Trinity Term 1811* (London, 1815); J. Haggard, *Reports of cases argued and determined in the High Court of Admiralty: During the time of the right hon. Lord Stowell* (London, 1825); W. Robinson, *Reports of cases argued and determined in the High Court of Admiralty: Commencing with the judgments of the right hon. Stephen Lushington* (London, 1844); Minot G. (ed.), *Reports of cases argued and determined in the High Court of Admiralty: Commencing with the Judgements of the Hon. Sir William Scott. Michaelmas Term, 1798* (Boston MA, 1853).

131 *Dictionary of Welsh Biography, Nicholl, Sir John (1759–1838): judge*, https://biography.wales/article/s-NICH-JOH-1759#?c=0&m=0&s=0&cv=0&manifest=https%3A%2F%2Fdamsssl.llgc.org.uk%2Fiiif%2F2.0%2F4674538%2Fmanifest.json&xywh=773%2C1748%2C3391%2C2736 (accessed 21 August 2023).

132 See table 5.

133 Lillich, 'The Jay Treaty Commissions', 277, fn. 68.

134 16 May 1795, NARA, *Letters Received from Samuel Bayard – NAID: 1170268*, p. 32.

135 NARA, *Opinions Filed by the Commissioners, 1797–99 – NAID: 1170266.*

136 For example, 12 December 1795; Bayard, *Diary of Samuel Bayard*, p. 44.

not only Bayard himself, but also his wife and on some occasions his children. It seems the only person not involved in this social interaction was Sir James Mariott, for whom Bayard had a distinct dislike.

Mr Bush, clerk of proctor Robert Jenner, may serve as an example here. Bayard not only had tea with him and his wife, they also went to see the 'newly discovered' Shakespeare play/manuscript "the Vortigern"[137] together. Sadly, the Vortigern and Rowena, as it is often referred to, turned out to be merely one of William Henry Ireland's forgeries.[138]

On 19 April 1796, Mr and Mrs Bayard attended a large ball. Mr Bayard wrote, "I have been at none since my arrival in England more splendid than this". There were about 180 to 200 people in attendance including several foreign ministers and "most of the consuls also from the powers",[139] with Bayard estimating the costs between £300 and £400. The ball had been organised by Crickett & Townley, the two admiralty proctors in partnership with whom Bayard had worked closely together during his first year of service.[140]

Bayard's relationship with Dr Nicholl can be described almost as a friendship, with his family spending several days at the Nicholls' seat in Edgegrove.[141] Mrs Bayard's diary excerpts mirror this relationship quite well, with her noting:

> We have just returned from a most agreeable visit to Dr. Nicholls, and, tho' it was the first time I had the pleasure of seeing either the Dr. or his Lady, in half an hour [...] I felt perfectly at home; so friendly and

[137] 24 August 1795/16 September 1795; ibid., pp. 26, 29.

[138] D. Stewart, 'To Be ... Or Not: The Greatest Shakespeare Forgery: William-Henry Ireland committed a scheme so grand that he fooled even himself into believing he was William Shakespeare's true literary heir', *Smithsonian Magazine Online* (2010).

[139] 19 April 1796, Bayard, *Diary of Samuel Bayard*, pp. 67–8.

[140] For more on Charles Alexander Crickitt and James (Sen.) Townley, see TNA, London: Index of Persons, Prob 39. Bayard met and dined with both Townley and Crickitt, as well as their senior clerk Mr Burchett in his first week at Doctors' Commons (13/16 May 1795) and later referred to "C&T" or "C&Townley" in his diary; for example, 25 May 1795, ibid., p. 8.

[141] 5 September 1795, ibid., p. 26; Today the Edge Grove estate is a school for children aged up to thirteen; Edge Grove, *History, Co-educational School, Watford, Edge Grove*, www.edgegrove.com/about-us/our-history/ (accessed 27 June 2023); A plan of the grounds was drawn up in 1804, when Dr Nicholls was still the owner of the estate; Hertfordshire Archives and Local Studies, D/EX 216 P4: *Plan of the Parish of Aldenham in the County of Hertford*; It was sold by Nicholls to the Thelluson Trustees of Wall Hall after an enlargement of the grounds; D. Wratten, *The Book of Radlett and Aldenham* (1990), p. 54. My thanks to Graham Taylor of the Radlett & Aldenham Museum, and to Sue Maughan, the Alumni Representative at Edge Grove School.

> affable is she that she must be loved and admired wherever known. I am exceedingly pleased with them both.[142]

Several further visits followed during the Bayards' time in London.[143]

Whereas his relationship with Dr Nicholl seems to have been almost like a friendship, Bayard's relations with Scott constantly permeated his business dealings. Bayard does not appear to have visited the Scotts in any private capacity, although his wife met both Sir William and his wife.[144] Bayard had also on occasion met up for a day's walk with the British civilian outside of Doctors' Commons to mull over business in the fresh air of Richmond.[145] In part, Scott passed on political information to Bayard that had been unknown to him before. For example, the diary shows that Scott passed on information from conversations with prime minister Pitt and foreign secretary Lord Grenville.[146]

Bayard attributed the activities of the High Court of Admiralty and the Lords of Appeal as critical in regard to maintaining peace. He considered the "just and equal"[147] conduct of judges in the United States and in the British ranks alike as crucial to maintaining a (peaceful) alliance between Great Britain and the United States. It is clear that he viewed Sir William Scott as an ally in this battle for justice, although it cannot be shown whether this was entirely honest. Certain passages from the diary make one wonder to which degree a strategy of flattery was being employed by Bayard, such as: "had a long conversation with him [Scott] on the subject of appeals. Stated our reliance on his influence & his talents, how much it was in his power to conciliate the 2 countries Am. & G.B. with each other."[148]

In several instances, such as with the category of costs and damages that were sorted out of court, Bayard first persuaded Scott and then contacted others, referring to the approval of said civilian.[149]

Bayard's third social circle consisted chiefly of a broad mix of American and a decent number of English politicians, as well as general US citizens

[142] Bayard, *Journal of Martha Bayard*, p. 83.

[143] For example, 12 December 1795, 16 July 1796, Bayard, *Diary of Samuel Bayard*, pp. 44, 79.

[144] 18 and 23 April 1796; ibid., pp. 67, 69.

[145] After their private walk, they met up with other members of Doctors' Commons to dine; 10 July 1796; ibid., p. 79.

[146] 7 July and 28 November 1795; ibid., pp. 19, 41.

[147] 5 July 1795; ibid., p. 18.

[148] 18 April 1796; ibid., p. 67.

[149] 30 November 1795, NARA, *Letters Received from Samuel Bayard – NAID: 1170268*, pp. 65–6.

residing in London. As one of the few scientific articles focusing on Bayard's diary put it:

> To have known Washington, Franklin, and Hamilton, and frequently to have seen the British King and his ministry [...]; to have been acquainted with many of the American generals [...] and with their antagonists [...]; to have been on terms of intimacy with six of the signers of the Declaration of Independence: and to have known Burke and Barré, Fox and Pitt, Sheridan, Wilberforce, and Warren Hastings is certainly a very remarkable record for a young American of thirty. This was doubtless owing in good part, at home, to his birth and family connections, and abroad, to his official position, but much more to his own charming character.[150]

One must point out that although Bayard did interact with all these people, his relations with many of them are rather overstretched in this portrait of his life. For example, Bayard was most certainly not part of the Royal family's inner circle. While these relationships, if one may even call them such, are indeed highly interesting and quite unusual, none of them can be considered regular social contacts of Bayard during his time in London.

However, figures such as Adams, Pinckney, Marshall, King and Jay were regular contacts of his. In addition, the Bayard family kept in close contact with the Vaughan[151] and Vandam[152] families, with whom Samuel met up at least once per week.

Several times Bayard attended or attempted to attend parliamentary debates, both on topics specifically relevant to overseas trade, and on general British politics. For example, he was present when a movement to ban the slave trade in the West Indies was forwarded in parliament.[153] On another occasion,

150 Wilson, 'Judge Bayard of New Jersey and his London diary of 1795–96', 216.

151 Benjamin Vaughan helped negotiate the Treaty of Paris. He had by this time been arrested on grounds of treason and left for first France, then America; however, his family remained influential in England (for example, his brother who was one of the leading members of the Royal Exchange). R. Thorne, *Vaughan, Benjamin (1751–1835)*, www.historyofparliamentonline.org/volume/1790-1820/member/vaughan-benjamin-1751-1835 (accessed 18 January 2021).

152 The Van Dam family had been very influential in New York at the time of the Revolution. They sided with the independence movement and Anthony Van Dam became one of the Committee of One Hundred alongside John Jay. He was socially considered part of "Jay's circle" when in London: S. C. Hutchins, *Civil List and Constitutional History of the Colony and State of New York* (Albany NY, 1882), p. 114; A. S. Collins (ed.), *Travels in Britain, 1794–1795: The Diary of John Aspinwall. Great-Grandfather of Franklin Delano Roosevelt. With a Brief History of His Aspinwall Forebears* (Tabor SD, 1994), fn 71, p. 163

153 21 May 1795, Bayard, *Diary of Samuel Bayard*, p. 7.

he listened to a debate on the Seditious Acts.[154] Bayard also attempted to hear various parliamentary candidates.[155] He enclosed some of their speeches from the House of Commons in his dispatches and forwarded them to the Secretary of State.[156] He also attended several orations by radical British politicians.[157] Moreover, talks with leading British politicians reoccurred throughout Bayard's time in London (for example, with prime minister Pitt).[158] This had been specifically encouraged by Jay who had pre-emptively written:

> Such is the nature and magnitude of the business of these capture cases, as that, on certain occasions, diplomatic and prudential, as well as legal proceeding may be advicable [...] I take the liberty of submitting to your consideration the propriety of giving Mr. Pinckney a general superintende over the business.[159]

Generally, Bayard followed Jay's advice and left the communication with British politicians to American diplomats of higher standing. Nevertheless, one can most certainly conclude that Bayard was not an insignificant American in London, despite having been by no means as famous as the 1885 report of the New Jersey Historical Society would have one believe. This level of being acquainted with famous personalities of the day, having a good reputation and being employed by the American government, most certainly qualified him to fulfil representative functions. His attendance at the Merchants Dinner of 1795 can be seen in this light, where most foreign representatives and various consuls were present.[160] Other events, such as attending large gatherings in honour of the King's and Queen's birthdays should be considered diplomatic, host country 'must-haves'.[161] American celebrations to mark Independence Day and the President's birthday seem to have aroused more enthusiasm with the Bayards.[162]

Bayard saw the court system as part of a larger political interaction between Britain and the United States, underlining how he drew a direct, continuous

[154] 16 November 1795, ibid., p. 39.

[155] 1 June 1796, ibid., p. 73.

[156] 31 March 1795, NARA, *Letters Received from Samuel Bayard – NAID: 1170268*, p. 19.

[157] Such as John Thelwall who had been tried and acquitted for treason in 1794; 10 June 1795, Bayard, *Diary of Samuel Bayard*, p. 13.

[158] 19 June 1795; ibid., pp. 14–15.

[159] *The debates and Proceedings in the Congress of the United States with an Appendix containing Important State Papers and Public Documents, and all the Laws of Public Nature with a Copious Index*, p. 2494.

[160] 5 December 1795, Bayard, *Diary of Samuel Bayard*, p. 43.

[161] For example, 4–5 June 1795, 18 January 1796, ibid., pp. 12, 49.

[162] For example, 4 July 1795, 22 February 1796, ibid., pp. 17, 57.

line between war and peace from the political sphere through the admiralty court system, following the path of Article VII.

By 1797, Bayard clearly felt a sense of defeat, going so far as to say he had been able to achieve "but little of what is due to our fellow citizens".[163] At the same time, he incessantly wrote of the insurmountable workload he was facing and how hard his occupation was.[164] When this reality was questioned and he met resistance from other American diplomats, labelling his work as inefficient and incompetent in all but name, Bayard resigned.[165] Naturally, it was his wife's homesickness and state of health that was given as the formal reason for requesting to return home.[166] Moreover, he handed in his resignation in August 1797, having stayed in London at least half a year longer than had originally been proposed to him.[167]

Samuel Williams was appointed as Bayard's successor. Although Bayard offered to continue aiding the prize affairs from the American mainland, the offer was declined.[168] He wrote to his clients, informing them of the change, and the British admiralty court system did not use the change of personnel to question the authority of the agent appointed by the Government of the United States, to prosecute Claims and Appeals in Prize Causes, on Behalf of Citizens of the said United States. The transfer of agents worked seamlessly.

[163] Bayard to Rufus King, 10 August 1797, NARA, *Letters Received from Samuel Bayard – NAID: 1170268*, p. 203.

[164] Fitzsimmons to Pickering, 27 July 1796; NARA, *Box 10, British Spoliations – NAID: 1170270*.

[165] Gore and Pinkney to Bayard, 29 April 1797, NARA, *Letters Received from Samuel Bayard – NAID: 1170268*, p. 189.

[166] Bayard to Rufus King, 10 August 1797, ibid., p. 203.

[167] They returned to America, settling in New Rochelle, where Bayard received the judgeship of Westchester county, New York, from now-Governor John Jay in 1800. Later, the Bayard family moved to Princeton, where Bayard served as the first borough mayor from 1813 to 1818. He also became a founding member of the American Bible Society and the New York Historical Society. Craven and Woodward, *Princetonians, 1784–1790*, p. 10; A. Leitch, *A Princeton Companion, Princeton Legacy Library* (Princeton NJ, 1978), p. 46; Fosdick, *French Blood in America*, p. 309; J. W. Francis, *Old New York; or, reminiscences of the past sixty years. Being an enlarged and revised edition of the anniversary discourse delivered before the New York Historical Society, etc.* [electronic resource] (New York, 1858), p. 73.

[168] Bayard to Rufus King, 10 August 1797, NARA, *Letters Received from Samuel Bayard – NAID: 1170268*, p. 204.

# 5

# Dependent and Entangled: The American Experience of British Prize Jurisdiction in London

US politicians hoped to enforce the US claim on independence, sovereignty and neutrality in the British prize law system. However, in practice the American experience was one of unavoidable dependence and entanglement.

Prize law, by its very nature, has always been a contested legal field nestled between domestic and international law. The Judge of the High Court of Admiralty was subordinate to and bound by British parliamentary decisions. In this constellation, he could be considered a conflicted judge, much like prize law itself, trapped between municipal interests and international principles. Sir William Scott would become the judge of the High Court of Admiralty in 1798, when Marriott retired. During the first years of the Jay Treaty commission, he was active as the King's Advocate.[1] He was intertwined with the political sphere both on a professional and familial level: in his role as King's Advocate he drafted opinions for the Foreign Office on various matters, including neutral rights.[2]

While Marriott's work was widely received, it is his successor Scott whose judgments were internationally cemented into admiralty law. Scott's predecessors argued that British law and international law were one and the same.[3]

In his original communications to Secretary of State Edmund Randolph on the treaty of amity and commerce, Jay noted: "It appeared to me advisable that our people should have precise and plain instructions relative to the

1 See table 5.

2 Bourguignon, *Sir William Scott* (1987), p. 49. For the family ties, see Chapter 4.

3 It must be pointed out that this narrative of one clear international law has in part simply been taken on by researchers and historians without questioning the statements made by individuals with their own agenda or outlook on the (legal) world order. Others simply omit differences in the interpretation of international law, by referring to instructions which were to make privateers "conform to the law of nations" or by pointing out that privateering was "conducted within the international law of the sea, its practitioners authorized and regulated by the legal and administrative institutions of their respective states". Such statements, though factually correct, smooth over the contested nature of the field. Kert, *Prize and Prejudice*, vol. 11, p. 43; Starkey, *British Privateering Enterprise in the Eighteenth Century*, vol. 4, p. 13.

prosecution of appeals and claims, in cases of capture. For that purpose, I applied to Sir William Scott, and requested him, in concert with Dr. Nicholl, to prepare them."[4]

On 10 September 1794, he received detailed instructions by both civilians, which they in turn based on a report given to the King by his legal advisors, including Lord Mansfield, in 1753.[5]

The text summed up the relationship between the Appeals Court and the law of nations as such: "this [...] court judges by the same rule which governs the court of admiralty, viz.: the law of nations."[6] The 'law of nations' is mentioned seven times in the explanatory statement, being depicted as a canon of accepted and uniform rules, reinforced through phrases such as "the law of nations has established",[7] "the law of nations requires",[8] "the law of nations allows"[9] and culminating in the statement: "By the maritime law of nations, universally and immemorially received, there is an established method of determination, whether the capture be, or be not, lawful prize."[10] In this concept, which depicts *British* admiralty practice, the perception of national boundaries and differences in the judicial interpretation of international law, which most certainly existed, is entirely omitted. Instead, it depicts the vision of a standardised and internationally accepted canon of the law of nations used worldwide when actually referring to its own, British system of prize law. This was backed up or arguably enforced by the existence of British sea power, to the point that Bayard felt the British "think they have a right to *dictate* the *law of nations* to the ocean".[11]

The 1753 summary of British admiralty court jurisdiction and practice was obviously still considered acceptable and representative by Scott and Nicholl in the 1790s, otherwise it would not have been forwarded in questions of international politics to Jay. Mansfield's vision of omitting any contradictions between the British and international, divergent interpretations of the law

4 John Jay to Edmund Randolph; Johnston, *Correspondence and Public Papers of John Jay*, p. 86.

5 Ibid., pp. 86–7.

6 Ibid., p. 89.

7 Ibid., p. 87.

8 Ibid., p. 88.

9 Ibid., p. 88.

10 Ibid., p. 88.

11 Letter from Samuel Bayard to Elias Boudinot concerning British maritime conduct and policy, 12 December 1795; Sterling, 'A Federalist opposes the Jay treaty', 423.

of nations was shared and continued by the British side of the commission under Article VII.[12]

Yet for Scott, most of the time being bound by British law in practice and the moral framework of international law in theory was not a contradiction during his tenure. In his opinion, generally British prize law was entirely congruent with international law.[13] He also believed himself to be uninfluenced by politics.[14]

Still, if one examines *Robinson's Reports*, the edited and collected published decrees under Scott's judgeship of the High Court of Admiralty, an evolution of thought compared to Mansfield's communiqué becomes apparent throughout Scott's tenure. The series contains a wide range of references, both in the substance of Scott's judgments and in the additional footnotes provided by Robinson, to the variation in prize law practice. The reports show a deep knowledge of other European legalists in the field of international law (for example, Vattel or Bynkershoek), as well as historic sources such as French ordinances and the rolls of Oléron or Rodes.[15] Bourguignon, Scott's biographer and an author relied on by almost all scholars concerning prize, points out that in prize courts, precedents were sometimes "a game of finding the most helpful version of a prior case"[16] – much like in many other courts of law – with Scott referring more and more to British precedents over time.[17] According to Bourguignon, this was not considered a bias or contradiction of the law of nations, it was merely down to Scott's belief that "The precedents of the British admiralty court [...] had expressed these supranational legal principles more accurately and reliably than any of the philosophical commentators".[18] However, the Reports show that Scott did not shy away from mentioning the disparities in other national prize court rulings and procedure, and clearly stated his motivation for using British precedents in the case of the *Santa Cruz* (Picoa):

> I am bound to decide them [the cases] according to my own best informed apprehensions of law and justice, of the general law of

12 As an example, see Dr Nicholl's statement: "the sentence of condemnation [of the Lord of Appeals] having been affirmed in this case [...] according to the law of nations, it is presumed that justice has been administered in matters of prize." Moore, *History and digest, Vol. IV*, vol. 212, p. 3160.

13 One exception to this vision concerning the case of the *Fox* will be discussed later in this chapter.

14 Bourguignon, Sir *William Scott, Lord Stowell* (2009), p. 264.

15 For example, Minot (ed.), *Reports of cases argued and determined in the High Court of Admiralty*, pp. 136, 289, 364.

16 Bourguignon, *Sir William Scott* (2009), p. 155.

17 Ibid., p. 262.

18 Ibid., p. 263.

> nations, *as it has been understood and administered in the British Courts of Admiralty* [emphasis added] [...] but the fact is, there is no such rule of practice; nations concur in principle indeed, so far as require firm and secure possession; but their rules of evidence respecting the possession are so discordant, and lead to such opposite conclusions, that the mere unity of principle forms no uniform rule to regulate the general practice. [19]

This statement makes Scott's position very clear, placing British admiralty court precedent and its legal interpretations of the law of nations at the top of his reference sheet. He openly acknowledges the disparity of opinions in the law of nations as opposed to omitting it. Two other statements also show why, in his opinion, it was precisely because of this disparity, that he put the biggest emphasis on his national court's precedents.

In the case of the *Flad Oyen* (Martenson) in 1799 he stated: "It is not my duty to admit, that because one nation has thought it proper to depart from the common usage of the world, [...] that I am on that account under the necessity of acknowledging the efficiency of such a novel institution."[20] Back in the case of the *Santa Cruz* he continued:

> But were the public opinion of European States more distinctly agreed, on any principle, as fit to form the rule of the law of nations on this subject, it by no means follows that any one nation would lie under an obligation to observe it. That obligation could arise only from a reciprocity of practice in other nations.[21]

It thus becomes apparent that Scott saw a common and shared set of principles of international law to which he did refer frequently, but he did not consider cases in any other court other than those of the British admiralty as binding for his own decrees. Nevertheless, historians have often overlooked this aspect of Scott's tenure, instead focusing on his self-depiction as a man above national rulings, who believed international "law itself has no locality".[22]

American politicians, however, clearly saw their rights as provided by 'international law', not British law, and, in the context of the commission, repeatedly referred to the multitude of different practices of adjudication found in Europe. US commissioner Gore phrased it simply: "To suppose the decisions of the [prize] courts of any country evidence of the law of nations

[19] Minot (ed.), *Reports of cases argued and determined in the High Court of Admiralty*, pp. 59–60.

[20] Ibid., p. 141.

[21] Ibid., pp. 59–60.

[22] Müller, *Neutrality in World History*, p. 73.

would be to suppose that nation always right who captures and condemns the effects of another."[23]

Regardless of this sentiment, Americans had to deal with a number of dependencies in British prize jurisdiction. First and foremost, only a select few British members of the admiralty court, the advocates, were permitted to represent parties in court. Consequently, the US government had to employ British legal counsel to represent them in court, but also to provide them with knowledge on their cases.[24] A host of proctors were also employed to do the legwork, alongside the American agent for prize cases who was attempting to learn the ropes as he went along. Bayard attempted to distribute the case load on which American captains, ship owners and merchants depended widely throughout the Doctors' Commons microcosm. Bush and Jenner received cases, as did Crickett and Townley, and Slade. The latter remained Bayard's favourite proctor, because of his record of taking on the cases of neutrals, not primarily those on behalf of British captors.[25] Up until that point, Crickett and Townley had secured a large part of their business without any special qualification through their connections with the consuls of the neutral powers, affording them a "monopoly"[26] of such neutral claims and securing what Bayard originally termed a 'large' sum, before changing it to a "handsome fortune"[27] in his letter. It may therefore not be surprising that Bayard noted seeing most of the consuls present at Crickett and Townley's "splendid"[28] ball in 1796 alongside a few foreign ministers.

23 Moore, *History and digest, Vol. IV*, vol. 212, pp. 3161–3.

24 This is not to understate the knowledge American commissioners brought to the table in the London commission. Yet the examination, management and sorting of cases into classes as well as the forwarding of suggested precedent cases could not be undertaken by them due to the sheer volume of claims. John Trumbull, the fifth commissioner, was a painter, not a legalist, and wrote to Jay upon receiving his position that he had not previously given much attention to the law of nations. Nonetheless, he was confident in writing that said law: "is neither so voluminous nor so intricate, but that the degree of attention which I have sometimes given to other subjects, applied to this, will I trust, render me sufficient to master it." Trumbull, *Autobiography*, p. 192.

25 Bayard, Letter to John Jay, 27 January 1795; Bayard to Randolph, 16 May 1795: NARA, *Letters Received from Samuel Bayard – NAID: 1170268*. Bayard stated he wished to allocate cases to those "who from principle are led to exert zeal in behalf of your injured Fellow Citizens. For these qualities no one of the Proctors is more eminent than Mr Slade."

26 Bayard to Randolph, 16 May 1795: NARA, *Letters Received from Samuel Bayard – NAID: 1170268*, p. 30.

27 Bayard to Randolph, 16 May 1795: ibid., p. 30.

28 19 April 1796, Bayard, *Diary of Samuel Bayard*, pp. 67–8.

Furthermore, British civilians were selected to give their opinions on cases: Dr Nicholl was the consistent consultant, and sometimes Scott's guidance was added to this. Their legal opinions were regularly copied and forwarded to the Secretary of State at considerable expense, and they met up with Bayard and the commissioners frequently.

One example of their involvement is the case of the vessel *George Washington* (Mason), laden with 612 barrels of flour.[29] She was captured by HMS *Thetis*, a naval vessel from Admiral Murray's squadron, on 14 July 1795 and carried into the Vice-Admiralty Court at Halifax. The vessel, belonging to the Philadelphia merchant James Yard, was restored as American property. But her cargo was wholly condemned as French.[30] The court also condemned her in taxed costs of the claim for freight, demurrage, and expenses.[31] The owners contacted the State Department and applied for help.[32] Bayard followed up the required steps and entered an appeal on behalf of the owners. The case was given to proctor Slade.[33] As American cases were severely delayed, Bayard found the time to write a letter to Dr Nicholl, asking him to determine whether "it is advisable in any View to bring the said appeal to a hearing".[34] He also asked for an honest assessment of how likely the chance of a reversal of the decree was. Dr Nicholl's opinion gave a detailed explanation of the fact that neutrals were permitted to carry enemy property. When seized by a belligerent, they were entitled to the freight and expenses, claims that the vice-admiralty court had previously dismissed. However, the *George Washington* had not been taken on a lonely journey. Alongside several other American ships, she had been protected by a French convoy, as (some of) her cargo was to be sold to the French government upon arrival. Thus, the neutral had ceded her right to freight and expenses.[35] Moreover, he added that on appeal the ship itself might also be considered liable to confiscation as legal prize and therefore concluded "I do not think it advisable to bring the appeal to a hearing".[36]

29 Nicholl: Case of the George Washington; NARA, *Letters Received from Samuel Bayard – NAID: 1170268*, p. 79.

30 NARA, *List of Claims, 12 May 1797 – NAID: 1170192*, p. 19; NARA, *List of Claims, 18 May 1797 – NAID: 1170192*, p. 14 Both lists contain the same information on this case.

31 Nicholl: Case of the George Washington; NARA, *Letters Received from Samuel Bayard – NAID: 1170268*, p. 79.

32 Wagner to Templeman, 30 August 1796; NARA, *Box 3, British Spoliations – NAID: 1170270*.

33 NARA, *List of Claims, 12 May 1797 – NAID: 1170192*, p. 19.

34 Nicholl: Case of the George Washington; NARA, *Letters Received from Samuel Bayard – NAID: 1170268*, p. 79.

35 Nicholl: Case of the George Washington; ibid., pp. 79–80.

36 Nicholl: Case of the George Washington; ibid., p. 80.

Nicholl's opinion was forwarded to the Secretary of State. The government decided to drop the case, entering it in their ledger as "suspended in consequence of Dr Nicholl's Opinion".[37] The owners of the *George Washington* were then contacted by the Chief Clerk of the State Department, explaining why their case would not be accepted by the government's commission to go on to appeal. Still, it was added that "nothing [...] will prevent you, sir, from doing it, if you think proper, at your own charge".[38]

The employment of British legal professionals created a strangely twisted dependency at the core of American prize claims, which the government fought through steps such as the publication of case precedents. However, prior to publication, the knowledge remained inaccessible to claimants without British counsel.

The other dependence was a temporal one: American claimants were reliant on the compliance and cooperation of various factions in the prize court system to obtain what Lord Grenville had promised to Jay, "the most complete & speedy justice".[39]

American claimants were all constantly and continuously losing time and money on their cases.[40] Not only had they suffered initial financial losses through the confiscation of their vessels and/or cargo, but losing a vessel also meant losing an opportunity for further trade.[41] It would still be costing insurance, maintenance and in some cases protection fees. Goods that were on board could rot and perish. To say nothing of the costs of court procedure, which claimants were by no means sure to recuperate. Merely to qualify for an appeal, claimants had to post a bond with a deposit of £150–300.[42] On top, there were the fees for copying, sending and printing pieces of evidence and court documents. Moreover, due to the physical distance, all the vice-admiralty

37 NARA, List *of Claims, 12 May 1797 – NAID: 1170192*, p. 19.

38 Wagner to Templeman, 30 August 1796; NARA, *Box 3, British Spoliations – NAID: 1170270*; One case that the American government dropped due to Nicholl's opinion, and that the claimants consequently decided to prosecute at their own expense was that of the brig *Potowmack* (Chunn). She had also been travelling in the presence of a French convoy and was carrying a cargo of flour. The owners of the *Potowmack* lost their appeal, resulting in £250 of legal fees. Williams to Pickering, 30 July 1798; NARA, *Box 2, General Records, ca. 1790–ca. 1820 – NAID: 1170269*: Unbound Records; Opinion of Dr Nicholl on the Brig *Potowmack* (Robert Chunn), 23 June 1796; NARA, *Box 1, British Spoliations – NAID: 1170270.*

39 27 January 1796; Bayard, *Diary of Samuel Bayard*, p. 50.

40 Bayard, *Letter to John Jay, 27 January 1795.*

41 Sometimes a vessel would be released to the claimants by interlocutory decree until all the evidence was ready. Starkey, *British Privateering Enterprise in the Eighteenth Century*, vol. 4, p. 26. But this was not always the case. The vessel might not be released, meaning it could not make any profits.

42 Kert, *Prize and Prejudice*, vol. 11, p. 71.

court records needed to be copied and sent to London, incurring high amounts of clerk and postage fees.[43] In Bayard's first diary entry, he noted his personal desire that "claimants [were] not to suffer by the delay".[44] Jay repeatedly told Bayard to spend his time efficiently and not cause any delays, but once a case had been entered in the appeals court,[45] it "could stretch into years".[46]

To Bayard, any avoidable delays were regarded as strategic blows to the economic interests of American citizens, incompatible with the treaty's provisions and intent (though he did not focus on avoidable American delays). In a letter to proctors Crickett and Townley, he wrote: "The Honor of the British Government is pledged to dispense to the American Claimants 'the most complete and impartial justice' and it will not I trust be necessary to remind any officer of his majestys Government that the delay of compensation is the Denial of Justice."[47]

US commissioners even went so far as to call (avoidable) delays "delinquency".[48] Recurrently, Bayard noted behaviour such as the premature ending of hearings or their postponement due to British judicial personnel's election campaigns or private engagements, which he considered the polar opposite of the American governmental mission.[49] He summed it up: "How strange is this delay. How little sympathy can they have with our merchants who by their postponements of discussions are hurt out of the money due them."[50]

43 Bayard to Butler and Norton, 27 September 1796; NARA, *Box 2, Ships E–F; British Spoliations, ca. 1796–ca. 1824 – NAID: 1170270*; Aside from the costs of delays, there was also always the risk of failure. Appealing a decree was something distinctly different from overturning it. Faye Kert states that there was only a "relatively low success rate" for the decrees of appeal cases to be reversed. Kert, *Prize and Prejudice*, vol. 11, p. 72.

44 8 May 1795; Bayard, *Diary of Samuel Bayard*, p. 5.

45 Hill, *The Prizes of War*, p. 17.

46 Jay, *Letter to Samuel Bayard, 5 January 1795*.

47 Bayard to Crickett and Townley, 27 October 1796, NARA, *Box 4, Ships L–N; British Spoliations, ca. 1796–ca. 1824 – NAID: 1170270*.

48 J. B. Moore, *Compensation for losses and damages caused by the violation of neutral rights, and by the failure to perform neutral duties: Mixed commission under article VII of the treaty between Great Britain and the United States of November 19, 1794, Vol IV, Publications of the Carnegie Endowment for International Peace, Div. of International Law, Washington, Modern Series* (Buffalo NY and New York [u.a.], 1931), International Adjudications Ancient and Modern, History and Documents, ed. by John Bassett Moore, vol. 4, p. 476.

49 25 May 1796 and 17 June 1796; Bayard, *Diary of Samuel Bayard*, pp. 73, 77.

50 13 February 1796; ibid., p. 54.

He ominously insinuated that the officers of the courts of admiralty had no desire to achieve swift justice as this would reduce their fees.[51] This seemed to him a simple matter of greed, as he noted every "expence thus incurred [by delay] is highly injurious to all the parties concerned except the Gentl[me]n of the profession".[52] In the case of the judge of the High Court of Admiralty, political motives and incompetency were also on Bayard's mind.[53]

A commission set up to look into prize agency shows how delays plagued all claimants, not just American ones. It determined that an average case would take at least seven months until distribution. In his research sample of 327 cases of captured merchant vessels, Richard Hill places the chances of closing a case and distributing the prize money attached to it at only 26.9%.[54] Anna Brinkman's work on the Appeals Court in the Seven Years' War also documents many complaints of long delays.[55] In her work, she clearly demonstrates how the close interaction between British politicians and members of Doctors' Commons enabled the Court of Appeals to be used as a political instrument towards neutral powers in the Seven Years' War.[56] In some of these cases, the government had even threatened citizens into withdrawing appeals cases by pointing to a lack of success and significant cost and expense.[57] A naval prize agent in the West Indies purposefully retained the proceeds of sale for years (possibly for investment purposes) knowing that legal redress would take years.[58] In the 1790s, Bayard voiced similar concerns, describing the courts of admiralty as political instruments.[59]

Bayard's confrontation with delays in the system deeply frustrated him, but at the same time he was unsure how to proceed. Although he deeply disliked the system, he needed to work within it to gain the best outcome for his clients.[60] The issue with prize jurisdiction was, that despite being based on international law, it was still being executed by domestic courts. As a

51 Though he exempted Mr Slade from this judgment. 16 May 1795; NARA, *Letters Received from Samuel Bayard – NAID: 1170268*, p. 28.

52 Bayard to Rufus King, 4 April 1797, ibid., p. 183.

53 3 February 1796, ibid., p. 84.

54 Hill, *The Prizes of War*, pp. 212–13.

55 Brinkman, *Balancing Strategy*, p. 140.

56 A. Brinkman, 'The Court of Prize Appeals as an Agent of British Wartime Foreign Policy: The Maintenance of Dutch and Spanish Neutrality during the Seven Years War' (dissertation, King's College London, 2017), p. 190.

57 Brinkman, *Balancing Strategy*, p. 242.

58 F. A. James, 'Making Money from the Royal Navy in the Late Eighteenth Century: Charles Kerr on Antigua "breathing the True Spirit of a West India agent"', *The Mariner's Mirror*, 107 (2021), 402–19, at 407.

59 Samuel Bayard to William Bradford, 9 June 1795; quoted in Sterling, 'A Federalist Opposes the Jay Treaty', 414.

60 17 February 1796; Bayard, *Diary of Samuel Bayard*, p. 55.

foreign citizen representing foreign citizens, Bayard was thus conflicted as to whether he should complain and risk negatively impacting his cases, or whether to accept the negative impact that delay was already causing. He thus described it as "an evil of which we can only complain, but which we are unable to remove".[61]

A further aspect of this difficulty did not actually lie with the court at all, but on claimants' dependency on the cooperation of the opposing party in court. As he candidly wrote to the Secretary of State:

> the proceeds of sale of every Vessel and cargo condemned as prize – when we consider the measures that will probably be taken by interested parties, proctors, agents & others to defend a suit to the last in hopes of a favourable decision, knowing the casualties that may happen in their favour the defect of evidence, the loss of ships papers, mistakes or prevarication of the Captain or crew, false testimony unfairly obtained & a thousand other circumstances which affect the ultimate decision of a cause that they have everything to expect and nothing to apprehend from a final decree.[62]

What did the opposing party have to gain from a swift settlement in court? Nevertheless, the US government also used delay as an instrument in their battle for compensation. When the case of the *Betsey* (Furlong) did not go as planned, Bayard immediately wrote to the Secretary of State to put all similar cases on hold until they could find a solution.[63] Prolonging cases on behalf of his clients seemed to him a very different matter than the same behaviour on his opponents' side.

Of all the captures documented in the HCA 45 dataset, 57.8% were conducted solely by privateers, whereas 38.4% were captures made by royal naval vessels, and only 2.5% of appeals cases were joint captures between privateers and naval vessels.[64] This meant that a large part of the American claimants was not facing British government employees, such as members of the Royal Navy, in the appeals court. Instead, they were combating private citizens, with private interests in the courtrooms, making the development of such appeals cases more erratic, diverse and unpredictable. Facing a party from the Royal Navy at least insinuated a stronger form of (governmental) power over said respondents.

But this did not mean that royal naval officials were easy to control. The cases of Sir John Jervis, Vice-Admiral of the blue, and Lieutenant General

61 12 April 1797, NARA, *Letters Received from Samuel Bayard – NAID: 1170268*, p. 174.

62 16 May 1795, ibid., p. 26.

63 29 July 1795; ibid., pp. 50–1.

64 See table 10.

Sir Charles Grey may serve as an example. In 1794 they led British forces in the successful capture of French Martinique, taking many prizes in the process.[65] Also known as the Martinique cases, these vehemently disputed captures were one of the early battle frontiers on which American and British visions of international law collided.

Alongside the Baltic, the Caribbean was one of the central theatres for naval action in the French Wars. The West Indies were a powerhouse of the British economy and have been described as the "hub of the trade and shipping of the Atlantic Ocean [...] a veritable money-box brimming with wealth for the benefit of the European Atlantic community".[66] British West Indian exports accounted for *c.* £7,250,000 of revenue in 1788 and the value of British investments and their associated services lay between 7% and 10% of the annual national income. Moreover, similar patterns emerge for the French economy, where 40% of foreign trade was West Indian. The trade employed roughly one-third of registered French seamen and contributed around £8,250,000 in exports before the 1793.[67]

The West Indies were therefore not only funding the British but also the French war efforts. Henry Dundas, Britain's Secretary of State for War from 1794 to 1801 and First Lord of the Admiralty 1804–5, therefore considered the capture of French Caribbean possessions as key steps in the defeat of the French.[68] Although the venture failed in the long run, resulting in roughly 50,000 casualties and deaths, mainly by disease, it was initially successful. By June 1794 various French Caribbean islands, such as Martinique, Guadeloupe and St Lucia had been captured by British forces under Jervis and Grey's command, in what was "probably the most successful expeditionary army sent to the Caribbean up to that date".[69]

Their capture of Martinique was highly lucrative in terms of prize-taking, especially as they did not distinguish between enemy and neutral vessels. British naval chaplain Cooper Willyams, who was present at the attacks,

65 P. D. Nelson, *Sir Charles Grey, First Earl Grey: Royal Soldier, Family Patriarch* (Madison WI, 1996), pp. 144–8; C. Harrison, *Sir John Jervis (1734/35–1823)*, https://threedecks.org/index.php?display_type=show_crewman&id=1503 (accessed 29 June 2023).

66 M. Duffy, *Soldiers, Sugar, and Seapower: The British Expeditions to the West Indies and the War Against Revolutionary France* (Oxford, 1987), pp. 6–7.

67 Robson, *A History of the Royal Navy*, pp. 75–6.

68 R. Thorne, *Dundas, Henry (1742–1811)*, www.historyofparliamentonline.org/volume/1790-1820/member/dundas-henry-1742-1811 (accessed 20 July 2024); P. Harling, 'A Tale of Two Conflicts: Critiques of the British War Effort, 1793–1815', in M. Philp (ed.), *Resisting Napoleon: The British Response to the Threat of Invasion, 1797–1815* (London and New York, 2016), at p. 19.

69 R. Harding, 'Review: By Fire and Bayonet. Grey's West Indies Campaign of 1794', *Journal of the Society for Army Historical Research*, 97 (2019), 184–6, at 184.

simply remarked: "If what is found in places or vessels taken by assault be not considered legal prize, what is? Is no booty, no prize money, to be the reward of successful heroism, after the dreadful fatigues, diseases and dangers of war?"[70] Not once did he consider a difference in the treatment of neutrals to be important in the military operations that he was involved in.

This did not only implicate American property, as the British military leaders also didn't differentiate between neutral and enemy seamen, imprisoning American and neutral mariners and "treating them in all respects as enemies"[71] on prison ships.

American politicians were outraged at this treatment as they were supposed to be neutrals, exempt from such behaviour: Edmond Randolph described Jervis's operation as a "system of plunder, prosecution, and cruelty […] unknown in the history of any warring towards a neutral nation". [72] Affected Americans' legal counsel also saw the behaviour as a clear violation as the law of nations, that needed to be rectified in court.[73] Furthermore, the actions of Jervis and Grey were not a case of ignorance, but clearly part of British strategy. It was in line with other military evaluations, such as those of Royal Navy officer Sir Charles Knowles, who had been sent to America in 1793 to report on French developments in the West Indies. In one of his accounts, he wrote that the Americans exhibited "treachery and implacable hatred […] to the British Nation".[74] Moreover, the idea that American estrangement could lead to a Franco–American alliance was plausible, as the two countries were in a mutual defensive Alliance already and strengthened their relationship through binational treaties until the Anglophile Jay Treaty upturned this political cooperation. The operations in Martinique were plainly presented as intentional, strategic and military decision-making before the House of Commons, as noted in the following report: "at this Time the *Americans* were very much attached to the *French*, and unfriendly to the *British* Government, and for this reason […] it [was judged] necessary to take Measures to prevent the *American* vessels, taken at *Martinique*, from giving Assistance to the Enemy."[75]

[70] C. Willyams, *An Account of the Campaign in the West Indies, in the Year 1794: Under the Command of their Excellencies Lieutenant General Sir Charles Grey, K.B., and Vice Admiral Sir John Jervis, K.B* (1794/2021), pp. 69–70.

[71] Report of the Relief (Cole), NARA, *Letters Received from Samuel Bayard – NAID: 1170268*, p. 115.

[72] Quoted in J. M. Fewster, 'The Jay Treaty and British Ship Seizures: The Martinique Cases', *William and Mary Quarterly*, 45 (1988), 426–52, at 427.

[73] Report of the Relief (Cole), NARA, *Letters Received from Samuel Bayard – NAID: 1170268*, pp. 114, 116.

[74] Quoted in Robson, *A History of the Royal Navy*, p. 11.

[75] House of Commons, *Journals of the House of Commons: 39 GEO. III*, Reprint (1803), vol. 54, p. 650.

French revolutionary politician Victor Hugues phrased it as such in regard to the occurrences on Martinique: "If they [the British officers] cannot get it [money] from their enemies they are base enough to turn pirates and ransack neutral vessels which are not able to defend themselves."[76]

The American ships, about 250 in number, were condemned by the Vice-Admiralty Court of Martinique.[77] On 11 May 1795, Lord Grenville, who publicly disagreed with the quick policy of expanding British prize jurisdiction abroad, mentioned the court in a letter alongside several others set up in the Caribbean and North American continent.[78] However, upon inspection, it was revealed that the court had never been authorised by the High Court of Admiralty. Without a great seal, it was an illegal shell, with no authority. The court had been set up by Jervis and Grey themselves.[79] As a member of Doctors' Commons phrased it, the vessels had been condemned in "a court without authority, one that had been illegally constituted by these Commanders".[80] On top of that, the court had not followed correct, or even, it would seem, any procedures at all. The extent of this disregard was immense: no standing interrogatories were taken, most of the American crews were imprisoned on prison ships without food for several days, some were impressed into the British Navy, while their ships were allegedly looted and vandalised. Several vessels were also damaged or lost through bad seamanship.[81] Therefore all vessels condemned and sold there had a right to appeal their decree. Strictly speaking though, these were not cases of appeal. As they had never been tried in a legal court, they all first went to the High Court of Admiralty, the first (true) instance of British admiralty jurisdiction.[82] Chaplain Willyams insisted the whole affair was a plot by treacherous British West Indian merchants, who had successfully "misrepresented the facts to England"[83] in hopes that they could oust the British naval presence and continue lucrative smuggling ventures with the French in the Caribbean.

76 Propaganda address, 21 February, third year of the Republic, quoted in Fewster, 'The Jay Treaty and British Ship Seizures', 448.

77 Ibid., p. 426.

78 Lord Grenville to John Jay, 11 May 1795; Johnston, *Correspondence and Public Papers of John Jay*, p. 139.

79 Fewster, 'The Jay Treaty and British Ship Seizures', 427.

80 Draft of proceedings concerning the Martinique cases, undated, NARA, *Box 5, British Spoliations – NAID: 1170270*.

81 Fewster, 'The Jay Treaty and British Ship Seizures', 431.

82 This procedure was explained to Bayard by Scott and Nicholl, cf.: Moore, *Compensation for losses and damages Vol. IV, International Adjudications Ancient and Modern. History and Documents*, ed. by John Bassett Moore, vol. 4, p. 48.

83 Willyams, *An Account of the Campaign in the West Indies, in the Year 1794*, p. 71.

Bayard's diary first mentions the cases on 9 June 1795.[84] He went on to file several claims relating to the incident.[85] The main case the Americans focused their efforts on was that of the *Relief* (Cole), which was a clear-cut example for a neutral American vessel being captured and illegally condemned and sold.[86] It had been selected together with the British legal counsel team.[87] Bayard hoped it would receive not only a complete exoneration (a reversal of the illegal sentence), but also be allowed costs and damages, thus forming a strong precedent for the other American claimants. As part of the (re-) trial, the ships' papers needed to be supplied to the court. These had been originally confiscated through Jervis's and Grey's men.[88] However, it seems they were never transported to Britain, despite the King's Proctor, representing the British captors, reassuring everyone that the papers would be arriving soon.[89] The agent for the two reputable English officers was Sir Charles Grey's son.[90] Repeatedly, Marriott gave Jervis and Grey additional time to procure the papers. The court case was adjourned five times, until, on 22 December 1795, Marriott refused to give the captors any more time for the collection of evidence, drawing a deadline for the middle of January.[91] Still, a decision had not been reached by February 1796.[92] A further five delays followed, with the first cases coming to court in March 1796.[93] When the *Relief* (Cole) finally came to court, Marriott wanted to condemn it to plead and prove, a procedural step that was connected with much delay and only issued in cases of extreme suspicion against the claimant. Both the captors' and claimants' representatives agreed that this was an unjust step, as the case was clear cut.[94] Marriott voiced his concern on making a decision in this case, pointing out that both Grey and Jervis were reputable gentlemen, and he did not wish to damage their social standing.[95] This went so far, that in another Martinique case, that of the *Lucy* (Treadwell), the creation of the Vice-Admiralty Court

84 9 June 1795; Bayard, *Diary of Samuel Bayard*, p. 13.

85 16 June 1795; ibid., p. 14.

86 TNA, HCA 32/820/23: *Relief* (Cole).

87 3 February 1796, NARA, *Letters Received from Samuel Bayard – NAID: 1170268*, p. 83.

88 Report of the *Relief* (Cole), ibid., pp. 113–4.

89 11 June 1795; Bayard, *Diary of Samuel Bayard*, p. 13.

90 NARA, *Letters Received from Samuel Bayard – NAID: 1170268*, p. 177.

91 22 December 1795; Bayard, *Diary of Samuel Bayard*, p. 46.

92 6 February 1796; ibid., p. 52.

93 7 March 1796; ibid., p. 60.

94 Report of the *Relief* (Cole), NARA, *Letters Received from Samuel Bayard – NAID: 1170268*, p. 115.

95 Moore, *Compensation for losses and damages Vol. IV*, International Adjudications Ancient and Modern, History and Documents, ed. by John Bassett Moore, vol. 4, p. 48.

in Martinique was diplomatically put down to a "misapprehension that they possessed the authority to erect such a court".[96]

Nevertheless, Judge Marriott was swayed by the opinions of both sides of the British legal counsel in the *Relief* (Cole).[97] He ordered her to be restored in February 1796, even including costs and damages.[98] Writing to the Secretary of State, Bayard noted that he should feel a sense of achievement, having set a precedent for the Martinique cases. However, he felt Marriott's judgments too wild and unreliable to celebrate.[99] Indeed, his intuition would prove correct. The other Martinique cases were dragged on further. The *Lucy* (Treadwell) only came to court in 1800. The remaining issue with most of these cases was that they were restored without costs and damages. An incomplete list from the House of Commons shows that at least fifty-eight American Martinique cases were taken to court, of which none were given costs and damages.[100] Bayard's dispatches to the Secretary of State shows that seven vessels did receive costs and damages, but that by far the larger part of American vessels (more than forty) were ordered to bring further proof, dragging out the cases even longer than expected.[101] Bayard was rightfully angry at this result, writing that the decree was:

> thus obliging us [Americans] to receive property (admitted by [Marriott] himself to have been most illegally and injuriously taken from us & most wrongfully condemned & sold) without interest from the time of seizure & without the costs we have unavoidably incurred here in the recovery of this property. In the Majority of these cases he exacts further proof which it will require at least 6 months to procure.[102]

Bayard was incensed at what he considered a partisan decision by a British judge, though maybe he found some solace in the fact that some of these cases would be solved in an extrajudicial, binational arrangement (see Chapter 7). In Bayard's eyes, delays coupled with the infrequent sittings of the court already

96 C. Robinson, *Reports of cases argued and determined in the High Court of Admiralty: Michalmas Term 1798*, 4th edn (London, 1812), p. 209.

97 Report of the Relief (Cole), NARA, *Letters Received from Samuel Bayard – NAID: 1170268*, pp. 121–2.

98 3 February 1796, ibid., p. 84.

99 3 February 1796, ibid., p. 84.

100 The list does not include, for example, the *Relief* (Cole), *House of Commons, 39 GEO. III*, vol. 54, pp. 652–3.

101 List dated 21 March 1796, NARA, *Letters Received from Samuel Bayard – NAID: 1170268*, pp. 109–10.

102 Copy Bayard to Pinkney, 14 March 1796, ibid., p. 102.

rendered it "incompatible with the principles of Justice".[103] As previously mentioned, he saw the delays as a strategic method employed by the British, remarking: "There appears to be a studied delay of our appeals."[104] It was thus that Bayard and the US cases that he was fighting for were being simultaneously blocked off at different sections within the British system of admiralty jurisdiction. Deciding that the impact of waiting was equally negative to his clients, Bayard actively endeavoured to undertake steps to counter this strategy. At least twice Bayard challenged the HCA's Judge, Sir James Marriott, with a list of all the delays/postponements that had occurred concerning a particular case. On some occasions, Bayard's lists of delays, at least in his own opinion, "had the desired effect",[105] deterring from further delays and resulting in (final) decrees. An example of such a scathing document can be found at NARA in Bayard's letter book, reading:

> That there are about 60 American cases now ready for hearing before your Lordships, about 30 of which are under the particular direction of your Memorialist […] That in the cases of the Essex, Liberty, Helen and Nancy, argued more than a twelve month ago; no judgment has yet been given, that the point to be determined in these cases is of Considerable Importance […] That the cases of the Charlotte, Peter Augustus, & Good Intent have long been ready for hearing […] That on no Subject is the Sensibility of the people of the United States more acute than on the event of the appeals now depending before your Lordships. […] That in most of those cases of appeals to your Lordships from the West Indies and Bermuda the American owners have been above two years deprived of the use of their Capitals Seized and condemned, to the extreme injury of all, & to absolute ruin of some of the claimants, and that were they immediately to have a decree of restitution in their favor, many months would probably elapse before they could receive the proceeds of their Vessels & Cargoes so decreed to be restored.[106]

On other occasions, Marriott seemed unfazed by Bayard's outrage. For example, in July 1797, when the Judge postponed the Martinique cases once more, simply replying, "They will not take cold".[107] Another time Marriott seemed to crack under the pressure, Bayard noted how he "plainly diggested

[103] 14 March 1795, ibid., p. 14.

[104] 30 January 1796; Bayard, *Diary of Samuel Bayard*, p. 51.

[105] 6 February 1796; ibid., p. 52.

[106] Memorial, undated, NARA, *Letters Received from Samuel Bayard – NAID: 1170268*, pp. 126–7.

[107] 14 July 1797, ibid., p. 191.

his wish to get rid of the business [current cases] & to drive us to an appeal".[108] US claimants were thus forced to overcome a British judicial tactic of delay, increased costs and harassment. As government funds were provided for appeals, this may also have been one factor why US appeals were so frequent in this period.

Bayard immediately advocated taking the Martinique cases without costs and damages on to the appeals court.[109] Simultaneously, he asked the Secretary of State to attempt to reason with Lord Grenville, trying to find a political solution to the situation.[110] Yet the stark reality for many of the American claimants was that they were glad to have even been given restitution of their property.[111] Undertaking another court case, this time before the Lords of Appeal, was increasing their risk. The only reason to move on to the appellate jurisdiction was a matter of principle and court fees, which themselves would increase through the action. Why attempt to change the system? Why not simply cut one's losses at this stage of what they considered a losing game? Bayard entered protests on behalf of all those condemned to further proofs, and wrote to the claimants about the deadlines by which they must enter an appeal if they wished.[112] The year before, the last payment of the regular Martinique cases had been issued, eight-and-a-half years after the original seizures.[113]An inquiry held into Grey and Jervis's behaviour in 1795 came to nothing.[114]

While some cases of costs and damages were later solved out of court, others ventured on to the appeals court; for example, the *Sally* (Smith), the *Sally* (Runey), the *Phoenix* (Harlow) and the *Nance* (Graves).[115] The last of these went before the Lords of Appeal in 1803, but none of them were granted costs and damages. In the case of the *Sally* (Smith) these were explicitly refused.[116]

The Martinique cases reveal several layers of dependencies that confronted US claimants. They were reliant on the good conduct of the judge and judicial personnel, as well as the opposing parties. In practice, there was little that could be done when either was lacking, and frustrations were high when

108 27 January 1796; Bayard, *Diary of Samuel Bayard*, p. 50.

109 15 March 1796, NARA, *Letters Received from Samuel Bayard – NAID: 1170268*, p. 103.

110 3 February 1796, ibid., p. 83.

111 15 March 1796, ibid., p. 103.

112 15 March 1796, list dated 21 March 1796, ibid., 103, 109.

113 Fewster, 'The Jay Treaty and British Ship Seizures', 446.

114 Thorne, *Dundas, Henry (1742–1811)*.

115 TNA, HCA 45/24/12: *Sally* (Hugh); TNA, HCA 45/27/1: *Sally* (Hugh); TNA, HCA 45/32/27: *Sally* (Runey); TNA, HCA 45/32/12: *Phoenix* (Harlow); TNA, HCA 45/41/28: *Nance* (Graves).

116 TNA, HCA 45/41/28; *House of Commons, 39 GEO. III*, vol. 54, p. 652.

captors like Jervis and Grey were afforded so much respect and leeway in contrast to the neutral claimants.

Taking a step back, the treatment suffered by American claimants was dependent on military developments and the tactics considered, enforced or retracted by the British government throughout the French Wars. The House of Commons' report on Jervis and Grey clearly showed that the original seizures were part of a wider strategy, fearing an open alliance between America and France, at a time when French privateers were intertwined with the American maritime community, although the creation of the court was not sanctioned.

The impact of governmental policy and military tactics, as well as international entanglements on US cases, can also be seen in the seizures that resulted from the secret order in Council of 25 April 1795. This order has been seen as part of Britain's embrace of "hard-line policies against Revolutionary France with […] starvation as a means of arresting French advances".[117]

The order permitted British warships to seize neutral vessels carrying grain bound for French ports or purchased by the French government or its agents. As the term 'secret' suggests, the order was not published, although knowledge of it circulated quickly and was openly discussed between politicians, national and international.[118]

At first glance this may seem to be part of the British war strategy that launched a blockade of French ports, not only to incapacitate its naval forces, but also to damage its economy and increase counter-revolutionary sentiment.[119] Heightening this economic warfare, foodstuffs were redefined as contraband of war, and instructions issued that enabled privateers and British naval vessels to bring in ships carrying provisions to France, turning grain into a military item, like ammunition.[120] The French had also made use of this tactic, issuing a decree in May 1793 that enabled them to capture neutral vessels with provisions, especially referring to the British practice of purchasing "flour […] for the service of the marine of France, [… from

117 C. Baker, 'Grains as a Weapon? Britain's Scheme to Starve Revolutionary France, 1793–1796', *Historical Geography*, 47 (2019), 72–99, at 73.

118 William Allen Deas, Pinckney's Secretary and representative while abroad, still complained that he had not been able to see the order on 28 October 1795. By this time, it had already been rescinded. B. Mayo and American Historical Association, *Instructions to the British Ministers to the United States: 1791–1812* (Washington DC, 1941), p. 88, footnote 37.

119 Lambert, *The Challenge*, p. 13.

120 P. Pourchasse, 'War of Hunger: Supplying the French Republic during the Revolutionary Wars (1793–1795)', in J. W. Veluwenkamp (ed.), *Early Modern Shipping and Trade: Novel Approaches Using Sound Toll Registers Online* (Boston MA, 2018), pp. 59–76, at pp. 59–60.

neutral vessels] detained in England by the Government, who would not pay for them, except at a price below that which flour had been sold".[121] It later rescinded these decrees, leaving a whole classification's worth of French spoliation claims for American diplomats to deal with.[122]

However, while on the surface the British order in council was an attack against France, it was also a sign of Britain "fighting for her very survival in Europe",[123] as the country was itself suffering from food shortages and needed to prevent the very reactions that it was attempting to foster in France.

Due to what environmental historians now term a 'low North Atlantic Oscillation index' (that is, a weather phenomenon encompassing ocean currents, participation and winds dominating the atmospheric pressure over the North Atlantic Ocean), the 1790s would be dominated by cold, wet weather in Europe, leading to a series of bad harvests.[124] In 1795, the average acre of British land yielded a mere fifteen bushels of wheat, as opposed to the expected average of twenty-four.[125] As a result, grain prices varied significantly throughout the end of the eighteenth century. With several bad harvests in succession, prices increased significantly from 1794. This was very important for the local population as "wheat or other cereals constituted the centerpiece of all meals"[126] and made up about 80% of the caloric intake of city populations in Britain in the 1790s.[127] It was also important for the Royal Navy as "the sheer physical effort demanded by sailing the ship meant that seamen needed to be well fed if they were to carry out orders effectively. They were required to manhandle guns weighing up to three tons, to furl heavy canvas sails and to haul up heavy anchors".[128]

121 Lowrie and St Claire Clarke (eds), *Class I – Foreign Relations*, vol. 1, www.napoleon-series.org/research/government/france/decrees/c_decrees2.html (accessed 13 March 2025).

122 Scattergood and Henry, *The French Spoliation Claims*, p. 165.

123 Lambert, *The Challenge*, p. 12.

124 T. D. Finger and A. Flagstaff, 'Harvesting Power: Transatlantic Merchants and the Anglo-American Grain Trade, 1795–1890' (dissertation, University of Virginia, 2015), p. 40.

125 W. M. Stern, 'The Bread Crisis in Britain: 1795–6', *Economica*, 122 (1964), 168–87, at 174.

126 Finger and Flagstaff, 'Harvesting Power', p. 35.

127 Ibid., p. 41.

128 Knight, *Britain against Napoleon*, p. 153.

The average price for a Winchester bushel of wheat had been around 6 shillings in January 1794.[129] In February 1795 it was at 7 shillings 3 pence.[130] Martha Bayard remarked in her diary that "the poor suffer exceedingly; […] bread [price] very high; a scarcity is apprehended".[131] At the end of June, the price had increased to 8 shillings 9 pence.[132] Bayard simply noted in his diary "scarcity of bread & grain".[133] By September 1795 it had spiked at 13 shillings 6 pence, and only sank to 10 shillings 10 pence by the end of the year, before slowly sinking to stable rates in 1797.[134]

Increased prices led to famines and caused widespread unrest in the British population. In April 1795 militia men from Sussex forcibly entered Seaford and Newhaven, fully armed, against the orders of their superior officers, to confiscate as much flour and provisions as they could get. The riot and insurrection were so disreputable that two of its leaders were executed.[135] Although the incident was not far from London, no remarks on it could be found in Bayard's records. But in July 1795 he candidly noted in one of his dispatches: "By the papers you will learn what a state of alarm & distress this country experiences in consequence of the present scarcity of provisions. Every part of the kingdom either feels or dreads the evil of popular insurrections from this cause."[136] Popular anger was not just directed at politicians and the elite, with the war easily identified as one of the contributing factors for the grain shortage. An anonymous pamphlet describes how King George III was attacked and harassed on his way to opening parliament by a crowd of allegedly 200,000 people chanting "No King, No Pitt, No War, Bread, Bread, Peace, Peace!"[137]

Anger was also levied at middlemen in the grain trade, especially millers, and merchants. Rumours persisted that British wheat was being sold overseas to line merchants' pockets with high profits, as higher returns could be expected there.[138]

129 While the importance of the 'cheap loaf' has often been highlighted, a large part of the population made its own bread from wheat/flour. Therefore, while the increase in the price of loaves for this period can be examined, the focus here has been put on the development of grain.

130 Stern, 'The Bread Crisis', 169.

131 13 February 1795; Bayard, *Journal of Martha Bayard*, p. 46.

132 Stern, 'The Bread Crisis', 169.

133 26 June 1795; Bayard, *Diary of Samuel Bayard*, p. 16.

134 Stern, 'The Bread Crisis', 169.

135 Ibid., p. 172.

136 Bayard to Randolph, 16 July 1795, marked "(not official)"; NARA, *Letters Received from Samuel Bayard – NAID: 1170268*, p. 44.

137 *Truth or Treason! A Narrative of the Royal Procession to the House of Peers, October 29th 1795* (1795), p. 1.

138 Stern, 'The Bread Crisis', 174–6.

The British government empowered Claude Scott to act as a governmental grain agent and until the end of 1795 all imported wheat was purchased by and transported on government owned or chartered vessels.[139] At a dinner party in early July 1795, Bayard wrote in his diary that there had been whispers of a plan accepted by Lord Hawkesbury, President of the Board of Trade, to secretly import grain from America to prevent a famine.[140] Yet Scott's attempts to buy up provisions from North America failed in 1795, partially because his French, Spanish and Portuguese equivalents were faster.[141] Just in the spring of 1794, France had already purchased 24,000,000 pounds of flour.[142] The French Navy had been able to break through the British blockade with 150 ships' worth of grain, preferentially to feed its armed forces.[143]

However, there remained not insignificant portions of grain that the British intercepted and seized off neutral vessels as a result of the secret order in council.[144] Whereas Bayard's wife noted some developments in the grain market with regard to the poor, Bayard took a decided interest in them in his professional capacity.

In May 1795, he noted in his diary that he had spoken to captain Howard (formerly master of the *James*, at that instant of the *Ocean*), who had been in Bordeaux "but a few days"[145] earlier. Howard described conditions in France as good, with plenty of provisions, "bread excepted".[146] It may well be that Howard's description was still in the back of Bayard's mind as he wrote to the Secretary of State on 12 June 1795. He wished to inform him "as fully as I am able in regard to the nature and operation of those late orders issued by the King's Council for bringing all neutral vessels laden with provisions & intended for France into British ports".[147] Despite the order not having been published, Bayard was able to give a good rough impression in his introductory

139 Ibid., p. 178.

140 2 July 1795; Bayard, *Diary of Samuel Bayard*, p. 17.

141 His attempts also failed, because the American harvests in the 1790s had, much like everyone else's, suffered from bad weather. Finger and Flagstaff, 'Harvesting Power', p. 40.

142 Dull, *American Naval History*, p. 40.

143 And this, despite British agents reporting on the events. Robson, *A History of the Royal Navy*, p. 11; Baker, 'Grain as a Weapon?', 89.

144 Stern phrases this behaviour as such: "War rendered them [grain imports] more difficult, except from one source: corn cargoes intercepted in enemy or neutral vessels bound for enemy ports were naturally diverted to Britain." How the seizure of ships and vessels may be considered a 'natural' phenomenon is questionable. Stern, 'The Bread Crisis', 176.

145 24 May 1795; Bayard, *Diary of Samuel Bayard*, p. 8.

146 24 May 1795; ibid., p. 8.

147 12 June 1795; NARA, *Letters Received from Samuel Bayard – NAID: 1170268*, p. 35.

paragraph. He attempted to draw more specific conclusions from the intelligence on the captured vessels brought into port, searching for commonalities to gain a clearer picture. From this he deduced:

> In short the plan is I understand to bring in all Neutral vessels carrying provisions from whatever port they may have cleared & to whatever port they may be bound if there is any ground to suspect their real destination to be for France. Hence you will perceive that the scheme of starving the French into submission is not yet relinquished notwithstanding every Account from this quarter proves them to be well provided with everything but grain. [148]

Bayard relayed how examinations were still to be taken in the first port where US/neutral vessels were brought into, then forwarded to London. Once brought to Britain, the government would seize the grain and planned, according to Bayard's intelligence, to give an additional 10% compensation (that is, the costs of the product plus a 10% profit margin) on the original invoice price of the neutral owners. Generously, the British government would permit freight, demurrage and expenses to be paid, but every cargo must be claimed as in a regular case of prize which gave Bayard much cause for concern regarding the constant delays already plaguing the court system.[149] Trying to err on the side of caution, Bayard added:

> There is little probability of neutral property on the Ocean being more secure than at present for this season. I have reason to think that the Gov[ernmen]t of this Country will be more vigilant than ever in preventing France from recovering supplies in neutral bottoms. [...] Our citizens will act prudently in trusting as little property as possible on the Ocean bound to France. Perhaps even that which may be coming from France may be unsafe, but on this nothing certain can be said till we learn more.[150]

Furthermore, he pointed to Denmark and Sweden, asserting that they were increasing the strength of their naval armaments on their neutral vessels to improve the security of their trade. He also added that the Danes were said to have instituted a general embargo, a rumour that he withdrew as a falsehood in his next dispatch.[151]

Six days later Bayard had been able to secure more founded knowledge on the secret order in council: he had spoken to Sir William Scott, who had

[148] 12 June 1795; ibid., pp. 35–6.
[149] 12 June 1795; ibid., p. 36.
[150] 12 June 1795; ibid., p. 37.
[151] 12 June 1795; ibid., p. 37.

clarified that the order only permitted the capture of vessels carrying grain or flour and permitted the British government to forcibly buy said cargo. But Bayard did not give this answer much credit, as reports had reached him that both Danish and American vessels with neither flour nor grain on board had already been seized and brought into English ports, allegedly justified through the order in council.[152] He persisted: "one would suppose that their [the Royal Navy's] orders were to bring in all neutral Vessel whatever their cargoes or destination might be."[153]

He had also been able to ascertain that the figure of 10% had been agreed between the Danish and British government at a prior incident and was thus to be maintained.[154] This Danish precedent would indeed govern the entire affair. The methods previously established were quickly reintroduced. It was up to appointed merchants to ascertain the amount of money that the British government was to pay "to the Neutral claimants"[155] and agree upon a sum with the Registrar of the Admiralty. The sum was to consist of the original sales invoice, plus an additional "10 % […] & no more".[156] These proofs needed to be presented to and accepted by Sir William Scott. The final account, with the addition of freight, demurrage and expenses, was to be brought before the Merchants and the Registrar and if agreed upon, immediately be paid out by Claude Scott, the agent of grain sales and imports on behalf of Government. Bayard attended such a meeting in the case of the *Patriot* (Lee) on 26 June 1795.[157]

In July, Bayard was happy to report that:

> In several of those recent cases of seizure and detention orders for the restitution of vessel and cargo have been obtained & the value of the cargo according to the original invoice price of the same with the addition of 10 % including freight demurrage and expenses have been paid in bills payable 2 Months after date for freight & in 3 Months for the Amount of the Cargo.[158]

Thus, it seemed that everything had gone according to the British government's plan. Bayard, conversely, strongly disagreed with this procedure. He requested and received a meeting with William Pitt, the British Prime Minister. To the Secretary of State he explained, "my object was if possible to procure

152 Bayard to Randolph, 18 June 1795; ibid., pp. 37–8.

153 Bayard to Randolph, 18 June 1795; ibid., p. 38.

154 Bayard to Randolph, 18 June 1795; ibid., p. 39.

155 Bayard to Randolph, 27 June 1795; ibid., p. 40.

156 Bayard to Randolph, 27 June 1795; ibid., p. 40.

157 26 June 1795; Bayard, *Diary of Samuel Bayard*, p. 16.

158 Bayard to Randolph, 16 July 1795, marked "(not official)"; NARA, *Letters Received from Samuel Bayard – NAID: 1170268*, p. 43.

a larger allowance than 10% on the invoice price of all kinds of grain, flour & other provisions coming directly from America".[159]

Bayard arrived for his appointment only to be informed that Pitt had had to leave at short-notice and was not home. It appears the meeting was never followed up. Bayard took the hint and two weeks later wrote to American politician Deas, whose position as substitute *Chargé d'Affaires* gave him more leverage than that of the American agent of claims and appeals. He pointed out his indignance that a cargo of grain, which would have realistically fetched returns of 150–200% on the Continental market, could be legally seized and bought for mere 10% profits by the British government. He pleaded with Deas to use his influence to change the form of compensation.[160] Even Scott revealed that he personally would also have considered 15% appropriate.[161] Though Deas was unsuccessful, the 10% ruling came under fire in the Jay commission through the case of the *Betsey* (Furlong). It was consequently overturned in favour of American interests. US commissioners argued for the use of papers documenting market prices at the planned destinations of captured vessels, dropping a uniform compensation and instead making each case individual and more realistic.[162] Neutral trade was not to be damaged by wars between other nations through court systems that limited the profits of legal trade. As one American commissioner pointed out, why should neutrals bear all the consequences of a war they had no part in?[163]

The British response was sceptical: if neutrals were to reap the profits of wartime trading, they need also to live with the consequences.[164] Moreover, the arrivals of merchant ships would alter the prices on the market. In theory, it would be possible for five vessels to be sailing towards the same market with similar cargo. The first vessel to arrive might receive extraordinarily high prices for goods in short supply with high demand, whereas the fifth vessel might receive below average market prices, as four other vessels had by now flooded the market. Determining which of the five captured vessels would have arrived first, was an act of economic fortune-telling that could not be attempted by the court.

American commissioner Pinkney went so far as to state that this was exactly the point:

[159] Bayard to Randolph, 16 July 1795, marked "(not official)"; ibid., p. 44.
[160] Bayard to Mr A. Deas, 28 July 1795; ibid., p. 55.
[161] 7 July 1795; Bayard, *Diary of Samuel Bayard*, p. 19.
[162] Moore, *History and digest Vol. IV*, vol. 212, p. 4208.
[163] Ibid., p. 4212.
[164] Ibid., p. 4216.

> If a thousand illegal captures had preceded that of the *Betsey* and raised the price of the articles with which she was freighted, the only consequence would be that the claimants had an undoubted right to avail themselves of that raised price, and that Great Britain, having no possible right to prevent them, but choosing (or at least her cruisers choosing) to interfere with their title, must make reparation equal to the damage *such as it was*.[165]

The financial results of such a legal precedent were not to be discussed. Much as some scholarship on the history of law regarded the legal sphere as a realm separate from politics and society, the US commissioners attempted to put pressure on the British commissioners by insinuating a negative response would be economically and politically motivated and insisting decisions be resolved according to the principles of the law of nations, aloft and away from national interests, much as Mansfield had insinuated.[166]

Surprisingly, the new method of compensation was agreed, although the captures made in consequence of the Orders in Council of April 1795 were exempted from the rule.[167]

Meanwhile, the secret order in council was so unpopular and misunderstood in America, that it added fuel to the dissatisfaction and public outrage already targeted at the Jay Treaty. Despite Bayard's presence in London and the creation of the commission, the Jay Treaty had at this point not yet been ratified by the Senate. The news made US opposition to the treaty reach the point at which both Washington and Hamilton accepted they should only ratify it on the condition that the order in council be revoked.[168] It was rescinded in September, as Bayard diligently reported.[169]

These case studies highlight the many dependencies that faced American claimants in the British prize system: US claimants were reliant on the goodwill of opposing parties at court and British legal staff from start to finish. Their vessels though in theory protected by a veil of neutrality, were bobbed along the waves of British military policy, sometimes left unharmed, sometimes sucked under and struck against the rocks of economic warfare. US claimants also needed to navigate the rules and agreements the British government had already established in cooperation with other nations. Whereas the American objective had been to deal with prize jurisdiction as a neutral player in a supranational framework of international law, the reality of cases

165 Ibid., pp. 4210–11.

166 Rose, 'Studying the Past', 118.

167 Moore, *History and digest Vol. IV*, vol. 212, p. 121.

168 Mayo and American Historical Association, *Instructions to British Ministers*, p. 88, footnote 37.

169 Bayard to Pickering, 10 September 1795; NARA*, Letters Received from Samuel Bayard – NAID: 1170268*, p. 56.

demonstrates how international entanglements were unavoidable in this field of law. Nevertheless, the 10% rule exemplifies how the United States was able to not just traverse but to overcome previously set precedents through binational agreements with Britain.

# 6

# “In Pursuit of a Shadow”: US Citizens, Prize Appeals and Vice-Admiralty Courts

Next to his responsibility for collecting and organising general claims in prize causes, Bayard was especially entrusted with working on US prize appeals. These appeals did not go to the High Court of Admiralty, but to its superior court, the High Court of Appeals for Prizes, a very different legal body from the first. Whereas the members of the High Court of Admiralty were chosen through a long process of legal training and specialised knowledge (embodied in the Doctors’ Commons microcosm), the members of the appeals court, known as the Lords Commissioners of Appeal (further referred to as the Lords of Appeal), did not require any legal training. Some of the Lords were eminent common law judges, but often, they were simply politicians, for the appeals court consisted of members of the Privy Council.[1] The president of the Privy Council was also president of the Lords of Appeal.[2] Four to six of the Lords of Appeal would meet up about once a week in the winter, generally from 12pm until 3pm, while in the summer they met less frequently and discussed several cases in a single session.[3] Whereas the American Federal Appeals Court would later go on to review its own cases, the final decree of the Lords of Appeal was just that: final. There does not seem to have been a single case in which it reviewed one of its own decisions.[4] The decrees they issued were simple and to the point. Most final judgments remain simple statements without explanation, declaring the what and not the why.[5]

Their distinction from the High Court of Admiralty was also reflected in their locality, with the Lords of Appeal meeting at a different law court, known as the Cockpit, in Westminster/Whitehall.[6] This once again clearly shows

1 Roscoe, *A History of the English Prize Court*, p. 37.

2 Moore, *Compensation for losses and damages Vol. IV*, International Adjudications Ancient and Modern, History and Documents, ed. by John Bassett Moore, vol. 4, p. 42.

3 Ibid., p. 40.

4 Bourguignon, *The First Federal Court*, vol. 122, p. 221.

5 TNA, HCA 45/19/9, fol. 163r.

6 This differentiation greatly aids in distinguishing Bayard’s fields work, cf.: 3 October 1795, “At Docts Coms – in the morning on business, at Change at noon”,

the proximity between the Lords of Appeal and political offices. Doctors' Commons in contrast was central, but not directly located in the heart of British rule and policy-making.

Usually, the Judge of the High Court of Admiralty, who was also a member of the Appeals Court, abstained from their cases as he had already made his views clear in the decrees he had issued. However, on occasion, he would also join as a Lord of Appeal in the Appellate Court. In these cases, the presence of the Judge was generally seen as a reason to uphold the decree. But most of the time the Lords of Appeal were left to their own devices. It was very rare for Judges to influence the decision through their physical presence.[7] Employing politicians (although many had trained at the bar themselves, though generally not in civil law) to review the work of trained civil law experts also had advantages for political activism. For Anglo-Spanish prize cases it has even been shown that British parties had been pressured into dropping appeals when the cases in question were seen as politically sensitive and could have led to diplomatic crises.[8]

Bayard found the constellation of the court a difficult one, revealing an extremely cautious and suspicious outlook on it from the very start of his work.[9] This outlook was strengthened, as he first noted how the Lords permitted only the King's Advocate to speak on behalf of the captors and forbade the claimants' party from being heard, instead demanding 'further proofs', which meant additional costs and waiting times.[10] About five months later, this practice was so usual that Bayard found it necessary to add that *both* sides were heard in a case.[11] Statements regarding the one-sided decisions of the Lords are found frequently throughout his diary.[12] His critical attitude quite quickly escalated into a consistently negative view of the institution, though Bayard did not refer to its political nature in his diary. He did not believe in the possibility of impartial justice due to the prize law staff, stating:

and 19 December 1795, "Attended Lords at the Cockpit"; Bayard, *Diary of Samuel Bayard*, pp. 42, 45.

7 Bourguignon, *Sir William Scott* (2009), p. 248.

8 Brinkman, *Balancing Strategy*, p. 224.

9 On one of his first visits to the Cockpit, he already notes "justice to claimants doubtful", 13 June 1795, Bayard, *Diary of Samuel Bayard*, p. 13.

10 20 February 1796; ibid., p. 57; The decree states in the regular form that both sides were heard; TNA, HCA 45/19/7: *Harriet* (Calder) fol. 134r.

11 16 July 1796; Bayard, *Diary of Samuel Bayard*, pp. 79–80.

12 For example, "case … of the Besty & Molly – the question whether there should be further proof – or sentence of condemnation affirmed – the Lords without hesitation adopted the latter – I never saw an instance of more direct partiality", 30 April 1796; ibid., p. 71.

> As these courts [High Court of Admiralty and the Appeals Court] are really *political*, *ministerial* and filled with characters not the most *independent* and *liberal* in sentiment, their decision will in all likelihood be found tempered with that *selfish* policy for which the Court of St. James has long been remarkable.[13]

Despite working for the commission and being subordinate to John Jay, Bayard himself was sure that the provisions agreed in the Jay Treaty were insufficient, writing: "in respect to the appeals under my care, they have absolutely deceived Mr. Jay as to the time in which the business would be finished, the expence attending it, and if *I* am not greatly deceived as to the *measure* of justice we shall ultimately experience."[14]

Bayard would go on to state:

> when it is known that he [Jay] has only secured the right of appeal and of eventual payment by the British government where a recovery fails as against the captors, and it is known what a length of time must probably elapse before the claimants can expect restitution, the expense that must be incurred, and at last the possibilities of being robbed of the whole by a contest between the two countries, there will be a broad foundation laid for dissatisfaction and complaint.[15]

He mainly justified this bleak outlook with the political nature of admiralty jurisdiction in Britain, which dominated judicial practice in his opinion.[16] As early as March 1795, Bayard commented that the Lords of Appeal's "judicial determinations are said often to be influenced by their political opinions".[17] So, Bayard followed a microcosmic strategy in the appeals cases, linking the decisions to the personalities of the Lords present. He noted down the members present in the Cockpit and which decisions they took (whether for or against American interests), which would give him some insight into the personalised mechanics of the court.[18] By July, Bayard could add his own experience to the circulated rumours:

> from what I have lately observed myself & from the best information I have been able to collect from others respecting the character and principles of those members of the privy Council who usually attend

13 Sterling, 'A Federalist Opposes the Jay Treaty', 414.

14 Ibid., p. 415.

15 Ibid., p. 423.

16 Ibid., p. 414.

17 14 March 1795, NARA, *Letters Received from Samuel Bayard – NAID: 1170268*, p. 18.

18 30 May 1795, Bayard, *Diary of Samuel Bayard*, p. 9.

> at the Cockpit, I do not draw the most flattering conclusions as to the fair and liberal extension of the principles of justice to american citizens, by this board.[19]

This impression seems to reflect political reality. Repeatedly, Bayard noted parallel developments between Anglo-American foreign policy and the success of his claims in the High Court of Admiralty and before the Lords of Appeal. At first, he phrased these as questions:

> A mysterious hesitancey in regard to hearing and deciding on the american appeals at the Cockpit- I have my fears that a cloud is Collecting there which nothing save the Resolute conduct of the Government of the U.S. will dissipate. Can the delay in Settling principles in cases from the U.S. arise from a wish to hear first of the ratification of the Treaty negotiated by Mr Jay?[20]

When the news of the Jay Treaty's ratification reached London, Bayard expressed his hope that "perhaps the Lords may in future proceed with greater expedition in the hearing and determination of the American cases".[21] Similarly, another dispatch linked the arrival of Mr Pinkney in London to "an auspicious influence on the business of the claims and appeals".[22] Bayard became certain that so long as politics in the United States were favourable to Britain, his work would be easier to conduct, happily reporting in February 1796: "I have hereby reason, at present to believe that we shall experience considerable aid in the amicable adjustment of our controversies with G.B. particularly in the settlement of the claims and appeals under my direction."[23]

About one year after the treaty had entered into force, he wrote in his diary that he had become aware of the fact that the commission had improved the chances of success for American citizens' claims in the other admiralty courts, labelling their sentences "a little more favourable than they would have been 6 months ago".[24]

Bayard was convinced that his work both in the High Court of Admiralty and the High Court of Appeals for Prizes, was linked to the Jay Treaty's London commission. Repeatedly he stressed that the political nature of the appeals court meant that American claimants had no chance to win there. In July 1795 he voiced: "I fear that after they have decided on our cases,

19 29 July 1795, NARA, *Letters Received from Samuel Bayard – NAID: 1170268*, p. 47.

20 11 July 1795, ibid., pp. 42–3.

21 29 July 1795, ibid., p. 46.

22 18 January 1796, ibid., p. 77.

23 3 February 1796, ibid., p. 83.

24 18 November 1796; Bayard, *Diary of Samuel Bayard*, p. 94.

the regard I owe to the interest of our citizens will oblige me to bring the greater part of these cases again before the commissioners contemplated in Mr Jay's Treaty."[25] A year later he reckoned: "we must seek that redress from a Board composed of persons from both nations, which we cannot fully obtain from a British Court of appeals."[26] By 1797, regarding the Martinique cases, he simply observed: "I fear there is little chance of our obtaining compensation thro[ugh] the medium of this [Appeals] Court."[27] Similarly, American merchants wrote that they had entered appeals in "little hopes of obtaining Justice".[28]

But this fear and irritation was at the same time a recurrent hope. Bayard's perception of the commission alternated between regarding it as the final, frustrating attempt at gaining compensation, and accepting it as the ultimate path to victory for his clients:

> It [the application of American claimants directly to the commission] would be the means of settling amicably and fairly points in which the national interest & prejudices of the present Court of Appeals will most probably so warp and perplex as to under negociation at last inevitably & it would I doubt not fully meet the wishes of our citizens and the approbation of all the liberal minds of the British Nation.[29]

Bayard thus started viewing the appeals court not as a true course to attain justice, but as a necessary step to move his cases on to the commission.

American cases made up a majority of all appeals cases between 1794 and 1804, reflecting the dominance of neutral US carriers in transatlantic trading. One way of examining American appeals' processes and the role that Bayard undertook with them, is by examining the HCA 45 series at the National Archives, London. These consist of various printed papers provided by the opposing parties in court for the use of the Lords Commissioners of Prize Appeals, including not only each side's legal arguments, but also appendices with pieces of evidence ranked according to importance for each case. They were bound together into volumes and have been digitised for researchers.[30] If we examine an overview of the HCA 45s, we can see that there were 1,144 printed appeals that came before the Lords of Appeal in the ten years studied.

25 29 July 1795, NARA, *Letters Received from Samuel Bayard – NAID: 1170268*, p. 47.

26 Bayard to Sec. State, 17 May 1796; ibid., p. 72.

27 28 February 1797, ibid., p. 170.

28 Ludlow to Randolph, 28 May 1795; NARA, *Box 8, British Spoliations – NAID: 1170270*.

29 Bayard to Sec. State, 29 July 1795; NARA, *Letters Received from Samuel Bayard – NAID: 1170268*, p. 52.

30 TNA, Catalogue Description HCA 45; Prize Papers Portal (2023).

Of these, 638 concerned American claimants or respondents, meaning nearly 56% of all appeals appear to be American.[31] However, this is not accurate, as there were also manuscript appeals, some of which were never printed and bound into volumes. These manuscript papers are in the HCA 42 series and contain a further 561 cases, of which 255 were American.[32] This gives us an estimate of about 38% of all appeals being American, still a clear majority. Not a single other country came close to prosecuting as many appeals before British jurisdiction.[33]

This does not necessarily mean that the United States was also the most frequently captured nation, such numbers are impossible to come by, as the records of not just the High Court of Admiralty, but all the global vice-admiralty courts would need to be assessed to derive the amount. But it does clearly show that a large volume of American vessels was captured and beyond that, it demonstrates how Americans had a strong interest in following up British prize jurisdiction in the appellate courts and considered the risks of appeals procedure tolerable. Indeed, Bayard considered it his personal and political mission to redress what he judged to be illegal decisions regularly made in the British prize courts. Bayard's work as "Agent appointed by the Government of the United States of America"[34] offered an opportunity, with government funds being used to fight cases of American citizens abroad. For claimants, it not only reduced the financial burden of appealing from what was considered an unjust sentence, it should also have reduced the amount of work, organisation and fear involved in the process.

The amount of appeals Bayard received was considerable. His diary contains regular entries of him swearing to large amounts of affidavits, as well as to receiving them in the first place.[35]

In addition to pending cases, the number of appeals in Bayard's care could also increase with every case British admiralty jurisdiction decided against American interests, both in London and abroad. Theoretically, every case could go on to appeal, but practically, there was no need to pursue cases with little chance of success. It "would only be throwing away money in pursuit of a shadow".[36] As Jay outlined in his strategy, those cases with only a small chance of succeeding in the superior court should be dropped by the

31 See table 10.

32 See table 11.

33 See table 12.

34 TNA, HCA 45/19/6: *Farmer* (Osborn) fol. 104r.

35 For example, 12, 18 and 22 May, 17 July and 30 September 1795, Bayard, *Diary of Samuel Bayard*, pp. 6, 7, 20, 34.

36 29 July 1795, NARA, *Letters Received from Samuel Bayard – NAID: 1170268*, pp. 50–1.

government due to the costs an appeal case incurred, instead prioritising cases that were likely to win and have a strong impact on precedent.[37]

Bayard took careful notes on the decisions made by the Lords of Appeal in the Cockpit. For example, in the case of the *Sally* (Hayes) Bayard remarked "this sentence holds out a premium for captors",[38] recognising the impact a single case could have as a precedent to other cases. In general, Bayard attempted to only attend if American cases were to come before the Lords, though this often did not work out, as US cases were regularly postponed at short notice once Bayard had already arrived.[39] Bayard also paid attention to other non-American cases that seemed to have a significant bearing on precedent and passed on the information gained from them.[40]

Of the printed appeals, Bayard acted on behalf of one or several American citizens as an appellant or respondent party in 237 cases. At least every third case went through Bayard's hands (37.1%).[41] His involvement in the manuscript appeals is currently unclear. When the banking company Bird, Savage & Bird spoke up in support for Bayard by offering a suitable financial arrangement, they specifically referred to the necessity of possessing funds to prosecute American appeals cases from the vice-admiralty courts.[42] A small government list of American cases concerned in restitution and reversals of decrees was issued by the Department of State in February 1798. In it, 66.7% of all cases listed were condemned in the vice-admiralty courts; however, Timothy Pickering himself admitted that his department had not systematically collected the data and was lacking cases.[43] If we examine Bayard's appeal cases, 96.8% came from vice-admiralty courts. He represented only five appeals cases that originated from the High Court of Admiralty, as opposed to the vice-admiralty courts overseas.[44] This appears extraordinarily high. Examining non-printed manuscript and printed American appeals together (almost 900 cases) still shows that less than 8% of US appeals originated from the High Court of Admiralty in London. This is not representative of the international experience, with the overall appeals from 1794 to 1804 showing that *c.* 14.7% of all cases originated from the High Court of Admiralty, when

37 Jay, *Letter to Samuel Bayard, 5 January 1795.*

38 16 April 1796, Bayard, *Diary of Samuel Bayard*, p. 66.

39 20 June 1795 and 23 February 1796, ibid., pp. 15, 57.

40 For example, 28 November 1795; ibid., p. 41.

41 See table 10.

42 *The Debates and Proceedings in the Congress of the United States with an Appendix containing Important State Papers and Public Documents, and all the Laws of Public Nature with a Copious Index*, p. 2484.

43 Lowrie and St Claire Clarke (eds), *Class I – Foreign Relations*, vol. 2, pp. 122–3.

44 See table 10.

we include other nations aside from the United States.[45] Maybe simply not as many American vessels were adjudicated in London, meaning there was less need for action. Otherwise, one can hypothesise that the High Court was more lenient towards American claimants than to other nations, or that American claimants were more wary of appealing from the London court. No definitive answer can be given here.

Either way, the vice-admiralty courts clearly were the focus of American appellate action. The Vice-Admiralty Courts of Jamaica, Bermuda and the Bahamas made up more than half of all American appeals and were among the five most appealed courts for international claimants too.[46] When we examine the percentage of American cases taken on by Bayard, his involvement varied exceedingly depending on the court's location, ranging from 0% (for example, in the Vice-Admiralty Court of Gibraltar) to 85.4% in the Vice-Admiralty Court of Dominica.[47]

From the end of the seventeenth century, official vice-admiralty courts had been set up throughout North America as part of colonial, imperial policy.[48] These additional courts aided merchants on several fronts; privateers were supposed to bring captured vessels to the nearest vice-admiralty court, saving time and money for merchants/captains, should their vessel be proven innocent. However, they did not always do this. Partially, because certain vice-admiralty courts had a bad reputation and were avoided despite the risk of ignoring this order.[49] But sometimes also, because captors might not wish to lose time and would rather, for example, use good winds to steer them in the direction of their next planned destination.[50] In 1795 Nelson wrote to his agents in Livorno asking whether it was truly necessary to send certain papers to London or whether prize jurisdiction could not be solved much faster in vice-admiralty courts.[51] Some Captors also had agents to represent them in particular ports, adding to these motives of selecting a specific vice-admiralty court as opposed to simply accessing the nearest one. In response, some ship owners and merchants also established networks of legal counsels in different ports for their legal defence.[52]

It was the lack of transparency that upset swathes of the US maritime community. Many American seamen wrote to the State Department with resembling experiences. The *Betsey* (Buckley) was taken over by a prize master

45 See table 12.
46 See tables 10–12.
47 See table 10.
48 Mangone, *United States Admiralty Law*, p. 26.
49 Hill, *The Prizes of War*, p. 98.
50 Ibid., pp. 99–100.
51 Ibid., p. 212.
52 TNA, HCA 45/18/9: *Betsey* (Furlong) fol. 259v.

and brought into Jamaica. The original captain wrote home to his employers, lamenting "the cause of her detention as yet I know not".[53] In his opinion, foreign diplomacy, specifically negotiations between France and the United States, had given British cruisers cause to capture every American vessel of value in a maritime expression of diplomatic revenge. Despite employing an attorney on the island, Buckley had still been unable to ascertain why his vessel had been libelled several days later and was thus unable to write a protest.[54]Another example is the case of the *Charlotte*, in which British captors refused to inform the crew why they had been captured and what was to be done with them.[55]

Other regular complaints were about delays and detainments in vice-admiralty courts, alongside corruption.[56] A correspondent to the Secretary of State highlighted:

> As my Sufferings in the case of the John & Jos. has been very heavy (upwards of £300 Stg.) owing to 111 days detention, plunder and distruction of the vessel, […] I shall be much Obliged, by your promoting as early a determination of the above case and compensation as possible.[57]

Captain Lore, who was detained with his vessel for five weeks in Kingston, not only lost two out of three crew members on the voyage to Jamaica, but described his distress seeing "the Vessel without care left to the weather, her loocks were soon injured by the Sun, which in few days admitted every Rain that fell upon them to the injury of the Cargo".[58]

In his capture by the Royal Navy frigate *Penelope*, Joshua Barney described very similar scenes:

> My ship has been libeld and unloaded, the cargo stored, and no trial granted altho here upwards of two months, I am not suffered, nor any person for me to go on board my ship, to take any care of her or the Cargo […] indeed Sir it is impossible to describe the distress

53 Buckley to Phelps and Sandford, 20 January 1801; NARA, *Box 1, British Spoliations – NAID: 1170270.*

54 Buckley to Phelps and Sandford, 23 January 1801; ibid.

55 For example, Brothers Coster & Co. to Pickering, 19 July 1799; ibid.

56 Similar issues were also communicated about French vice-admiralty courts, though these are harder for historians to trace as they often left no legal records or only rare, complex, fragmented ones. Williams, *French Assault on US Shipping*, p. 4.

57 Truxtun to Pickering, 16 October 1796; NARA, *Box 3, British Spoliations – NAID: 1170270.*

58 Lore to Pickering, 15 May 1797; NARA, *Box 6, Ships S–W; British Spoliations, ca. 1796–ca. 1824 – NAID: 1170270.*

> [...], at this moment before my eyes, the Cargoes are thrown upon the wharves, the vessels without any person to take care of them, and the Worm is so destructive here that a ship is rendered useless in three months, add to all this the enormous expences attending Admiralty suits [...] exclusive of the loss America sustains by having her seamen taken from her.[59]

Indeed, the Vice-Admiralty Court system was considered so corrupt by some US merchants that they took great care to avoid it. One captain wrote home to his employers that he was given the:

> choice either to have the vessel libelled or to deliver the 13 Casks Nails, and proceed on my voyage. I applied to several Gentlemen, particularly Mr. Armstrong who advised me to deliver them up, as he said there was no hope of recovering for the expences of carrying on the Suit, would be more than the nails were worth besides the detention of the Brig.[60]

In the end, the costs were still over $100, and his correspondence was forwarded to the State Department.

Thomas Lynch described how he attempted to use public pressure to influence a British government official to drop prize charges against the American vessel *Eliza* at Barbados, which at first seemed to succeed. In the end, the man in question had instead proposed dropping the charges in exchange for a sum of money. Lynch advised the ship owners to take up the offer, as he was certain this would still be considerably less costly than a court case.[61] While corruption was thus tolerated, even encouraged, it still entered the political radar of US officials.

One of the categories in which compensation was frequently asked for was also the case of vessels detained but then released without further trial. Such stratagems caused damages mainly through negligence, as the vessels could no longer be treated to cope with the elements and often large parts of the cargo would be spoilt due to exposure to water. At least twenty-one American vessels were brought into Nassau, detained and then released according to government files.[62]

59 Barney to Jefferson, 17 February 1794; NARA, *Box 10, British Spoliations – NAID: 1170270.*

60 Hudson to Gibbs and Channing, 26 December 1798; NARA, *Box 4, British Spoliations – NAID: 1170270.*

61 Lynch to illegible, 25 May 1794; NARA, Box 2, *British Spoliations – NAID: 1170270.*

62 List of US vessels brought into Nassau and illegally detained; NARA, *Box 10, British Spoliations – NAID: 1170270.*

Whereas the lack of transparency immediately influenced the crews of vessels, it also affected ship owners, merchants with cargo on board, underwriters and insurance companies, and many more. However, the work of the commission and Bayard's new position as agent offered some relief. Lore closed his letter on an upbeat tone, stating, "But now Sir I'm informed the United States has an Agent at London for such business" and asking for government aid.

Explicit negative references were identified in letters concerning the Vice-Admiralty Courts of Bermuda and Jamaica.

The Vice-Admiralty Court of Jamaica was described as "an infernal hole"[63] by the American captain of the *Betsey*. The owners of the *Three Brothers* barely believed: "the Injuries and grievances we have suffered from those Robbers, Pirates and thieves of Bermuda – the Villany of their Judge appears so obvious in every part of the trial that it is needless for us to comment on it."[64]

And Robert Oliver went on to state that the Jamaican Judge based his decrees on "no principal of justice and unless some steps are taken to put astop to them infamous proceedings, the wil will [*sic*] increase. Our trading People are sensibly alarmed."[65]

Even some British citizens apologised, admitting that: "The number of American Vessels & Cargoes Condemned in this [Bermudan] Court of Admiralty is great. It would give us much Satisfaction if we could say at the present that there was any apparent disposition to discontinue such practices."[66]

Indeed, a look at printed and manuscript appeals shows that in the time frame of Jay's Treaty and the commission's work, 207 American cases were appealed from Jamaica. Internationally, 270 cases were brought before the Lords of Appeal. This means, that Americans constituted 43.4% of all Jamaican appeals cases. In the Bahamas, Bermuda, Dominica, Saint Domingue as well as the British North American courts in Nova Scotia and Newfoundland, they made up more than half of all cases.

When examining Bayard's work on appeals, we also come across cases from the Antigua, Barbados, Grenada, Jamaica, Martinique, Montserrat, Nevis, Nova Scotia, St Kitts, St Vincent, Tobago and Tortola.[67] The West Indies were clearly the dominant force here, both in terms of the amount of vice-admiralty

63 Buckley to Phelps and Sandford, 20 January 1801; NARA, *Box 1, British Spoliations – NAID: 1170270*.

64 Hallam to Wolcot, July 1796; NARA, *Box 7, British Spoliations – NAID: 1170270*.

65 Oliver to unknown, 5 September 1799; NARA, *Box 10, British Spoliations – NAID: 1170270*.

66 Ellinston and Perot to Randolph, 1 November 1794; ibid.

67 See table 10.

courts located there and their caseloads.[68] This is in line with the important dual economic function the Caribbean fulfilled, as a major component of American trade on the one hand – between 1790 and 1814, one-third of all American exports can be attributed to the West Indies trade – and as a centre for British economic warfare on the other.[69] Brinkman has demonstrated how the Caribbean was already identified as key strategic point in the Seven Years' War.[70] Jarvis has convincingly argued that Bermuda exhibited "geographical centrality"[71] to British America, with weather patterns and the Gulf stream leading most sailing vessels from the Caribbean past the island. Bayard took on more than sixty cases from this small British colony in the North Atlantic.[72] The court staff in Bermuda generally overlapped with those of the governor and the island's council, so there were no specialist admiralty lawyers present.[73] In 1780 the new governor of Bermuda, George Junior Bruere, politically cleansed the court, making way for speedy condemnations, which would continue throughout Bermuda's history.[74] In the 1790s, Bermudan Vice-Admiralty Judge John Green had such a reputation that a Boston newspaper decreed: "Such is the venality and wickedness of Green [...] that everything of value is sure to be condemned, so great is the partiality of the said judge"[75] and went on to state that American cargoes had been condemned against all international principles of the law of nations. Sadly, only patchy documentation of the Vice-Admiralty Court of Bermuda exists; however, for the period 1794 to 1804 we can see from the Appeals Court records that ninety appeals cases from Bermuda were examined. Of these all but four of the original rulings were overturned.[76]

68 See table 12.

69 This figure includes US exports to European colonies in South America; however, as Coatsworth's graph demonstrates, these are negligible for the early 1790s, see J. H. Coatsworth, 'American Trade with European Colonies in the Caribbean and South America, 1790–1812', *William and Mary Quarterly*, 24 (1967), pp. 243–66, at 243, 266.

70 Brinkman, *Balancing Strategy*, p. 34.

71 M. J. Jarvis, *In the eye of all trade: Bermuda, Bermudians, and the maritime Atlantic world, 1680–1783, Published for the Omohundro Institute of Early American History and Culture, Williamsburg, Virginia* (Chapel Hill NC, 2010), p. 3.

72 See table 10.

73 H. J. Crump, *Colonial Admiralty Jurisdiction in the Seventeenth Century* (London, 1931), vol. 5, pp. 81–2, 90.

74 Jarvis, *In the Eye of all Trade*, pp. 428–9. Between 1812 and 1813, notes of a prize agent on the island depict a 75% condemnation rate; Royal Museums Greenwich, HUL/7, Hulbert, George Redmond, Naval Agent, 1774–1825.

75 'Bermuda Homes with American Connections: Verdmont Interior', *Bermuda Historical Quarterly*, 25–7 (1968), at 19.

76 See table 10.

The bad reputation of the Bermudan court must have been well known among all legal professionals dealing with prize. A watershed moment for the commission and Bayard's work in it, came with the case of the *Betsey* (Furlong). She had been captured on 20 March 1794 and brought into the island's admiralty court by the British privateer *Agenoria* (Morgan).[77] In the heated debates on the case, commissioner Pinkney would state:

> The sentence of the vice admiralty of Bermudas, founded upon a ridiculous falsehood abandoned by everybody, is no evidence of anything but the folly of the judge who passed it. The sentence of the lords is that of a tribunal respectable in the highest degree for talents, integrity, and station; but even the commissioner who recommends it to us, as conclusive proof of *probable cause*, confesses that it was an *erroneous sentence*, inasmuch as it condemned the property of *William* Patterson as well as that of George Patterson.[78]

There were many vice-admiralty courts in the British Empire and a significant number in the West Indies. Despite the appeals court in London clearly having the higher and more central authority, it was internationally apparent that the British court system was not as strictly controlled as the government would have liked. Yet precisely this perception may have been a key component of British strategy.

In part, vice-admiralty courts could only loosely follow the rulings of the High Court of Admiralty, because barely any materials from that court or the Lords of Appeal were published.[79] Therefore, it was difficult for the vice-admiralty to stick to the precedents their decisions should have provided. Much as American parties at court were attempting to understand the system in order to partake in it to their advantage, the vice-admiralty courts were not informed of the decisions made by the Lords of Appeal or the High Court of Admiralty due to the secretive nature of Doctors' Commons. In this form, the limbs of British admiralty jurisdiction were unaware of what the head was doing, creating a jumbled and disjointed pattern of what was supposed to be a uniform body of international law.

British admiralty jurists and politicians alike could use the alleged misconduct of vice-admiralty judges as an alibi for illegal condemnations.

Lord Grenville clearly stated to John Jay relating:

> to the Admiralty Courts in the West Indies, which it is in contemplation immediately to diminish in point of number so as to have them only at Jamaica, Barbados, Grenada, Antigua, and Martinique. Knowing

77 TNA, HCA 45/19/9, fol. 253r.

78 Moore, *History and digest Vol. III*, vol. 212, pp. 3205–6.

79 Petrie, *The Prize Game*, pp. 130–1.

> as I do how much evil has been produced by the multiplication of these Courts I look to this reduction with very sanguine hopes. But I hope the regulation will not stop there, but that the effect of it may lead to render the practice of those which still remain, more correct and cautious than I fear it has hitherto been.[80]

As the Vice-Admiralty Court of Martinique had not even been legally set up, Grenville's statement rings even more true in retrospect than it would have at the time. The Duke of Portland pointed out to the Lords Commissioners of the Admiralty on 30 March 1801 that in a specific case: "the sentence of the Vice Admiralty Court is erroneous, and founded in a misapprehension and misapplication of the principles laid down in the decision of the High Court of Admiralty."[81] The way to prevent such cases from reoccurring was to issue more precise instructions "for their future guidance and direction".[82] In this manner, courts abroad were seen in an almost child-like manner, whose decisions stemmed from innocent misguidance, to be adapted for the better through leadership, control and aid, instead of facing reprimands and personal consequences.[83]

By promising that they were working to improve the weaknesses of the global British prize system, British politicians could attempt to pacify foreign governments. Illegal condemnations were portrayed as individual failings or put down to failed communication. That claimants could bring their case before the Appeals Court for correction was seen as a conciliatory measure, simultaneously disregarding the costs to individual merchants or ship owners.[84] At the same time, political promises need not actually be followed up. There would be no reduction of Admiralty Courts. In fact, additional courts would be created along-side British colonial expansion when considered necessary.[85]

80 Lord Grenville to John Jay, 11 May 1795; Johnston, *Correspondence and Public Papers of John Jay*, p. 139.

81 W. Lowrie and M. St Clair Clarke, *Foreign Relations: Class I, Vol II, American State Papers Documents, legislative and executive, of the Congress of the United States* (Washington DC, 1832), vols 1 and 2, p. 491.

82 Ibid.

83 Delving deeper into letters written by the Duke of Portland underscores this argument. His reasoning for informing the judges in the colonies that "the principle […] lately adopted in the Courts of Vice Admiralty […] is in direct opposition to the decisions daily passing in the High Court of Admiralty and the Court of Appeal" was not to correct the course of justice. Actually, it was merely "to put a stop to the inconveniences arising from these erroneous sentences". Lowrie and St Claire Clarke (eds), *Class I – Foreign Relations*, vol. 2, p. 491.

84 Sterling, 'A Federalist Opposes the Jay treaty', 416.

85 For example, the vice-admiralty court at Freetown, Sierra Leone was founded in 1808; T. Helfman, 'The Court of Vice Admiralty at Sierra Leone and the Abolition of the West African Slave Trade', *Yale Law Journal*, 115 (2006), 1122–56, at 1143.

This trope of the uncontrolled vice-admiralty jurisdiction far from London was hence employed by British and American politicians and legal professionals. However, it made up a backbone of the US strategy in strengthening American cases under Article VII of the Jay Treaty commission.

For example, in the case of the *Farmer* (Obsborne), the vessel had been condemned in the Vice-Admiralty Court of Jamaica, went to the London Appeal's court, lost, and then applied to the commission. The American master of the vessel had hidden papers inside a barrel of coffee that proved a significant part of the cargo belonged to a French merchant and was being shipped on his behalf.[86] The papers were discovered and all the cargo condemned except for two ventures.[87] Bayard represented the case on behalf of the claimants in the Appeals court.[88] In his diary he referred explicitly to receiving preparations of the case from Mr Kurnan, proctor Slade's assistant.[89] He also recorded a further discussion of the case with Dr Nicholl.[90] Nevertheless, Bayard's attempt to have the property which had not been French restored, was for the most part unsuccessful. The Lords of Appeal only restored the master's small, private venture.[91]

Bayard was displeased with the result of an American case at the appeals court. He noted down how the case was "I think very unjustly"[92] (note the phrasing) condemned. In response, he wrote to the owners, stating:

> as I take this sentence to be contrary to 'justice and the law of nations' I would advise [... for the case to be] laid before the commission under the treaty [...] You may then probably obtain restitution of your property and of the charges you have been put to in pursuit of it.[93]

He then outlined how to obtain further evidence to aid in their success before the commission. Although the case itself is not considered one of the key cases of the commission, it gives great insights into the relationship between the Lords of Appeal and the British vice-admiralty court system.

The American commissioners used the bad reputation of vice-admiralty courts to strengthen their own position. Commissioner Pinkney merely pointed

86 The master deposed that they had merely been deposited in the coffee for safe keeping. TNA, HCA 45/19/6, 106v.

87 Ibid., fol. 122r, 107r.

88 Ibid., fol. 104r.

89 13 January 1796, Bayard, *Diary of Samuel Bayard*, p. 47; Bayard, *Letter to John Jay, 27 January 1795.*

90 15 January 1796; Bayard, *Diary of Samuel Bayard*, p. 48.

91 TNA, HCA 45/19/6, fol. 108r.

92 20 February 1796; Bayard, *Diary of Samuel Bayard*, p. 57.

93 Bayard to Adam and Mendenhall, 29 February 1796; NARA, *Box 2, British Spoliations – NAID: 1170270.*

out that the claimants should be entitled to compensation as the "vice admiralty ought to have restored [...] instead of condemning".[94] But such lines of argument could be dangerously misinterpreted, as they did not explain how the Lords of Appeal in London could have agreed to uphold such a decree and thus implicated them in misconduct. Commissioner Trumbull supplied the solution by insisting that the case must have been misrepresented in front of the Lords of Appeal, as clearly "the court of vice admiralty proceeded on [...] imperfect grounds to condemn and confiscate. To my mind this condemnation appears to have been in manifest contradiction to the above rule of admiralty proceedings, and justice".[95]

John Jay displayed this strategy beautifully in a letter written to Commissioner Trumbull on 27 October 1797:

> The delays of the court of admiralty do not surprise me. I have no faith in any British court of admiralty, though I have the greatest respect for, and the highest confidence in their courts of justice, in the number of which, those courts do not deserve to be ranked. I do not extend this stricture to the lords of appeal.[96]

In this way, the commissioners attempted to discredit vice-admiralty court decrees without implicating the microcosms of Doctors' Commons or the Appeals Court in any misconduct or misjudgement.

Even when Bayard successfully gained compensation for American claimants in the appeals court, he was often dissatisfied with the results. Bayard viewed the court as a political body and aside from correlations and political entanglements of its members, the results sometimes also subtly reflected this attitude regarding maritime law. When Bayard prepared the cases of the *Farmer* (Osbourne), the *Harriet* (Calder) and the *Nancy* (Florence), he was hoping to gain a clear precedent on the legality of US trade with the French West Indies. However, the court avoided issuing such a precedent, simply voting in favour of the American claimants, but "[they] do not intend making a question respecting this trade, but will for the present suffer it to pass without argument in our favour."[97] Bayard did not rejoice in the single victories of the individuals he was representing, as was already shown in the case of the *Relief* (Cole). He instead desired precedents that seemed to

[94] Moore, *Compensation for losses and damages Vol. IV*, International Adjudications Ancient and Modern, History and Documents, ed. by John Bassett Moore, Vol. 4, p. 355.

[95] Ibid., p. 366.

[96] Johnston, *Correspondence and Public Papers of John Jay*, p. 188.

[97] 29 February 1796, NARA, *Letters Received from Samuel Bayard – NAID: 1170268*, p. 98.

acknowledge the maritime rights of US citizens. This is encapsulated by his reaction in May 1796, when the Lords of Appeal announced that all seizures made under the later revoked British Orders-in-Council of 6 November 1793, were of questionable legality; that is, had good chances of being overturned in the appeals court. Bayard railed at the fact that the court stated the order had been revoked "from a Spirit of concession to America, it did not follow that the first orders were contrary to the law of nations".[98] The principles behind the decision were more important to him than the practicalities of the Lords' statement.

This highlights the different position Bayard, as US agent, was in compared to private agents and their clients, who surely would have rejoiced at individual wins as opposed to fuming over missing principles. Bayard only represented 37.1% of all American cases before the appeals court, though he certainly aided in more cases than the dataset captures here.[99] This reflects how many US citizens still relied on private representation, networks and finances to follow up their cases in appellate court, though it is hard to judge how business was conducted in the High Court of Admiralty, where a general overview of all cases has yet to be compiled.

In general, a clear distinction must be drawn between the legal body of the British appeals court and its lower court in London, the High Court of Admiralty. The Lords of Appeal were politicians, as opposed to maritime legalists, and their perception as a political body is understandable. The fact that neither the High Court nor the appeals court had published decrees in the 1790s reinforced this perception, with opaque decisions making the judicial principles hard to follow. Nevertheless, the American commissioners maintained at least public regard for this British institution, instead deflecting their anger and criticism toward the vice-admiralty courts that were dotted throughout the British Empire. Americans were particularly affected by those located in the West Indies, with each court having an individual reputation depending on location and staff.

Criticism of the vice-admiralty courts was wide-reaching, voiced by politicians and merchants alike, centring on a lack of competency alongside allegations of corruption. The lack of publications issued by the appeals court made it hard for vice-admiralty courts to grasp and follow precedents, but also provided the British politicians seated in the appeals court and the halls of

98 17 May 1796, ibid., p. 70.

99 That Bayard aided in other cases where he was not officially sworn in, but still acted as an advisor or mediator to the American party involved, becomes clear from other sources. He is not always tangible or traceable in the HCA 45 court records, which is why it would be impossible to compile a complete list of all his court activities through this source alone. However, as a base, the data provided by HCA 45 is enough to give an overall impression of his work at the appeals court.

parliament with easy answers to decisions that neutrals took offence at. A lack of knowledge could be seen as a flaw by ill-treated claimants, but it also provided a defence strategy in British prize jurisdiction.

Examinations of the total appeals cases show the vice-admiralty court decrees accounted for roughly nine out of ten cases that came before the appeals court, proving that this phenomenon was not purely American (where these decrees accounted for 92.6% of appeals cases), but a general reality faced by many international claimants in British prize courts.[100]

Claimants knew appeals procedures were expensive, time-consuming and prone to unfavourable outcomes. The extent of American appeals should therefore be attributed to the governmental funds provided in the prosecution of cases here, which probably is why the US was the most frequent petitioner of the court from 1793 and 1804. This need for financial as well as legal assistance is reflected in the quick acceptance of the government agent. It is astonishing that Bayard was already representing nearly 40% of all US cases, despite the position being in its infancy and not even officially acknowledged by Congress, still adrift in a legal grey zone. It was the initiative of the US government that provided American claimants with the vehicles to chase their rights through the British lawcourts. In addition, prosecuting cases before the appellate court was a necessary step if claimants wanted to bring their case before the binational arbitration committee established under Article VII of the Jay Treaty. One may therefore speculate that the prominence of American appeals at this time went hand in hand with Jay's Treaty. US claims must therefore be seen as at the very least a byproduct, maybe even as an intentional component, of American foreign policy.

[100] See table 10.

# 7

# Finding Common Ground: The London Commission of the Jay Treaty

Bayard had vested many of his hopes in the commission of the Jay Treaty's London commission. In Article VII, the Jay Treaty specified that five commissioners were to meet in London for eighteen months to discern and evaluate: "Complaints […] made by divers Merchants and others, Citizens of the United States, that during the course of the War in which His Majesty is now engaged they have sustained considerable losses and damage by reason of irregular or illegal Captures or Condemnations of their vessels."[1]

The aim of this commission was to agree on and pay out an "adequate Compensation"[2] to such merchants, to be covered by the British (or American) government. This systematic and formalised arbitration was new, introducing what has been termed as "the modern era of arbitral or judicial settlement of international disputes".[3]

For the London commission, American commissioners Christopher Gore and William Pinckney were 'mixed' with British commissioners, Dr Nicholl (who later resigned to take on the position of King's Advocate and was replaced by Maurice Swabey) and John Anstey.[4] Therefore, the commission "consisted chiefly of lawyers with a wide cultural background".[5] Gore had studied law under John Lowell, a judge on the US Court of Appeals in Cases of Capture – the first federal US court and incidentally a law court that dealt in prize.[6] William Pinkney, not to be confused with Thomas Pinckney the US Minister to Great Britain until 1796, had studied law under Samuel Chase,

1 *Treaty of amity, commerce, and navigation, between His Britannick Majesty and the United States of America*, Article 7.

2 Ibid., Article 7.

3 J. H. Ralston, *International Arbitration from Athens to Locarno* [Nachdr. d. Ausg. Stanford 1929] (Clark NJ, 2004), p. 191.

4 Lillich, 'The Jay Treaty Commissions', 277, fn 68; Schwarzenberger, 'Present-Day Relevance of the Jay Treaty Arbitrations', 722.

5 Schwarzenberger, 'Present-Day Relevance of the Jay Treaty Arbitrations', 721.

6 F. W. P. Greenwood, *Funeral Sermon [on Rev. xx. 6] on the late Hon. C. Gore: formerly Governor of Massachusetts., Preached at King's Chapel, Boston* (Boston MA, 1827), p. 9; E. Everett, *A memoir of Mr. John Lowell, jun. delivered as the introduction*

one of the first judges on the Supreme Court.[7] Dr Nicholl has already been introduced in Chapter 4. He was a set member of Doctors' Commons, who was on amicable terms with Bayard. John Anstey was already personally known in the United States. He was a trained barrister and a member of parliament, who had previously been tasked with the "Authority to verify the Claims of the Loyalists, as they call themselves"[8] on behalf of the British government. It was laid out that the fifth member of the commission was to be randomly drawn by lot, should the two parties/nations be unable to agree upon a common nominee.[9] To select the fifth commissioner, the American and British commissioners each proposed a list of eight candidates to the other side. As they could not agree on a candidate through this method, they then selected a name from the list provided by the other nation's commissioners. Gore and Pinkney chose Maurice Swabey, Nicholl and Anstey selected John Trumbull. The names were "deposited in an urn […] and […] Mr. Pinkney, […] drew out the name".[10] The lucky candidate to be drawn was the American John Trumbull. Considered the "most colorful member of the Commission"[11] by Schwarzenberger, Trumbull is mainly remembered for his work as an artist, in which capacity he painted portraits not only of Washington and Hamilton, but also of Rufus King, John Jay and William Bayard Jr.[12]

*to the lectures on his foundation, in the Odeon, thirty-first of December, 1839* (Boston MA, 1840), p. 11; Bourguignon, *The First Federal Court*, vol. 122.

7 H. Wheaton, 'Life of William Pinkney', in J. Sparks, H. Wheaton, E. T. Channing and W. B. O. Peabody (eds), *Lives of William Pinkney, William Ellery and Cotton Mather* (Boston MA and London, 1836), pp. 1–84, at p. 5.

8 John Adams to John Jay, 26 January 1796, quoted in Giunta, *The Emerging Nation*, vol. 3, p. 75.

9 *Treaty of amity, commerce, and navigation, between His Britannick Majesty and the United States of America*, Articles 6 and 7.

10 J. B. Moore, *History and digest of the international arbitrations to which the United States has been a party: Vol I, The Miscellaneous Documents of the House of Representatives, 1893–94* (Washington DC, 1898), vol. 212, pp. 320–1.

11 Schwarzenberger, 'Present-Day Relevance of the Jay Treaty Arbitrations', 722.

12 The Metropolitan Museum of Art (Met), *George Washington and William Lee, 1780*, www.metmuseum.org/art/collection/search/12822 (accessed 17 January 2021); Met, *Alexander Hamilton, 1792*, www.metmuseum.org/art/collection/search/20893 (accessed 17 January 2021); Yale University Art Gallery, *Artist: John Trumbull, Subject: Rufus King, 1792*, https://artgallery.yale.edu/collections/objects/70 (accessed 17 January 2021); John Jay Homestead, *John Jay by John Trumbull, 1793*, http://johnjayhomestead.org/collections/fine-art/john-jay-by-john-trumbull/ (accessed 17 January 2021); New York Historical Society, William Bayard: Gallery of Peers, in Exhibition 'Alexander Hamilton: The Man Who Made Modern America', www.alexanderhamiltonexhibition.org/gallery/bayard_w.html (accessed 17 August 2023).

In addition to the commissioners, further actors from Doctors' Commons and beyond were involved. Both national parties selected an agent to deal with the 'nitty-gritty' of everyday judicial practice. The British one was Nathaniel Gostling, the American Samuel Bayard (later succeeded by Samuel Williams who in turn was succeeded by Samuel Cabot).[13] In the archives, they would be preserved as antagonists, with Bayard filing a plethora of memorials on behalf of American claimants, and his papers being archived alongside an equal amount of protests, denying those claims, filed by Gostling.[14] Yet, at the end of the day, they were both merely national representatives attempting to strengthen their governments' foreign policies.

Before the commissioners had even agreed to draw their fifth member by lot, Bayard had already taken up his position as a government agent fighting for American citizens in the High Court of Admiralty and in its appeals court. As part of this process, he had established connections that would also benefit the commission and its work. The success of the commission must therefore be seen within the context of the Doctors' Commons microcosm, and the interlocking activities of Bayard's mission, in which he laid the groundwork for the commissioners. He was aided and assisted by the counsel of Sir William Scott and Dr Nicholl, as well as by the proctors, clerks, register, and others. Much like Scott, despite not being a commissioner, his contributions were instrumental in the implementation and success of Article VII.

Bayard's wife, Martha, enjoyed spending time with the commissioners and their wives, but appears to have taken little interest in her husband's work.[15] Samuel Bayard described their joint dinners, observing "such parties often will be agreeable – some at parties are insufferable".[16] In this regard, the situation in which the commission was placed seems unique: The Doctors' Commons microcosm created a tight-knit community that interacted on both a social/familial, political and professional level, and the American legal professionals were at least partially integrated into this British network.

This community may have played a part in the achievements of the London commission. Despite initial setbacks, it was the only one of the Jay Treaty's three commissions that can be considered a success in judicial arbitration; the commission concerning the Mississippi River (Article IV) barely met and finally came to an agreement through political negotiation rather than judicial rulings.[17] The second commission (Article VI), considering Americans'

13 *Register of the department of state in four parts: Corrected to March 1. 1874* (Washington DC, 1874), p. 126.

14 This can be beautifully observed in NARA, *Box 2, General Records – NAID: 1170269*.

15 Bayard, *Journal of Martha Bayard*, p. 117.

16 23 August 1796, Bayard, *Diary of Samuel Bayard*, p. 85.

17 Lillich, 'The Jay Treaty Commissions', 267.

debts to British creditors, swiftly came to a deadlock. Unlike in the London commission of Article VII, the fifth commissioner here had been a British man, tilting the group in favour of Great Britain with three British and two American commissioners.[18] As the majority, this British group decided to push national interests as far as possible, attempting to not simply repay the debts due, but also to include interest on all the debt owed by American citizens.[19] In response, the US commissioners no longer attended meetings, as the British majority could overrule them on such occasions.[20] Due to the treaty requirement of at least one commissioner from either party having to be present, no decisions could be made against US interests – or indeed against British interests – without the American commissioners' presence.[21] The commission could no longer function at all.

A stalemate resulted, which was finally resolved through a political negotiation spearheaded by Rufus King instead of the mixed commission.[22] Until a lump sum settlement had been negotiated, the British withdrew their commissioners from the London commission in retaliation for American lack of cooperation in the Philadelphia commission.[23] This is why the original eighteen-month time frame set out for the commission and its accompanying position of agent in disputed prize cases was vastly overstepped.[24] In the end, the commission lasted roughly eight years, from 16 August 1796 to 24 February 1804, and required three American agents.[25] Indeed, the various Jay Treaty commissions had been intertwined from their very conception, with letters sent from Lord Grenville to Jay remarking:

> Mr. Gore delivered to me [...] your letter of introduction. He seems a sensible and moderate man [...] I think he and his colleague will be well satisfied with the colleague which has been made here for that commission [...] If I do not deceive myself, the choice of the commissioners who are going to America will not be less satisfactory.[26]

18 Schwarzenberger, 'Present-Day Relevance of the Jay Treaty Arbitrations', 722.

19 Lillich, 'The Jay Treaty Commissions', 272–3.

20 Ibid., p. 273.

21 *Treaty of amity, commerce, and navigation, between His Britannick Majesty and the United States of America*, Article 6.

22 Lillich, 'The Jay Treaty Commissions', 274.

23 Ibid., p. 277.

24 Schwarzenberger, 'Present-Day Relevance of the Jay Treaty Arbitrations', 718.

25 Lillich, 'The Jay Treaty Commissions', 280.

26 Lord Grenville to Jay, 9 July 1796; Johnston, *Correspondence and Public Papers of John Jay*, p. 178.

A register of the commission's cases found in the British records gives an impression of the London commission's success as well as insights into Bayard's bearing upon its work.[27]

Bayard presented thirty-five cases before the commission, the last of his memorials coming before the commission in February 1798, after his resignation.[28] During his tenure, he prepared all but one case for the commissioners.[29] Beyond a doubt, Bayard was therefore the main force of American claimants for the commission at this time. Of his thirty-five cases, twenty-two received compensation (a 63% success rate), the rest were dismissed or withdrawn (if we remove the withdrawn cases, the success rate rises to nearly 71%).[30] Bayard had hoped that some of his cases might bypass the Court of Appeals altogether, going straight to the commission, but the phrasing in the Jay Treaty was clear:[31] claimants had to have exhausted all regular possibilities of the British legal system before being considered by the commission.[32] Most of the dismissals were due to the fact that the cases either had not yet been through the British appellate system or because the case fell outside the commission's jurisdiction, such as the *Harriet* (Daddy), which had been captured after the treaty had been signed.[33] There were no reasons listed for the withdrawing of cases. Some may have required further preparation and deliberation, such as the *Rising Sun* (Rossiter) and the *Diana* (Gardner), which were withdrawn at first, but later reapplied and received compensation within Bayard's tenure.[34]

The most frequently carried cargo on board the vessels in disputed vessels were flour (including wheat), coffee and sugar. Such cargo could be presumed to be destined for France or occupied Europe, if they were not designated as exports to Britain, and particularly grain remained an important foodstuff due to national shortfalls and the restricted access that Britain had to wartime markets, such as the Baltic in 1799 to 1800.[35] But the breadth of captured cargo was wide, including wine, tobacco, cotton, soap, cocoa, rice, beans, fish, indigo, hemp, iron, beef and staves.[36] Most frequently, the captured vessels

27 TNA, FO 304/27.

28 See the case of the *Harriet* (Daddy), listed as case 71A in ibid.

29 See the case of the *Ann* (Black), brought by Charles Murray and James Hamilton, listed as case 65A in ibid.

30 See table 14.

31 29 July 1795, NARA, *Letters Received from Samuel Bayard – NAID: 1170268*, p. 51.

32 *Treaty of amity, commerce, and navigation, between His Britannick Majesty and the United States of America*, Article 7.

33 TNA, FO 304/27, listed as case 71A.

34 See fig. 3.

35 See Chapter 5.

36 See table 15.

were bound for France (seventeen cases), and bound from the United States (eighteen cases).[37]

All vessels presented by Bayard were captured between 1793 and 1796. Generally, these vessels had been processed in regular admiralty courts within the first year, latest within three years of being captured. None of them went before the appeals court until at least a year had passed since their first decree, though this may be a flaw in the data set, as the dates of appeals sentences have generally been neglected in FO 304/27. Despite the data in the FO 304/27 register being relatively detailed for Bayard's period, it becomes consecutively less reliable with increasingly empty columns, coming to a standstill by 1799. More reliable data on the processing of appeals can be compiled from the HCA 45 series as has been done in the previous chapter. Concerning Bayard's commission work, all cases brought before the commission by him were concluded by 1798, with his peak in 1797. The payment of compensation generally occurred about six to twelve months after the decision had been made.[38]

In total, Bayard's cases resulted in more than £70,000[39] of compensation. The median compensation was in the £1,000–2,000 bracket.[40] During his tenure, the US government paid out just under £5,000 of compensation to British claimants in the American–French privateer cases of the *Citizen Genêt*.[41]

Looking at the total amount of compensation achieved by the commission until its conclusion in 1804, it can clearly be said that despite the character of establishment and precedent that Bayard's commission work carried with it, the awards he received were only insignificantly raised by his successors. The financial success of the commission for American claimants is reflected in the awards issued by the commission. Writing to Elias Boudinot on 30 July 1797, Bayard noted how the commission had so far awarded payments of £34,000. In addition, his own deliberations with Scott and Nicholl had resulted in £56,000 worth of awards: "Here is *something* for which we are indebted to Mr. Jay's treaty",[42] he remarked. By 9 May 1798, Samuel Cabot felt confident in saying "the claims preferred under that article [VII of the Jay

37 See table 16.

38 TNA, FO 304/27, lists one case before the commission in 1796, eighteen in 1797 and eight in 1798, alongside four undated entries for commission cases. Aside from one undated award of compensation by the commission, the others were all dated 1797 (thirteen) and 1798 (fifteen) and the average time was computed from the individual cases.

39 Equivalent to $318,500.

40 See fig. 6.

41 Listed as case 19 in TNA, FO 304/27.

42 Bayard to Elias Boudinot, 30 July 1797; quoted in Sterling, 'A Federalist Opposes the Jay treaty', 424.

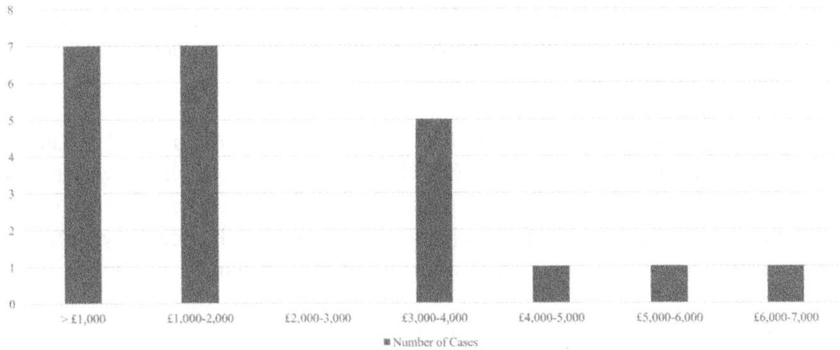


Fig. 6: Compensation claimed by Bayard's cases before the commission of Article VII of the Jay Treaty, compiled from FO 304/27.

Treaty] amounted to the sum of one million two hundred and fifty thousand pounds sterling".[43] By the conclusion of the committee on 24 February 1804, $11,650,000 – the equivalent of £2,560,440[44] – had been awarded to American claimants.[45] Both Bayard's cases and the overall caseload of the commission must be seen as clear financial victories on the side of the United States.

Yet, despite all Bayard's efforts, it was actually the commissioners who determined the outcome and amount of compensation in each case. The impact of their behaviour – their cooperation, argument and choice of words – is therefore equally, if not more, important than the legwork provided by Bayard and his associates at Doctors' Commons.

Once the London commission had been established, the US commissioners struck up a series of strategies to improve the chances of American claimants. At first, they emphasised the importance of the commission's work and its authority, stressing that the commission was an implementor of international law, not British national interest.

In the case of the *Betsey* (Furlong), it was phrased as such:

> if it should appear to us, that in any case the high court of appeal had decided, rather in conformity with the *laws and usages of England*,

43 James Madison to Thomas Jefferson, 16 April 1802; quoted in Lowrie and St Claire Clarke (eds), *Class I – Foreign Relations*, vol. 2, p. 427.

44 For historic exchange rates of British Sterling pounds and US dollars, see the website *Measuring Worth*, kindly recommended by Dr Gardner of the London School of Economics, www.measuringworth.com/datasets/exchangepound/ (accessed 14 March 2025).

45 In contrast $143,428.14 was awarded to British claimants; Lillich, 'The Jay Treaty Commissions', 280.

> than in consonance *with the law of nations, and the principles of equity and justice*, it will become our duty [to address these cases], as it is clearly within our power.[46]

In the case of the *Sally* (Choate), Pinckney stated that "the orders [in council of the British government] of the 6th November 1793, which, however they might have bound him [Sir James Marriott, Judge of the British High Court of Admiralty], are no rule for us [commissioners]".[47] Repeatedly, international principles were contrasted with the domestic nature of British prize jurisdiction.

This clashed with the British vision of international law and its British implementation in the courts of admiralty being congruent, as described by Mansfield.

Dr Nicholl argued:

> That the sentence of condemnation [of the *Betsey* (Furlong)] having been affirmed in this case upon an appeal to the supreme tribunal, credit is to be given inasmuch as, according to the general law of nations, it is presumed that justice has been administered in matters of prize by the supreme tribunal of the capturing state.[48]

Commissioner Gostling added that British decrees should be respected, as they were "proceeding on the same law".[49] He was thus upholding the image of British prize jurisdiction and the law of nations being one and the same.

While this strategy may at first glance seem suited to strengthening American claimants' cases by reducing the impact of British policy and legal thought, it actually led to what Bayard described as a "momentous crisis!"[50] in his diary in November 1796.

The *Betsey* (Furlong) was one of the first cases which Bayard prepared for the commission, furnishing the commission members with a respective memorial.[51] She has already been mentioned in the context of compensation (Chapter 5), but furthermore it was her case that determined the very jurisdiction of the commission. As always, Bayard had high hopes for a speedy determination, compensation and "justice"[52] for his American claimants. Aside

46 Trumbull, *Autobiography*, p. 193.

47 Moore, *History and digest Vol. III*, vol. 212, p. 3824.

48 Moore, *History and digest Vol. IV*, vol. 212, p. 3160.

49 Ibid., p. 3161.

50 24 November 1796; Bayard, *Diary of Samuel Bayard*, p. 94.

51 She was actually captured by the British twice, but the commission discussed her first capture in 1794. For more on her second capture in 1808, see TNA, HCA 45/40/20: *Betsey* (Furlong).

52 10 October 1796; Bayard, *Diary of Samuel Bayard*, p. 91.

from Bayard's memorials, the commissioners also referred to the papers now preserved as the HCA 45 series. Commissioner Trumbull dispels any doubt in this regard, when he refers to "That paper as printed in the cases and appendixes of both appellant and respondent".[53] It thus seems that most of the time the commissioners were referring to the same papers that are available to researchers today in the HCA 45 series, the American claimants' papers generally being prepared by Bayard.

The decrees issued by the Lords of Appeal in every case, were noted down by hand on the printed case papers of either the appellants or respondents. These decisions generally lacked an explanation of the legal principles or reasoning for the decree, instead simply recording the outcome. At one stage commissioner Gore pointed out that although the King's agent, Nathaniel Gostling, was capable of voicing the reasons behind the judgments of the Appeals Court (from his recollections of such cases as a member of Doctors' Commons), the commissioners themselves had merely the physical, written statement as true evidence. He diplomatically phrased that the memory of a case could be incomplete. It was clearly implied that the British members of the commission were unreliable sources to the American commissioners, to be placed on one level with the critically viewed oral testimony of claimants.[54]

This was due to the financial interests the British government had in denying cases and thus not having to compensate American claims (although equally the American commissioners were also interested in gaining compensation for their clients). In turn it was hard to view the King's Advocate, the British representative of the government and generally of the captors' interest, as impartial, devoid of these interests. Without the argumentation of the Lords of Appeal noted down, oral testimony of British legal professionals could not be considered in any form binding or reliable. In this regard, the commission found itself in a similar position to the vice-admiralty courts: the lack of binding, written legal precedents resulted in a significant degree of judicial freedom. A leeway that clearly provided British interests with convenient space to manoeuvre. This would change when the judicial reports prepared by Robinson were published for all, but the work was still years away at this time of the commission's work.

However, while American commissioners were happy to point out the untrustworthiness of the King's Agent's recollections, they were careful to point out that the judgment of the Lords of Appeal should in no way be less respected due to their close links with the Crown and the British government.[55]

53 Moore, *Compensation for losses and damages Vol. IV*, International Adjudications Ancient and Modern, History and Documents, ed. by John Bassett Moore, vol. 4, p. 363.

54 Moore, *History and digest Vol. III*, vol. 212, pp. 3177–8.

55 Ibid., p. 3181.

That this cloak of respectability was wrapped around the British admiralty institutions by the American commissioners, is down to the case of the *Betsey* (Furlong).

In this, their very first case, the British participants questioned the whole premise of the commission. Gostling stated that despite all the lofty and derogatory statements made by the American commissioners above, the British High Court of Appeals for Prizes could by no means be overruled by a mere commission. Article VII could not in any form alter the results of what they considered a truly final decree with no superior court to go to and no possibility of review. By refuting the decision of the Appeals Court, the commission would, in essence, be declaring itself superior to the highest court in British prize jurisdiction.[56] Consequently, the work not just of the commission, but also of Bayard's cases in the lower courts, was put on hold.

Yet if the commission were unable to alter any of those decisions from the superior court, in which way could it act at all? Commissioner Gore described the commission under such conditions as "a board with great and important powers to decide on their inability to act, but possessing no faculty of judging or acting".[57] Pinkney spoke of how this interpretation of the commission's jurisdiction would "leave the 7th article of the Treaty perfectly lifeless & intrinsically a Nullity".[58] If not resolved, this disagreement would have made the commission inactive and futile.

As it was, British political will quickly resolved the issue. First, Rufus King, US Minister to Britain, conferred with Lord Grenville on the subject. Subsequently, Lord Loughborough, the Lord Chancellor of Great Britain, sent out the message that the commissioners were to take on their responsibility. Technically, the commission was not a superior court. It never reversed any decisions of the High Court of Appeals for Prizes, it merely offered an opportunity to give compensation.[59] This meant that it was able to financially recompense parties that had been denied justice before the highest prize court of Britain, but did not overturn their decrees in any way. If this had not been the case, a mixed binational panel would have been legally superior to a municipal British court – a phenomenon unheard of at this time. Still, the commission was a pioneer effort of its day as regards international arbitration.[60] In order to maintain this vision of an inferior panel with compensation rights, the phrasing of paperwork became very important as well as treating British legal institutions diplomatically and tactfully. Phrases sometimes noted in

56 Ibid., pp. 3160–1.
57 Moore, *History and digest Vol. IV*, vol. 212, p. 193.
58 Ibid., p. 196.
59 Ibid., p. 84.
60 Schwarzenberger, 'Present-Day Relevance of the Jay Treaty Arbitrations', 715.

Bayard's diary such as "illegal"[61] or "unjust"[62] were to be removed from any memorials and papers of the commission. They were considered an affront to the British prize jurisdictional system and were considered both inappropriate and contrary to the efficient workings of the commission.[63]

Practically, this arrangement enabled American claimants to receive financial recompense from the British government through the commission, although the tone for discussions had been set and officially no reversals of decrees would ever take place. In response, the American commissioners needed to adapt their strategy. Instead of constantly hammering on the superiority of the commission, they started undercutting the very norms on which Mansfield's claims were built; the idea that a standardised canon of international law existed.

When referring to the *Betsey*'s case regarding her compensation precedent, a US commissioner voiced: "it is not likely that there is to be found any one rule which has been received and adhered to in the courts of admiralty of all countries or even of many countries"[64] and described the 10% denomination as an arbitrary number chosen by the British. Considering the case of the *Farmer* (Osborne), where an entire vessel and almost the entirety of the cargo had been condemned because of partial enemy property/cargo on board, Pinkney pointedly remarked: "I cannot find in any writer on the law of nations, or in any approved practice of nations, the least color for this [British] system of penalty."[65] One American commissioner contrasted French and British prize law when considering the case of the *Sally* (Choate), which hinged on the discussion of whether bills of lading were required on board, or whether other proofs of ownership were equally acceptable. In France a missing bill of lading justified condemnation of ship and cargo.[66] However, as Gore pointed out:

> The Government of France has always been uncommonly rigid in requiring plenary and minute proof of property on board ships in times of war. The edicts of Louis XIV. on this subject have been extremely severe, and in many instances unsupported by the law or practice of nations; but even these do not extend so far as to require bills of lading *and* [emphasis added] invoices.[67]

61 7 May 1796; Bayard, *Diary of Samuel Bayard*, p. 71.

62 25 February 1796; ibid., p. 58.

63 Moore, *Compensation for losses and damages Vol. IV*, International Adjudications Ancient and Modern, History and Documents, ed. by John Bassett Moore, vol. 4, p. 84.

64 Moore, *History and digest Vol. IV*, vol. 212, p. 4213.

65 Ibid., p. 358.

66 Ibid., p. 309.

67 Moore, *History and digest Vol. III*, vol. 212, p. 3819.

In another case, he simply summed up: “In the practice of nations there are many instances of difference of opinion as to what acts are, or are not, correspondent with the law of nations, and each asserting and maintaining its right to decide for itself against the express opinion of the other.”[68]

When examining the influence of international law on the so-called founding fathers’ generation, it has been stated that “no group of America’s leaders have ever been more mindful of the discipline”.[69] Scholars have remarked how “citations of Grotius, Pufendorf, and Vattel are scattered in about equal numbers”[70] throughout their writings, and that they relied on “a canon [of law-of-nations writers] that was at once broad, diverse, and authoritative”.[71] Yet, while these legalists were common and internationally accepted authorities on the law of nations, they each supported a “different understanding”[72] of how to interpret principles of international law, enabling their words and arguments to be used to very different ends.[73]

As well as referring to law of nations authorities, the US commissioners also tapped into the trope of the uncontrollable vice-admiralty courts. By employing thoughtful wording and distinguishing between the vice-admiralty courts and the Appeals Court, the commissioners disassociated the vice-admiralty courts from the London prize courts, preserving an image of respect for these British institutions, but repeating allegations against the system that were widespread and acceptable to voice.

Through a three-pronged attack, this trident of US strategy employed not only the multitude of legalists and their opinions but also referenced the diverse range of practices employed in European admiralty courts and even the range of decisions made within the body of the British Empire itself.

In the words of commissioner Gore:

> It appears to me that in considering this subject much error has arisen […] in supposing the sentence of the supreme court of the nation […] conclusive as to the law, [and binding] not only on the subjects of their own government, but on foreign nations […] [T]hat the decision of

68 Moore, *History and digest Vol. IV*, vol. 212, p. 3163.

69 Janis, *America and the Law of Nations, 1776–1939*, p. 24.

70 J. S. Reeves, ‘The Influence of the Law of Nations Upon International Law in the United States’, *American Journal of International Law*, 3 (1909), 547–61, at 547.

71 B. Richardson, ‘The Use of Vattel in the American Law of Nations’, *American Journal of International Law*, 161 (2012), 547–71, at 571.

72 Müller, *Neutrality in World History*, p. 26.

73 In a pamphlet *The Compact Maritime* responding to one of Scott’s decisions, Thomas Paine argued that there was no one law of nations and that even legalists such as Vattel, Pufendorf *et al.* were only theorists, while an actual law of nations in practice could only be found in the First League of Armed Neutrality, where several nations had concurred on a shared set of principles and conduct; ibid., p. 74.

> any court, however respectable its members, is conclusive on foreign governments, as to the law of nations, and that the principles on which it is founded may not be rightfully contested, as contrary to that law, is not, in my belief, warranted by just ideas of the equal independence of nations or by their practice […] To suppose the decisions of the courts of any country evidence of the law of nations would be to suppose that nation always right who captures and condemns the effects of another.[74]

Clearly, despite diplomatically phrasing his respect for the British admiralty court system, there would have been no need for the commission's work if there had been no disagreements on the conduct of British prize jurisdiction.

It also once again showcased the potential that a law of nations framework provided to the United States, to portray itself as a sovereign, equal partner with the same privileges and obligations as long-standing European states, including Britain, regardless of military power.[75] Notwithstanding their interpretations, all players of the London commission referred to the law of nations. Gore went so far as to consider himself under "equal obligations of duty to both nations"[76] and stressing that the commission needed to function as a court of two nations, reflecting the visions of both parties concerning international law.[77]

However, this vision came into conflict with the entanglements and realpolitik faced by Americans in the British prize system. Officially, the commission was set up as a platform of equal negotiation for two partners. In theory, the odds of the Article VII commission were skewed in favour of the United States due to them receiving three out of five commissioners. In reality, the debate over jurisdiction in the case of the *Betsey* (Furlong) showed how the United States was entirely dependent on the goodwill of their British counterparts in even starting the endeavour. In the case of the *Sally* (Hayes), the American side bitterly stated: "We are told every time we meet that it is owing to the great condescension of the British government that the board is permitted to examine and decide on cases."[78] Bayard criticised the Jay Treaty as not egalitarian enough, seeing it as one-sided in favour of British demands, and he was especially wary of the discrepancy between signing

74 Moore, *History and digest Vol. IV*, vol. 212, pp. 3161–3.

75 Janis, *America and the Law of Nations, 1776–1939*, p. 30.

76 Moore, *Compensation for losses and damages Vol. IV*, International Adjudications Ancient and Modern, History and Documents, ed. by John Bassett Moore, vol. 4, p. 190.

77 Moore, *History and digest Vol. III*, vol. 212, p. 3166.

78 Moore, *History and digest Vol. IV*, vol. 212, p. 472.

treaty provisions and actually fulfilling them.[79] American claimants needed to pass through all levels of British admiralty jurisdiction before reaching the committee, financing their path all the way. Thus, an American claimant "cannot enter our [commission's] doors; the key by which alone you can gain admission is held by the party of whom you complain".[80] At the same time, it had been demonstrated that tactics of delay could be successfully deployed against claimants at court, drawing out processes, increasing costs and potentially even offering the opportunity of extending cases to the point they could no longer be entered before the commission.

While the American commissioners appealed to a feeling of unison and shared values (international law), they also followed a more practical approach: The asymmetrical distribution of naval power was evident to all players in the commission under Article VII. Despite negotiated rights and theoretical obligations to the law of nations, the need for British cooperation was clear. Rufus King noted: "It is evident that a new principle of maritime Law cannot be established against the will of the first maritime Powers. It is equally evident that they will not assent to a principle which takes from them the advantage of their naval superiority."[81] But there was one class of precedents that was exceedingly hard for British commissioners to refute: British precedents. American commissioners used the "British accent"[82] of prize law to voice their own interests and be heard, regularly quoting English authorities on prize and admiralty law.

In the case of the *Betsey* (Furlong), Pinkney referred to Thomas Rutherford's *Institutes of Natural Law; being the substance of a Course of Lectures on Grotius de Jure Belli et Pacis*[83] when outlining an acceptable method of obtaining justice.[84] Rutherford is now considered part of an "unmistakably British"[85] legal tradition. Gore referred to a statement of Lord Mansfield's in the case of the *Sally* (Choate).[86] In his opinion on the *Farmer* (Osborne), Pinkney mentioned various English legalists on the one hand, referencing, for

[79] Bayard to Elias Boudinot, July 1795; Sterling, 'A Federalist Opposes the Jay Treaty', 416.

[80] Moore, *History and digest Vol. IV*, vol. 212, p. 187.

[81] King and King, *The Life and Correspondence of Rufus King*, p. 588.

[82] Bourguignon, *Sir William Scott* (2009), p. 271.

[83] T. Rutherforth, *Institutes of natural law: Being the substance of a course of lectures on Grotius De jure belli et pacis, read in S. John's College, Cambridge* (London, 1754).

[84] Moore, *History and digest Vol. IV*, vol. 212, pp. 3183–4.

[85] M. G.-S. Rovira, 'Early Twentieth-Century Positivism Revisited', in A. Orford, F. Hoffmann and M. Clark (eds), *The Oxford Handbook of the Theory of International Law*, 1st edn (Oxford, 2016), pp. 173–91, at p. 181.

[86] Moore, *History and digest Vol. IV*, vol. 212, p. 3819.

example, passages from Sir James Mariott's work *Dutch Ships Considered* or Lord Hawkesbury/Charles Jenkinson's earlier text *A Discourse on the Conduct of the Government of Great Britain: In Respect to Neutral Nations.*[87] On the other hand, he also was able to refer to concrete and modern cases in the High Court of Admiralty, such as the case of the *Molly* (Young).[88]

Such references were incorporated into the broader American strategy. For example, Pinkney not only quoted Rutherford's *Institutes*, but also backed up his point with references to Grotius and Pufendorf.[89] In this way, he used references to British legalists, but at the same time counteracted the impression of considering British legalists more important than other law of nations writers.

Once the commission's jurisdiction had been established through the deliberations of the *Betsey* (Furlong) and the ensuing political push, Bayard's work, which had been put on hold until a decision was made, was allowed to recommence in the High Court of Admiralty and before the Lords of Appeal. This opened the door for more appellate decrees to be brought before the commission.

Generally, merchants appealed their cases due to financial motivation. When examining the cases Bayard prepared for the commission, the British register detailed losses for twenty-three vessels. These show, when regarding the mode, that most losses registered were valued in the £2,000 to £3,000 bracket. The mean average lay just below £7,000, but this is the result of several high value losses, which spiked at more than £9,289 in the case of the *Light Horse* (Townsend).[90]

If one compares the detailed losses with the compensation those cases received, it becomes apparent that despite compensation, most cases still made a loss according to the costs and damages claimed by the American parties. If we consider this small dataset, the average loss per compensated case amounted to approximately £1,427, a significant sum. Only three cases received more compensation than the losses they detailed.[91] However, it was probably in the claimants' interest to overstate losses within reasonable bounds. While a large loss and a small loss were still significantly different outcomes to merchants and their lives, this does emphasise the importance that claims

87 C. Jenkinson, *A Discourse on the Conduct of the Government of Great Britain: In Respect to Neutral Nations* (London, 1794); Moore, *History and digest Vol. IV*, vol. 212, 356, 359.

88 Moore, *Compensation for losses and damages Vol. IV*, International Adjudications Ancient and Modern, History and Documents, ed. by John Bassett Moore, vol. 4, p. 358.

89 Moore, *History and digest Vol. IV*, vol. 212, p. 4207.

90 See fig. 7.

91 See table 17, compiled through fig. 7 and table 18.

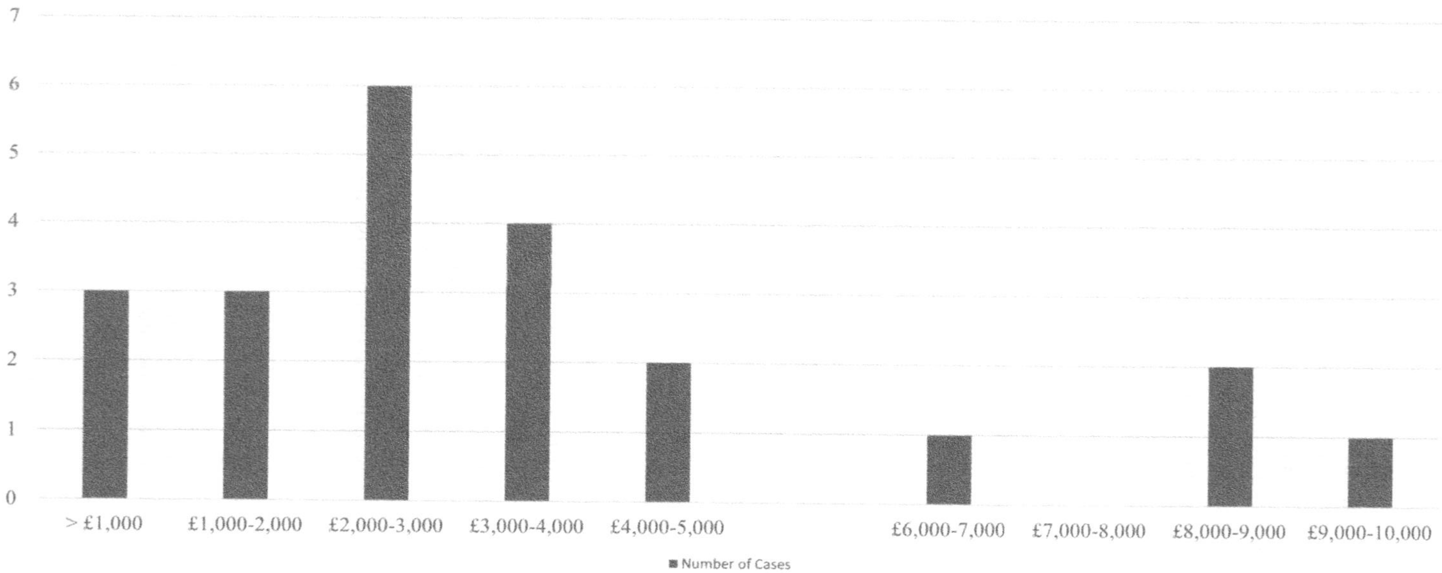


Fig. 7: Losses claimed in Bayard's cases before the commission of Article VII of the Jay Treaty, compiled from FO 304/27.

had on a political stage. The public funding provided by the US government for the commission was the catalyst for the flow of capital from the British government to American citizens and enabled claimants to bring their cases before the commission despite their failures in the appellate court. Whereas the total amount of the compensation of the Jay Treaty's Article VII commission has always been celebrated, statistics on the individual losses and gains thus suggest that the importance of presenting the American nation as a sovereign and equal independent player on the stage of international law may have been more important than the financial gains for individual merchants.

Moreover, many American cases that Bayard pursued in the High Court of Admiralty or the appeals court had costs and damages as one of their points of contention, with an entire class of cases in which the *only* point of contention was the costs and damages. The sums in question, though still significant to individual merchants, were small fry compared to cases that involved property such as vessels or cargo, or additional services such as freight, demurrage, insurance, and so forth. When Bayard considered entering appeals for these claims, he found it difficult to weigh the costs and benefits of such courses of action, as the "loss sustained appeared to be inconsiderable".[92] The issue at hand was thus whether it was worth the American government's time, effort or money to pursue these cases at all, as each case in court would cause more financial loss than could be gained from a successful case, simply through legal fees in the system. And yet the cases were so frequent that to drop them seemed to be giving up on a major part of the international maritime rights of the United States. It appears the British civilian Scott originally suggested to Bayard that a solution could be found by mutual consent outside of court to the advantage of both nations and their parties.[93] In theory, all such cases would need to go to appeal and then potentially on to the commission of the Jay Treaty before compensation might be agreed. A settlement by consent out of court would avoid this course of action and:

> from his [Scott's] knowledge of the sentiments of [the British] Ministry he had no doubt they would wave this right, & consent that himself, Dr. Nicholl & myself [Bayard] should consider & ascertain what allowance ought Justly to be made to the Citizens of the United States and that once some basic principles have been settled at court, those principles may be applied without court cases by consent too.[94]

92 Bayard to Sec. State, 17 April 1795: NARA, *Letters Received from Samuel Bayard – NAID: 1170268*, p. 22.

93 The 1797 letter written by the proctors at Doctors' Commons, reveals that consensual agreements were nearly four times as fast as an actual hearing and final decree in court; Crickett & Townley, Slade, Bush to Wolff, Grill, Fridag and Bayard, 1 February 1797: NARA, *Box 10, British Spoliations – NAID: 1170270*.

94 Bayard to Sec. State, 17 April 1795: NARA, *Letters Received from Samuel Bayard – NAID: 1170268*, pp. 22–3.

Astonishingly, Scott suggested circumventing his own, British system of admiralty jurisdiction and cooperating binationally in the interest of American claimants. An extrajudicial solution would relieve pressure on the admiralty system, which was under considerable strain through the number of cases requiring prize jurisdiction. Any member of Doctors' Commons could assume that a large backlog of cases would ensue through the war and could guess that diplomatic pressures would be exerted to attempt to speed up the adjudication of neutral nations' cases. Thus, encouraging extrajudicial processes could alleviate stress not just off the admiralty court system, but also off British international relations. Additionally, Scott's suggestion also strictly adhered to the vision of a top-down judicial hierarchy, implying that an arbitration committee would be following precedents already set by the British admiralty judges and not have any independent capacity for setting new precedents itself.

About a month later, Bayard mentioned another discussion with Scott on the subject, contrasting their productive conversation on the class of costs and damages with the injurious strategies employed by those defending British captors.[95] Yet the hint was too subtle to reap a reward from the Secretary of State. Nearly half a year passed, with no governmental instructions issued as to which course he should take. The entry deadline for appeals was approaching fast and Bayard did not wish to let it expire due to untimely orders. Consequently, Bayard asked Fitzsimmons, who represented US merchant interests in the American government, to remind the Secretary of State that he still had received no instructions on the cases of costs and damages. He also added further counsel from Doctors' Commons, supplementing Scott's verdict with recommendations from different members of staff, and concluded that the general proposal to attempt to settle out of court by consent was much encouraged. Importantly, Bayard had been reminded that every case they had to settle in court would add to the long delays already experienced by their clients there.[96] It was thus truly in the interest of American clients to take the option of an out-of-court settlement, if possible.

Two months later, Bayard still had no definitive instructions, however, he was glad to report that his attentions on the class of costs and damages had been forwarded to Lord Grenville, and once again to Scott, who still approved the proposed measures. Bayard was thus hopeful that his efforts would bear fruit in the near future.[97] By January 1796, he was reporting that no progress had been made.[98] Another month later he wrote that despite speaking with Pinkney, they were still awaiting instructions from the State Department.[99]

95 Bayard to Sec. State, 16 May 1795: ibid., p. 28.

96 Bayard to Fitzsimmons, 2 October 1795: ibid., pp. 59–61.

97 Bayard to Pinckney, 30 November 1795: ibid., pp. 65–6.

98 Bayard to Sec. State, 5 January 1796: ibid., p. 72.

99 Bayard to Sec. State, 9 February 1796: ibid., p. 86.

In July 1796, Lord Grenville finally proposed a clear line of action: "For the Settlement of cases merely of cost & damage – To shorten the Proceedings in many of the Cases of American captures, in which it is conceived that the expence and delay of proceedings by appeal might throw difficulties in the way of obtaining adequate compensation, where it might be due."[100] He proposed that such cases should be brought forward by "the American Government (Mr. Bayard) [...] before the arbitration of two persons";[101] namely, the King's Advocate and either Mr Adams or Mr Bayard. The process envisioned both parties to agree on the amount of compensation, in which case that amount would be binding on both governments, but should either side disagree, then the case should follow the usual court process. Attached was a list of thirty-six vessels that immediately could fall into said category.[102] Seven months later, Bayard was finally able to outline further progress.

Grenville's original idea had been adapted to have the amount of compensation determined by a set of British professionals, before continuing the plan outlined in his original letter: Scott and Nicholl considered the class of costs and damages and had moved on to pronounce both conditional and definitive awards by the end of February 1797. In the case of conditional awards, the award would only be granted after specific further proofs had been acquired and shown in London. Bayard celebrated both the conditional and definitive awards as "liberal" sums, favourable to American interests.[103] In an undated letter to Grenville, Scott and Nicholl wrote that most of the proofs they had been provided with had been insufficient and would not hold up in a 'proper' British admiralty court. Yet they considered the speedy conclusion of the business their duty and had decided to overlook these standards in favour of quick, decisive redress.[104] Consequently, they forwarded their recommendations for award sums to both government agents (Bayard and Heseltine, the King's Proctor), who could now decide. The process was incredibly efficient and appears in stark contrast to regular admiralty proceedings.

100 Copy of Lord Grenville's letter, undated, enclosed in Bayard to Sec. State, 14 July 1796: ibid., pp. 127–8.

101 Copy of Lord Grenville's letter, undated, enclosed in Bayard to Sec. State, 14 July 1796: ibid., p. 128.

102 Copy of Lord Grenville's letter, undated, enclosed in Bayard to Sec. State, 14 July 1796: ibid., pp. 128–9.

103 Bayard to Sec. State, 28 February 1797: ibid., p. 171.

104 Naturally, when absolutely requisite, they had ordered further proofs, but as opposed to vaguely asking for more evidence, they had concretely specified which forms of further proofs were needed, adding they "ought most deliberately & conscientiously to approve" the awards as soon as those particular papers were received. Copy of Letter by Scott and Nicholl to Grenville, undated: ibid., p. 171.

Nevertheless, Bayard and Heseltine were able to approve by consent more than fifty cases of definitive awards in their joint meeting. The amount of the conditional awards could not be ascertained. All that remained was for the two governments to determine a mode of payment and to communicate the good news to the American citizens involved.[105] Three weeks later, Bayard had informed all the respective claimants and was considering recommending the process for additional cases – this in itself indicates the level of success attributed to this approach.[106] However, Scott and Nicholl declared they would only examine cases until 1 May 1797.[107] In July 1797 Bayard noted that he had still not been permitted to collect the sums awarded by Scott and Nicholl in the cases.[108] In the end, the compensation was only paid out at the same time as the first awards issued by the commission under Article VII of the Jay Treaty. But, despite all this, compensation was granted and legal fees from the court system were avoided in the financial interest of individual claimants, although the speed of arbitration was perhaps not as swift as desired.

It was noted at the beginning of this chapter that all players sitting at the commission's table not only built on their own national and binational interests but also adhered to (their own visions of) international law. The framework of the law of nations provided a common ground between both sides, while also leaving room for interpretation and negotiation. Maybe it was exactly the contested legal nature of prize that aided the participants in this undertaking. Another commonality was the integration of and interaction with the community at the Doctors' Commons, which may have helped in the arbitration processes. Whereas the other arbitration committees failed, the London commission under Article VII was able to compromise and find methods of cooperation, even beyond the vision laid down in the Jay Treaty. They were able to produce significant results both for individuals trapped in the prize court system as well as on a binational level. A detailed picture of individual claims furthermore shows that the commission's success should not only be reduced to its financial outcomes but also needs to be viewed in terms of US commissioners' self-identification as standing up for America's maritime rights and community and as an equal player at the negotiating table.

105 Samuel Bayard to Rufus King, 7 February 1797: NARA, *Box 10, British Spoliations – NAID: 1170270.*

106 Bayard to Sec. State, 28 February 1797, and Bayard to Sec. of State, 12 April 1797: NARA, *Letters Received from Samuel Bayard – NAID: 1170268*, pp. 171 and 175.

107 Bayard to King, 4 April 1797: ibid., p. 182.

108 Bayard to King, 6 July 1797: ibid., pp. 195–6.

# 8

# "The Distress of our Commerce": US Merchants and the Transatlantic Communication Cycles for Claims and Compensation

The Jay Treaty was published by the US government and widely disseminated in the press. Known as one of the first outcries in American politics and infamous for the public reaction to it, its circulation can barely be underestimated.[1] But how did US merchants interact with the commission or with Bayard in his capacity for assistance in claims and appeals? What information did the US government provide to mercantile communities, in which manner did they themselves interfere with the court process, and how was such information circulated?

Merchants were already following regular updates on condemnations and captures, both in the vice-admiralty courts and in the High Court of Admiralty. Decrees and lines of argumentation in court were published in newspapers.[2] John Proctor obtained knowledge "by a late Bermudian paper, that the Ship Hamilton, Capt. Farrett, was taken by the Thetis British Frigate, and carried into Bermudas"[3] and thus took up correspondence with the US government. Some government instructions had been printed in American newspapers, even printed in their entirety, with specific references made to the importance of providing merchants with information.[4] The merchant community also functioned as a communication network in itself, with two merchants corresponding in 1797, whether they should contact other persons who might be in a similar position concerning captured property and get them in touch

1 Estes, *The Jay Treaty debate, public opinion, and the evolution of early American political culture*, p. 212.

2 See, for example, newspaper clipping 'Admiralty Court', in NARA, *Box 9, British Spoliations – NAID: 1170270.*

3 Proctor to Pickering, 21 September 1795; NARA, *Box 3, British Spoliations – NAID: 1170270.*

4 Printed pamphlet of Instructions by Scott and Nicholl, 22 November 1794, NARA, *Box 9, British Spoliations – NAID: 1170270*; John Jay to Edmund Randolph, Johnston, Correspondence and public papers of John Jay, p. 92.

with Samuel Bayard.[5] Yet the knowledge of what exactly the Treaty meant for their private cases remained unclear to many. The main initial point of governmental contact for most queries was the Secretary of State, although individual members of the commission, and additional staff on both sides, such as Jacob Wagner, Chief Clerk at the State Department, or Samuel Bayard, all received letters. Occasionally, citizens were referred there by other government officials.[6]

The *Sidney* had been captured by the British privateer the *Portland* and condemned at the Vice-Admiralty Court at St Kitts. Following the captain's suggestion and at the behest of their legal counsel, the decision had been made to appeal the decree. Smith, whose two merchant houses made him the sole owner of the vessel and cargo, wrote:

> I am not certain of any Immediate Service you can render. If any I have the fullest confidence that it will be afforded. I have for the present to request to be informed whether our Government still continues to prosecute the claims of our citizen thro[ugh] the courts of Great Britain. If so, which I presume is the case, I shall on receiving the papers forward them to you with such other vouchers as I may think will be necessary to substantiate our claim.[7]

Harrison, sole owner of the uninsured vessel *Susanna* and her entire cargo, summed up:

> I see no other remedy but that of seeking an indemnification from the British [...], but am unacquainted which is the best mode of prosecuting our claim, and whether I should make application [...] direct to London, your advise on the Subject would be greatly received and any interference of our Government in behalf of Capt. Smith and myself.[8]

Other merchants simply asked the government to take any steps necessary, as they themselves did not know how to gain compensation.[9] However,

5 Sewall to unknown, 10 October 1797; NARA, *Box 8, British Spoliations – NAID: 1170270.*

6 In the case of the *Charlotte* 'Major Hamilton' passed on the necessary information. Brothers Coster & Co. to Pickering, 19 July 1799; NARA, *Box 1, British Spoliations – NAID: 1170270.*

7 Smith to unknown, 30 June 1797; NARA, *Box 8, British Spoliations – NAID: 1170270.*

8 Harrison to Pickering, 4 November 1799; ibid.

9 Hallam to Wolcot, July 1796; NARA, *Box 7, British Spoliations – NAID: 1170270.*

these merchants felt sure that the government would take on their cases. Other applicants were wondering whether their misfortunes could be helped by the London Jay commission or the government at all. For example, the *Circumnavigator* had been captured by a British privateer and detained for five months, only for the capturing party to abscond before costs and damages could be brought.[10] The *Susanna* had accidentally been wrecked by a British prize crew.[11] Zobdiel Coffin described how his whaling season had been ruined when a British vessel threatened him into leaving his regular hunting grounds. In consequence, he had been captured by the French.[12] In such cases, claimants felt wronged by British adversaries, but needed clarifications to the London commission's jurisdiction.

Generally, merchants who contacted the State Department or those involved in the London commission were financially motivated. Abrial Hathaway, master of the *Betsey*, wrote to the Secretary of State that his capture and his desired restitution thereof at appeal were "a matter of very considerable consequence to me as I own'd the whole of the vessel myself".[13] For some, the admiralty court processes were also personal; for example, with Thomas Robinson who felt his "honor & credibility"[14] had been attacked by the King's Advocate and consequently planned on printing a pamphlet to show his innocence and the extent of British injustice.

Such pamphlets often drew connections between the fate suffered by an individual merchant and the entire American mercantile community, as well as tying personal and national suffering together.[15] Barney simply spoke of the "distress of our commerce",[16] on a collective and personal level. These were typical strategies employed by US merchants in their communications with the State Department.[17]

10 Adams & Loring to Pickering, 18 April 1798; NARA, *Box 1, British Spoliations – NAID: 1170270.*

11 Letter extract, Wagner to Harrison, 9 November 1799; NARA, *Box 8, British Spoliations – NAID: 1170270.*

12 Coffin to unknown, 25 February 1799; NARA, *Box 3, British Spoliations – NAID: 1170270.*

13 Hathaway to Pickering, 10 March 1797; NARA, *Box 1, British Spoliations – NAID: 1170270.*

14 Robinson to King, 10 December 1799; NARA, *Box 6, British Spoliations – NAID: 1170270.*

15 *Proceedings of the Trial of the Ship Two Friends in the Court of Vice Admiralty in Bermuda: Copy* (Philadelphia PA, 1795), p. 1.

16 Barney to Jefferson, 17 February 1794; NARA, *Box 10, British Spoliations – NAID: 1170270.*

17 Backett and James are a good example for the personal angle. They wrote they would be pleased for "the Interest you shall take in this Concern, which though small

Furthermore, merchants referred to their lack of connections in England, pointing out that they had nobody else to turn to, as beautifully illustrated by Butler and Norton's phrasing: "You will excuse us for [...] requesting so many favours on account of our living so remote and can get no information only what we have from you."[18]

While one might assume that interactions mainly took place between London and individual merchants, the records at NARA prove that the State Department played a key role in the processes of knowledge circulation concerning prize cases. This was not only true for the initial stages, but throughout the entire judicial process.

For American prize cases that wanted to go on to appeal or be heard before the commission, it was vital that the required paperwork reached London, specifically the resident agent there. However, individual merchants first had to face three overarching challenges in this regard. First, they did not know which proofs would be accepted or were desired by the British court system. Second, they often did not know who would be procuring or indeed how to procure said proofs. Third, there was a general disarray concerning to whom to send the relevant papers.

To help with the first issue regarding which papers were required, Samuel Bayard's correspondence was invaluable. Scott and Nicholl's instructions on British prize court procedure, originally found in the correspondence between Jay and Greenville, were published by the US government on 22 November 1794 for all to read. From this small pamphlet general sets of required papers could be identified; for example, the standing interrogatories of crew members or the papers on board (ship's papers).[19] However, it was not much to go on for claimants an ocean away. By 5 May 1795, various letters of Bayard's regarding necessary proofs had been published for the mercantile community.[20] But the main set of directions seems to have been issued by him or, occasionally, the Secretary of State, in hand-written form for each individual case. It was quite usual for several bundles of proofs to be sent, one after another, with more information trickling through as time passed.

Corresponding with George Crowninshield in October 1796, Bayard explained in great detail which papers were important. He mentioned foremost

---

in itself is of Consederable consequence to us". Backett and James to Pickering, 5 February 1796; NARA, *Box 6, British Spoliations – NAID: 1170270.*

[18] Butler and Norton to Pickering, 27 August 1798; NARA, *Box 2, British Spoliations – NAID: 1170270.*

[19] A Letter and Instructions from Sir William Scott and Doctor John Nicholl, prepared at the instance of Mr Jay, 1794; NARA, *Box 9, British Spoliations – NAID: 1170270.*

[20] Bear & Judah to Pickering, 5 May 1795; NARA, *Box 1, British Spoliations – NAID: 1170270.*

the vice-admiralty court proceedings, explicitly mentioning the retrieval of the ship's papers and the standing interrogatories as part of these proceedings, and added that all the papers were to be authenticated under the court's seal. He continued that "it is useful to accompany them with the protest of the Master – if any has been made – statement under oath of costs paid or damages sustained – affidavits as to the value of the vessel & cargo & Furnishment thereof".[21] In a letter to the merchants of the *Commerce*, Bayard assured them that while the first set of proofs they had forwarded had been insufficient, the second bundle seemed a "great assistance, but whether it will be sufficient to satisfy the Judge of the Admiralty, I cannot possibly say at present".[22] Yet he was swift to add that he would inform them as soon as he knew of any further evidence that would aid their cause, stating "Nothing in my power shall be wanting to assure your success".[23] Writing to Ricard Blow about the captured vessel *David & George*, Bayard asked specifically to send an affidavit as to the ownership of the cargo and highlighting "that such property was really your own, and that no citizen of France or of Holland had or were to have any interest in the same".[24] It also becomes apparent that extracts of such letters were published in newspapers and their content exchanged within the merchant community; for example, in Baltimore, where a small article highlighted some favourable decisions in the court and a plea was added "that those who have not already forwarded their vouchers and estimate of loss to Mr. Bayard may do so immediately, either direct to him, or through their agents in London".[25]

By November 1797, Bayard was asking certain claimants to also add a declaration "of the Neutrality of brig & cargo"[26] to the papers forwarded. Such individual recommendations were key to successful cases, as often merchants considered their cases clear-cut and were at a loss how to prove their case any more plainly. Writing to the Secretary of State, David Pearce stated: "I know not what further evidence I can give that will throw light on the matter."[27]

Whereas protections were sought by the maritime community to protect their vessels, cargo and crew, similar documentation was also sought by some US claimants regarding their official documents. Thus, some merchants added

[21] Bayard to Crowninshield, 4 October 1796; ibid.

[22] Bayard to Bear & Judah, 15 June 1796; ibid.

[23] Bayard to Bear & Judah, 15 June 1796; ibid.

[24] Bayard to Blow, 11 July 1796; ibid.

[25] Clipping attached to a letter of Wagner's to Tyler, Winslow & Attwood Jun., 26 December 1794; TNA, FO 304/10.

[26] Bulkey, Curtis & Goodwich to Pickering, 17 November 1797; NARA, *Box 4, British Spoliations – NAID: 1170270.*

[27] Pierce to Pickering, 28 November 1796; NARA, *Box 5, British Spoliations – NAID: 1170270.*

certifications by Phineas Bond, the British Consul-General for the Middle and Southern States of America, declaring that a specific notarial act was granted by a qualified notary public in the United States. This behaviour shows both the distrust merchants placed in the value attached to the American judicial system by the British admiralty courts, but also displays how important the recognition of their papers was to them.[28] Supplementary certificates were never specifically required or encouraged by Bayard, but were obtained by merchants at their own initiative.

In a draft by the State Department's chief clerk, Wagner, various alterations show some of the issues faced by the government. Captain Truxton had been enquiring about his vessel, the *John & Joseph*, specifically to find out if the papers that he had sent would be enough to win his case at the appeals court. Wagner replied that he was unable to answer said question as the papers had been forwarded to London just a few days before and he could no longer examine them. Still, he attempted to reassure Truxton that he would hear back from London should any further papers be required. Some alterations in the letter show that even Wagner was unsure which papers were necessary:

> if the counsel of our Agent there should think that other proofs than those which appeared in the court below are necessary you will ~~doubtlessly~~ certainly be informed of it. In the mean time ~~from the enclosed paper you will be able to discover the nature of the proofs which are requisite and~~ if there ~~are any such~~ is any document within your reach, tending to set the affair in a clearer light, [...] it will be proper to send it on immediately.[29]

Specific instructions were edited out in favour of an all-encompassing phrase that could be read to mean almost anything. But there was some knowledge of which papers were expected in a standard British admiralty cause. Before Bayard sent out any individualised instructions, he would send out the same, standardised message to every American claimant, listing the required papers and adding the status of that claimant's case, as follows:

> In every case of appeal from a Vice-Admiralty Court in the W. Indies to the Court of Appeal here, the first Step that is Necessary and without which no Sentence of Restitution in favor of the American Claimants can be obtained, is to send forward a Complete Copy of

[28] Various examples found in NARA, *Box 9, British Spoliations – NAID: 1170270.*

[29] Wagner to Truxton, 20 April 1796; NARA, *Box 3, British Spoliations – NAID: 1170270.*

> the proceedings in the Vice-Admiralty Court below. In your Case of the Schooner Friendship W. Worth, none has yet been received.[30]

Attaining the vice-admiralty court proceedings was the crux of every case and often the most difficult part of the entire process. Bayard described them as "indesputibly necessary"[31] and had to inform the owners of the *Argo*, that an Appeal had been turned down due to the lack of said papers. The number of such cases must have been substantial, generating significant income to the clerks and registrars at the vice-admiralty courts.[32] Some Americans procured the paperwork from the vice-admiralty courts straight after their condemnation.[33] However, this does not often seem to have been the case; for example, the master of the *Ceres* did not have "money sufficient to defray the Expenses"[34] of obtaining the papers after his trial and thus proceeded on his journey without them.

The owners of the brig *Nobby* pointed out that "being Deprived of our property in the manner we were has placed us under So very Destressing Circumstances that we are utterly unable to do any thing of that kind and if ever the prosess is proceeded it must be Done by Government".[35]

Having applied to the government for assistance, many merchants leant back and waited for the State Department to procure the required proceedings. The owner of several condemned cases of glass on the vessel *Minerva*, clearly expressed his desire to be rid of the business, stating: "I Cannot now prosecute an Appeal without paying down one hundred & fifty Dollars which I am not Inclined to do but rather trust in the Justice of my Country to demand of the British Government Restitution for my Property. I Submit the whole business to your Superior Judgement."[36]

30 Bayard to Butler and Norton, 27 September 1796; NARA, *Box 2, British Spoliations – NAID: 1170270*.

31 Bayard to Wall, 21 August 1797; TNA, FO 304/1/21: *Argo* (Spurr).

32 At least forty-seven ships were mentioned just in the list of authenticated proceedings for US vessels in the Bahamas; NARA, *Box 10, British Spoliations – NAID: 1170270*.

33 Story to Pickering, 6 December 1796; NARA, *Box 5, British Spoliations – NAID: 1170270*.

34 Hedge to Pickering, 4 December 1796; NARA, *Box 1, British Spoliations – NAID: 1170270*.

35 Owners of the Brig *Nobby* to Pickering, 6 June 1798; NARA, Box *4, British Spoliations – NAID: 1170270*.

36 Coffin to Pickering, 18 August 1796; ibid.

Another motive for US merchants to wait for the US government to procure the papers, was that the government then immediately covered the not insubstantial cost of the copies.[37]

Yet it was precisely this attitude that Bayard would later determine as one of the major factors for excessive delays in prosecuting American cases.[38] There was a decided lack of clear communication when it came to who was responsible for acquiring copies of the vice-admiralty court proceedings: The government or the merchants themselves?

In the case of the *Ceres*, the claimant wrote:

> I have supposed that our Government had procured all the necessary Papers from the West Indies, and that the Sufferers in their private Capacity had nothing further to do – should this not be the Case, I wish to be informed, and whether it is expected of me to procure the abovementioned Papers, or not. [39]

On behalf of his client's son, Foster Junior, Prescott wrote to Pickering of a similar incident:

> In the autumn of that year [1794] Mr Foster [Sen.] sent a statement of the Fact, and the circumstances of his case, together with an estimate of the value of his Vessel & Cargo to the late Secretary of State, and received the answer which is inclosed – After this he rested easy, presuming the necessary Copies would by Government be procured from the West Indies, and forwarded to England; nor did he suspect that it had not been done until the receipt of Mr. Bayard's Letter.[40]

When glitches in the system caused delays, the result could be that the deadline for appealing decrees was irrevocably passed. Affected in this manner, American merchant Norris bitterly moaned: "I had assurances […] that the Proper Papers should be obtained & sent on to our Agent in London, on this assurance I rested easy, and did not take any Steps myself to send out to the West Indies to procure these Papers. I cannot account for this failure."[41]

37 Unknown quoting from a letter of Samuel Cabot's to Pickering, 23 November 1797; NARA, *Box 2, British Spoliations – NAID: 1170270*.

38 Bayard to the Commissioners under Article VII of the Jay Treaty, 7 December 1796; TNA, FO 304/7.

39 Hedge to Pickering, 4 December 1796; NARA, *Box 1, British Spoliations – NAID: 1170270*.

40 Prescott to Pickering, 7 December 1796; NARA, *Box 8, British Spoliations – NAID: 1170270*.

41 Norris to Pickering, 30 November 1799; NARA, *Box 10, British Spoliations – NAID: 1170270*.

Similarly, Sewall wrote to the Secretary of State about the case of the schooner *Jeremiah*. He had "supposed till now that the Adm[iralt]y Copies of this Case had been obtained with others, in the course which was taken by the Care of the Gov. of the US, and had been daily transmitted to Mr. Bayard".[42] However, the copies of the proceedings never arrived in London and thus the appeal was turned down. The only option left was "now in an application to the Comm[ission] under the British Treaty",[43] for which the papers would again be needed.

To Bayard's chagrin, the knowledge about the commission as an alternative means of compensation also meant that many US merchants no longer believed the usual time frame applied. They incorrectly thought that they could simply send their cases to the commissioners at their leisure, so long as the commission was still active, and thus simply let the deadlines for appealing decrees pass.[44] Yet, to be eligible for the commission, cases had to have passed through, or at least applied for an appeal within the regular time frame of nine months after their first decree. Negotiations led to a special dispensation that permitted American claimants an additional three months.[45] Further regulations were in place for applying to the commission.

Missed deadlines for acquiring proceedings and necessary papers were so frequent that Bayard established a method of having US claimants explain their reasons for delays in a sworn affidavit that was annexed to said papers.[46] The King's Advocate, Nathaniel Gostling, angrily pronounced that if American claimants paid "proper diligence"[47] they would be able to obtain papers on time and if they did not, they must apply to get extensions within the regular, British court system, especially since Britain was graciously giving "special Accommodation"[48] to American suitors. Using the case of the *Friendship* (Tuttle) to explain which general issues American claimants faced and why they were so prone to delays, Bayard's letter, sent four days later, can hardly been seen as anything other than a reply to Gostling's allegations.[49] Sadly, his

42 Sewall to Pickering, 28 September 1797; NARA, *Box 3, British Spoliations – NAID: 1170270*.

43 Sewall to Pickering, 28 September 1797; ibid.

44 Bayard to the Commissioners under Article VII of the Jay Treaty, 7 December 1796; TNA, FO 304/7.

45 18 July 1795; Bayard, *Diary of Samuel Bayard*, p. 20.

46 Clarkson to Bayard, 15 May 1797; TNA, FO 304/7.

47 Gostling to the Commissioners under Article VII of the Jay Treaty, 3 December 1796; ibid.

48 Gostling to the Commissioners under Article VII of the Jay Treaty, 3 December 1796; ibid.

49 Bayard to the Commissioners under Article VII of the Jay Treaty, 7 December 1796; ibid.

main reasons would only have stoked British prejudice. Of the four reasons given, three were down to American misconceptions and communications: ignorance of required deadlines, confusion of regular appeal deadlines with the time frame of the commission's work, and miscommunication on whether the government or individual parties were to organise the vice-admiralty court proceedings. His statement closed with the fact that the "delay & expence attending the procuring of copies of proceedings of the Vice-Admiralty Courts have prevented the parties from obtaining such copies".[50]

A large proportion of American merchants constantly worried about preparing their cases in time, especially those who were organising the necessary copies and proofs themselves. In the case of the *Argo*, a claimant wrote to George Irving, the US consul in London, that: "the Captors put it [...] out of my power to either lay in a Claim or to appeal from the sentence within the time prescribed by the British Laws in prize Cases" by "my not knowing where they had sent her [the vessel]."[51] The firm Oliver & Thompson complained that they had been unable to enter appeals in time for several cases as "we have good reason to believe that the detention of these papers was occasioned by an infamous Agent of the Captors, of the name of Waterhouse, who has done much mischief to this country and even to England".[52] Some merchants wanted to obtain the paperwork independently of the government, but simply lacked contacts in the respective area, making the process cumbersome and ineffective.[53] Yet the British court system, at least in theory, had the same rules and deadlines regardless of one's wealth or circumstances, and Gostling had little sympathy for these situations.[54]

However, the government did help obtain the required vice-admiralty papers in many cases. On two occasions they sent government agents to the West Indies to procure large sets of proceedings.[55] They also cooperated with the Committee of Merchants in Philadelphia chaired by Thomas Fitzsimmons. It published a Notice "for the Information of the Suffering Merchants in the

50 Bayard to the Commissioners under Article VII of the Jay Treaty, 7 December 1796; ibid.

51 Wall to Irving, 5 September 1801; TNA, FO 304/01/21.

52 Oliver to Pickering, 29 April 1799; NARA, *Box 10, British Spoliations – NAID: 1170270.*

53 Bayard to the Commissioners under Article VII of the Jay Treaty, 7 December 1796; TNA, FO 304/7.

54 This mindset seems unconvincing when regarding the leeway provided to Grey and Jervis in the Martinique cases. Gostling to the Commissioners under Article VII of the Jay Treaty, 3 December 1796; ibid.

55 Bayard to the Commissioners under Article VII of the Jay Treaty, 7 December 1796; ibid.

United States"[56] and forged a plan to send one joint agent to the West Indies to procure copies of the many proceedings needed by different, individual merchants there.[57] Publicly advertised, they offered to acquire all necessary papers if applied to by a particular deadline.[58] A similar strategy had previously been employed in the Martinique cases, where a newspaper clipping read:

> A gentleman lately from Martinique was requested to make known in Philadelphia for the information of those concerned, that a complete collection is made of all documentary papers relative to captures and adjudications on the part of the British government, and that the same may be expected shortly to arrive in the brig Venus, capt. Burrows, for this port. [59]

B. Amory would take on such duties as the Committee of Merchants in Philadelphia's Agent at St Kitts. There, he spoke with the Registrar, producing "a list of all the Cases in which it would be necessary to have Copies from the Records of the Court [...] as expeditious as possible in getting them ready".[60] Despite mainly communicating with Fitzsimmons, the interaction between Bayard and Amory was actively encouraged by the Committee.[61] And the State Department referred (for example, the case of Foster Sen./Jr), to the Committee.[62] Correspondence between another merchant company and Fitzsimmons also shows that Bayard was supplying information on which vessels needed vice-admiralty court papers at another location.[63] Secretary of State Randolph had already started communicating with merchants on the island of Bermuda to obtain copies of the vice-admiralty court proceedings there before November 1794.[64] Indeed, a government agent had been appointed

56 Wagner to Bear & Judah, 8 December 1794; NARA, *Box 1, British Spoliations – NAID: 1170270.*

57 Bear & Judah to unknown, undated; ibid.

58 Barttet to Pickering, 2 December 1796; NARA, *Box 8, British Spoliations – NAID: 1170270.*

59 Clipping attached to a letter of Wagner's to Tyler, Winslow & Attwood Jun., 26 December 1794; TNA, FO 304/10.

60 B. Amory Jr to Fitzsimmons, 24 July 1797; NARA, *Box 8, British Spoliations – NAID: 1170270*; Ellinston and Perot to Randolph, 1 November 1794; NARA, *Box 10, British Spoliations – NAID: 1170270.*

61 Fitzsimmons to Wagner, 21 October 1797; NARA, *Box 10, British Spoliations – NAID: 1170270.*

62 Wagner to Forster, 2 January 1795; NARA, *Box 8, British Spoliations – NAID: 1170270.*

63 Dan and Brade to Fitzsimmons, 21 November 1797; NARA, *Box 10, British Spoliations – NAID: 1170270.*

64 Ellinston and Perot to Randolph, 1 November 1794; ibid.

to travel to the West Indies and aid in disputed prize cases there in April 1794. But Nathaniel Higginson, the lawyer chosen and provided with a $5,000 warrant for his cause, had inconveniently died in Dominica, having ordered sets of proofs in various Caribbean islands. [65] The West Indian copyists, now unsure what to do with the papers they had made, and not knowing from whom to receive their payment, declared him a "fraud".[66]

But even when the communication worked out and copies were obtained, they still needed to survive the transport to London. They were not only exposed to the elements and risks of ocean-bound travel, but also to other captures. The brig *Peggy* (Hayer) is a catastrophic example. She was carrying numerous copies of proceedings of American cases in the West Indies. How many precisely she was carrying is unknown and for a while even the State Department was unsure which papers had actually been on board. The vessel was wrecked off the English coast. At least eighty-seven sets of papers needed to be reordered from Dominica and St Kitts alone.[67] Bayard informed some merchants that their copies were lost and had been requested by the government once more.[68] Others wrote to the Secretary of State, attempting to ascertain the fate of their own papers, repeatedly hoping some had been saved at the site of the wreckage.[69] Edward Hallam & Co. wrote to find out the fate of his case. Knowing the copies for the case of the *Three Brothers* had been on board the *Peggy*, he had heard about her loss through commissioner Trumbull's brother.[70] Whatever their fate, they were not on the governmental list for secondary orders. Merchant Derby contrarily did not even know in which vessel his papers had been transported and was thus left in the realm of utter uncertainty, suffering from the inconsistent and slow American procedure.[71]

The risk of communications and papers going astray was quite high, as it was unusual for the papers to be sent straight from the lower admiralty courts to London. It was general practice for American merchants to send documents

[65] NARA, *Letters Received from Samuel Bayard – NAID: 1170268*, p. 88; Moats, *Navigation Neutrality*, p. 130.

[66] NARA, *Letters Received from Samuel Bayard – NAID: 1170268*, p. 57.

[67] Copies of the Proceedings of the Courts of Vice Admiralty at Dominica and St Kitts are wanted in the following cases only, being such as were lost in the Brig *Peggy*, Capt. Hayer; NARA, *Box 10, British Spoliations – NAID: 1170270*.

[68] Bayard to Woodward, 21 August 1797; NARA, *Box 4, British Spoliations – NAID: 1170270*.

[69] Jackson to Pickering, 18 November 1795; NARA, *Box 3, British Spoliations – NAID: 1170270*.

[70] Hallam to Pickering, 4 September 1797; NARA, *Box 7, British Spoliations – NAID: 1170270*.

[71] Derby to Pickering, 20 November 1796; NARA, *Box 3, British Spoliations – NAID: 1170270*.

for the commission to the State Department, which in turn was supposed to forward them to London.

A typical letter to the Secretary of State in June 1795 read: "Be so good Sir, as to forward them [the annexed papers relative to the capture and condemnation of the *Salome*] to London by the first vessel to the care of the Agent for Claims and Appeals, where I hope that justice may be done me."[72]

This process left much room for error, both in the case of allocating responsibilities, but also from a simple geographic perspective. In an ideal version of this envisioned communication cycle, US merchants spread throughout the country applied for assistance at the State Department. Their cases were forwarded by said department to London, where Samuel Bayard took up correspondence and sent out information on which papers to obtain back to the individual claimants in the United States. The papers were then organised from the respective vice-admiralty courts, located somewhere across the vastness of the British Empire, but most frequently in the West Indies. They were obtained partially by the government, partially by individual parties or their middlemen. The documents were sent to and collected in the State Department. Finally, they would be forwarded to London for the actual use by Bayard or the commission. This was the fastest cycle of information the US government envisioned for claimants. Should any questions concerning types of proof come up, application again had to be made to London, sometimes via the State Department. This overly engineered system left many, many loopholes for confusion, and was far removed from the most efficient system.

The Philadelphia Committee's private agents in the West Indies, for example, had received word from Bayard that certain ships no longer required copies of their proceedings. Not only did the communication arrive so late that some of these had already been completed, once the papers had been copied, they were forwarded from the West Indies to the Committee first, instead of being forwarded directly to Bayard.[73] As other correspondence has illustrated, the correct addressees were hard for US claimants to discern, ranging from Jay to Bayard to the Secretary of State. Eliphalet Ladd had already contacted Bird, Jefferson, Pickering and Wagner in an attempt to find out how he could gain compensation for the brig *Mary*, sunk in 1794.[74]

72 Vasse to Randolph, 16 June 1795; NARA, *Box 8, British Spoliations – NAID: 1170270.*

73 Dan and Brade to Fitzsimmons, 21 November 1797; NARA, *Box 10, British Spoliations – NAID: 1170270.*

74 Ladd to Pickering, 31 August 1797; NARA, *Box 4, British Spoliations – NAID: 1170270.*

Fig. 8: Information cycles in the Jay Treaty commission under Article VII and communications for government assistance in Prize Appeals cases, compiled from NARA, Boxes 1–10; British Spoliations, *c.* 1796–*c.* 1824 – NAID: 1170270.

8.1: Most efficient cycle of information.

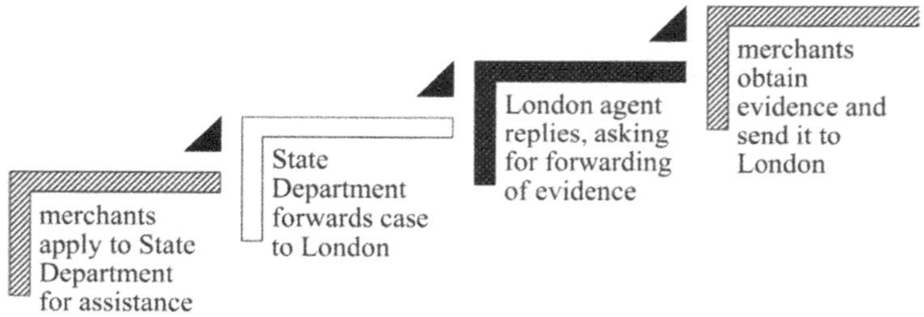


8.2: Cycle of information desired by the US government.

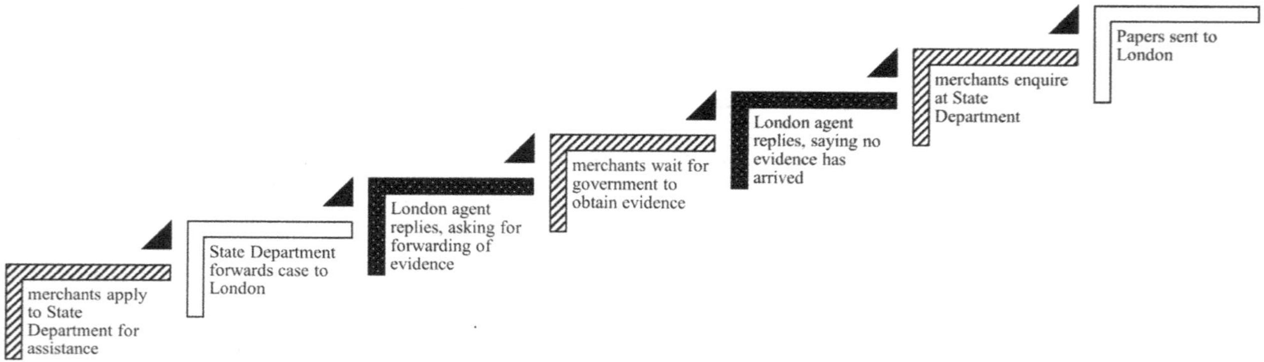


8.3: Regular cycle of information in practice.

In several cases, the vice-admiralty court proceedings were individually organised by merchants, only for them to be lost by the State Department.[75] After their original copies had gone missing in the department, the owners of the *Rachel* angrily, but pragmatically, scrawled: "It will be very expensive to me to send out to the West Indies and get the Copies, but if there is no prospect of its being done by Government, It seems necessary I should immediately attend to the Business myself."[76] Prescott, writing on behalf of Foster Junior, descried how after his father's passing: "It is an object of importance to him, and rather than not have the Copies forwarded to the Court of Appeal in time, he would endeavour to procure them himself, altho it would be very inconvenient & expensive to him to do it."[77]

The system was made even more complicated by the inclusion of private agents as merchant representatives in London, acting in parallel alongside Bayard. In some cases, they cooperated with him, but in others they acted separately and from 1794 to 1804 private representation still accounted for 62.9% of all American appeals.[78]

In one case a merchant noted:

> one copy of the appeal papers you will please forward to me & transmit two copies thereof to our London friends Ja[me]s Mackenzie & Glennie, with a request to prosecute the appeal in behalf of the Maryland Insurance Co. the responsibility of which instruction is added to my own, for the repayment of any advances which you may be subjected to.[79]

In another, concerning the brig *Minerva*, it was written that all the papers were transmitted to George Barclay & Co. of London:

> with Orders to adopt the necessary measures for the recovery of that property. As it appears those Gentlemen have intirely neglected the business. I shall take the earliest Opp[ortunit]y in desiring them to put the papers into the hands of Mr. Bayard to whom I Shall write on the Subject[80].

75 For example, Hathaway to Pickering, 10 March 1797; NARA, *Box 1, British Spoliations – NAID: 1170270.*

76 Story to Pickering, 6 December 1796; NARA, *Box 5, British Spoliations – NAID: 1170270.*

77 Prescott to Pickering, 7 December 1796; NARA, *Box 8, British Spoliations – NAID: 1170270.*

78 See table 10.

79 Buchanan to Hardlman, 2 March 1804; NARA, *Box 4, British Spoliations – NAID: 1170270.*

80 Moore to Wagner, 26 May 1797; ibid.

More people were sometimes involved simply due to the maritime nature of all causes. Thus, Willman asked for the correspondence concerning his case to be forwarded by the State Department to an associate of his, as "tis likely I may be at Sea when you write".[81]

Bayard's departure from London in 1798 started a frequent change of resident agent for the commission. Described as an additional agent with a more established knowledge on maritime commerce, Samuel Cabot would take over Bayard's role until the suspension of the Commission.[82] Such changes of hands caused some merchants additional distress. The claimants, Bear and Judah, of the *Commerce* wrote:

> Mr. Bayard [...] informs us that he must recommend our appointing some other Gentleman resident in London in his place as our Attorney. And we being unacquainted in London & Concluding that Mr. Bayard derived his agency from the Executive of our Government, are at a loss to know how to proceed in the business & have thought it most prudent to solicit your advice explanatory therein[83].

These claimants, whose vessel had been captured in 1794, went on to have Samuel Bayard, Samuel Cabot and Samuel Williams all handle their case in succession. Bayard took their case to the Appeals Court, after it had been condemned at St Kitts, at an estimated value of more than $15,000 for ship and cargo.[84] The appeal concluded on 26 January 1799, with a decree of restitution, but forcing the claimants to pay interest.[85] It appears that this case was then forwarded to the commission, though no award seems to have been made.

The complex cycle of knowledge circulation across the Atlantic, also led to regular enquiries by various parties trying to ascertain where their papers were, whether they had been lost or if they needed to be acquired again.

Discussing the documents of the *Hawke*, condemned in Antigua and then lost on board the *Peggy*, Jackson asked the Secretary of State "wether it is best for us to forward coppies of those Documents to Mr. Bayard direct, or to the Secretary of State".[86]

[81] Willman to Pickering, 25 February 1797; NARA, *Box 8, British Spoliations – NAID: 1170270.*

[82] 16 Boston merchants to Gore, 6 May 1796; NARA, *Box 10, British Spoliations – NAID: 1170270.*

[83] Bear & Judah to unknown, 8 illegible 1797; NARA, *Box 1, British Spoliations – NAID: 1170270.*

[84] Bear & Judah to James Madison, 26 February 1802; ibid.

[85] TNA, HCA 45/24/6: *Commerce* (Bouton).

[86] Jackson to Pickering, 18 November 1795; NARA, *Box 3, British Spoliations – NAID: 1170270.*

Generally, attempting to keep track of their court papers appears to have been a challenge for many merchants. Charles Ligourrey did not even find out if his papers had been procured by the government at all, writing: "I never have learnt what has been done by our gov[ernmen]t Agents, who went out to the West Indies upon this business [of retrieving court papers]".[87] He continued: "I'm at a loss to know in what manner I am to proceed."[88]

Almost as regular as Bayard's standard letter on the necessary forms of evidence and the need for swift action, was his response to merchants enquiring about their cases. To this, he would often reply that no papers had been received from the State Department and that enquiries were to be made at said department quickly and diligently by the merchants themselves: "You had best ascertain whether our Government has been able to send forward a Copy of the Court-proceedings in your case & if not, it is highly expedient that you should take measures as early as possible to have such Copies forwarded to me without delay."[89]

A lack of note of receipt by Bayard was already enough to set merchants' nerves on edge. Had the copies of the court proceedings arrived? In the case of the *Friendship*, Butler, Wheaton & Jackson stated that a letter of Bayard's did not mention receiving any papers and they were "apprehensive they have not reached Mr. Bayard".[90] Another merchant enquired anxiously about the state of his papers, admitting: "It may be possible the papers respecting my vessel & others being directed to Mr. Jay may not have fallen into Mr. Bayard's hands."[91] The usual route of enquiry taken by merchants seems to have been to contact Bayard directly or to enquire whether he had received the papers at the State Department.[92] Interestingly, Bayard, in part, also told claimants to get in touch with the State Department when concerning the state of their case, as opposed to answering all queries himself.[93] One supposes this may have reduced his workload somewhat, which seems to have been quite high considering the amount of correspondence required in the system of communication established for his work.

87 Ligourrey to Pickering, 28 November 1799; ibid.

88 Ligourrey to Pickering, 28 November 1799; ibid.

89 Bayard to Hedge, [illegible]; NARA, *Box 1, British Spoliations – NAID: 1170270.*

90 Butler, Wheaton & Jackson to Pickering, 20 September 1797; NARA, *Box 2, British Spoliations – NAID: 1170270.*

91 Derby to Pickering, 20 November 1796; NARA, *Box 3, British Spoliations – NAID: 1170270.*

92 Anderson to Pickering, 14 August 1798; NARA, *Box 4, British Spoliations – NAID: 1170270.*

93 Brantingham to Wagner, 22 August 1798; NARA, *Box 5, British Spoliations – NAID: 1170270.*

Elias Hasket Derby complained concerning the vessel *Hope* (Felt) "I have frequently received Letters from Mr. Bayard respecting this Case [...] but not so particular as I could wish".[94] As papers had been sent in several bundles, Bayard's phrasing had not been precise enough: the claimant was still unsure as to which set of proofs he had received, and which had got lost in transit.[95] Yet, in this case, Derby decided against asking Bayard, and simply asked the Secretary of State to ascertain whether the vessel by which the papers had been sent had successfully arrived in London.

The *Hope*, however, had bigger fish to fry. It belonged to an unfortunate group of claimants that needed to have inhibitions served upon absent captors. In these cases, when the capturing party did not react to a summons to court, or indeed interact at all with the opposing party, an inhibition had to be served upon them, compelling them to appear. A register held in the American archives dated May 1797, listed seven cases in which inhibitions had been served in the vice-admiralty courts of the West Indies and a further seventy-one in process, not yet completed.[96] Finding captors was not easy and more often than not also involved sending agents to islands in the West Indies. In the *Hope*'s case, Bayard had forwarded the Inhibition to the Secretary of State, who in turn was to send it on "to the West Indies & there serve [...] on the Captors. This must first be returned before the cause can advance".[97] A similar case was that of the *John & Joseph*, where an inhibition needed to be served in Bermuda.[98] The state of an inhibition could also be enquired at the State Department, but sometimes US claimants applied directly to their allocated proctors at Doctors' Commons for news.[99] The Philadelphia Committee of Merchants also aided in organising the serving of inhibitions.[100] Their West Indies agent, Armory, confirmed that he had served an inhibition forwarded to him and added that he would post it back to the Committee.[101]

94 Derby to Pickering, 16 May 1797; NARA, *Box 3, British Spoliations – NAID: 1170270*; The Derby family was heavily involved in American privateering, with both Elias Hasket Derby (Sr) (1739–99) of Salem and his son, Elias Hasket Derby Jr (1766–1826) investing in privateering from the Revolutionary War. For more, see Williams, *French Assault on US Shipping*, p. 251; Hulbert, *Untold War*, pp. 25–6.

95 Derby to Pickering, 20 November 1796; ibid.

96 NARA, *List of Claims, 18 May 1797 – NAID: 1170192, 39v–64r.*

97 Bayard to Derby, 9 March 1797; NARA, *Box 3, British Spoliations – NAID: 1170270.*

98 Truxtun to Pickering, 16 October 1796; ibid.

99 Slade to William and Ross, 16 February 1796; NARA, *Box 4, British Spoliations – NAID: 1170270.*

100 Dan and Brade to Fitzsimmons, 21 November 1797; NARA, *Box 10, British Spoliations – NAID: 1170270.*

101 Amory Jr to Fitzsimmons, 24 July 1797; NARA, *Box 8, British Spoliations – NAID: 1170270.*

Despite their misfortunes, the vessels condemned at illegal vice-admiralty courts, such as the one at Martinique, could consider themselves lucky: no copies of those proceedings need be acquired for the appeals process. The proctors Crickett & Townley even went so far as to declare this a kindness at the behest of their (American) claimants, saving the capturing party unnecessary costs and delays should they lose their case in the appeals court.[102]

With such views on the British admiralty court system, the creation of the Commission should have been a welcome relief. As has been clearly demonstrated above, many merchants did appreciate government assistance. They not only applied and actively engaged with the commission but admitted to being unable to follow up cases on their own, mainly due to the financial strain this created.

Their opinions of the process and its members, however, were as varied as their cases. While some described Bayard as "our Agent in London",[103] others kept their distance, naming him simply "the agent in London for conducting appeal cases",[104] and some merchants considered him incompetent, as Fitzsimmons told Secretary of State Pickering in July 1796. He concluded: "I have no doubt but the Multiplicity of cases under Mr Bayards direction and the extensive Correspondence he is expected to maintain would require an assistant, but I am sorry to observe that an Opinion prevails […] that he is himself unequal to the great trust Committed to him."[105]

Yet the clearest denominator of wide public support for the commission's work can be found in the reactions to its suspension in retaliation to the failures of the other arbitration boards under Articles IV and VI.

In the case of the *Commerce*, which went through the hands of all agents residing in London, and had finally reached the last possible instance for legal redress in front of the commission just in time for those proceedings to be suspended, the claimants wrote to Secretary of State Madison. With a bitter undertone, they asked to be informed as to *why* the commission's activities had been halted, despite them *not* having received compensation, and desired to be informed when the work would resume and who would be responsible for them this time.[106]

102 Cricket & Townley to Heseltine, 21 April 1796; NARA, *Box 4, British Spoliations – NAID: 1170270.*

103 Hedge to Pickering, 4 December 1796; NARA, *Box 1, British Spoliations – NAID: 1170270.*

104 Patterson to Pickering, 30 June 1796; NARA, *Box 5, British Spoliations – NAID: 1170270.*

105 Fitzsimmons to Pickering, 27 July 1796; NARA, *Box 10, British Spoliations – NAID: 1170270.*

106 Bear & Judah to James Madison, 26 February 1802; NARA, *Box 1, British Spoliations – NAID: 1170270.*

In a petition to the government the "Subscribers of the Committee of the Sufferers by British Spoliations in the State of Massachusetts" addressed the President on the subject. They considered the sheer volume of captures undertaken by the British in 1793 and 1794 so large, that they described them as "a great public calamity [more] than a source of individual embarrassment".[107] They termed Britain the "aggressor nation"[108] and went on to conclude that they would not allow themselves to believe that the attempt: "to revive the Board of Commissioners should be unsuccessful, their just claims [...] abandoned. They cannot conceive that the public interest requires, or that national honor permits, so great and **such** a sacrifice."[109]

If the commission should be disbanded, they expect their losses to be covered by the US government instead. Moreover, they expressed their frustration: they had considered the Commission under Article VII of the Jay Treaty a good idea, describing its members as competent and capable, and had allegedly been "sanguinely expecting the result[s of their cases] within a few months and by the restoration of their capital to resume & extend their commercial enterprises".[110]

While some merchants delicately phrased that they hoped the extent of British seizures and admiralty jurisdiction might not give "cause to regret the destruction of the French and Spanish fleets",[111] the Sufferers' petition openly acknowledged that: "a nation has, with respect to others, no effective rights, but such as it will vindicate."[112] The Commission was thus not just as a tool to compensate individual merchants, but much more a method of asserting American rights at sea and was actively seen as such by the American merchant community. It was not a mere discussion field of international law, but a concrete aspect of foreign policy on the world stage, and while most

[107] Petition of the Subscribers of the Committee of the Sufferers by British Spoliations in the State of Massachusetts, to the President of the United States, 15 December 1801; NARA, *Box 9, British Spoliations – NAID: 1170270.*

[108] Petition of the Subscribers of the Committee of the Sufferers by British Spoliations in the State of Massachusetts, to the President of the United States, 15 December 1801; ibid.

[109] Petition of the Subscribers of the Committee of the Sufferers by British Spoliations in the State of Massachusetts, to the President of the United States, 15 December 1801; ibid.

[110] Petition of the Subscribers of the Committee of the Sufferers by British Spoliations in the State of Massachusetts, to the President of the United States, 15 December 1801; ibid.

[111] Oliver to unknown, 5 September 1799; NARA, *Box 10, British Spoliations – NAID: 1170270.*

[112] Petition of the Subscribers of the Committee of the Sufferers by British Spoliations in the State of Massachusetts, to the President of the United States, 15 December 1801; NARA, *Box 9, British Spoliations – NAID: 1170270.*

merchants applied for personal financial reasons, they frequently referred to national honour, their right to international trade and a common sense of justice. It was understood that the merchant community was a crucial pillar in maintaining the economy of the new, American democratic experiment, and government aid was accepted as a path to strengthen and protect it.

# 9

# Looking Forward: Prize and Independence Post-1804

On 1 September 1807 the privateer *Betsey* (Chant) successfully captured the American merchant vessel *Minerva* (Caldwell). She had been bound from New York to Amsterdam, laden with sugar, coffee, hides and other articles. The vessel was brought into Plymouth, and, on 29 September, was restored along with all the cargo except 5,839 hides, which were condemned as legal prize.[1] The captors alleged that the hides had been transferred to the *Minerva* from the *Eagle*, an American vessel that had purchased them at Monte Video.[2] The owners of the hides disagreed and went on to appeal. The work of the arbitration commission under Article VII had been concluded for three years, thus there was no governmental assistance in the case. Nevertheless, through their merchant connections, the American owners found a way to get British aid: Charles Wall, a partner in the London merchant company Baring, Brothers & Co., appealed the case on their behalf. He took on the case for the New York owners of the goods in question: LeRoy, Bayard and Co. Sadly, the Lords of Appeal did not alter the decree issued by the High Court of Admiralty. LeRoy, Bayard & Co. had to accept the verdict of the British admiralty system.

William Bayard Jr (1761–1826) was a few years older than his distant relative, Samuel Bayard. Unlike his uncle, Robert Bayard, who had been condemning American 'rebels' during the War of Independence, or his father, William Bayard Sr, who had fled the country and whose property had largely been confiscated, William Bayard Jr remained in the United States and attained American citizenship. In 1786, he set up the mercantile firm of LeRoy, Bayard & Co. alongside his brother-in-law Herman LeRoy. The company was funded largely with the credit provided by his family, relying on loyalist and familial ties. In 1796, James McEvers, son of the New York stamp collector, joined the company, rebranded as LeRoy, Bayard & McEvers.[3] The company lost at least three vessels to British privateers; alongside the *Minerva* (Caldwell), the

1 TNA, HCA 45/57/14: *Minerva* (Caldwell) 270r.

2 Ibid., 272v.

3 James McEvers' parents were James McEvers and Elisabeth Bayard, who had married Robert Bayard after her husband's death, making him William Jr's step-cousin. Founders Online and NARA, *LeRoy, Bayard & McEvers to Thomas Jefferson, 19 March 1816.*

*Catherina Augusta* (Center) was captured in 1811 and the *Herman* (Horn) in 1812.[4] In addition, another four vessels were captured by the French between 1793 and 1813.[5]

As William Bayard Jr's experiences show, upon the completion of the Jay Treaty's commission in London in 1804, prize taking was not a thing of the past for American citizens. Throughout the French Wars, French, Spanish and North African privateering remained a "major difficulty"[6] to US commerce in the Mediterranean, to the point that the fledgling US Navy was dispatched to deal with the latter in 1801.[7]

As the London commission concluded, Thomas Fitzsimmons, who had been aiding merchants in their claims as a lobbyist with governmental influence, published a declaration, emphasising how Americans were suffering from illegal European captures. In addition, the group feared that the Haitian Revolution would lead to what was termed "Algerians in the western hemisphere";[8] that is, an outbreak of piratical or privateering activity in the Caribbean that would threaten US commerce.[9]

The Napoleonic Wars were still raging. With the Jay Treaty and Washington's Neutrality Proclamation, the United States had done its best

4 These three cases went on to appeal. It is highly likely that significantly more vessels were captured and that the records have either been lost or are currently hidden among the vast amount of prize papers waiting to be catalogued. TNA, HCA 45/64/14: *Catherina Augusta* (Center); TNA, HCA 42/434/580: *Herman* (Horn).

5 Williams, *French Assault on US Shipping*, pp. 101, 164, 318, 336.

6 Marzagalli, 'However illegal', 118.

7 Ibid., p. 121. For instance, the Derby family, which continually invested in American privateering, was not only embroiled in the British prize system, but also had run-ins with the French. The *Mount Vernon* (Derby Jr) received her commission in 1799 and was engaged in a "famous action" with several French privateers off Gibraltar. Williams, *French Assault on US Shipping*, p. 251. In addition, the family was embroiled in the French prize court system, reclaiming awards under a prize commission with France in the first half of the nineteenth century, as can be seen from the following governmental publication: *Statement showing the Payments of Awards of the Commissioners appointed under the Conventions between the United States and France, Concluded April 30, 1803, and July 4, 1831, and Between the United States and Spain, Concluded February 22, 1819; also Abstract Containing the Names of the Persons and the Vessels Concerned in those Cases allowed as Valid by the Respective Commissions, with other Important Data Relative to Amounts Awarded and Payments of the Same* (Washington DC, 1886), p. 16.

8 T. Fitzsimmons, 'Representation of the Philadelphia Chamber of Commerce', in American Antiquarian Society (ed.), *Early American Imprints, 1639–1800: A Readex Microprint of the Works Listed in Evan's American Bibliography, Evans Numbers 1–39162* (Worcester MA, 1804), at p. 6.

9 Incidentally, Fitzsimmons was also a commissioner for the Jay Treaty's commission under Article VI (debts). Perkins, *The First Rapprochement*, p. 53.

to maintain peaceful relations. Despite the Quasi-War with France leading to many captures, the Convention of 1800 laid the foundations for summary restorations and took concrete steps (for example, in establishing proofs of ownership).[10] The Americans had not joined the Second League of Armed Neutrality and had watched from the sidelines, as the death of the League's patron and the British destruction of the Danish fleet had ended the venture within a year.[11]

Back at home, by the turn of the century, William Jr's business was doing well. His friend, Alexander Hamilton, was also involved, communicating on issues of business.[12] Yet 1804 would see him take his last breath at the Bayards' family estate in Greenwich village, after his infamous duel with Aaron Burr.[13] He had been a driving force in the development of federal American admiralty courts. The American system of prize courts had been revolutionised since 1776. With the dissolution of the British vice-admiralty courts, the states had established a plethora of different court styles and rulings, questioning the very foundations of civil, international law.[14] In the end, the realisation that "[admiralty] law was not a game; it was, among other things, a branch of foreign policy",.[15] had led to American prize courts falling under federal jurisdiction. That they held the key to war and peace meant their implementation required standardisation, or as Alexander Hamilton had famously remarked in The Federalist Paper No. 80:

> The most bigoted idolizers of state authority have not thus far shewn a disposition to deny the national judiciary the cognizance of maritime cause. These so generally depend on the law of nations, and so commonly affect the rights of foreigners, that they fall within the considerations which are relative to the public peace.[16]

Although the American Revolutionary War and Independence did bring many freedoms and new opportunities with it, in the long-term American legalists mainly adhered to a vision of international law as it was negotiated

10 France – Convention of 1800: Avalon Project – Documents in Law, History and Diplomacy, Yale Law School/Lillian Goldman Law Library, https://avalon.law.yale.edu/19th_century/fr1800.asp (accessed 27 July 2024), esp. Articles III, IV.

11 Robson, *A History of the Royal Navy*, pp. 32, 36.

12 Founders Online and NARA, *William Bayard*, https://founders.archives.gov/search/Recipient%3A%22Bayard%2C%20William%22 (accessed 17 August 2023).

13 New York Historical Society 2004.

14 August, 'Trial by Jury in a Court of Admiralty', 176.

15 Friedman, *A History of American Law*, p. 190.

16 Quoted in Casto, 'Origins of Federal Admiralty Jurisdiction', 136.

on the international stage.[17] The first ever federal court of the United States had been an appellate board for cases of prize, though it was disbanded with the ratification of the US Constitution in 1789 and its powers transferred to the Supreme Court.[18] From 1789 to 1801, "prize cases arising from the wars following the French Revolution utterly dominated the Supreme Court's appellate jurisdiction over maritime cases",[19] in which 77% of all cases concerned privateering.[20] Thus, while American politicians viewed prize as a valuable component of foreign policy abroad, its implementation on national ground was equally important to the maintenance of peaceful relations.

However, much as piracy and privateering could blend into one another, prize also bled into other maritime disputes, such as fishing rights or impressment. In the case of the *Camillus* (Kennard), the owner of the vessel wrote to James Madison, enclosing a report on the treatment of the American seamen employed on his vessel and several affidavits of varying crew members. After a successful chase, Nathaniel Kennard, the *Camillus*'s captain, had been asked to come aboard the British privateer, being rowed over by members of his own crew. Arriving on deck, he had been detained for fourteen hours, while his rowers were asked to sign up for service with the Royal Navy. For refusing to serve on any naval vessel other than an American one in a defensive war, Thomas Carpenter, one of Kennard's crew, was forcibly stripped of his shirt and then severely flogged, while his own captain was still confined.[21] Whereas Carpenter referred to bad pain and the loss of large parts of skin, his captain described his back as being "in a shocking condition appearing like black bruised meat […] that […] might mortify"[22] and had ordered several treatments of vinegar and brandy to prevent infection and death in the tropical climate. In addition to bodily harm, the cargo had also been damaged through negligence and the hold plundered by the captors.

Such cases of illegal impressment are well known to historians and would contribute to the War of 1812. They stemmed in part from the severe British need for naval personnel, but also from the presumption that all English-speaking sailors without an accepted proof of US nationality were British subjects. American mariners had attempted to guard themselves from such

17 Janis states that some American jurists even believed the law of nations had been adopted into the American legal system. Janis, *America and the Law of Nations, 1776–1939*, p. 33.

18 Library of Congress and United States Congress, Constitution Article III.

19 Casto, 'Origins of Federal Admiralty Jurisdiction', 150.

20 Ibid., pp. 150–1.

21 Testimony of Thomas Carpenter, noted in Manning to Madison, 11 September 1804; NARA, *Box 1, British Spoliations – NAID: 1170270*.

22 Testimony of captain Nathaniel Kennard on the treatment of Thomas Carpenter, noted in Manning to Madison, 11 September 1804; ibid.

allegations by obtaining 'protections' (that is, certificates proving nationality). In 1796 Thomas Pinckney wrote to Grenville: "no Article of the existing Treaty requires nor does […] the Law of Nations impose upon Americans the hard condition of not being able to navigate the Seas without taking with them […] Proof of their being Citizens of the United States."[23] Often acquiring protections was futile, as there was no need for British officials to accept them and they could easily be forged/falsified. Sir John Nicholl would state to the British Secretary of Foreign Affairs in 1804, "that it was 'impossible' for him to offer general guidelines to the Admiralty about how to decide who was a Briton. There were too many different circumstances that could potentially complicate the determination".[24] Thus, reiterated grievances of the American government were repeatedly set aside in preference of a British vision of dominant sea power on the high seas as opposed to the shared realm of the law of nations. While a few US seamen decided to tattoo their bodies with patriotic symbols, the most attempted to prove their nationality through officially issued protection papers.[25] Yet the commander of the British vessel *L'Éclair* (Sutton) refused to acknowledge those carried by the *Camillus* (Kennard), stating that there were "no protections good for any thing"[26] and he could obtain a whole ship load of said papers for a miserly $2. The disappointment at this reality was also explicitly mentioned by the owner of the vessel.[27]

The outrage was not just over the mistreatment of sailors and individuals, it was tied up with the continual disregard for American citizenship itself.[28] In his war message, President Madison described British impressment as "a series of acts, hostile to the United States as an independent and neutral nation"[29] and went on to clearly label impressment as "not […] founded on the Law of Nations […] but […] a municipal prerogative".[30]

23 Quoted in Perl-Rosenthal, *Citizen Sailors*, p. 134.

24 Ibid., p. 259.

25 Ibid., p. 174. Yet it should be pointed out that Dye, whose work Perl-Rosenthal relies on, points out that patriotic symbols were a very small proportion of ink marks in the 1790s; I. Dye, 'The Tattoos of Early American Seafarers: 1796–1818', *Proceedings in the American Philosophical Society*, 133 (1989), 520–54, at 527, 541.

26 Testimony of Thomas Carpenter, noted in Manning to Madison, 11 September 1804; NARA, *Box 1, British Spoliations – NAID: 1170270.*

27 He referenced the "causeless lawless cruelties inflicted on a peaceable, native citizen, of good behaviour having a protection"; Manning to Madison, 11 September 1804; ibid.

28 Perl-Rosenthal, *Citizen Sailors*, p. 270.

29 J. Madison, *President James Madison's war message, June 1, 1812*, www.visitthecapitol.gov/artifact/president-james-madisons-war-message-june-1-1812-0 (accessed 14 March 2025).

30 Ibid.

After the painstaking work undertaken by all those involved in the Jay Treaty and its implementation, peace between Britain and America was finally disbanded. By this point, British sea power had been clearly established. The League of Armed Neutrality had been broken, the French defeated in the West Indies and again alongside the Spanish at Trafalgar.[31] Napoleon had attempted to shift from naval to economic warfare, attempting to blockade Britain through the implementation of his Continental system, which was repeatedly enshrined into the treaties of the nations he had defeated.[32]

In the War of 1812, the asymmetry of naval power became strikingly clear: At the time of Madison's declaration, the Royal Navy had 584 ships, including 102 ships-of-the-line and 124 frigates. The fledgling US Navy had about twenty vessels, consisting of eight frigates and twelve sloops.[33] The result was a flourish in American privateering activity, the only other maritime defence the US had aside from the navy.[34] For example, the privateer *Comet* (Boyle) was commissioned on 29 June 1812, eleven days after declaration of war. She left harbour on 12 July and captured her first prize exactly two weeks later, barely a month passed since her commission.[35] Both in the Revolutionary War and the War of 1812, American privateers, which vastly outnumbered their national naval vessels, played a vital role.[36] John Latimer states the "weakness in historical writing about the war [...] is the failure to evaluate the effect of privateering".[37] There is a strong cleft in scholarly opinion on this issue. In Latimer's opinion, the impact of privateering has been overestimated. He focuses on Lloyd's insurance in Britain, which reported 1,175 British captured vessels (out of an estimated merchant fleet of 25,000). For Latimer, a loss of not even 5% of all national shipping is negligible. He goes on to emphasise that privateering was motivated by profit, as opposed to national defence, with American privateering ventures declining as soon as investors believed that they wouldn't bring sufficient returns.[38] However, Brian Arthur has proven

31 Robson, *A History of the Royal Navy*, p. 143.

32 Although economic warfare had of course been ongoing throughout the wars, as has been demonstrated, for example, with the orders in council of 1794 in Chapter 5. F. Crouzet, 'Wars, Blockade, and Economic Change in Europe, 1792–1815', *The Journal of Economic History*, 24 (1964), 567–88, at 567–8; For example, fondation Napoléon, *The Treaty of Vienna, 14 October 1809*, www.napoleon.org/en/history-of-the-two-empires/articles/39720/ (accessed 27 July 2024), Articles VII, XVI.

33 J. Latimer, *1812: War with America* (Cambridge, 2010), p. 84.

34 Hulbert, *Untold War*, p. 176.

35 A. Tabarrok, 'The Rise, Fall, and Rise Again of Privateers', *The Independent Review*, 11 (2007), 565–77, at 567.

36 M. Cancian and B. Schwartz, 'Unleash the Privateers! The United States should issue letters of marque to fight Chinese aggression at sea', *Proceedings*, 146 (2020).

37 Latimer, *1812*, p. 242.

38 Ibid., pp. 242–3.

that Lloyd's did not include the capture of uninsured vessels and therefore disregarded the capture at least 500 additional vessels, bringing the estimate up to approximately 7%.[39] The tendency to discount the role played by privateers and focus on their allegedly solely economic motives was already identified by Coggeshall in 1856, who wrote that US privateers were:

> brave and patriotic men who [...] instead of being awarded a proud niche [...] have encountered neglect, and even obloquy. No testimonials of national gratitude have rewarded their blood-bought victories, and their invaluable services in crippling the resources of the common enemy. But their motives have been assailed, and cupidity and a desire for booty imputed to them as the impulses which led to their bold achievements.[40]

Similarly, Hulbert describes privateers' lives and impact as a "story [...] largely untold"[41] in the Revolutionary War. In 2014, Leiner described the lack of scholarly research on privateers in the War of 1812 as an omission, partly due to the complicated nature of researching privateering, which may result in the loss of "a critical aspect of American maritime history".[42]

Lambert reinforces Latimer's point of view, considering privateers as insignificant, as they did not force decisive military action to be taken.[43] With the implementation of the convoy system, privateering successes reduced and as Kert states "privateer captures of weak or unarmed merchant vessels served no strategic purpose beyond annoying and embarrassing their respective governments".[44]

39 Fn 257, B. Arthur, *How Britain Won the War of 1812: The Royal Navy's Blockades of the United States, 1812–1815* (Suffolk, 2011), p. 301.

40 G. Coggeshall, *History of the American privateers: And letters-of-marque, during our war with England in the years 1812, '13 and '14. Interspersed with several naval battles between American and British ships-of-war* (New York, 1856), p. 5.

41 Hulbert, *Untold War*, p. 3.

42 F. C. Leiner, 'Yes, Privateers Mattered: History is ill-served by a peculiar recent trend to downplay the significance of American privateering in the War of 1812', *Naval History Magazine*, 28 (2014). Understanding some captures and privateering ventures is highly complicated, due to their international entanglements and the turbulent events they were trapped in; for example, in the case of the destruction of the brig *Mary* (Josiah). She had been captured by a British privateer in March 1794, but was recaptured by the French when they seized control of the West Indies port where she was moored. Subsequently, "the English from a battery on the other Side, Sunk her with 11 Americans more", allegedly despite knowing she was a neutral vessel; Ladd to Pickering, 31 August 1797; NARA, *Box 4, British Spoliations – NAID: 1170270.*

43 Lambert, *The Challenge*, pp. 136, 394–5.

44 F. Kert, *Patriots and Profits in the War of 1812* (Baltimore MD, 2015), p. 13.

Either way, it can be firmly concluded that the War of 1812 would have been very different without US privateers: The American government commissioned 515 of them, including 102 from New York.[45]

One of these was the *Benjamin Franklin* (Ingersoll), which left New York harbour on 24 July 1812, a few days after the *Comet* (Boyle), and returned one month later, having made seven prizes.[46] The realities of privateering, both as a risk factor to national commerce and as a chance of investment, surrounded William Bayard Jr throughout the war and beyond.[47] In 1813, William Bayard Jr received an American letter of marque for one of his schooners, becoming not only a victim of privateering, but an active player and investor in this system of naval warfare.[48]

The War of 1812 would be remembered, or forgotten, in very different terms on either side of the Atlantic. Whereas some Americans styled the conflict as a victory, it was not important for British popular memory, that instead focused on Nelson and Napoleon.[49] Nearly a century later, the conflict would be used as a case study by Alfred Thayer Mahan to advocate for "an American ocean-going battlefleet".[50]

William Bayard Jr's company successfully overcame the setbacks of captured vessels, continuing to function into at least the late 1820s. Alongside his mercantile adventures, William Bayard Jr set himself up in the banking business. LeRoy, Bayard & McEvers also provided banking services.[51] Bayard himself became the director of the Bank of America in 1818 and the President of a Savings Bank in New York in 1819.[52] Moreover, he was also "President of Chamber of Commerce, governor of New York Hospital, trustee of Sailors' Snug Harbor, chairman of Greek Committee, member of New York Society Library and of St. John's Society, and one of the owners of Tontine Coffee House".[53]

In other words, William Bayard Jr successfully established himself in New York. In 1824, representing "Sundry Merchants [...] and Citizens of New

45 E. S. Maclay, *A History of American Privateers* (Cambridge, 1899; 2011), p. 506.

46 Ibid., p. 439.

47 Although Lambert describes New York as "barely affected" in the first years of the war, by the end of 1814 he describes the city as "full of prime seamen". Lambert, *The Challenge*, pp. 351–2.

48 J. Clement, 'Neither United States Citizens Nor British Nationalists: A Postwar Loyalist Trade Diaspora' (master's thesis, College of William & Mary, 2010), p. 52.

49 Lambert, *The Challenge*, pp. 449–51.

50 Ibid., p. 451.

51 Founders Online and NARA, *LeRoy, Bayard & McEvers to Thomas Jefferson, 19 March 1816*.

52 Hess, *America's Political Dynasties*, p. 277.

53 Pelletreau, *Historic Homes*, vol. 1, p. 110.

York"[54] he sent a memorial to Congress, presenting the plight of American merchants trading with Cuba and stating:

> It is a lawful commerce, and our citizens have a right to claim the protection of Government in its pursuit [...] We should respectfully submit to the consideration of Congress, whether it would not be expedient that a law should be passed authorizing merchant vessels to arm for their own protection, under [...] regulation [...], and which may avoid the danger of committing the peace of the nation to the discretion of individuals.[55]

This memorial demonstrates that governmental assistance concerning prizes was accepted by the merchant community. What had been a little-understood initiative at the beginning of the Jay Treaty was now a right being claimed by American merchants and their representative bodies. Samuel Bayard and the London commission's work, probably accompanied by US political rhetoric, had cemented themselves into the American mercantile psyche. In the same year, William Jr published another memorial, this time in his capacity as President of the Chamber of Commerce of New York, describing how "in the late war with Great Britain"[56] tariffs had been tolerated as protections in the mercantile community, but that further duties were unacceptable and damaging to the nation's merchants and international commerce. Life as an American merchant moved on. Privateering and prize-taking remained parts of mercantile life, but US merchants also needed to keep an eye on many other developments, including the economic policies of their own government, the building or strengthening of a national navy and their own domestic expansion. Before Napoleon had invaded Russia, he had sold Louisiana to the American government for roughly $15 million, and while the interactions with European and North African countries have been mentioned, we must not forget that some of the earliest international treaties were forged with the nations already living on American soil.[57]

54 W. Bayard, *Memorial of Sundry Merchants, (and others,) Citizens of New York, Praying Congress to take into Consideration The Subject of Piracies Committed on the Commerce of the United States by Vessels from the Island of Cuba, &c.* (Washington DC, 1824).

55 Ibid., pp. 3–4.

56 W. Bayard, *Memorial of the New York Chamber of Commerce to the Hon. The Senate and House of Representatives of the United States in Congress Assembled: With Statements Prepared by Order of the Chamber to show the Present Rate of Duties and the Rate of Duties Proposed by the Tariff Bill, Now before Congress with Remarks & C.* (New York, 1824), p. 3.

57 S. S. Harjo, 'American Indian Land and American Empire: An Interview with Philip J. Deloria', in S. S. Harjo (ed.), *Nation to Nation: Treaties Between the United*

Additionally, US prize jurisdiction started to forge its own path after the War of 1812. Under Justice Story's tenure, contracts relating to "navigation, business or commerce of the sea"[58] were established as clearly falling into admiralty courts in the United States in 1815 (*De Lovio v. Boit*), breaking with British precedent.[59] US admiralty jurisdiction was also widened after his tenure, for example to include the bodies of inland water(way)s in its jurisdiction, as opposed to the United Kingdom where the tide marks the admiralty court's jurisdiction (*Genessee Chief v. Fitzhugh*, 1852).[60]

While the colonial Vice-Admiralty Court of New York had once been located on New York's Wall Street, in the post-Revolutionary period, William Bayard Jr resided there with his wife.[61] They had married in 1783 and had several children together. William Jr's second son, Robert Bayard (1797–1878), was born six years after Lewis, Samuel and Martha (Pintard) Bayard's son.[62] Robert Bayard would be the last of the New York Bayards to carry the surname and passed away in Brooklyn, New York, in 1878.[63] In a twist of fate, Lewis Bayard (1791–1840) actually ended up living in the close vicinity of William Bayard Jr and his family.[64] It is tantalising to envision them meeting,

---

*States and American Indian Nations*, Catalogue for the New Exhibition of the National Museum of the American Indian, Washington DC, 1st edn (Washington DC, 2014), pp. 1–14, at p. 12; Dull, *American Naval History*, p. 51.

58 Quoting Justice Story's decision, S. F. Friedell, 'Admiralty and Maritime Law', in K. L. Hall (ed.), *The Oxford Companion to the Supreme Court of the United States*, 2nd edn (Oxford, 2005), pp. 18–20, at p. 19.

59 Justice Story (1779–1845, tenure as Associate Justice on the US Supreme Court: 1812–45) saw American admiralty jurisdiction in an expansive manner, to the point that "according to legend, [he] would declare admiralty jurisdiction over a cob in a bucket of water if someone happened to bring one into his Court". R. K. Newmyer, *Supreme Court Justice Joseph Story: Statesman of the Old Republic* (Chapel Hill NC, 1985), p. 207.

60 J. W. Ely, '*Genesee Chief v. Fitzhugh*', in K. L. Hall (ed.), *The Oxford Companion to the Supreme Court of the United States*, 2nd edn (Oxford, 2005), p. 388.

61 H. Liston, *The Travel Journals of Henrietta Marchant Liston: North America and Lower Canada, 1796–1800*, ed. by Louise V. North (Lanham MD, 2014), p. 100.

62 W. S. Powell, *Dictionary of North Carolina Biography: Vol. 1, A–C* (1979), vol. 1, p. 121.

63 Pelletreau, *Historic Homes*, vol. 1, p. 110.

64 Following his religious calling, Lewis was made a Deacon at Grace Church in New York in 1812. He spent a significant time in New York state, before moving to the city in 1830, where he built up St Clement's Episcopal Church. Ten years later, Lewis Pintard Bayard followed his religious path and set out on a pilgrimage to Jerusalem. He visited the Holy Land, writing busily in a journal, much as his parents had done during their travels in London. On the return journey, he succumbed to a fatal illness, on 16 October 1840, never returning home. Onderdonk, *Memorial of the Rev. Lewis P. Bayard*, pp. 26, 53–5, 64, 144.

especially as William Jr was a member of the New York Historical Society, which Samuel Bayard had co-founded and where today original furnishings from his time in London can be found.[65] While Lewis had moved to New York, Samuel and his family had relocated to the Princeton area after their stay in London and remained in the vicinity.[66] In 1784 Samuel had graduated there as valedictorian, along with his cousin James Asheton Bayard, who would be one of the American signatories of the Treaty of Ghent, which brought the War of 1812 to a close and instituted more binational arbitration committees like those established by Jay, as well as a summary restoration policy for prizes with clear geographical demarcations and time frames for claimants.[67]

With the Paris Declaration Respecting Maritime Law, generally known as the Declaration of Paris, in 1856, the age of privateering came to an end in popular memory. Its' first clause simply stated: "Privateering is and remains abolished."[68] Most of the Western maritime powers agreed to abolish this substantial part of maritime warfare. This did not mean the end of prize law, but it did mean that prize-taking moved into the realm of the state, into the catalogue of powers allotted to naval vessels as opposed to privately owned ships and their crews.[69] Attempts to create an international appeals court for nationally adjudicated prize cases (for example, in the Hague Convention (XII) of 1907) failed.[70]

Prize law was thus still an active part of warfare and municipal adjudication during both World Wars, although Tucker stresses: "that the second World War added very little in the way of substantive developments to the law of prize."[71]

The more governmental control increased and public armed forces became available, and the fewer merchant marine vessels were prevalent for potential

65 New York Historical Society Museum and Library, Side chair (one of a set of three), https://emuseum.nyhistory.org/objects/26591/side-chair-one-of-a-set-of-three?ctx=99017ac997eeb9eb2e5f547720932e0cd4d9358e&idx=19 (accessed 27 July 2024); Various plates and a worktable owned by Martha Pintard Bayard are also in the collection; New York Historical Society Museum and Library, 2024; Francis, *Old New York*, p. 73.

66 Stockton, '"Cleremont" – Historic Mansion'.

67 Craven and Woodward, *Princetonians, 1784–1790*, pp. 9–10; National Archives, *Treaty of Ghent (1814)*.

68 C. H. Stockton, 'The Declaration of Paris', *American Journal of International Law*, 14 (1920), 356–68, at 356.

69 P. Mankowski, *Rechtskultur, Beiträge zum ausländischen und internationalen Privatrecht, 1. Aufl.* (Tübingen, 2016), vol. 115, p. 114.

70 D. Schindler and J. Toman, *The Laws of Armed Conflicts: A Collection of Conventions, Resolutions and Other Documents*, 3rd rev. and completed edn (Dordrecht and Geneva, 1988), p. 825.

71 R. W. Tucker, *The Law of War and Neutrality at Sea* (Washington DC, 1957), vol. 49, p. 4.

captures, the less the importance of privateers became in warfare. On the one hand, this reflected the additional capabilities of state navies, that not only attacked enemy commerce but also enabled the prevention and facilitation of land-troops for invasions as well as protection one's own, national commerce at sea.[72] On the other hand, economists have argued that a declined interest in privateering as viable economic ventures was also responsible. They view the decline of privateering as starting with the end of the American Revolutionary War and the rise in safe and profitable long-distance trade instead.[73] For the United States, the tide of privateering was certainly already turning in the War of 1812. This is not to say that privateering was one, if not *the* main, naval defence strategy, but that the military thought was moving away from the humanitarian approach of civilised naval warfare as regulated through the prize system.[74] Despite its violent nature, prize limited the deaths and injury done to crew and passengers, as well as the destruction to property, through its provision of legal regulations. Yet in 1813 the American government created incentives to increase the financial desirability of privateers destroying vessels as opposed to capturing them.[75] A (re)captured vessel could continue to sail, a wreck was no good to either party. It was edited out of the military equation.

Crucially, it was the leaps in technology that left privateering by the wayside: "As military technology developed [...] substitution between private and military use became more difficult, and the cost-saving advantages of privateering declined. It was one thing to transform a merchant vessel into a privateer and quite another to build a nuclear submarine."[76]

The invention and introduction of the submarine cemented this prior change in the now fundamentally altered realities of naval warfare. How could the small crew of a submersible forcibly stop a much larger vessel to board and search it for papers? During World War II German submarine commanders would be issued with a simplified, government legal aid to understand how they were allowed to deal with other vessels.[77] By turning two wheels to select the type of vessel, its flag, the nationality of its cargo and its behaviour

72 N. J. Ross, 'The Provision of Naval Defense in the Early American Republic: A Comparison of the US Navy and Privateers, 1789–1815', *The Independent Review* (2011), at 422–4.

73 H. Hillmann and C. Gathmann, 'Overseas Trade and the Decline of Privateering', *The Journal of Economic History* (2011), at 731–2.

74 J. R. Garitee, *The Republic's Private Navy: The American Privateering Business as Practiced by Baltimore During the War of 1812*, 1st edn (Middletown CT, 1977), vol. 8, pp. 244–5.

75 Tabarrok, 'Rise and Fall', 574.

76 Ibid., p. 575.

77 Widmannsche Prisenscheibe, International Military Tribunal (ITM) Nuremberg Archives, H-1600: Dönitz Beweisstück Nr. 95, International Court of Justice.

at sea, this paper construction would reveal one of five options on how to proceed. Two of these options included the destruction of the vessels, in theory after the papers had been seized on board. In Britain, the distribution of prize money to naval officers was only formally ended in the Prize Act of 1948.[78] By this point Doctors' Commons had been disestablished for nearly a hundred years, with the right for common lawyers to represent clients in admiralty courts established in 1859 and the dissolution of the premises in 1867.[79] All the while, prize law traditions remained distinct throughout Europe and the United States. The issue of what exactly was international law would not be solved in this issue, despite continuous attempts, turning maritime warfare and prize into one of the topics hotly debated in the Nuremberg trials.[80]

In the United States, privateering is legal to this day. The country never signed the Declaration of Paris, which Lemnitzer has described as "an essentially anti-American package deal" [81] aiming at US isolation.[82] The United States was unwilling to give up the right to privateering that was still seen as a crucial component in a potential war against Britain.[83] Some confusion, however, has arisen, from various government statements over the American willingness to uphold the Declaration without being a signatory thereof. For example, in 1861, Secretary of State Seward wrote:

> The United States have never disclaimed the employment of letters of marque as a means of maritime war. [...] While still willing and desirous to have that further principle incorporated in the law of

78 Colombos, *A Treatise on the Law of Prize*, p. 338.

79 Thompson, *Admiralty Registrars*, p. 32; P. Barber, 'The Fall and Rise of Doctors' Commons?', *Ecclesiastical Law Journal*, 4 (1996), 462–9, at 466. While most historians equate the disappearance of Doctors' Commons as a location with the end of the High Court of Admiralty and the society of the College of Advocates, some insist that society only ended with the death of its last member. Squibb, *Doctors' Commons*, pp. 108–9; Barber even goes so far as to say that the office of the Dean of the Arches remains to this day, the one and only member of Doctors' Commons since its dissolution, asking whether a modern revival of the society would be possible. Barber, 'The Fall and Rise of Doctors' Commons?', 469.

80 See, for example, Henricus – Edition Deutsche Klassik GmbH, Nürnberger Prozesse, Hauptverhandlungen, XXI, Tag/Dienstag, 14 May 1946, Nachmittagssitzung, www.zeno.org/Geschichte/M/Der+N%C3%BCrnberger+Proze%C3%9F/Hauptverhandlungen/Einhundertneunundzwanzigster+Tag.+Dienstag,+14.+Mai+1946/Nachmittagssitzung (accessed 23 August 2023).

81 J. M. Lemnitzer, *Power, Law and the End of Privateering* (London, 2014), p. 95.

82 Ibid., pp. 74–5.

83 A. Lambert, *The British Way of War: Julian Corbett and the Battle for a National Strategy* (New Haven CT, 2021), p. 206.

> nations, we nevertheless instructed you, and all our representatives in foreign countries, to waive it, if necessary, and to stipulate, subject to the concurrence of the Senate of the United States, our adhesion to the declaration of the congress of Paris as a whole and unmodified.[84]

Charles Stockton emphasises how in the Spanish-American War and in World War I the United States upheld parts of the Declaration of Paris.[85] He does not take the time to reflect that it is the clause on privateering which was not incorporated and meant the Declaration was, in reality, not adopted in its entirety.

In the Hague Convention of 1907, American governmental representatives once again emphasised that "The United States has not renounced the right to resort to privateering",[86] though the Convention was still able to "slowly adapt the rules of maritime warfare to the technological realities of the 20th century".[87] This results in Schwartz stating that the avoidance of issuing letters of marque since the mid-nineteenth century has been the result of individual policies and strategic national interests, as opposed to a legal obligation.[88] After the War of 1812, Congress issued a large amount of privateering licences to American citizens during the Civil War and in the Wars with Spanish-America, though much research still needs to be done in these fields.[89]

Tabarrok ascribes a new relevance to privateering in the modern day, regarding the flexibility, quick responses and labour skill encapsulated in private enterprise as superior to governmental forces. However, he appears

84 *S. o. S. Seward, Message of the President of the United States to the Two Houses of Congress, at the Commencement of the Second Session of the Thirty-seventh Congress: Mr. Seward to Mr. Dayton*, https://history.state.gov/historicaldocuments/frus1861/d131 (accessed 23 August 2023), pp. 225–6.

85 Stockton, 'Declaration of Paris', 367–8.

86 James Brown Scott, *The Hague Peace Conferences of 1899 and 1907: A Series of Lectures Delivered before the Johns Hopkins University in the Year 1908*, vol. 2 (Baltimore MD, 1909), 222–23, quoted in B. Schwartz, 'U.S. Privateering Is Legal', *Proceedings*, 146 (2020).

87 Lemnitzer, *The End of Privateering*, p. 187.

88 Ibid.

89 V. S. Buford, *The Militia of the Seas: A guide to the Confederate privateers of the American Civil War, 1861–1865* (2000); W. M. Robinson, *The Confederate Privateers*, reprint of the ed. New Haven CT Yale University Press, 1928 (Columbia SC, 1990); D. Head, *Privateers of the Americas: Spanish American privateering from the United States in the early republic, Early American places* (Athens GA, 2015); M. McCarthy, *Privateering, Piracy and British Policy in Spanish America, 1810–1830* (Suffolk, 2013).

to simply equate privateering to (private) government contractors.[90] The potential for Congress to issue letters of marque has been voiced in many different contexts in the twenty-first century. Its principles were discussed in relation to the attacks of 11 September 2001, arguing that licences could be issued to private citizens against (individual) terrorists as opposed to state entities, fundamentally questioning our understanding of modern warfare, as well as transforming privateers from agents on the seas into actors in the skies.[91] Privateering was also suggested as an alternative form of combating modern piracy in Somalia and off the African coast.[92] For several decades this threat of piracy, now cemented in popular culture through films such as *Captain Phillips*, was one of the largest threats facing global navies, suddenly challenged with asymmetric warfare and hostage-taking at sea.[93] Various military operations were set up to deal with the regional threat, some of which, such as the European Naval Forces' Operation ATALANTA mission and the Combined Maritime Forces' CTF 151, are still active today.[94]

In 2022, a bill was put forward in the House of Representatives asking members to consider Congress's ability to issue letters of marque and reprisal to seize the property of "certain Russian citizens"[95] (oligarchs) at sea. Introduced

90 Tabarrok, 'Rise and Fall', 576.

91 R. P. DeWitte, 'Let Privateers Marque Terrorism: A Proposal for a Reawakening', *Indiana Law Journal*, 82 (2007), 131–58, at 145; R. Paul, *H.R.3074 – 107th Congress (2001–2002): Air Piracy Reprisal and Capture Act of 2001*, www.congress.gov/bill/107th-congress/house-bill/3074?s=1&r=89 (accessed 24 July 2023); R. Paul, *H.R.3076 – 107th Congress (2001–2002): September 11 Marque and Reprisal Act of 2001*, www.congress.gov/bill/107th-congress/house-bill/3076 (accessed 24 July 2023).

92 J. C. Coito, 'Pirates vs. Private Security: Commercial Shipping, the Montreux Document, and the Battle for the Gulf of Aden', *California Law Review*, 101 (2013), 173–226; T. E. Hutchins, 'Structuring a Sustainable Letters of Marque Regime: How Commissioning Privateers Can Defeat the Somali Pirates', *California Law Review*, 99 (2011), 819–84; T. T. Richard, 'Reconsidering the Letter of Marque: Utilizing Private Security Providers against Piracy', *Public Contract Law Journal*, 39 (2010), 411–64; C. Spearin, 'Promising Privateers?: Understanding the Constraints of Contemporary Private Security at Sea', *Naval War College Review*, 67 (2014), 97–116.

93 Danoff describes the film as a narrative that "might seem like a simple tale of American heroism and transform[s] it into a story that is far more tragic and morally complex", B. Danoff, '"I'm the Captain Now": Power, Justice, and Tragedy in "Benito Cereno" and Captain Phillips', *American Political Thought*, 6 (2017), 30–53.

94 Combined Maritime Forces (CMF), *CTF 151: Counter-piracy*, https://combined-maritimeforces.com/ctf-151-counter-piracy/ (accessed 25 July 2023); EUNAVFOR, Operation ATALANTA, https://eunavfor.eu/ (accessed 25 July 2023).

95 R. Gooden, H.*R.6869 – 117th Congress (2021–2022): To authorize the President of the United States to issue letters of marque and reprisal for the purpose of seizing the assets of certain Russian citizens, and for other purposes*, www.congress.gov/bill/117th-congress/house-bill/6869/text (accessed 24 July 2023).

by Lance Gooden, this bill envisioned privateering as a measure that the United States could introduce to support Ukraine in its current conflict with Russia. However, with the transition to the second Trump administration, foreign policy objectives have changed once again, now focussing on China. American privateering has also been suggested as a method to "attack [...] Chinese global trade [...] undermine China's entire economy and threaten the regime's stability"[96] and as a deterrent strategy in peacetime to counter the might of the Chinese merchant fleet at sea.[97] A counter-article is simply titled: "Hiring Privateers to Combat China is a Ridiculous and Risky Idea".[98] A London-based intelligence firm contradictorily both cites privateering as a way to fight Chinese naval militias "without involving the US Navy"[99] on its website, while warning that such action could lead to retaliation and escalation. This article is ironically emblematic for the issue of many modern articles on the subject, which lack the basic understanding of privateering as a method of warfare involving private parties, rather than a peaceful method of circumventing war through private actors.

96 Cancian and Schwartz, 'Unleash the Privateers!'.

97 C. Spearin, 'U.S. privateering and China in the 21st century: Tied at anchor', *Comparative Strategy*, 42 (2023), 1–13.

98 D. Axe, 'Hiring Privateers to Combat China is a Ridiculous and Risky Idea', *The National Interest*, 28 October 2021.

99 M. G. Ribera, *Little Blue Men: China & US Privateering*, https://greydynamics.com/little-blue-men-china-us-privateering/#h-privateering (accessed 27 July 2024).

# Conclusion

At first glance the development of Anglo-American prize law may seem like a topic with little practical relevance for modern readers, of use to scholars only. But the topic will continually resurface in the future in relation to the development of the (geo)politics in the maritime world, so long as the United States does not agree to remove it from its catalogue of military strategies.

Robert Bayard's life has shown how such a system of law was successfully used to the detriment of independence-supporting seafarers during the Revolutionary War by the Vice-Admiralty Court of New York. It also demonstrated that colonial jurisdiction, though in theory following the same principles as in London, had massively diverged, with major consequences for claimants. The different approaches to judicial procedures and staff made New York's Vice-Admiralty Court a far more liberal and efficient system, governed practically by a different set of rules than its metropolitan counterparts. HCA 49/92 is a great tool for gaining an overview of the court's workings, but more in-depth research must be done here, particularly regarding the court's impact on military operations during the War of Independence and its development throughout the conflict.

Samuel Bayard's experiences on the other hand demonstrate that a generation later, America and Britain would be able to come together and forge a new way forward together, impacting on the development of maritime law worldwide. The transformation from illegitimate rebels and objects of adjudication in the Revolution, to adjudicators and recognised players in the global system by the 1790s is remarkable. The Jay Treaty's arbitration committees were the first of their kind and would lead to a global plethora of similar commissions; for example, regarding the abolition of the slave trade in Sierra Leone in the nineteenth century, or the United Nations Compensation Commission arbitrating losses and damage suffered in consequence of Iraq's unlawful invasion and occupation of Kuwait in 1990–1, concluded in 2022.[1]

Prize was an important component in American foreign policy during the French Wars, and the importance the US government attributed to it caused far-reaching changes, such as the issuing of *Robinson's Reports*, which actively influence prize jurisdiction to this day. The concept of 'lawfare',

[1] J. S. Martinez, *The Courts of Mixed Commission for the Abolition of the Slave Trade* (2012); United Nations, United Nations Compensation Commission, https://uncc.ch/home (accessed 23 August 2023).

instrumentalising (international) law as a proxy for traditional warfare, does not truly grasp the reality faced by Americans at this time. It is only natural that every government attempted to shape international law in their favour and clearly prize was woven into the fabric of national policies, including defence and wartime strategies, to the point that it cannot be analysed without understanding the political circumstances that surround it.[2] Yet, the negotiation of this legal framework was not simply a measure to gain strategic advantages, but also a step to prevent war. While differences in policy and opinion continued to rage between the two Anglophone nations, in the commission established under Article VII of the Jay Treaty, methods were found to aid individual citizens on either side of the divide through binational cooperation, lessening the economic impact the war had on American citizens. Indeed, despite the complaints issued against British (and French, Spanish or any other) privateering, one must not forget that as neutrals Americans were making major profits from the French Wars. The British government in contrast was busy fighting an existential battle in Europe, which would ultimately lead to an undeniable dominance at sea in the nineteenth century.

As part of American and British international relations, prize was constantly entangled in political considerations that cannot be reduced to the binational sphere. It is exactly this international framework, encapsulated by prize through international law, that provided a common ground to build on together. William Bayard Jr's life reveals how US merchants did not only care for their financial losses through British privateering enterprises, but that justice on the high seas was seen more and more as a right to which US citizens should be entitled, and the Jay commission's efforts must be seen as part of this wider goal.

Major developments such as the introduction of the submarine, asymmetric warfare and international treaties have altered the importance of prize today, relegating it largely to the shelves of history. Yet prize continues to develop and shape the American experience of international and maritime affairs to this day, as a potential tomb in the bookshelf of military strategies. While it remains to be seen how these will impact US citizens in the future, we already have the power to learn about the past lives inscribed on its pages. The archival sources for the period of 1776 to 1804 mean that the key to understanding their stories lies in our hands. This book has begun to unlock those experiences, providing us with important insights into national, binational and international affairs. By delving deeper into these historical narratives, we not only preserve the legacy of the past but also gain a richer understanding of our present and potential future maritime challenges.

2 Although, Dunlap's original definition of lawfare replacing traditional 'kinetic' warfare can be applied to the negotiation process of the Jay Treaty, it is critically flawed when applied to prize law itself, as this branch of law does not exist in times of peace and therefore can never fully substitute physical violence. O. F. Kittrie, *Lawfare: Law as a Weapon of War* (New York 2016), pp. 1–2.

# APPENDIX

Representation of the Bayard family tree, focusing on the Delaware and New York branches with regard to the male line as relevant for this study. Starting with Samuel Bayard and Anne Stuyvesant, who first immigrated to the United States in the seventeenth century. On branches displaying two marriages, the next generation of Bayard sons sprang from the second marriage. The lifespans of family members were compiled from Hess, Bulloch and the New York Historical Society.[1] The Bayard family was perpetuated by the three brothers – Nicolas, Balthazar and Petrus – upon their arrival in New Netherland in the seventeenth century. Nicolas established the New York branch, one of the foremost politically and economically influential in that area, from the time of its first European settlement. From that branch sprang Robert and William Bayard, proponents of the Crown, supporting the loyalist cause in the American Revolution.[2] Petrus, however, would break with the family, both religiously and geographically, leaving New York and moving to the Delaware region, more specifically, to Cecil County, Maryland, to join a colony of Labadists.[3] While the New York Bayards would be overwhelmingly loyalist in 1776, the Delaware branch embraced independence and became embedded in the new republic's governmental service.[4]

1 Bulloch, *A History and Genealogy of the Families of Bayard, Houstoun of Georgia*; Hess, *America's Political Dynasties*; New York Historical Society, *Mr and Mrs Samuel Bayard*, c. 1644, oil on canvas, 1915.7, https://emuseum.nyhistory.org/objects/18977/mr-and-mrs-samuel-bayard (accessed 31 August 2023).

2 Testimony of Willliam Bayard, TNA, AO 12/20, 130r.

3 C. P. Mallery, *Ancient Families of Bohemia Manor: Their Homes and their Graves* (Wilmington DE, 1888), pp. 49–51; B. B. James, *The Labadist Colony in Maryland*, Johns Hopkins University studies in historical and political science Economic history – Maryland and the South (Baltimore MD, 1899), 17/6, p. 42.

4 Hess, *America's Political Dynasties*.

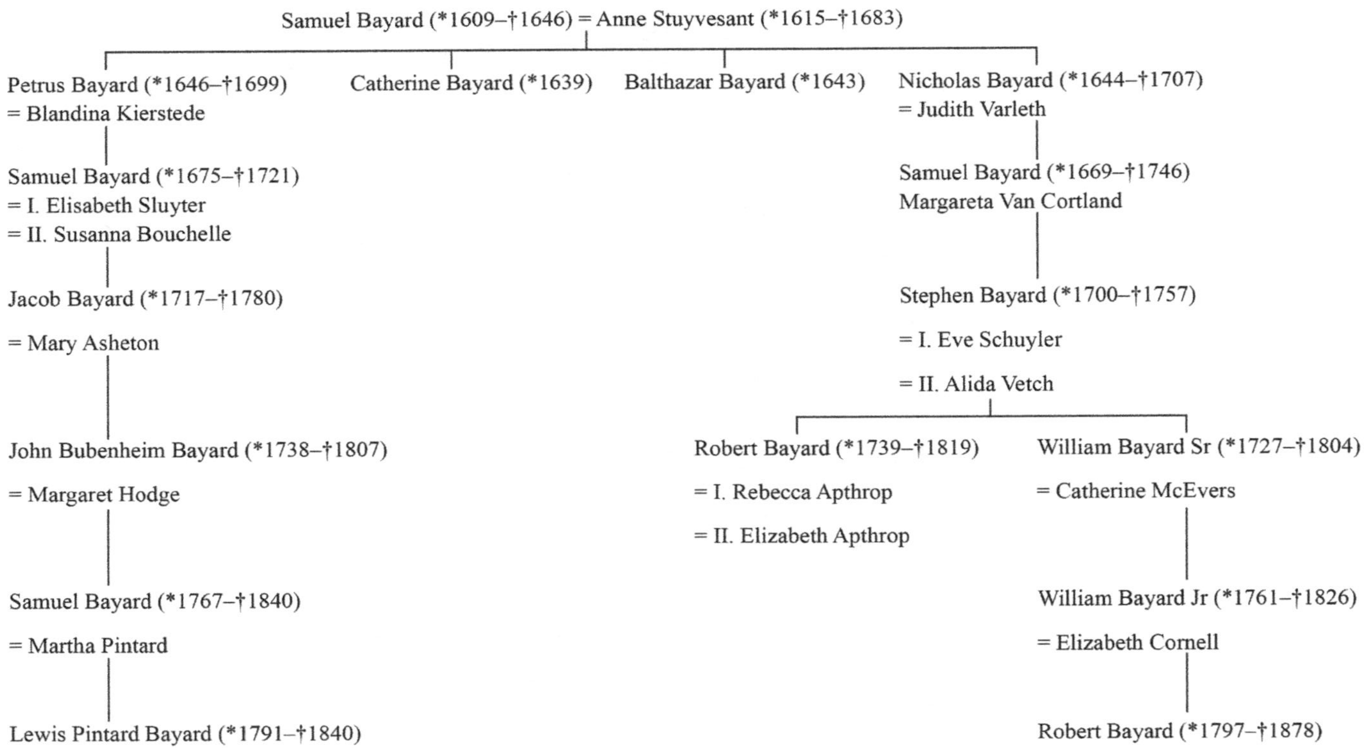


Fig. 1: The Bayard Family Tree.

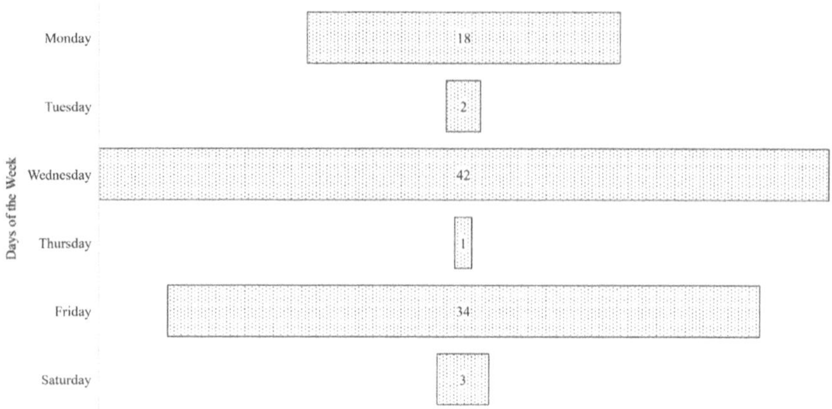


Fig. 2: Distribution of court sittings per weekday in the New York Vice-Admiralty Court, from 31 December 1777–31 December 1778 according to the Minute Books HCA 49/92/1–4.

Table 1: Overview of entries in the New York Vice-Admiralty Court minute books, from 31 December 1777–31 December 1778 according to the Minute Books HCA 49/92/1–4.

| | **Number** |
|---|---|
| *In personam* entries | 115 |
| Entries by the Advocate General on behalf of the British government | 46 |
| Entries by the Advocate General on behalf of private persons | 907 |
| Entries against the Advocate General | 86 |
| Entries by claimants/libellant representing themselves | 654 |
| Number of different claimants representing themselves | 133 |
| All entries involving the Advocate General as one of the parties at court | 1,039 |
| **Total entries** | **1,607** |

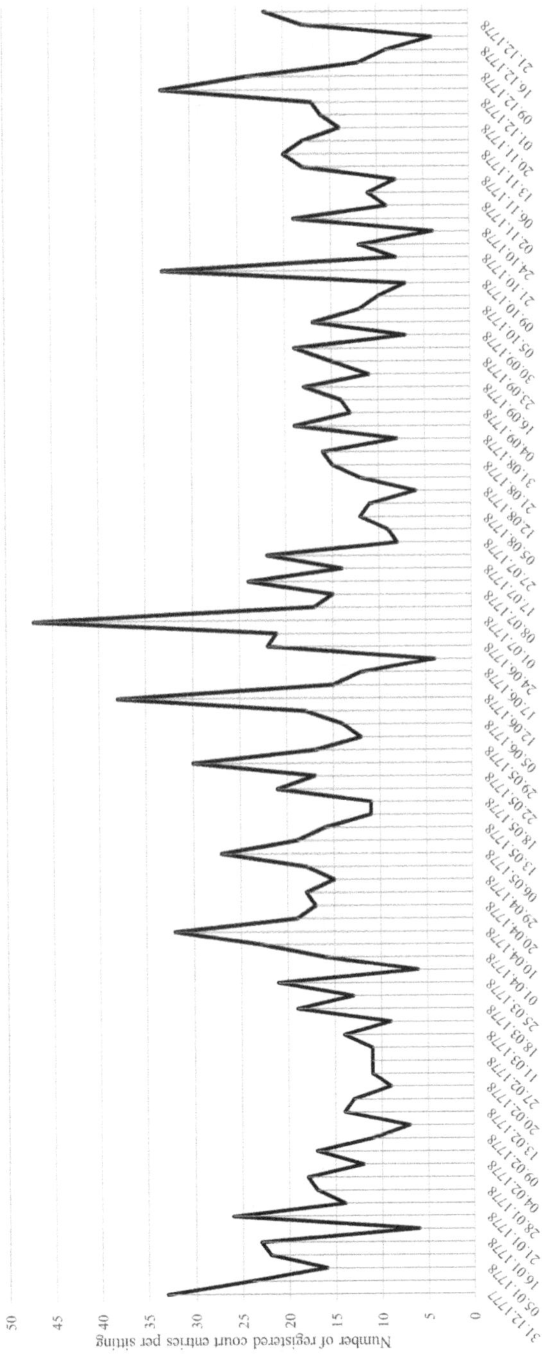


Fig. 3: Court entries registered in the Vice-Admiralty Court of New York per sitting, from 31 December 1777–31 December 1778 according to the Minute Books HCA 49/92/1–4.

Table 2: Correlation of court procedural steps in the New York Vice-Admiralty Court, from 31 December 1777–31 December 1778 according to the Minute Books HCA 49/92/1–4.

| | **Libels filed** | **Motion for monition** | **First proclamation filed** | **Third proclamation filed** | **Publication** | **Monition returned** | **Affidavit as to papers** | **Hearings** |
|---|---|---|---|---|---|---|---|---|
| In total | 272 | 270 | 275 | 319 | 200 | 315<br>*Returned by the air marshal*: 303 | 307<br>*Affidavit as to no papers on*: 17 | 443<br>Regular (R): 373<br>*Instanter* (I): 70<br>*(With decree: 312)* |
| Filed on same day as Libel | – | 220 | 224 | 0 | 3 | 0 | 3 | 5<br>(R) 3 (I) 2 |
| Filed on same entry as motion for monition | 220 | – | 241 | 2 | 1 | 0 | 0 | 1<br>(R) 0 (I) 1 |
| Filed on same entry as first proclamation | 224 | 241 | – | 0 | 0 | 1 | 1 | 1<br>(R) 1 (I) 0 |
| Filed on same entry as third proclamation filed | 0 | 2 | 0 | – | 110 | 308 | 3 | 87<br>(R) 63 (I) 24 |

| | Libels filed | Motion for monition | First procla-mation filed | Third procla-mation filed | Publication | Monition returned | Affidavit as to papers | Hearings |
|---|---|---|---|---|---|---|---|---|
| Filed on same entry as publication | 3 | 1 | 0 | 110 | – | 110 | 76 | 163<br>(R) 139 (I) 24 |
| Filed on same entry as monition returned | 0 | 0 | 1 | 308 | 110 | – | 1 | 24<br>(R) 0 (I) 24 |
| Filed on same entry as affidavit as to papers | 3 | 0 | 1 | 3 | 76 | 1 | – | 307<br>(R) 273 (I) 44 |
| Filed on same entry as hearing | 5<br>(R) 3 (I) 2 | 1<br>(R) 0 (I) 1 | 1<br>(R) 1 (I) 0 | 87<br>(R) 63 (I) 24 | 163<br>(R) 139 (I) 24 | 24<br>(R) 0 (I) 24 | 307<br>(R) 273 (I) 44 | – |

Table 3: Overview of decrees issued by the New York Vice-Admiralty Court, from 31 December 1777–31 December 1778 according to the Minute Books HCA 49/92/1–4.

| | Regular hearings | Hearings instanter | Total |
|---|---|---|---|
| | 373 | 70 | 443 |
| Hearings without a decree | 87 | 25 | 112 |
| Condemnations | 269 | 43.5 | 312.5 |
| Restorations | 17 | 1.5 | 18.5 |

Partial restorations and condemnations were recorded as 0.5 in each category.

Table 4: Overview of rebel privateers in the New York Vice-Admiralty Court, from 31 December 1777–31 December 1778 according to the Minute Books HCA 49/92/1–4.

| Vessel | Libelled on | Condemned on | Vessel type |
|---|---|---|---|
| *Fly* | 11 September 1778 | 5 October 1778 | schooner |
| *General Arnold* | 1 July 1778 | 22 July 1778 | sloop |
| *General Gadsen* | 11 September 1778 | 2 October 1778 | brigantine |
| *Greenwich* | 6 May 1778 | 29 May 1778 | sloop |
| *Mehitabel* | 1 July 1778 | Probably: 22 July 1778* | schooner |
| *New Broom* | 28 October 1778 | 20 November 1778 | brigantine |
| *Portsmouth* | 29 May 1778 | 24 June 1778 | sloop |
| *Retaliation* | 26 August 1778 | 16 September 1778 | sloop |
| *Wexford* | 10 June 1778 | 3 July 1778 | brigantine |

* The *Mehitabel*'s hearing does not actually mention any decree being issued. However, it appears as if the scribe entering the minute book simply forgot to note the last passage (condemnation). All the other steps were noted in an identical fashion to the other privateers.

Table 5: The position of King's Advocate as a stepping stone.

| King's Advocate | Judge of the High Court of Admiralty | Dean of the Arches |
|---|---|---|
| A1) George Hay<br>23 April 1755 | Thomas Salisbury<br>1751–1773 † | George Lee<br>1751–1758 † |
| B1) James Marriott<br>11 September 1764 | A3*) George Hay<br>1773–1778 | Edward Simpson<br>1758–1764 † |
| C1) William Wynne<br>2 November 1778 | B2) James Marriott<br>1778–1798 | A2) George Hay<br>1764–1778 |
| D1) William Scott<br>1788 | D2) William Scott<br>1798–1828 | Peter Calvert<br>1778–1788 † |
| E1) John Nicholl<br>6 November 1798 | F2) Christopher Robinson<br>1828–1833 † | C2) William Wynne<br>1788–1809 |
| F1) Christopher Robinson<br>1 March 1809 | E3*) John Nicholl<br>1833–1838 † | E2) John Nicholl<br>1809–1834 |
| G1) Herbert Jenner<br>28 February 1828 | K1) Stephen Lushington<br>1838–1867 | G2) Herbert Jenner<br>1834–1852 † |
| H1) John Dodson<br>18 October 1834 | J3*) Robert Phillimore<br>1867–1875 | H2) John Dodson<br>1852–1858 |
| John Dorney Harding<br>1852 [retired and died due to bad health] | | K2) Stephen Lushington<br>1858–1867 |
| J1) Robert Phillimore<br>1862 | | J2) Robert Phillimore<br>1867–1875 |

The table shows the order in which the King's advocates were promoted. Every official who features in the table more than once has been given an alphabetical denominator and his positions have been numbered chronologically; for example, George Hay (denominator A), who was first King's Advocate (1), then promoted to Dean of the Arches (2) and then became Judge of the High Court of Admiralty simultaneously (3).

The practice of the King's Advocate either receiving the Judgeship of the High Court of Admiralty or becoming Dean of the Arches (or both) can be traced up to the abolition of the court. Ecclesiastic and maritime law shared their (Roman) civil law tradition, as opposed to being rooted in endemic common law. Generally, the King's Advocate would take on whichever superior position became free first, either the role of Dean of the Arches, the head of the ecclesiastical courts, or that of the Judge of the High Court of Admiralty, head of the admiralty courts. Various members also took on both roles (marked above with an asterisk). The only exception to the rule of King's

Advocates taking on a higher position is John Dorney Harding, who retired from his post as Queen's Advocate in 1862 due to bad health and died four years later at his estate in Wales, and thus did not move up the professional ladder.[5] In all other cases, attaining the position of King's/Queen's Advocate was a promise to move on to higher judicial callings, and their accompanied paygrades. In contrast, the tenure as King's/Queen's Proctors did not show any promotions to leading judicial positions in civil law.

Table 6: Stipulations made in the Vice-Admiralty Court of New York, from 31 December 1777–31 December 1778 according to the Minute Books HCA 49/92/1–4.

| **Stipulations** | ***In rem*** | ***In personam*** | **Total** |
|---|---|---|---|
| Running cases: NY £200 | 15 | 34 | 49 |
| Running cases: NY £35 | 1 | 0 | 1 |
| Running cases: NY £60 | 0 | 2 | 2 |
| Running cases: NY £100 | 0 | 2 | 2 |
| Appeals: GB £200 | 4 | 2 | 6 |
| Running appeals cases: NY £1,000 | 2 | 0 | 2 |
| Running appeals cases: NY £4,000 | 1 | 0 | 1 |
| Running appeals cases: NY £3,900 | 1 | 0 | 1 |
| **Totals** | 23 | 38 | 0 |

The table lists the number of entries for stipulations in the minute books, not the number of stipulants. Sometimes a stipulation was made by a single man, sometimes by two men. There were no female stipulants in the examined records.

5 A. Ray-Jones, *John Dorney Harding Kt: A History of the Ray-Jones Family*, https://family.ray-jones.org.uk/rootspersona-tree/john-dorney-harding-kt/ (accessed 04 August 2020).

Table 7: Moneys paid into the hands of Judge Robert Bayard by the Marshal, from 31 December 1777–31 December 1778 according to the Minute Books HCA 49/92/1–4.

| Amount in NY currency (£sd) | Vessel | Date of Payment |
|---|---|---|
| 441.0.9 | *Charming Polly* | 5 January 1778 |
| 345.12.4 | *Harliquin* | 5 January 1778 |
| 796.4.1 | *L'Este* | 5 January 1778 |
| 609.10.3 | *Hawke* | 5 January 1778 |
| 14425.18.12 | *Boreas* | 16 January 1778 |
| 790.14.8 | *Eagle* | 17 January 1778 |
| 957.17.3 | *Neptune* | 17 January 1778 |
| 1165.2.7 | *Molly* | 17 January 1778 |
| 4153.19 | *Rebecca* | 10 April 1778 |
| 1024.9.3 | *St Jacques* | 1 May 1778 |
| 1069.18.5 | *Betsy* | 15 May 1778 |
| 07/09/2102 | *Sea Nymph* | 12 June 1778 |
| 597.17.7 | *Congress* | 1 July 1778 |
| 02/07/5929 | *L'Esperance* | 14 August 1778 |
| 192.9 | *Patriarch Jacob* | 14 August 1778 |
| 06/12/3249 | *Amphitrion* | 21 August 1778 |
| 641.2.4 | *Liberty* | 14 October 1778 |
| 1657.0.8 | *L'aimable Jannet* | 2 November 1778 |
| 409.6. | *Lark* | 6 November 1778 |
| 1368.3.8 | *Bon Basque* | 9 November 1778 |
| 235.12.6 | *Bon Basque* (embezzlement sum) | 9 November 1778 |
| 1186.13.5 | *Marquis d'Entragues* | 1 December 1778 |
| 03/08/4204 | *St Jago* | 9 December 1778 |
| 642.1.10 | *Sea Nymph* | 21 December 1778 |
| **£48,196 15s 10d** | | |

This dataset is has excluded two entries. The minute book records £1,761 7s 1d being the total sum of accounts brought in by the Marshal in the case of the *Hawke* on 1 December 1778. However, the minutes do not specifically record this amount being paid into the hands of the judge, as is always noted in the other cases. Although this seems likely from the precedents set in the time frame, the sum was therefore not included, as the analysis is source-driven. The second entry was excluded as it was entered without an exact sum, merely noted as the "value of 542 tierces of rice". The entry is from part of the cargo of the *St Jago*, entered into the minute book on 16 September 1778.

Table 8: Overview of costs issued by the New York Vice-Admiralty Court, from 31 December 1777–31 December 1778 according to the Minute Books HCA 49/92/1–4.

| **Vessel** | **Date** | **Costs decreed against whom?** | **Condemnation** | **Restoration** |
|---|---|---|---|---|
| *Joli Cocur* | 11 February 1778 | Captor | X | |
| *Polly* | 27 February 1778 | Reclaimant | X | |
| *Fonbonne* | 20 May 1779 | Reclaimant | X | |
| (cargo) *Vryheid* | 11 February 1778 | Captor | | X |
| (cargo) *Vryheid* | 13 February 1778 | Captor | | X |
| *Lively* | 24 June 1778 | Reclaimant | | X |
| (cargo) *Providence* | 6 October 1778 | Reclaimant | | X |
| *Hawke* | 4 November 1778 | Reclaimant | | X |

Table 9: Causes for the (partial) sale of cargo by the Marshal of the Vice-Admiralty Court of New York, from 31 December 1777–31 December 1778 according to the Minute Books HCA 49/92/1–4.

| Vessel | Goods | Reason for sale | Date |
|---|---|---|---|
| *Four Sisters* | Molasses | Leakiness of containers (hogsheads) | 17 January 1778 |
| *Mary* | Flour | By consent of the parties | 23 January 1778 |
| *Alexandrine* | Tobacco | Leakiness of vessel | 28 January 1778 |
| *Congress* | Sundry dry goods | Leakiness of vessel | 4 February 1778 |
| *Le Hardie* | Dry goods | Leakiness of vessel | 4 February 1778 |
| [unspecified] | Tobacco and turpentine | By consent of the parties | 27 February 1778 |
| *Betsy* | Flour and tobacco | Leakiness of vessel | 20 March 1778 |
| *Le Hardie* (in court storage) | Sundry dry goods | Bad weather | 30 March 1778 |
| *Friendship* | [unspecified] | Perishable nature of cargo | 13 May 1778 |
| *Exchange* | Sugar | [unspecified] | 15 May 1778 |
| *Lively* | [unspecified] | Perishable nature of cargo | 20 May 1778 |
| *Polly* | Rice | Leakiness of vessel and infestation of the cargo with weevils (pests) | 26 August 1778 |
| *Port au Prince* | [unspecified] | [unspecified] | 4 September 1778 |
| *Sea Flower* | [unspecified] | Leakiness of vessel | 21 September 1778 |
| *Charming Nancy* | Fish and oil | Leakiness of containers (barrels) | 28 September 1778 |

| Vessel | Goods | Reason for sale | Date |
|---|---|---|---|
| *Liberty* | Rum and sugar | Leakiness of vessel | 9 October 1778 |
| *Liberty* | Tobacco | Leakiness of vessel | 14 October 1778 |
| *Salisbury* | Wheat | [unspecified] | 21 October 1778 |
| *Whim* | Rum | Leakiness of containers (casks) | 21 October 1778 |
| *Le Devin* | [unspecified] | [unspecified] | 13 November 1778 |
| *Three Friends* | Salt | Leakiness of vessel | 13 November 1778 |
| *Success* | [unspecified] | [unspecified] | 23 November 1778 |
| *Experiment* | Mainly fruit | Perishable nature of cargo | 1 December 1778 |
| *Abringden* | Mainly fruit | Perishable nature of cargo | 1 December 1778 |
| *L'aimable Genevieve* | Mainly fruit | Perishable nature of cargo | 1 December 1778 |
| *King Bird* | Flour | [unspecified] | 1 December 1778 |
| *Le Devin* | Tobacco and flour | Bad weather | 4 December 1778 |
| *Tyrall* | Tobacco | Leakiness of vessel | 4 December 1778 |
| *St Croix Pacquet* | [unspecified] | Leakiness of vessel | 4 December 1778 |
| *Polly* | Mainly molasses | Bad Weather | 18 December 1778 |
| *Polly* | Wine | Leakiness of containers (casks), bad stowing of casks | 21 December 1778 |
| *Friendship* | Fruit | Perishable nature of cargo | 28 December 1778 |

Table 10: Overview of Prize Appeals Court cases from 1794–1804.

| Court of origin | Number of cases with Bayard as appellant | Percentage of total cases for Bayard | Ranking of Bayard's cases listed by court of origin; most to least cases | Total cases appealed | Bayard's percentage of total cases | Number of American cases | Number of American cases excluding captors as appellants | Percentage of American cases in the appeals court (incl. captors as appellants) | Bayard's percentage of total American cases as appellants (incl. captors as appellants) |
|---|---|---|---|---|---|---|---|---|---|
| High Court of Admiralty | 5 (two cases for Bayard Company) | 2.1% | 11 | 156 | 3.2% | 47 | 43 | 30.1% | 10.6% |
| Vice-Admiralty Court of Antigua | 9 | 3.8% | 8 | 23 | 39.1% | 16 | 16 | 69.6% | 56.3% |
| Vice-Admiralty Court of the Bahamans | 6 | 2.5% | 10 | 87 | 6.9% | 76 | 63 | 87.4% | 7.9% |
| Vice-Admiralty Court of Barbados | 14 | 5.9% | 6 | 21 | 66.7% | 17 | 17 | 81% | 82.4% |
| Vice-Admiralty Court of Bermuda | 61 | 25.7% | 1 | 108 | 56.5% | 99 | 95 | 91.7% | 61.6% |
| Vice-Admiralty Court of the Cape of Good Hope | 0 | 0 | - | 7 | 0% | 2 | 2 | 12.5% | 0% |
| Vice-Admiralty Court of Dominica | 35 | 14.8% | 2 | 44 | 79.5% | 41 | 41 | 93.2% | 85.4% |
| Vice-Admiralty Court of Gibraltar | 0 | 0% | - | 112 | 0% | 4 | 0 | 3.6% | 0% |
| Vice-Admiralty Court of Grenada | 1 | 0.4% | 14 | 19 | 5.3% | 7 | 6 | 36.8% | 14.3% |
| Vice-Admiralty Court of Jamaica | 22 | 9.3% | 5 | 221 | 10% | 131 | 128 | 59.3% | 16.8% |

| Court of origin | Number of cases with Bayard as appellant | Percentage of total cases for Bayard | Ranking of Bayard's cases listed by court of origin; most to least cases | Total cases appealed | Bayard's percentage of total cases | Number of American cases | Number of American cases excluding captors as appellants | Percentage of American cases in the appeals court (incl. captors as appellants) | Bayard's percentage of total American cases as appellants (incl. captors as appellants) |
|---|---|---|---|---|---|---|---|---|---|
| Vice-Admiralty Court of Martinique | 3 | 1.3% | 12 | 64 | 4.7% | 23 | 23 | 35.9% | 13% |
| Vice-Admiralty Court of Minorca | 0 | 0 | - | 6 | 0% | 1 | 1 | 16.7% | 0% |
| Vice-Admiralty Court of Montserrat | 26 | 11% | 4 | 63 | 41.3% | 39 | 39 | 61.9% | 66.7% |
| Vice-Admiralty Court of Nevis | 1 | 0.4% | 14 | 10 | 10% | 2 | 2 | 20% | 50% |
| Vice-Admiralty Court of Newfoundland | 0 | 0 | - | 3 | 0% | 3 | 3 | 100% | 0% |
| Vice-Admiralty Court of Nova Scotia | 13 | 5.5% | 7 | 69 | 18.9% | 56 | 54 | 81.2% | 23.2% |
| Vice-Admiralty Court of St Kitts | 30 | 12.7% | 3 | 52 | 57.7% | 42 | 42 | 80.8% | 71.4% |
| Vice-Admiralty Court of St Vincent | 2 | 0.8% | 13 | 3 | 66.7% | 3 | 3 | 100% | 66.7% |
| Vice-Admiralty Court of Tobago | 1 | 0.4% | 14 | 2 | 50% | 2 | 2 | 100% | 50% |
| Vice-Admiralty Court of Tortola | 8 | 3.4% | 9 | 74 | 10.8% | 27 | 27 | 36.5% | 29.6% |
| **Total** | **237** | **100%** | | **1144** | | **638** | | **55.8%** | **37.1%** |

This data was compiled using the single entries from HCA 45/17 to HCA 45/71, spanning the time from 1793 to 1804. Many thanks to the team at the National Archives, London, for their help and support in this endeavour without whom this table would have not been possible to make. Last digits have been rounded after the decimal point. Of the total cases, 369 captures were solely conducted by privateers, sixteen cases were joint captures between HMS and privateer vessels, 245 cases were captures conducted solely by Royal naval vessels.

Table 11: Overview of never printed manuscript appeals by the Vice-Admiralty Court from 1794–1804, compiled from the online catalogue entries for HCA 42.

| Court | American caseload | Percentage of American cases | Non-American caseload | Total caseload | Percentage of total cases |
|---|---|---|---|---|---|
| HCA | 23 | 9.02% | 119 | 142 | 25.31% |
| Antigua | 6 | 2.35% | 8 | 14 | 2.50% |
| Bahamas | 33 | 12.94% | 6 | 39 | 6.95% |
| Barbados | 5 | 1.96% | 4 | 9 | 1.60% |
| Bermuda | 23 | 9.02% | 3 | 26 | 4.63% |
| Cape of Good Hope | 0 | 0% | 5 | 5 | 0.89% |
| Dominica | 5 | 1.96% | 0 | 5 | 0.89% |
| Gibraltar | 2 | 0.78% | 36 | 38 | 6.77% |
| Grenada | 2 | 0.78% | 3 | 5 | 0.89% |
| Halifax, Nova Scotia | 8 | 3.14% | 2 | 10 | 1.78% |
| Jamaica | 76 | 29.80% | 49 | 125 | 22.28% |
| Martinique | 3 | 1.18% | 13 | 16 | 2.85% |
| Minorca | 2 | 0.78% | 8 | 10 | 1.78% |
| Montserat | 10 | 3.92% | 8 | 18 | 3.21% |
| Nevis | 1 | 0.39% | 5 | 6 | 1.07% |
| New Foundland | 2 | 0.78% | 0 | 2 | 0.36% |
| Nova Scotia | 28 | 10.98% | 3 | 31 | 5.53% |
| Saint Domingue | 5 | 1.96% | 3 | 8 | 1.43% |
| St Kitts | 9 | 3.53% | 9 | 18 | 3.21% |
| St Vincent | 1 | 0.39% | 2 | 3 | 0.53% |
| Tortola | 11 | 4.31% | 18 | 29 | 5.17% |
| Trinidad | 0 | 0% | 1 | 1 | 0.18% |
| Unknown | 0 | 0% | 1 | 1 | 0.18% |
| **Total** | **255** | **100%** | **306** | **561** | **100%** |

This table was compiled by downloading the entries from TNA's online catalogue entries for "HCA 42" "Never printed" "1794–1804" as a CVS file. The data from the file was extracting into the table using OpenAI's ChatGPT.

There were twenty-six cases of disputed nationality, where the TNA descriptions listed two different nationalities, three of which concerned American cases (two disputed Danish, one disputed French nationality). These cases were entered into the table above as regular cases; however, they need to be taken into consideration for the international make-up of the never printed manuscript appeals. This is as follows, the front number giving the total cases with said nationality (totalling 575 thanks to twenty-six disputed, duplicate entries). The bracketed number was multiplied all disputed cases by a factor of 0.5 in order to not inflate the numbers: 255 (253.5) American, 117 (114) Danish, 35 (34.5) Swedish, 29 (28) British, 23 (20.5) Dutch, 22 (21) Hamburg and 22 (22) Prussian, 16 (15) Spanish, 14 (14) unidentified, 12 (10.5) French, 6 (6) Neapolitan and (6) Bremen, 3 (3) Portuguese, 2 (2) Tuscan and (2) Venetian cases. A single case of ascribed (1) Austria, (1) Dalmatian, (1) Genoese, (0.5) 'German', (1) Ligurian, (0.5) Lubeck, (1) Lucca, (1) Moroccan, (1) Ragusan, (1) Russian and (1) Turkish vessel nationality.

Table 12: Overview of printed and manuscript appeals from 1794–1804, compiled from the online catalogue entries for HCA 42 and HCA 45.

| Court | Caseload American HCA 42 | Caseload American HCA 45 | Total American caseload | Percentage of American cases overall | Caseload international (excluding American) HCA 42 | Caseload international (excluding American) HCA 45 | Total inter-national (excluding American) caseload | Total caseload all nations | Percentage of American cases from total caseload |
|---|---|---|---|---|---|---|---|---|---|
| HCA | 23 | 47 | 70 | 7.84% | 119 | 156 | 275 | 345 | 20.29% |
| Antigua | 6 | 16 | 22 | 2.46% | 8 | 23 | 31 | 53 | 41.51% |
| Bahamas | 33 | 76 | 109 | 12.21% | 6 | 87 | 93 | 202 | 53.96% |
| Barbados | 5 | 17 | 22 | 2.46% | 4 | 21 | 25 | 47 | 46.81% |
| Bermuda | 23 | 99 | 122 | 13.66% | 3 | 108 | 111 | 233 | 52.36% |
| Cape of Good Hope | 0 | 2 | 2 | 0.22% | 5 | 7 | 12 | 14 | 14.29% |
| Dominica | 5 | 41 | 46 | 5.15% | 0 | 44 | 44 | 90 | 51.11% |
| Gibraltar | 2 | 4 | 6 | 0.67% | 36 | 112 | 148 | 154 | 3.90% |
| Grenada | 2 | 7 | 9 | 1.01% | 3 | 19 | 22 | 31 | 29.03% |
| Halifax, Nova Scotia | 8 | 0 | 8 | 0.90% | 2 | 0 | 2 | 10 | 80% |
| Jamaica | 76 | 131 | 207 | 23.18% | 49 | 221 | 270 | 477 | 43.40% |
| Martinique | 3 | 23 | 26 | 2.91% | 13 | 64 | 77 | 103 | 25.24% |
| Minorca | 2 | 1 | 3 | 0.34% | 8 | 6 | 14 | 17 | 17.65% |
| Montserat | 10 | 39 | 49 | 5.49% | 8 | 63 | 71 | 120 | 40.83% |

| Court | Caseload American HCA 42 | Caseload American HCA 45 | Total American caseload | Percentage of American cases overall | Caseload international (excluding American) HCA 42 | Caseload international (excluding American) HCA 45 | Total international (excluding American) caseload | Total caseload all nations | Percentage of American cases from total caseload |
|---|---|---|---|---|---|---|---|---|---|
| Nevis | 1 | 2 | 3 | 0.34% | 5 | 10 | 15 | 18 | 16.67% |
| New Foundland | 2 | 3 | 5 | 0.56% | 0 | 3 | 3 | 8 | 62.50% |
| Nova Scotia | 28 | 56 | 84 | 9.41% | 3 | 69 | 72 | 156 | 53.85% |
| Saint Domingue | 5 | | 5 | 0.56% | 3 | 0 | 3 | 8 | 62.50% |
| St Kitts | 9 | 42 | 51 | 5.71% | 9 | 52 | 61 | 112 | 45.54% |
| St Vincent | 1 | 3 | 4 | 0.45% | 2 | 3 | 5 | 9 | 44.44% |
| Tobago | 11 | 2 | 13 | 1.46% | 18 | 2 | 20 | 33 | 39.39% |
| Tortola | 0 | 27 | 27 | 3.02% | 1 | 74 | 75 | 102 | 26.47% |
| Unknown | 0 | | 0 | 0% | 1 | 0 | 1 | 1 | 0% |
| **Total** | **255** | **638** | **893** | **100%** | **306** | **1144** | **1450** | **2343** | **38.11%** |

This data was compiled using the figures *Overview of never printed manuscript appeals by vice-admiralty court from 1794–1804 and Overview of Prize Appeals Court Cases from 1794–1804.*

Table 13: Overview of Nicholl's and Scott's costs and damages cases.

| Vessel | Master | Awards in £sd | Costs in £sd | Net in £sd |
|---|---|---|---|---|
| *Apollo* | Hempsted | 166.7.8 | 13.8.10 | 152.18.10 |
| *Ann* | Wright | 74.2.8 | 10.2.8 | 64.0.0 |
| *Amelia* | Whittlesey | 191.3.0 | 14.2.2 | 177.0.10 |
| *Betsey* | Caulkins | 853.13.3 | 15.3.6 | 838.9.9 |
| *Betsey* | Burr | 518.13.7 | 14.4.10 | 504.8.9 |
| *Bayonne* | Lawton | 165.8.10 | 14.6.6 | 151.2.4 |
| *Three Brothers* | Edgarton | 748.19.0 | 16.10.10 | 752.8.2 |
| *Betsey* | Trefethen | 321.9.7 | 13.10.2 | 307.19.5 |
| *Chloe* | Lord | 176.2.0 | 13.13.2 | 162.8.10 |
| *Eleven Sons* | M'Intire | 1,325.7.6 | 14.0.8 | 1,311.6.10 |
| *Friendship* | Downe | 290.16.0 | 16.4.2 | 274.11.10 |
| *Harriet* | Brock | 430.16.0 | 15.16.10 | 414.19.2 |
| *Maria* | Peoples | 28.8.5 | 4.13.5 | 23.10.0 |
| *Ranger* | Clark | 2,768.12.4 | 15.17.6 | 2,752.14.1 |
| *Sally* | Edgarton | 234.8.8 | 14.12.2 | 220.16.6 |
| *Sally* | Noyes | 194.2.0 | 13.12.2 | 180.9.10 |
| *Success* | Holmes | 1,147.10.0 | 46.7.6 | 1,101.2.6 |
| *Tryall* | Boyle | 293.6.0 | 31.12.8 | 261.13.4 |
| *Two Sisters* | Calvert | 59.9.7 | 9.9.7 | 50.0.0 |
| *Union* | Cottle | 434.8.4 | 14.15.2 | 419.13.2 |
| *Columbus* | Trevitt | 522.12.9 | 19.6.2 | 503.6.7 |
| *Chance* | Earl | 88.11.9 | 12.11.9 | 76.0.0 |
| *Dolphin* | Graves | 1,751.10.0 | 15.10.6 | 1,735.19.6 |
| *Fox* | Adams | 92.3.0 | 12.19.0 | 79.4.0 |
| *Friendship* | Pate | 348.2.6 | 14.18.2 | 333.4.4 |
| *Nancy* | Ingersol | 289.14.4 | 15.15.6 | 273.18.19 |
| *Polly* | Knight | 519.12.9 | 15.12.6 | 504.0.3 |
| *Vassalboro* | Porter | 1,160.8.4 | 36.5.0 | 1124.3.4 |
| *Commerce* | Pope | 1,099.13.0 | 17.12.2 | 1,082.0.10 |
| *Dolphin* | Barker | 197.6.10 | 13.18.10 | 183.8.0 |
| *Fox* | Adams | 676.5.4 | 14.7.6 | 668.18.2 |
| *Harriet* | Bradbury | 231.15.0 | 13.5.6 | 218.9.6 |

| Vessel | Master | Awards in £sd | Costs in £sd | Net in £sd |
|---|---|---|---|---|
| *James* | Morris | 1,299.17.6 | 14.7.2 | 1,285.0.4 |
| *Milly Huntress* | Eastwood | 283.3.6 | 14.10.6 | 268.13.0 |
| *Neptune* | Barr | 492.3.9 | 55.37.11 | 435.5.10 |
| *NY Packet* | Shaw | 359.17.7 | 14.17.2 | 345.10.5 |
| *Polly* | Shillabar | 503.2.6 | 39.17.8 | 446.4.10 |
| *Sally* | Grafton | 254.1.6 | 14.0.6 | 240.1.0 |
| *Betsey* | Porter | 190.1.8 | 13.15.6 | 176.6.2 |
| *Delight* | Sturgis | 2,239.1.1 | 19.4.2 | 2,273.16.11 |
| *Endeavour* | Everton | 119.5.4 | 13.5.6 | 105.19.10 |
| *Jerusha* | Woodberry | 249.11.11 | 15.12.2 | 233.19.9 |
| *Lark* | Tittle | 115.14.2 | 14.3.8 | 101.10.6 |
| *Norfolk* | Walsh | 1,097.1.0 | 15.10.2 | 1,081.10.10 |
| *Betsey* | Wheelright | 775.6.11 | 15.18.10 | 759.8.1 |
| *John* | Wallace | 812.5.10 | 15.5.6 | 797.0.4 |
| *Russel* | Holbrook | 875.7.3 | 14.5.6 | 861.1.9 |
| *Neptune* | Woodberry | 279.5.10 | 16.9.10 | 262.16.0 |
| *Roby* | Bradish | 431.18.10 | 55.7.2 | 376.11.8 |
| *Peggy* | Bryan | 289.6.5 | 17.12.10 | 271.13.7 |
| *John* | Mahool | 881.5.0 | 20.12.2 | 860.12.10 |
| *Success* | Holmes | 1,543.12.6 | 20.3.10 | 1523.8.8 |
| *Olive Branch* | Provost | 227.6.8 | 16.5.6 | 211.1.2 |
| *Ranger* | Atwood | 101.12.2 | 14.2.2 | 87.10.0 |
| *Betsey* | Tait | 352.10.0 | 7.1.6 | 345.8.6 |
| *Roebuck* | Wharfe | 984.10.0 | 15.0.10 | 969.9.2 |
| *Molly* | Mercer | 2,231.5.0 | 35.12.6 | 2,195.12.6 |
| **Total (£sd)** | | **£3,4389 13s 11d** | **£1,034 7s 4d** | **£3,3420 1s 11d** |

The data used to compile this list was taken from the US Department of State's papers submitted to Congress.[6] The awards agreed by Sir Scott and Dr Nicholl were awarded until 28 July 1798. The figure clearly illustrates that the costs incurred by these cases were significantly smaller than their awards, leaving the US government with a clear financial gain, even when one considers that Bayard's salary is not included in the costs here.

6 Lowrie and St Claire Clarke (eds), *Class I – Foreign Relations*, vol. 2, pp. 119–21.

Table 14: Results of Bayard's cases before the commission under Article VII of the Jay Treaty, compiled from FO 304/27.

| Case Results | Number |
|---|---|
| Compensation to be paid by Great Britain | 22 |
| Compensation to be paid by the United States | 0 |
| Dismissed | 9 |
| Withdrawn | 4 |
| **Total** | **35** |

Two cases were left blank in FO 304/27, that of the *Sally* (Hayes) and the *Nancy* (Florence). The results of these cases (compensation to be granted by Great Britain), were added and directly integrated into the table above.[7] The *Sally* (Griffith) was accidentally entered into the registry twice. Her case has only been entered once.

Table 15: Cargo of Bayard's cases before the commission under Article VII of the Jay Treaty, compiled from FO 304/27.

| Cargo listed | Number of vessels listed as carrying said cargo |
|---|---|
| Flour (including wheat) | 18 |
| Coffee | 13 |
| Sugar | 12 |
| Cotton | 4 |
| Wine | 2 |
| Rum | 2 |
| Tobacco | 2 |
| Molasses | 2 |
| Rice | 2 |
| Beans | 1 |
| Beef | 1 |
| Cocoa | 1 |
| Codfish | 1 |
| Hemp | 1 |

7 Moore, *Compensation for losses and damages Vol. IV*, International Adjudications Ancient and Modern, History and Documents, ed. by John Bassett Moore, vol. 4, 482, 488.

| **Cargo listed** | **Number of vessels listed as carrying said cargo** |
|---|---|
| Indigo | 1 |
| Iron | 1 |
| Soap | 1 |
| Staves | 1 |

This list consists only of the items of cargo specifically listed in FO 304/27. The cargo lists printed in most HCA 45 case files are generally more specific, but also include individual items not representative of the vessels' main cargo items. Provisions have not been included in the table.

Table 16: Destinations of Bayard's cases (according to American claimants) before the Commission under Article VII of the Jay Treaty, compiled from FO 304/27.

| | | |
|---|---|---|
| **Bound to** | United States | 9 |
| | France | 17 |
| | Netherlands | 2 |
| | Other | 3 |
| | Unspecified | 4 |
| **Bound from** | United States | 18 |
| | France | 7 |
| | Other | 5 |
| | Unspecified | 5 |

Table 17: Difference between claimed losses and compensation granted in Bayard's cases before the commission under Article VII of the Jay Treaty, compiled from FO 304/27.

| Vessel | Amount in £sd |
|---|---|
| *Betsey* (Furlong) | -1,454.19.6 |
| *Farmer* (Osbourne) | -838.7.10 |
| *Sally* (Choate) | -810.19.4 |
| *Rising Sun* (Rossiter) | -3,068.12.1 |
| *Diana* (Gardner) | +501.0.6 |
| *Bacchus* (Robins) | -2,118.17.10 |
| *St John* (Ives) | -1,658.3.12 |
| *Light Horse* (Townsend) | -8,739.14.4 |
| *Bald Eagle* (Atkins) | -286.17.6 |
| *Mary* (Flughes) | -997.12.6 |
| *Barbara* (Holland) | -1,987.4.8 |
| *Jason* (West Jr) | -378.16.4 |
| *Phoenix* (Gale) | -725.0.0 |
| *Catherine* (McCullom) | -706.2.2 |
| *Harmony* (Robinson) | -2,686.7.1 |
| *Betsey* (Fletcher) | -2,716.11.9 |
| *Pomona* (Bamard) | -1,701.0.11 |
| *Columbia* (Kelby) | -1,314.0.4 |
| *Patty* (Wickham) | +1,521.15.11 |
| *Margaret* (McLellan) | -937.3.1 |
| *General Washington* (Price) | +189.11.10 |
| **Total** | **£30,914 2s 4d** |

The total loss, amounting to £30,914 2s 4d (dataset: twenty-one), gives us an average loss of about £1,427. The list contains only cases that received compensation and detailed losses. For example, the *Harriet* (Daddy) claimed losses, but the case was dismissed as it did not comply with the parameters set during the ratification of the treaty. It is therefore not featured in this table.

Table 18: Losses claimed in Bayard's cases before the commission under Article VII of the Jay Treaty, compiled from FO 304/27.

| Vessel | Loss in £sd |
|---|---|
| *Betsey* (Furlong) | 8,138.2.0 |
| *Farmer* (Osbourne) | 2,000.0.0 |
| *Sally* (Choate) | 2,000.0.0 |
| *Nancy* (Florence) | 2,000.0.0 |
| *Rising Sun* (Rossiter) | 4,488.3.0 |
| *Bacchus* (Robins) | 8,000.0.0 |
| *St John* (Ives) | 1,899.2.2 |
| *Light Horse* (Townsend) | 9,289.15.3 |
| *Bald Eagle* (Atkins) | 407.6.6 |
| *Mary* (Flughes) | 2,852.12.0 |
| *Barbara* (Holland) | 1,987.4.8 |
| *Jason* (West Jr) | 1,010.14.10 |
| *Phoenix* (Gale) | 824.0.0 |
| *Catherine* (McCullom) | 2,081.5.6 |
| *Harmony* (Robinson) | 6,000.3.1 |
| *Betsey* (Fletcher) | 3,294.17.9 |
| *Pomona* (Bamard) | 3,000.0.0 |
| *Columbia* (Kelby) | 3,000.0.0 |
| *Margaret* (McLellan) | 2,000.0.0 |
| *General Washington* (Price) | 4,000.0.0 |
| *Eagle* (Williams) | 3,000.0.0 |
| *Harriet* (Daddy) | 600.0.0 |
| **Total (£sd)** | **£71,873 6s 8d** |

# BIBLIOGRAPHY


## Archival Sources, including historic objects

### *American Philosophical Society*

Bayard, S., *London Diary of Judge Samuel Bayard*, contained in 'Samuel Bayard Papers', *American Philosophical Society* (1795).

### *British Library*

Marriott, J., *A Letter to the Dutch Merchants in England* (London, 1759).
Marriott, J., *Collectanea Juridica: Consisting of Tracts relative to the Law and Constitutions of England* (London, 1792), vol. 1.
*Truth or Treason! A Narrative of the Royal Procession to the House of Peers, October 29th 1795* (1795).

### *Columbia University Library*

Adair J. M., *Letter to John Jay, 19 December 1794*, https://dlc.library.columbia.edu/jay/ldpd:35688 (12 January 2021).
Bayard S., *Letter to John Jay, 16 May 1796*, https://dlc.library.columbia.edu/jay/ldpd:78762.
— *Letter to John Jay, 27 January 1795*, https://dlc.library.columbia.edu/jay/ldpd:29850 (12 January 2021).
— *Letter to John Jay, 27 January 1795*, https://dlc.library.columbia.edu/jay/ldpd:29850 (12 January 2021).
— *Letter to John Jay, 31 March 1795*, https://dlc.library.columbia.edu/jay/ldpd:78754 (12 January 2021).
— *Note to John Jay, 20 January 1795*, https://dlc.library.columbia.edu/jay/ldpd:78784 (12 January 2021).
Bayard W., *Letter to John Jay, 16 August 1794*, https://dlc.library.columbia.edu/jay/ldpd:54720 (18 August 2023).
Crickett and Townley, *Letter to John Jay, 20 January 1795*, https://dlc.library.columbia.edu/jay/ldpd:48732 (12 January 2021).
Jay J., *Draft of letter to Samuel Bayard, 27 January 1795*, https://dlc.library.columbia.edu/jay/ldpd:78792 (12 January 2021).
— *Letter to Edmund Randolph, 7 January 1795*, https://dlc.library.columbia.edu/jay/ldpd:29908 (12 January 2021).

— *Letter to Samuel Bayard, 5 January 1795*, https://dlc.library.columbia.edu/jay/ldpd:29908.

Trumbull J., and Jay J., *Draft of Samuel Bayard's indemnity, 5 January 1795*, https://dlc.library.columbia.edu/jay/ldpd:78802 (12 January 2021).

*Founders Online, National Archives*

Founders Online and NARA, *To Alexander Hamilton from Samuel Bayard, 23 April 1794*, https://founders.archives.gov/documents/Hamilton/01-16-02-0246 (7 October 2020).

Founders Online and NARA, *To James Madison from Robert Slade, 24 September 1805*, https://founders.archives.gov/documents/Madison/02-10-02-0343.

Founders Online and NARA, *To Thomas Jefferson from LeRoy, Bayard & McEvers, 19 March 1816*, https://founders.archives.gov/documents/Jefferson/03-09-02-0400-0001 (17 August 2023).

Founders Online and NARA, *To William Bayard from John Jay, 24 August 1794*, https://founders.archives.gov/?q=Recipient%3A%22Bayard%2C%20William%22&s=1111311111&r=1 (18 August 2023).

Founders Online and NARA, *Letter to James Madison from S. and A. Bird, 10 February 1803*, https://founders.archives.gov/documents/Madison/02-04-02-0385 (12 January 2021).

*Frick Art Reference Library*

The Frick Digital Collections, 4107100224500: *Mrs. James McEvers (Elizabeth Apthrop) (Later Mrs Bayard)*, https://digitalcollections.frick.org/digico/#/archive/Photoarchive (1 August 2024).

*Gilder Lehrman Institute of American History*

Boudinot E., *Letter to Sammuel Bayard, 2 April 1796*, www.gilderlehrman.org/collection/glc03627 (18 September 2023).

*Hertfordshire Archives and Local Studies Library*

Hertfordshire Archives and Local Studies Library, D/EX 216 P4: *Plan of the Parish of Aldenham in the County of Hertford.*

*John Jay Homestead Fine Art Collection*

John Jay Homestead, *John Jay by John Trumbull, 1793*, http://johnjayhomestead.org/collections/fine-art/john-jay-by-john-trumbull/ (17 January 2021).

*International Court of Justice Archive*

International Military Tribunal (ITM) Nuremberg Archives, *H-1600: Dönitz Beweisstück Nr. 95*, International Court of Justice.

*Metropolitan Museum of Art*

Metropolitan Museum of Art (Met), *Alexander Hamilton, 1792*, www.metmuseum.org/art/collection/search/20893 (17 January 2021).

Metropolitan Museum of Art (Met*), George Washington and William Lee, 1780*, www.metmuseum.org/art/collection/search/12822 (17 January 2021).

*National Archives and Records Administration (NARA), Washington/United States*

NARA, *Box 1–2, General Records, ca. 1790–ca. 1820 – NAID: 1170269*: Unbound Records.

NARA, *Box 1, Records Relating to Claims, ca. 1796–1804 – NAID: 1438808*: Miscellaneous Records Relating to Claims.

NARA, *Box 1, Ships A–C; British Spoliations, ca. 1796–ca. 1824 – NAID: 1170270.*

NARA, *Box 2, Ships E–F; British Spoliations, ca. 1796–ca. 1824 – NAID: 1170270.*

NARA, *Box 3, Ships G–K; British Spoliations, ca. 1796–ca. 1824 – NAID: 1170270.*

NARA, *Box 4, Ships L–N; British Spoliations, ca. 1796–ca. 1824 – NAID: 1170270.*

NARA, *Box 5, Ships O–R; British Spoliations, ca. 1796–ca. 1824 – NAID: 1170270.*

NARA, *Box 6, Ships S–W; British Spoliations, ca. 1796–ca. 1824 – NAID: 1170270.*

NARA, *Box 7–10, Unsorted Papers; British Spoliations, ca. 1796–ca. 1824 – NAID: 1170270.*

NARA, *Letters Received from Samuel Bayard, ca. 1796 – NAID: 1170268.*

NARA, *List of Claims, 1797, dated 12 and 18 May 1797 – NAID: 1170192.*

NARA, *Opinions Filed by the Commissioners, 1797 and 1797–99 – NAID: 1170266.*

NARA, *Vol. 1 – Papers Relative to the Commissioners, 1796–1804 – NAID: 1170191.*

*New York Historical Society*

New York Historical Society, *Works by Martha Pintard Bayard and Lewis Pintard*, https://emuseum.nyhistory.org/people/1849/martha-pintard-bayard/objects (19 July 2023).

New York Historical Society, *Mr and Mrs Samuel Bayard – Oil on Canvas: 1915.7*, https://emuseum.nyhistory.org/objects/18977/mr-and-mrs-samuel-bayard (31 August 2023).

New York Historical Society Museum and Library, *Robert Bayard (1739–1819) commissions and letters, 1757–1830: New-York Historical Society MSS Collection*, https://bobcat.library.nyu.edu/permalink/f/22u4kq/nyu_aleph004034186.

New York Historical Society Museum and Library, *Side chair (one of a set of three)*, https://emuseum.nyhistory.org/objects/26591/side-chair-one-of-a-set-of-three?ctx=99017ac997eeb9eb2e5f547720932e0cd4d9358e&idx=19 (27 July 2024).

*New York Public Library*

New York Public Library, *Minute Book of the New York Court of Vice Admiralty: MssCol 2230*, https://archives.nypl.org/mss/2230 (31 January 2023).

*Office of the Historian, US Department of State*

*Seward S. o. S., Message of the President of the United States to the Two Houses of Congress, at the Commencement of the Second Session of the Thirty-seventh Congress: Mr. Seward to Mr. Dayton*, https://history.state.gov/historicaldocuments/frus1861/d131 (23 August 2023).

*Royal Museums Greenwich, Caird Library*

Royal Museums Greenwich, *HUL/7, Hulbert, George Redmond, Naval Agent, 1774–1825.*

*The National Archives (TNA), London/United Kingdom*

TNA, AO 12/20: *American Loyalist, Claims Series I, Evidence, New York.*
TNA, AO 13/113 A: *American Loyalists Claims, Series II, Temporary Assistance, New York, A–D.*
TNA, AO 13/63: *American Loyalist Claims, Series II, Temporary Support, New York, A–B.*
TNA, CO 5/330/022.
TNA, FO 304/1/1: *Polly* (Smith), *Atlantic* (Marshall), *Industry* (Grozer).
TNA, FO 304/1/21: *Argo* (Spurr).
TNA, FO 304/10.
TNA, FO 304/25: Office copies of awards, volume I.
TNA, FO 304/26: Office copies of awards, volume II.
TNA, FO 304/27: Register of Awards.
TNA, FO 304/7.
TNA, HCA 32/267/10: *L'Amitié* (Pascal).
TNA, HCA 32/327/3A: *Exchange* (unknown).
TNA, HCA 32/333/7: *Le Fortune* (Masse), https://discovery.nationalarchives.gov.uk/details/r/C13505832.
TNA, HCA 32/350/9: *Hawke* (Yell).
TNA, HCA 32/401/11: *Mehitabel* (Jackson).
TNA, HCA 32/401/20: *Mercury* (Banker).
TNA, HCA 32/820/23: *Relief* (Cole).
TNA, HCA 42: Search Results "Never printed" and "1794–1804", https://discovery.nationalarchives.gov.uk/results/r?_q=%22never+printed%22+AND+%22HCA+42%22&_sd=1794&_ed=1804&_hb=.
TNA, HCA 42/247/599: *Hope* (Felt).
TNA, HCA 42/331/1224: *Sally* (Choate).
TNA, HCA 42/434/580: *Herman* (Horn).
TNA, HCA: 45/3/1: Jenkins, C., *A Discourse on the Conduct of the Government of Great Britain: In Respect to Neutral Nations* (London, 1794).
TNA, HCA 45/3/3: *The Case of the Dutch Ships. Considered* (London, 1758).
TNA, HCA 45/18/9: *Betsey* (Furlong).
TNA, HCA 45/18/15: *Orion* (Christoffers).
TNA, HCA 45/19/6: *Farmer* (Osborn).
TNA, HCA 45/19/7: *Harriet* (Calder).

TNA, HCA 45/19/9: *Sally* (Choate).
TNA, HCA 45/20/8: *Salome* (Wassen).
TNA, HCA 45/24/12: *Sally* (Hugh).
TNA, HCA 45/24/6: *Commerce* (Bouton).
TNA, HCA 45/27/1: *Sally* (Hugh).
TNA, HCA 45/32/12: *Phoenix* (Harlow).
TNA, HCA 45/32/27: *Sally* (Runey).
TNA, HCA 45/41/28: *Nance* (Graves).
TNA, HCA 45/57/14: *Minerva* (Caldwell).
TNA, HCA 45/64/14: *Catherina Augusta* (Center).
TNA, HCA 45/7/4: *Appeal of Thomas Symonds against the Hawke (Yell).*
TNA, HCA 49/92/1–9: *[British] New York Vice-Admiralty Court: Assignation books.*
TNA, HCA 49/93: *Register for the Vice-Admiralty Court of the province of New York.*
TNA, HCA 49/94: *Register for the Vice-Admiralty Court of the province of New York.*
TNA, HCA 49/96: *Volume 2 of 'Letters of Agency', compiled by the registry of the British New York Vice-Admiralty Court.*
TNA, IR 26/772, 1003: *Death Duties of Robert Bayard.*
TNA, PRO 30/26/9: *Doctors' Commons Library Accounts.*
TNA, PRO 30/55/41: *Thomas Murray to Robert Bayard, 29 March 1782.*
TNA, PRO 30/55/42: *Robert Bayard to Major Murray, 6 June 1782.*
TNA, PRO 30/55/44: *Deposition of John Barlow, 12 July 1782.*
TNA, PRO 30/55/44: *Robert Bayard to Maurice Morgan, 3 July 1782.*
TNA, PRO 30/55/77/72: 8672: *New York Governor to John Parr, Nova Scotia.*
TNA, PROB 11/1621/289: *Will of Robert Bayard.*
TNA, T 1/557: *Commissioners for the Office of Lord High Admiral of Britain and Ireland to the Judge, Register and Marshal at New York, undated.*
TNA, T 1/557: *Robert Bayard to John Robinson, 9 December 1780.*

*The Prize Papers Portal*

PrizePapers-Portal, Search: *Appeals HCA 45*: https://portal.prizepapers.de/search/-/%28ISWORK%3Atrue+ISANCHOR%3Atrue%29+-IDDOC_PARENT%3A*/1/SORT_ALL_NAME/MD_DOCUMENT_DOCUMENT_TYPE%3ACase+book+of+prize+appeals%3B%3B/ (19 July 2023).

*US Capitol Visitor Center*

Madison J., *President James Madison's war message, June 1, 1812*, www.visitthecapitol.gov/exhibitions/artifact/president-james-madisons-war-message-june-1-1812.

*Yale University Art Gallery*

Yale University Art Gallery, *Artist: John Trumbull, Subject: Rufus King, 1792*, https://artgallery.yale.edu/collections/objects/70 (17 January 2021).

## Printed Primary Sources

### *Contemporary books and articles*

Bayard, M., *The Journal of Martha Pintard Bayard*, ed. by S. Bayard Dodd (New York, 1894).

Bayard, W., *Memorial of Sundry Merchants, (and others,) Citizens of New York, Praying Congress to take into Consideration The Subject of Piracies Committed on the Commerce of the United States by Vessels from the Island of Cuba, &c.* (Washington DC, 1824).

— *Memorial of the New York Chamber of Commerce to the Hon. The Senate and House of Representatives of the United States in Congress Assembled: With Statements Prepared by Order of the Chamber to show the Present Rate of Duties and the Rate of Duties Proposed by the Tariff Bill, Now before Congress with Remarks & C.* (New York, 1824).

Collins, A. S. (ed.), *Travels in Britain, 1794–1795: The Diary of John Aspinwall. Great-Grandfather of Franklin Delano Roosevelt. With a Brief History of His Aspinwall Forebears* (Tabor SD, 1994).

Dodson, J., *Reports of cases argued and determined in the high court of admiralty: Commencing with the judgments of the right hon. Sir William Scott, Trinity Term 1811* (London, 1815).

Edwards, T., *Reports of cases argued and determined in the High Court of Admiralty: Commencing with the judgments of the right hon. Sir William Scott, Easter term, 1808* (London, 1812).

Fitzsimmons, T., 'Representation of the Philadelphia Chamber of Commerce', in American Antiquarian Society (ed.), *Early American Imprints, 1639–1800: A Readex Microprint of the Works Listed in Evan's American Bibliography, Evans Numbers 1-39162* (Worcester MA, 1804).

Haggard, J., *Reports of cases argued and determined in the High Court of Admiralty: During the time of the right hon. Lord Stowell* (London, 1825).

Johnston, H. P., *The Correspondence and public papers of John Jay: Vol. 4 (1794–1826)* (New York, London, 1893).

King, C., and King, R., *The Life and Correspondence of Rufus King: Comprising his letters, private and official, his public documents and his speeches, Vol. IV 1801–1806* (New York, 1897).

Lowrie, W., and St Claire Clarke, M. (eds), *Class I – Foreign Relations: Documents, legislative, and executive, Congress of the United States, From the first Session of the First to the Third Session of the Thirteenth Congress, Inclusive: Commencing March 3, 1789 and Ending March 3, 1813, American State Papers* (Washington DC, 1832), vols 1 and 2.

Mayo, B., and American Historical Association, *Instructions to the British Ministers to the United States: 1791–1812* (Washington DC, 1941).

Melikan, R. A., *John Scott, Lord Eldon, 1751–1838: The Duty of Loyalty* (Cambridge, 1999).

Minot, G. (ed.), *Reports of cases argued and determined in the High Court of Admiralty: Commencing with the Judgements of the Hon. Sir William Scott. Michaelmas Term, 1798* (Boston MA, 1853).

Nichols, J., *Literary Anecdotes of the Eighteenth Century* (London, 1812).

Onderdonk, B. T., *Memorial of the Rev. Lewis P. Bayard: Containing a memoir of his life, extracts from his journals and correspondence, notices of his tour through Europe and the Holy Land, selections from his sermons, and the discourse preached on the occasion of his decease* (New York, 1841).

Pinkney, W., and Wheaton, H., *Some account of the life, writings, and speeches of William Pinkney* (New York, 1826).

*Proceedings of the Trial of the Ship Two Friends in the Court of Vice Admiralty in Bermuda: Copy* (Philadelphia PA, 1795).

Robinson, C., *Reports of cases argued and determined in the High Court of Admiralty; commencing with the judgments of the Right Hon. Sir William Scott, Michaelmas term 1798. By Chr. Robinson* (London, 1799).

— *Reports of cases argued and determined in the High Court of Admiralty: Michaelmas Term 1798*, 4th edn (London, 1812).

Robinson, W., *Reports of cases argued and determined in the High Court of Admiralty: Commencing with the judgments of the right hon. Stephen Lushington* (London, 1844).

*Statement showing the Payments of Awards of the Commissioners appointed under the Conventions between the United States and France, Concluded April 30, 1803, and July 4, 1831, and Between the United States and Spain, Concluded February 22, 1819; also Abstract Containing the Names of the Persons and the Vessels Concerned in those Cases allowed as Valid by the Respective Commissions, with other Important Data Relative to Amounts Awarded and Payments of the Same* (Washington DC, 1886).

*The annual biography and obituary for the year 1837: Part I –Memoirs of celebrated persons, who have Died Within the Years 1835–1836, Vol. XXI* (London, 1837).

*The debates and Proceedings in the Congress of the United States with an Appendix containing Important State Papers and Public Documents, and all the Laws of Public Nature with a Copious Index: Fourth Congress-Second Session; Comprising the Period from December 5, 1796, to March 3, 1797, inclusive., Compiled from Authentic Materials, Annals of the Congress of the United States* (Washington DC, 1849).

Trumbull, J., *Autobiography, Reminiscences, and Letters of John Trumbull from 1756 to 1841* (1841).

Tucker, G. J., *New York Marriages previous to 1784: A reprint of the original edition of 1860 with additions and corrections* (Clearfield, 1999).

Twiss, H., *The public and private life of Lord Chancellor Eldon, with selections from his correspondence: Vol. III*, 2 edn, 3 vols (London, 1844).

Willyams, C., *An Account of the Campaign in the West Indies, in the Year 1794: Under the Command of their Excellencies Lieutenant General Sir Charles Grey, K.B., and Vice Admiral Sir John Jervis, K.B* (1794/2021).

## *Official Documents and Publications*

*An act for granting and applying certain stamp duties, and other duties, in the British colonies and plantations in America: Stamp Act* (1765).

*An act for granting certain duties in the British colonies and plantations in America: The Sugar Act* (1764).

*An Act to prohibit all trade and intercourse with the colonies* (1775).

*Articles of Capitulation; October 18, 1781*: Avalon Project – Documents in Law, History and Diplomacy, Yale Law School/Lillian Goldman Law Library, https://avalon.law.yale.edu/18th_century/art_of_cap_1781.asp (8 June 2023).

*Decisions in the High Court of Admiralty: During the time of Sir George Hay, and of Sir James Marriott, late Judges of that Court, Vol. 1. 1776 to 1779* (London, 1801), vol. 1.

fondation Napoléon, *The Treaty of Vienna, 14 October 1809*, www.napoleon.org/en/history-of-the-two-empires/articles/39720/ (27 July 2024).

*France – Convention of 1800*: Avalon Project – Documents in Law, History and Diplomacy, Yale Law School/Lillian Goldman Law Library, https://avalon.law.yale.edu/19th_century/fr1800.asp (27 July 2024).

House of Commons, *Journals of the House of Commons, 39 GEO. III*, Reprint (1803), vol. 54.

Library of Congress and United States Congress, *Constitution Annotated: Article III*, https://constitution.congress.gov/constitution/article-3/ (2 February 2023).

Library of Congress, Law Library, *Fifth Congress, Sess. I, Ch. 6: June 30, 1797*, www.loc.gov/law/help/statutes-at-large/5th-congress/session-1/c5s1ch6.pdf.

Library of Congress, *Law Library, Fourth Congress, Sess II, Ch. 23: March 3, 1797*, www.loc.gov/law/help/statutes-at-large/4th-congress/session-2/c4s2ch23.pdf (17 January 2021).

Lowrie, W., and St Clair Clarke, M., *Foreign relations: Class I, Vol II, American State Papers Documents, legislative and executive, of the Congress of the United States* (Washington DC, 1832), vols 1 and 2.

National Archives, *Treaty of Alliance with France (1778)*: Milestone Documents Series, www.archives.gov/milestone-documents/treaty-of-alliance-with-france (19 July 2024).

National Archives, *Treaty of Ghent (1814)*: Milestone Documents Series, www.archives.gov/milestone-documents/treaty-of-ghent (19 July 2024).

National Archives, *Treaty of Paris (1783)*: Milestone Documents Series, www.archives.gov/milestone-documents/treaty-of-paris#transcript (19 July 2024).

*Register of the department of state in four parts: Corrected to March 1, 1874* (Washington DC, 1874).

*Treaty of Amity and Commerce Between The United States and France; February 6, 1778*: Avalon Project – Documents in Law, History and Diplomacy, Yale Law School/Lillian Goldman Law Library, https://avalon.law.yale.edu/18th_century/fr1788-1.asp#1 (19 July 2024).

*Treaty of amity, commerce, and navigation, between His Britannick Majesty and the United States of America: Signed at London, the 19th of November, 1794* (London, 1795).

### *Newspapers*

'War Office announcement 12 April', *London Gazette*, 18 April 1769.

## Secondary Sources

### *Contemporary Books and Articles*

*A Century of Lawmaking for a New Nation: U.S. Congressional Documents and Debates: 1774–1875, Journals of the Continental Congress; American Memory* (Washington DC, 2003), vol. 24.

Andrews, C. M., *Guide to the Materials for American History, to 1783, in the Public Record Office of Great Britain* (Washington DC, 1914), vol. 2.

Arthur, B., *How Britain Won the War of 1812: The Royal Navy's Blockades of the United States, 1812–1815* (Suffolk, 2011).

Aslanian, S., 'Trade Diaspora versus Colonial State: Armenian Merchants, the English East India Company, and the High Court of Admiralty in London, 1748–1752', *Diaspora: A Journal of Transnational Studies,* 13 (2004), 37–100.

August, R. S., 'Trial by Jury in a Court of Admiralty: A Constitutional Right Buried Under Historical Ignorance', *Journal of Maritime Law and Commerce,* 13 (1982), 149–76.

Axe, D., 'Hiring Privateers to Combat China is a Ridiculous and Risky Idea', *The National Interest* (28 October 2021).

Baker, C., 'Grains as a Weapon? Britain's scheme to Starve Revolutionary France, 1793–1796', *Historical Geography,* 47 (2019), 72–99.

Barber, P., 'The Fall and Rise of Doctors' Commons?', *Ecclesiastical Law Journal,* 4 (1996), 462–9.

Bemis, S. F., 'The United States and the Abortive Armed Neutrality of 1794', *The American Historical Review,* 24 (1918), 26–47.

— *Jay's Treaty: A Study in Commerce and Diplomacy, The Making of Modern Law: Foreign, Comparative, and International Law, 1600–1926* (Gale, 2013).

Benedict, E. C., *The Law of Admiralty: Its Jurisdiction and Practice with Forms and Directions*, 6th rev. edn (New York, 1940), vol. 4.

Benton, L. A., and Ford, L., *Rage for Order: The British Empire and the Origins of International Law, 1800–1850* (Cambridge MA, London, 2016).

Bergen, T. G., *Genealogies of the State of New York: A Record of the Achievements of her People in the Making of a Commonwealth and the Founding of a Nation*, Long Island edn (New York, 1915).

'Bermuda Homes with American Connections: Verdmont Interior', *Bermuda Historical Quarterly,* 25–7 (1968).

Bevan, Amanda, and Cock, Randolph, 'High Court of Admiralty prize papers, 1652–1815: Challenges in Improving Access to Older Records', *Archives* (2018), 34–58.

Biber, K., Luker, T., and Vaughan, P., 'Law's Documents: Authority, Materiality, Aesthetics', in K. Biber, T. Luker and P. Vaughan (eds), *Law's Documents: Authority, Materiality, Aesthetics* (London and New York, 2022), pp. 3–25.

Black, H. C., *Black's Law Dictionary: Definitions of the Terms and Phrases of American and English Jurisprudence, Ancient and Modern*, 4th rev. edn (St Paul MN, 1968).

Bolton, R., *The History of the Several Towns, Manors, and Patents of the County of Westchester: From its First Settlement to the Present Time, Volume II* (New York, 1881).

Boot, M., *The Savage Wars of Peace: Small Wars and the Rise of American Power* (New York, 2014).

Bourguignon, H. J., *The First Federal Court: The Federal Appellate Prize Court of the American Revolution, 1775–1787, Memoirs of the American Philosophical Society* (Philadelphia PA, 1977), vol. 122.

— *Sir William Scott, Lord Stowell, judge of the High Court of Admiralty, 1798–1828* (Cambridge, 1987).

— *Sir William Scott, Lord Stowell* (2009).

Boyle, F., 'The Law of the Sea', *Proceedings of the Annual Meeting (American Society of International Law)*, 76 (1982), 135–9.

Bradford, J. C., 'The First United States Navy', in J. P. Greene and J. R. Pole (eds), *A Companion to the American Revolution*, 1st edn (Malden MA, 2000), pp. 326–32.

— *America, Sea Power, and the World* (New York, 2016).

Brinkman, A., *Balancing Strategy: Sea Power, Neutrality, and Prize Law in the Seven Years' War*, 1st edn (Cambridge, 2024).

Broers, M., 'The Concept of "Total War" in the Revolutionary-Napoleonic Period', *War in History*, 15 (2008), 247–68.

Brougham, H., *Historical sketches of statesmen who flourished in the time of George III: Volume II, Works of Henry Brougham* (London and Glasgow, 1856), vols 3 and 4.

Brundage, J. A., *The Medieval Origins of the Legal Profession: Canonists, Civilians, and Courts* (Chicago IL, 2008).

Buford, V. S., *The Militia of the Seas: A guide to the Confederate privateers of the American Civil War, 1861–1865* (2000).

Bulloch, J. G. B., *A history and genealogy of the families of Bayard, Houstoun of Georgia: And the descent of the Bolton family from Assheton, Byron and Hulton of Hulton Park, by Joseph Gaston Baillie Bulloch* (Washington DC, 1919).

Burke, J., and Burke, J. B., *Dictionary of the Landed Gentry of Great Britain and Ireland: Vol. II, M to Z* (London, 1847), vol. 2.

Burrows, E. G., *Forgotten Patriots: The Untold Story of American Prisoners During the Revolutionary War* (New York, 2008).

Burrows, M., *The Life of Edward Lord Hawke: Admiral of the Fleet, Vice-Admiral of Great Britain and First Lord of the Admiralty from 1766 to 1771* (London, 1896).

Caliendo, R. J., *New York City Mayors: Part I: The Mayors of New York City before 1898* (Bloomington IN, 2010).

Cancian, M., and Schwartz, B., 'Unleash the Privateers! The United States should issue letters of marque to fight Chinese aggression at sea', *Proceedings*, 146 (2020).

Carp, B. L., *The Great New York Fire of 1776: A Lost Story of the American Revolution* (New Haven CT, 2023).

Casto, W. R., 'The Origins of Federal Admiralty Jurisdiction in an Age of Privateers, Smugglers, and Pirates', *The American Journal of Legal History*, 37 (1993), 117–57.

Chamberlayne, J., *Magnæ Britanniæ Notitia: Or, The present state of Great-Britain: With diverse remarks upon the ancient state thereof. By John Chamberlayne,*

*Esq; The thirty- seventh edition of the south part, called England; and the sixteenth of the north part, called Scotland. To which is added, a compleat list of their Royal Highnesses the Prince and Princess of Wales' household; as also those of their Royal Highnesses the Duke of Cumberland, the Princess Amelia, and the Princess Caroline. In two parts. With His Majesty's royal privillege*, Eighteenth century collections online (London, 1748).

Chambers, J. W., Anderson, F., and Piehler, G. K., *The Oxford Guide to American Military History* (New York, 1999).

Clarfield, G. H., 'Postscript to the Jay Treaty: Timothy Pickering and Anglo-American Relations, 1795–1797', *William and Mary Quarterly,* 23 (1966), 108–20.

Clark, B. R., and Bellia, A. J., *The Law of Nations and the United States Constitution* (Oxford, 2017).

Clement, J., 'Neither United States Citizens Nor British Nationalists: A Postwar Loyalist Trade Diaspora' (master's thesis, College of William and Mary, 2010).

J. H. Coatsworth, 'American Trade with European Colonies in the Caribbean and South America, 1790–1812', *William and Mary Quarterly*, 24 (1967).

Coggeshall, G., *History of the American privateers: And letters-of-marque, during our war with England in the years 1812, '13 and '14. Interspersed with several naval battles between American and British ships-of-war* (New York, 1856).

Coito, J. C., 'Pirates vs. Private Security: Commercial Shipping, the Montreux Document, and the Battle for the Gulf of Aden', *California Law Review,* 101 (2013), 173–226.

Colombos, C. J., *A Treatise on the Law of Prize*, 2nd edn (London, 1940).

Combs, J. A., *Jay Treaty: Political Battleground of the Founding Fathers* ([S.l.], 2022).

Cooperstein, T. M., 'Letters of Marque and Reprisal: The Constitutional Law and Practice of Privateering', *Journal of Maritime Law and Commerce* (2009).

Coote, H. C., *Sketches of the Lives and Characters op [sic] Eminent English Civilians, with an historical introduction relative to the College of Advocates, and an enumeration of the whole series of academic graduates admitted into that society, from the beginning of the reign of Henry VIII. to the close of the year 1803; by one of the members of the College [i.e. C. Coote]* (London, 1804).

Corbly, D., *Pennsylvania's Traitors and Criminals During the Revolutionary War* (Raleigh NC, 2013).

Cornell, J., *Genealogy of the Cornell Family: Being an Account of the Descendants of Thomas Cornell* (New York, 1902).

Cowrie, L. W., 'Doctors' Commons: "A cosey, dosey, old-fashioned little family party", wrote Dickens in 1849', *History Today*, 20 (1970), 419–26.

Craven W. F., and Woodward R. L., *Princetonians, 1784–1790: A Biographical Dictionary* (*Princeton NJ, 1991*).

Cronshagen, J., '"A Loyal Heart to God and the Governor": Missions and Colonial Policy in the Surinamese Saramaccan Mission (c. 1750–1813)', *Journal of Moravian History* (2019).

Crouzet, F., 'Wars, Blockade, and Economic Change in Europe, 1792–1815', *The Journal of Economic History*, 24 (1964), 567–88.

Crump, H. J., *Colonial Admiralty Jurisdiction in the Seventeenth Century* (London, 1931), vol. 5.

Culley, M., *A Day at a Time: The Diary Literature of American Women from 1764 to the Present* (New York, 1985).

Danoff, B., '"I'm the Captain Now": Power, Justice, and Tragedy in "Benito Cereno" and Captain Phillips', *American Political Thought,* 6 (2017), 30–53.

Dawson, H. B., *Westchester County, New York, during the American Revolution* (New York, 1886).

Deák, F., and Jessup, P. C., 'Early Prize Court Procedure: Part One', *University of Pennsylvania law review*, 82/7–8 (1934), 677–94.

Desmarais, N., *America's First Ally: France in the Revolutionary War* (Newburyport, 2019).

DeWitte, R. P., 'Let Privateers Marque Terrorism: A Proposal for a Reawakening', *Indiana Law Journal,* 82 (2007), 131–58.

Drake, F. S., *Dictionary of American Biography: Including Men of the Time, containing nearly ten thousand natives of Persons of both Sexes, of Native and Foreign Birth, who have been Remarkable, or Prominently Connected with the Arts, Sciences, Literature, Politics, or History of the American Continent* (Boston MA, 1879).

Duffy, M., Soldiers, *Sugar, and Seapower: The British Expeditions to the West Indies and the War Against Revolutionary France* (Oxford, 1987).

Dull, J. R., *American Naval History, 1607–1865: Overcoming the Colonial Legacy* (Lincoln NE, 2012).

Duncan, G. I. O., *The High Court of Delegates* (Cambridge, 1971).

Durston, G., *The Admiralty Sessions, 1536–1834: Maritime Crime and the Silver Oar* (Newcastle-upon-Tyne, 2017).

Dye, B., Genel-Gonzalez, G., Lawry, L. L., Hannan, C., and Herman, J. L. (eds), *Georgia Biographical Dictionary, 2008–2009* (Hamburg MI, 2008).

Dye, I., 'The Tattoos of Early American Seafarers: 1796–1818', *Proceedings in the American Philosophical Society,* 133 (1989), 520–54.

Egle, W. H., *Pennsylvania in the War of the Revolution: Associated Battalions and Militia 1775–1783* (Harrisburg PA, 1892), vol. 2.

Ely, J. W., 'Genesee Chief v. Fitzhugh', in K. L. Hall (ed.), *The Oxford Companion to the Supreme Court of the United States*, 2nd edn (Oxford, 2005), p. 388.

Estes, T., *The Jay Treaty Debate, Public Opinion, and the Evolution of Early American Political Culture: Political Development of the American Nation* (Amherst MA, 2006).

Etting T. M., *The Admiralty Jurisdiction in America* (Philadelphia PA, 1879).

Everett, E., *A memoir of Mr. John Lowell, jun. delivered as the introduction to the lectures on his foundation, in the Odeon, thirty-first of December, 1839* (Boston MA, 1840).

Fassbender, B., Peters, A., and Peter, S. (eds), *The Oxford Handbook of the History of International Law*, 1st edn (Oxford, 2012).

Fewster, J. M., 'The Jay Treaty and British Ship Seizures: The Martinique Cases', *William and Mary Quarterly,* 45 (1988), 426–52.

Flavell, J., *When London was Capital of America* (New Haven CT, 2010).

Flick, A., *Loyalism in New York During the American Revolution* (New York, 1901), 16/1.

Forsyth, A., *Common Law and Natural Law in America: From the Puritans to the Legal Realists* (Cambridge and New York, 2019).

Fosdick, L. J., *French Blood in America* (Boston MA, 1911).

Friedell, S. F., 'Admiralty and Maritime Law', in K. L. Hall (ed.), *The Oxford Companion to the Supreme Court of the United States*, 2nd edn (Oxford, 2005), pp. 18–20.

Friedman, L. M., *A History of American Law*, 3rd edn (New York, 2005).

Garitee, J. R., *The Republic's Private Navy: The American Privateering Business as Practiced by Baltimore During the War of 1812*, 1st edn (Middletown CT, 1977), vol. 8.

Gilmore, G., and Black, C. L., *The Law of Admiralty*, 2nd edn (Mineola NY, 1975).

Giunta, M. A., *The Emerging Nation: A Documentary History of the Foreign Relations of the United States under the Articles of Confederation 1780–1789* (Washington DC, 1996), vol. 3.

Gordan, J. D., 'Publishing Robinson's *Reports of Cases Argued and Determined in The High Court of Admiralty*', *Law and History Review* (2014), 1–49.

Green, N. C., *'The Focus of the Wills of Converging Millions': Public Opposition to the Jay Treaty and Origins of the People's Presidency* (Philadelphia PA, 2017).

Greenwood, F. W. P., *Funeral Sermon [on Rev. xx. 6] on the late Hon. C. Gore: formerly Governor of Massachusetts., Preached at King's Chapel, Boston* (Boston MA, 1827).

Grossman, M., *World Military Leaders: A Biographical Dictionary*, 1st edn (New York, 2007).

Harding, R., 'Review: By Fire and Bayonet. Grey's West Indies Campaign of 1794', *Journal of the Society for Army Historical Research,* 97 (2019), 184–6.

Harjo, S. S., 'American Indian Land and American Empire: An Interview with Philip J. Deloria', in S. S. Harjo (ed.), *Nation to Nation: Treaties Between the United States and American Indian Nations*, Catalogue for the New Exhibition of the National Museum of the American Indian, Washington DC, 1st edn (Washington DC, 2014), pp. 1–14.

Harling, P., 'A tale of Two Conflicts: Critiques of the British War Effort, 1793–1815', in M. Philp (ed.), *Resisting Napoleon: The British Response to the Threat of Invasion, 1797–1815* (London and New York, 2016).

Harrington, M. P., 'The Legacy of the Colonial Vice-Admiralty Courts: Part I', *Journal of Maritime Law and Commerce*, 26 (1995), 581–600.

— 'The Legacy of the Colonial Vice-Admiralty Courts: Part II', *Journal of Maritime Law and Commerce* (1996), 323–51.

Head, D., *Privateers of the Americas: Spanish American privateering from the United States in the early republic* (Athens GA, 2015).

Helfman, T., 'The Court of Vice Admiralty at Sierra Leone and the Abolition of the West African Slave Trade', *Yale Law Journal*, 115 (2006), 1122–56.

Henrietta, J., 'Magistrates, Common Law Lawyers, Legislators: The Three Legal Systems of British America', in M. Grossberg and C. L. Tomlins (eds), *The*

*Cambridge History of Law in America* (Cambridge and New York, 2008), vol. 1, pp. 555–92.

Hess, S., *America's Political Dynasties: From Adams to Clinton* (Washington DC, 2016).

Hill, R., *The Prizes of War: The Naval Prize System in the Napoleonic Wars, 1793–1815* (Stroud, 1998).

Hillmann, H., and Gathmann, C., 'Overseas Trade and the Decline of Privateering', *The Journal of Economic History* (2011).

Hodge, C. C., and Nolan, C. J. (eds), *U.S. Presidents and Foreign Policy: From 1789 to the Present* (Santa Barbara CA, 2007).

Hoffer, P. C., Hoffer, W., and Hull, N. E. H., *The Supreme Court: An Essential History*, 2nd edn (Lawrence KS, 2018).

Holdsworth, W. S., Goodhart, A. L., Hanbury, H. G., and Chrimes, S. B., *A History of English Law*, volume 1, 4th edn (London, 2009 [1938]).

Horgan, L. E., *Forged in War: The Continental Congress and the Origin of Military Supply and Acquisition Policy* (Westport CT, 2002), vol. 219.

Hough, C. M., *Reports of Cases in the Vice Admiralty of the Province of New York and in the Court of Admiralty of the State of New York, 1715–1788: With an Introduction and Appendix* (New Haven CT, 1925).

— *1789–1919, The United States District Court for the Southern District of New York: Its Growth, and the Men Who Have Done Its Work* (New York, 1934).

Hulbert, K. A., *The Untold War at Sea: America's Revolutionary Privateers* (Athens GA, 2022).

Hull, N. E. H., Hoffer, P. C., and Allen, S. L., 'Choosing Sides: A Quantitative Study of the Personality Determinants of Loyalist and Revolutionary Political Affiliation in New York', *The Journal of American History,* 65 (1978), 344–66.

Hunting, P., 'The Survey of Hatton Garden in 1694 by Abraham Arlidge', in A. Saunders (ed.), *London topographical Record* (London, 1985), pp. 83–110.

Hutchins, S. C., *Civil List and Constitutional History of the Colony and State of New York* (Albany NY, 1882).

Hutchins, T. E., 'Structuring a Sustainable Letters of Marque Regime: How Commissioning Privateers Can Defeat the Somali Pirates', *California Law Review,* 99 (2011), 819–84.

James, B. B., *The Labadist Colony in Maryland, Johns Hopkins University Studies in historical and Political Science Economic History – Maryland and the South* (Baltimore MD, 1899), 17/6.

James, F. A., 'Making Money from the Royal Navy in the Late Eighteenth Century: Charles Kerr on Antigua "breathing the True Spirit of a West India agent"', *The Mariner's Mirror*, 107 (2021), 402–19.

Janis, M. W., *America and the Law of Nations, 1776–1939* (Oxford, 2010).

— 'North America: American Exceptionalism in International Law', in B. Fassbender, A. Peters and S. Peter (eds), *The Oxford Handbook of the History of International Law*, 1st edn (Oxford, 2012), pp. 525–52.

Jarvis, M. J., *In the Eye of all Trade: Bermuda, Bermudians, and the Maritime Atlantic World, 1680–1783*, Published for the Omohundro Institute of Early American History and Culture, Williamsburg, Virginia (Chapel Hill NC, 2010).

Jasanoff, M., 'The Other Side of Revolution: Loyalists in the British Empire', *William and Mary Quarterly,* 65 (2008), 205–32.

Jenkins, H. J. K., 'The Heyday of French Privateering from Guadeloupe, 1796–98', *The Mariner's Mirror,* 64 (1978), 245–50.

Jones, B. A., *Resisting Independence: Popular Loyalism in the Revolutionary British Atlantic* (Ithaca NY, 2021).

Kaminski, J. P., 'Honor and Interest: John Jay's Diplomacy During the Confederation', *New York History,* 83 (2002), 293–327.

Keegan, N. M., *US Consular Representation in Britain since 1790* (London, 2018).

Kennedy, R. G., *Mr. Jefferson's Lost Cause: Land, Farmers, Slavery, and the Louisiana Purchase* (Oxford, 2003).

Kert, F. M., *Patriots and Profits in the War of 1812* (Baltimore MD, 2015).

— *Prize and prejudice: Privateering and Naval Prize in Atlantic Canada in the War of 1812* (St John's, Newfoundland, 1997), vol. 11.

Kilbride, D., *Being American in Europe, 1750–1860* (Baltimore MD, 2013).

King, G. A., 'The French Spoliation Claims', *The American Journal of International Law,* 6 (1912), 359–80.

Kittrie, O. F., *Lawfare. Law as a Weapon of War* (New York 2016).

Knight, R., *Britain against Napoleon: The Organization of Victory 1793–1815* (London, 2014).

Lamb, M. J., *Wall Street in History* (New York, 2005).

Lambert, A. D., *The Challenge: America, Britain and the War of 1812* (London, 2012).

— *The British Way of War: Julian Corbett and the Battle for a National Strategy* (New Haven CT, 2021).

Land, J., 'Trade and the New Republic: American Trade During the Napoleonic Wars, 1783–1839', chapter provided as an e-resource by the University of Helsinki in J. Eloranta, E. Golson, P. Hedberg and M. C. Moreira (eds), *Small and Medium Powers in Global History: Trade, Conflicts and Neutrality from the 18th to the 20th Centuries* (London and New York, 2019).

Latimer, J., *1812: War with America* (Cambridge, 2010).

Leane, J., and Harkin, N., 'When Records Speak We Listen: Conversations with the Archive', in K. Biber, T. Luker and P. Vaughan (eds), *Law's Documents: Authority, Materiality, Aesthetics* (London and New York, 2022), pp. 51–70.

Leiner, F. C., 'Yes, Privateers Mattered: History is ill-served by a peculiar recent trend to downplay the significance of American privateering in the War of 1812', *Naval History Magazine,* 28 (2014).

Leitch, A., *A Princeton Companion* (Princeton NJ, 1978).

Lemnitzer, J. M., *Power, Law and the End of Privateering* (London, 2014).

Leonard, G., 'A History of Violence: American Constitutional History and the Criminal System', in *The Oxford Handbook of Legal History* (Oxford, 2018).

Leopore, J., ' Historians Who Love Too Much: Reflections on Microhistory and Biography', *Journal of American History,* 88 (2001), 129–44.

Lillich, R.B., 'The Jay Commissions', *St John's Law Review,* 32 (1963), 260–83.

Liston, H. *The Travel Journals of Henrietta Marchant Liston: North America and Lower Canada, 1796–1800*, ed. By Louise V. North (Lanham MD, 2014).

Maclay, E. S., *A History of American Privateers* (Cambridge, 2011 [1899]).

Mallery, C. P., *Ancient Families of Bohemia Manor: Their Homes and their Graves* (Wilmington DE, 1888).

Mangone, G. J., *United States Admiralty Law* (The Hague, 1997).

Mankowski, P., *Rechtskultur*, Beiträge zum ausländischen und internationalen Privatrecht, 1. Aufl. (Tübingen, 2016), vol. 115.

Marsh, N. S., 'Lord Stowell: A New Assessment', *International and Comparative Law Quarterly*, 37, 668–74.

Martinez, J. S., *The Courts of Mixed Commission for the Abolition of the Slave Trade* (2012).

Marzagalli, S., '"However illegal, extraordinary or almost incredible such conduct might be": Americans and Neutrality Issues in the Mediterranean During the French War', *International Journal of Maritime History* (2016).

— and Müller, L., '"In apparent disagreement with all law of nations in the world": Negotiating Neutrality for Shipping and Trade During the French Revolutionary and Napoleonic Wars', *International Journal of Maritime History* (2016).

McCarthy, M., *Privateering, Piracy and British Policy in Spanish America, 1810–1830* (Suffolk, 2013).

McGinty, G. W., 'Reviewed Work: *The Parisian American: Fulwar Skipwith of Virginia* by Henry Bartholomew Cox', *Louisiana History: The Journal of the Louisiana Historical Association,* 6 (1965), 410–12.

Mekeel, A. J., 'The Quaker-Loyalist Migration to New Brunswick and Nova Scotia in 1783', *Bulletin of Friends' Historical Association,* 32 (1943), 65–75.

Melikan, R. A., *John Scott, Lord Eldon, 1751–1838: The Duty of Loyalty* (Cambridge, 1999).

Mikaberije, A., *The Napoleonic Wars: A Global History* (New York, 2020).

Moats, S., *Navigating Neutrality: Early American Governance in the Turbulent Atlantic* (Charlottesville VA, 2021).

Moore, J. B., *History and digest of the international arbitrations to which the United States has been a party: Vol I, III, IV*, The Miscellaneous Documents of the House of Representatives, 1893–94 (Washington DC, 1898), vol. 212.

Moore, J. B., *Compensation for losses and damages caused by the violation of neutral rights, and by the failure to perform neutral duties: Mixed commission under article VII of the treaty between Great Britain and the United States of November 19, 1794*, Vol. IV, Publications of the Carnegie Endowment for International Peace, Div. of International Law, Washington, Modern Series (Buffalo NY, 1931), International Adjudications Ancient and Modern, History and Documents, ed. by John Bassett Moore, vol. 4.

Morgan, E. S., and Morgan Helen M., *The Stamp Act Crisis: Prologue to Revolution* (Chapel Hill NC and London, 1995).

Müller, L., *Nordic Neutrals and Anglo-French Wars: 1689–1815*, The Northern Mediterranean, XIVth International Economic History Congress (Helsinki, 2006).

Müller, L., *Neutrality in World History* (New York and London, 2019).

Multhauf, R. P., ' The French Crash Program for Saltpeter Production: 1776–94', *Technology and Culture,* 12 (1971), 162–81.

Nagel, S., *Patriotism and Profit: Washington, Hamilton, Schuyler and the Rivalry for America's Capital City* (New York, 2021).

Namier, Lewis, and Brooke, John (eds), *The History of Parliament: The House of Commons 1754–1790, III Members K–Y*, 2nd edn (London, 1984).
Nelson, P. D., *Sir Charles Grey, First Earl Grey: Royal Soldier, Family Patriarch* (Madison WI, 1996).
New York County Lawyers' Association Committee on the Federal Courts, *The United States District Court for the Southern District of New York: A Retrospective (2000–2010)* (New York, 2012).
New York Genealogical and Biographical Society, *The New York Genealogical and Biographical Record: Devoted to the Interests of American Genealogy and Biography* (New York, 1890), XXI.
Newmyer, R. K., *Supreme Court Justice Joseph Story: Statesman of the Old Republic* (Chapel Hill NC, 1985).
Oldham, J., *English Common Law in the Age of Mansfield* (Chapel Hill NC, 2004).
Onuf, P., and Onuf, N., *Federal Union, Modern World: The Law of Nations in an Age of Revolutions 1776–1814* (Madison WI, 1993).
Paulsen, G. W., 'An historical overview of development of uniformity in international maritime law', *Tulane Law Review: Devoted to the Civil Law, Comparative Law and Admiralty Law* (1983), 1065–91.
Pelletreau, W. S., *Historic Homes and Institutions and Genealogical and Family History of New York: Volume I*, 4 vols (New York and Chicago IL, 1907), vol. 1.
Pellew, G., *John Jay* (Boston MA and New York, 1890).
Perkins, B., *The First Rapprochement* (Berkeley CA and Los Angeles CA, 1967).
Perl-Rosenthal, N., *Citizen Sailors: Becoming American in the Age of Revolution* (Cambridge MA and London, 2015).
Petrie, D. A., *The Prize Game: Lawful Looting on the High Seas in the Days of Fighting Sail* (New York, 1999).
Pleck, E. H., *Celebrating the Family: Ethnicity, Consumer Culture, And Family Rituals* (Cambridge MA, 2000).
Pourchasse, P., 'War of Hunger: Supplying the French Republic during the Revolutionary Wars (1793–1795)', in J. W. Veluwenkamp (ed.), *Early Modern Shipping and Trade: Novel Approaches Using Sound Toll Registers Online* (Boston MA, 2018), pp. 59–76.
Powell, W. S., *Dictionary of North Carolina Biography: Vol. 1, A–C* (1979), vol. 1.
Pratt, W. F., 'Judicial Disability and the Good Behavior Clause', *Yale Law Journal,* 85 (1976), 706–20.
Putnam, H., 'How the Federal Courts Were Given Admiralty Jurisdiction', *Cornell Law Review,* 10 (1925), 460–70.
Raapke, A., '"Dieses verfluchte Land"', transcript Verlag (2019).
Ralston, J. H., *International Arbitration from Athens to Locarno* [Nachdr. d. Ausg. Stanford 1929] (Clark NJ, 2004).
Read, J. E., *The Rule of Law on the International Plane, The W.M. Martin Lectures* (Toronto, 1961), vol. 1960.
Reeves, J. S., 'The Influence of the Law of Nations Upon International Law in the United States', *American Journal of International Law,* 3 (1909), 547–61.
Richard, T. T., 'Reconsidering the Letter of Marque: Utilizing Private Security Providers against Piracy', *Public Contract Law Journal,* 39 (2010), 411–64.

Richardson, B., 'The Use of Vattel in the American Law of Nations', *American Journal of International Law,* 161 (2012), 547–71.

Robinson, W. M., *The Confederate Privateers*, Repr. [of the ed.] New Haven, 1928 (Columbia SC, 1990).

Robson, M., *A History of the Royal Navy: The Napoleonic Wars* (London, 2014).

Roelofsen, C. G., 'International Arbitration and Courts', in B. Fassbender, A. Peters and S. Peter (eds), *The Oxford Handbook of the History of International Law*, 1st edn (Oxford, 2012), pp. 145–69.

Roscoe, E. S., *A History of the English Prize Court* (London, 1924).

Rose, J., ' Studying the Past: The Nature and Development of Legal History as an Academic Discipline', *The Journal of Legal History,* 31 (2010), 101–28.

Ross, N. J., 'The provision of naval defense in the early American republic: A comparison of the US Navy and privateers, 1789–1815', *The Independent Review* (2011).

Rovira, M. G.-S., ' Early Twentieth-Century Positivism Revisited' , in A. Orford, F. Hoffmann and M. Clark (eds), *The Oxford Handbook of the Theory of International Law*, 1st edn (Oxford, 2016), pp. 173–91.

Rutherforth, T., *Institutes of natural law: Being the substance of a course of lectures on Grotius De jure belli et pacis, read in S. John's College, Cambridge* (London, 1754).

Sabine, L., *Biographical Sketches of Loyalists of the American Revolution, with an Historical Essay: In Two Volumes*, 2 vols (Boston MA, 1864), vol. 1.

Scattergood, J. H., and Henry, B., *The French Spoliation Claims: With special reference to insurance companies* (Washington DC, 1910).

Schindler, D., and Toman, J., *The Laws of Armed Conflicts: A Collection of Conventions, Resolutions and Other Documents*, 3rd rev. and completed edn (Dordrecht and Geneva, 1988).

Schoenbaum, T. J., *Admiralty and Maritime Law*, 6th edn (St Paul MN, 2019).

Schwartz, B., 'U.S. Privateering Is Legal', *Proceedings,* 146 (2020).

Schwarzenberger, G., ' Present-Day Relevance of the Jay Treaty Arbitrations', *Notre Dame Law Review,* 53 (1978), 715–33.

Scott, D., 'The Spanish Armada and England's Conflict with Spain, 1585–1604', in J. Davey (ed.), *Tudors and Stuart Seafarers: The Emergence of a Maritime Nation, 1485–1707*, 1st edn, 1 vol. (London, 2018), pp. 55–79.

Sechrest, L. J., 'Privately Funded and Built U.S. Warships in the Quasi-War of 1797–1801', *The Independent Review,* 12 (2007), 101–13.

Selig, R. A., 'Washington, Rochambeau, and the Yorktown Campaign of 1781', in E. G. Lengel (ed.), *A Companion to George Washington* (Hoboken NJ, 2012), pp. 266–87.

Senior, W., 'Judges of the High Court of Admiralty', *The Mariner's Mirror*, 13 (1927), 333–47.

Shoenberger, A., 'Loyola Law School, State Secrets, the American Revolution, the War of 1812: The Maritime Connections of the Middle Temple', *Journal of Maritime Law and Commerce* (2012), 293–300.

Southern District Court of New York, *Proceedings: Gift of Silver Oar* (1941).

Spearin, C., 'Promising Privateers? Understanding the Constraints of Contemporary Private Security at Sea', *Naval War College Review,* 67 (2014), 97–116.

— 'U.S. Privateering and China in the 21st Century: Tied at Anchor', *Comparative Strategy,* 42 (2023), 1–13.

Spencer, F., 'Lord Sandwich, Russian Masts, and American Independence', *The Mariner's Mirror,* 44 (1958), 116–27.

Squibb, G. D., *Doctors' Commons: A History of the College of Advocates and Doctors of Law* (Oxford etc., 1977).

Starkey, D. J., *British Privateering Enterprise in the Eighteenth Century* (Exeter, 1990), vol. 4.

— 'Voluntaries and Sea Robbers: A Review of the Academic Literature on Privateering, Corsairing, Buccaneering and Piracy', *The Mariner's Mirror*, 97 (2011), 127–47.

Sterling, D. L., 'A Federalist Opposes the Jay treaty: The Letters of Samuel Bayard', *William and Mary Quarterly,* 18 (1961), 408–24.

Stern, W. M., 'The Bread Crisis in Britain: 1795–6', *Economica*, 122 (1964), 168–87.

Stewart, D., 'To Be … Or Not: The Greatest Shakespeare Forgery: William-Henry Ireland committed a scheme so grand that he fooled even himself into believing he was William Shakespeare's true literary heir', *Smithsonian Magazine Online* (2010).

Stockton, C. H., 'The Declaration of Paris', *American Journal of International Law,* 14 (1920), 356–68.

Stockton, H. H., '"Cleremont" – Historic Mansion', *Daughters of the American Revolution* (1931), 546–50.

Street, A. B., *The Council of Revision of the State of New York: Its History, a History of the Courts with which its Members were connected, Biographical Sketches of its Members and its Vetoes* (Albany NY, 1859).

Sturm-Lind, L., *Actors of Globalization: New York Merchants in the Global Trade, 1784–1812*, (Leiden and Boston MA, 2018), vol. 10.

Surrency, E. C., 'The Transition from Colonialism to Independence', *The American Journal of Legal History*, 46 (2004), 55–81.

Symonds, W., and Sharp, J. A., *Memoirs of the life and services of Rear-Admiral Sir William Symonds: Surveyor of the navy from 1832 to 1847, British naval history in the nineteenth century* (London, 1858).

Tabarrok, A., 'The Rise, Fall, and Rise Again of Privateers', *The Independent Review,* 11 (2007), 565–77.

Tiedemann, J. S., *Reluctant Revolutionaries: New York City and the Road to Independence, 1763–1776* (Ithaca NY, 2008).

Towle, D. S., *Records of the Vice-Admiralty Court of Rhode Island, 1716–1752: With an Introduction by Charles M. Andrews, American Legal Records* (Washington DC, 1936), III.

Trautsch, J. M., *The Genesis of America: US Foreign Policy and the Formation of National Identity, 1793–1815* (New York, 2018).

Tucker, R. W., *The Law of War and Neutrality at Sea* (Washington DC, 1957), vol. 49.

Ubbelohde, C., *The Vice-Admiralty Courts and the American Revolution* (Chapel Hill NC, 1960).

Vries, J. de, 'Playing with Scales: The Global and the Micro, the Macro and the Nano', *Past and Present* (2019), 23–36.

Wagner, E.-M., and Ahmed, M. A. H., 'From Tuscany to Egypt: Eighteenth Century Arabic Letters in the Prize Paper Collections', *Journal of Semitic Studies* (2017).

Wallace, N. W., *A regimental chronicle and list of officers of the 60th, or the King's Royal Rifle Corps: Formerly the 62nd, or the Royal American Regiment of Foot* [Microfiche ed.] (London, 1879).

Watson, M., 'Judge Lewis Morris, the New York Vice-Admiralty Court, and Colonial Privateering: 1739–1762', *New York History,* 78 (1997), 117–46.

Werner, E. A., *Civil List and Constitutional History of the Colony and State of New York* (New York, 1886).

Wertheimer, J., 'Counting as a Tool of Legal History', in D. J. Hulsebosch and R. B. Bernstein (eds), *Making Legal History: Essays in Honor of William E. Nelson* (New York, 2013), pp. 162–78.

Wheaton, H., 'Life of William Pinkney', in J. Sparks, H. Wheaton, E. T. Channing and W. B. O. Peabody (eds), *Lives of William Pinkney, William Ellery and Cotton Mather, The Library of American Biography* (Boston MA and London, 1836), pp. 1–84.

Williams, G. H., *The French Assault on American Shipping, 1793–1813: A History and Comprehensive Record of Merchant Marine Losses* (Jefferson NC, 2009).

Wilson, J. G., *Colonel John Bayard (1738–1807) and the Bayard family of America: The anniversary address before the New York genealogical and biographical society, February 27, 1885* (New York, 1885).

— 'Judge Bayard of New Jersey and his London diary of 1795–96: Read before the New Jersey Hist. Soc. May 21, 1885', *Proceedings of the New Jersey Historical Society,* 8 (1885), 203–16.

Winter, J. D., and Maidman, R., 'Retelling the History of the United States District Court for the Southern District of New York', *NY Litigator* (2012).

— *The Federal Court in New York: 225 Years and Counting* (2014).

Wiswall, F. L., *The Development of Admiralty Jurisdiction and Practice Since 1800*, 2nd edn (Cambridge, 1970/2011).

Wold, A. L., *Privateering and Diplomacy, 1793–1807: Great Britain, Denmark-Norway and the Question of Neutral Ports* (Cham, 2020).

Wratten, D., *The Book of Radlett and Aldenham* (1990).

Wright, J. F., 'British government borrowing in wartime, 1750–1815', *Economic History Review,* 52 (1999), 355–61.

Wroth, K. L., 'The Massachusetts Vice Admiralty Court and the Federal Admiralty Jurisdiction', *American Journal of Legal History,* 6 (1962), 250–68.

Ying, C. A., 'Colonial and Federal Admiralty Jurisdiction', *Federal Law Review,* 12 (1981), 236–70.

Yirush, C. B., 'The Imperial Crisis', in J. Kamensky and E. G. Gray (eds), *The Oxford Handbook of the American Revolution* (Oxford, 2012), pp. 85–102.

## *Unpublished Theses*

A. Brinkman, 'The Court of Prize Appeals as an Agent of British Wartime Foreign Policy: The Maintenance of Dutch and Spanish Neutrality during the Seven Years War' (dissertation, King's College London, 2017).

Carton, M. J., 'The Caribbean Vice Admiralty Courts 1763–1815: Indispensable Agents of an Imperial System' (dissertation, 1968).

Finger, T. D., and Flagstaff, A., 'Harvesting Power: Transatlantic Merchants and the Anglo-American Grain Trade, 1795–1890' (dissertation, University of Virginia, 2015).

Martin, E. J., 'Prize Game in the Borderlands: Privateering in New England and the Maritime Provinces, 1775–1815' (dissertation, University of Maine, 2014).

## *Web-based Sources*

Cambridge Alumni Database, *Marriott, James*, http://venn.lib.cam.ac.uk/cgi-bin/search-2018.pl?sur=&suro=w&fir=&firo=c&cit=&cito=c&c=all&z=all&tex=MRT746J&sye= &eye=&col=all&maxcount=50 (13 July 2020).

*Charles Apthorp (1698–1758) – HouseHistree*, https://househistree.com/people/charles-apthorp (20 May 2023).

Columbia University, *The History of Columbia University*, www.columbia.edu/content/history-columbia-university (20 May 2023).

Combined Maritime Forces (CMF), *CTF 151: Counter-piracy*, https://combined-maritimeforces.com/ctf-151-counter-piracy/ (25 July 2023).

Coote H. C., *The new practice of the High Court of Admiralty of England: With the Rules of 1859, and a collection of forms, and bills of costs, &c., &c*, http://galenet.galegroup.com/servlet/MOML?af=RN&ae=F106188149&srchtp=a&ste=14.

Crawford M. J., and Hughes C. F., *The reestablishment of the Navy, 1787-1801: Historical overview and select bibliography*, www.history.navy.mil/research/library/bibliographies/reestablishment-navy-1787-1801.html.

Dictionary of Welsh Biography, *Nicholl, Sir John (1759–1838): judge*, https://biography.wales/article/s-NICH-JOH-1759#?c=0&m=0&s=0&cv=0&manifest=https%3A%2F%2Fdamsssl.llgc.org.uk%2Fiiif%2F2.0%2F4674538%2Fmanifest.json&xywh=773%2C1748%2C3391%2C2736 (21 August 2023).

Edge Grove, *History, Co-educational School, Watford, Edge Grove*, www.edgegrove.com/about-us/our-history/ (27 June 2023).

Federal Bar Association of New York, New Jersey and Connecticut, *History of the United States District Court for the Southern District of New York* (New York, 1962).

EUNAVFOR, *Operation ATALANTA*, https://eunavfor.eu/.

Gooden R., *H.R.6869 – 117th Congress (2021–2022): To authorize the President of the United States to issue letters of marque and reprisal for the purpose of seizing the assets of certain Russian citizens, and for other purposes*, www.congress.gov/bill/117th-congress/house-bill/6869/text (24 July 2023).

Harrison C., *Thomas Symonds (c.1720–1792)*, https://threedecks.org/index.php?display_type=show_crewman&id=13868 (8 June 2023).

— *Sir John Jervis (1734/35–1823)*, https://threedecks.org/index.php?display_type=show_crewman&id=1503 (29 June 2023).

Historical Society of the New York Courts, *The New York Court of Admiralty, 1775–1789*, https://history.nycourts.gov/case/court-admiralty/ (26 May 2023).

Historical Society of the New York Courts, *Richard Morris*, https://history.nycourts.gov/figure/richard-morris/ (26 May 2023).

Henricus – Edition Deutsche Klassik GmbH, *Nürnberger Prozesse, Hauptverhandlungen, XXI. Tag/Dienstag, 14 Mai 1946, Nachmittagssitzung*, www.zeno.org/Geschichte/M/Der+N%C3%BCrnberger+Proze%C3%9F/Hauptverhandlungen/Einhundertneunundzwanzigster+Tag.+Dienstag,+14.+Mai+1946/Nachmittagssitzung (23 August 2023).

*James McEvers (1763–1818) – HouseHistree*, https://househistree.com/people/james-mcevers (23 May 2023).

NARA, *Records Relating to British Spoliations, ca. 1796–ca. 1824 – NAID 1170270: Catalogue Description*, https://catalog.archives.gov/id/1170270 (23 March 2023).

NARA, *Catalogue Entry: Records created by the Organizational Unit New York (State) Court of Vice Admiralty: 4 Series*, https://catalog.archives.gov/search?q=record.creators.naId:10490821 (26 May 2023).

NARA, *New York (State). Court of Vice Admiralty: Organizational entity*, https://catalog.archives.gov/id/10678313.

NARA, *Signers of the Declaration of Independence*, www.archives.gov/founding-docs/signers-factsheet (2 September 2023).

New York Historical Society, *William Bayard: Gallery of Peers, in Exhibition 'Alexander Hamilton. The Man Who Made Modern America'*, www.alexanderhamiltonexhibition.org/gallery/bayard_w.html (17 August 2023).

Paul R., *H.R.3074 – 107th Congress (2001–2002): Air Piracy Reprisal and Capture Act of 2001*, www.congress.gov/bill/107th-congress/house-bill/3074?s=1&r=89 (24 July 2023).

— *H.R.3076 – 107th Congress (2001–2002): September 11 Marque and Reprisal Act of 2001*, www.congress.gov/bill/107th-congress/house-bill/3076 (24 July 2023).

Pougher, Richard D., '"Averse … to Remaining Idle Spectators": The Emergence of Loyalist Privateering During the American Revolution, 1775–1778. Volume I. Introduction to Chapter 8' (dissertation, University of Maine, 2002), http://digitalcommons.library.umaine.edu/etd/207.

Prize Papers Portal, *Document Types: Standing Interrogatories*, https://portal.prizepapers.de/documenttype/ (9 June 2023).

Prize Papers Project, *What is the Prize Papers Collection?* www.prizepapers.de/what-is-the-price-papers-collection (13 July 2020).

Ray-Jones A., *John Dorney Harding Kt: A History of the Ray-Jones Family*, https://family.ray-jones.org.uk/rootspersona-tree/john-dorney-harding-kt/ (4 August 2020).

Ribera M. G., *Little Blue Men: China and US Privateering*, https://greydynamics.com/little-blue-men-china-us-privateering/#h-privateering (27 July 2024).

Thompson, G. H. M., *Admiralty Registrars: Some Historical Notes* ([London], 1958).

Thornbury, W., *Old and New London: A Narrative of its History, its People, and its Places*, A new edition, carefully revised and corrected (London, Paris and New York, 1881).

Thorne R., *Dundas, Henry (1742–1811)*, www.historyofparliamentonline.org/volume/1790-1820/member/dundas-henry-1742-1811 (20 July 2024).

— *Marriott, Sir James (1730–1803)*, www.historyofparliamentonline.org/volume/1790-1820/member/marriott-sir- james-1730-1803#footnote1_81440wp.+ (13 July 2020).

— *Scott, Sir John (1751–1838)*, www.historyofparliamentonline.org/volume/1790-1820/member/scott-sir-john-1751-1838 (26 August 2020).

— *Scott, Sir William (1745–1836)*, www.historyofparliamentonline.org/volume/1790-1820/member/scott-sir- william-1745-1836#footnoteref3_uxjdk4y (26 August 2020).

— *Vaughan, Benjamin (1751–1835)*, www.historyofparliamentonline.org/volume/1790-1820/member/vaughan- benjamin-1751-1835 (18 January 2021).

TNA, *High Court of Appeals for Prizes: Case Books (Printed Appeal Papers): Catalogue Description HCA 45*, http://discovery.nationalarchives.gov.uk/details/r/C8643 (26 May 2021).

TNA, *High Court of Appeals for Prizes: Papers: Catalogue Description HCA 42*, https://discovery.nationalarchives.gov.uk/details/r/C8640 (26 May 2021).

TNA, *Volume 2 of 'Letters of Agency', compiled by the registry of the British New York Vice-Admiralty Court: Catalogue Description of HCA 49/96*, https://discovery.nationalarchives.gov.uk/details/r/C3301416 (6 June 2023).

TNA, *Court of Exchequer: Research Guide*, www.nationalarchives.gov.uk/help-with-your-research/research-guides/court-exchequer/ (1 February 2023).

TNA, *Archives of American Claims Commission (1794): Catalogue Description FO 304*, https://discovery.nationalarchives.gov.uk/details/r/C7618 (23 March 2023).

TNA, *High Court of Admiralty: Prize Court: Prize Papers: Catalogue Description HCA 32*, https://discovery.nationalarchives.gov.uk/details/r/C8630 (23 March 2023).

TNA, *High Court of Admiralty, and Supreme Court of Judicature: Admiralty Miscellanea: Catalogue Description HCA 30*, https://discovery.nationalarchives.gov.uk/details/r/C8628 (19 July 2023).

TNA, *Vice-Admiralty Courts: Proceedings: Catalogue description HCA 49*, https://discovery.nationalarchives.gov.uk/details/r/C8647 (11 September 2023).

United Nations, *United Nations Compensation Commission*, https://uncc.ch/home (23 August 2023).

van Lottum, J., Lucassen, J., and van Voss, L. H., 'Sailors, National and International Labour Markets and National Identity,1600–1850', in R. W. Unger (ed.), *Shipping and Economic Growth, 1350–1850* (Leiden, 2011), pp. 309–52.

van Niekerk, J. P., 'The Story of the Silver Oar Mace of the Vice-Admiralty Court of the Cape of Good Hope', *Fundamina,* 18 (2012), 135–73.

Verzijl, J. H. W., Heere, W. P., and Offerhaus, J. P., *The Law of Maritime Prize*, Nova et vetera iuris gentium. Ser. A, Modern international law (Leiden, 1992), vol. 16.

Vito, C. G. de, 'History Without Scale: The Micro-Spatial Perspective', *Past and Present* (2019), 348–72.

Wikipedia, *Thomas Symonds (Royal Navy officer, died 1792)*, https://en.wikipedia.org/wiki/Thomas_Symonds_(Royal_Navy_officer,_died_1792).

William Nelson Cromwell Foundation, *William Nelson Cromwell Foundation*, https://cromwellfoundation.org/ (11 September 2023).

Yale University Art Gallery, *Artist: John Trumbull, Subject: Rufus King, 1792*, https://artgallery.yale.edu/collections/objects/70 (17 January 2021).

# INDEX

Printed and bound by CPI Group (UK) Ltd, Croydon, CR0 4YY

29/07/2025

14710921-0001